T0246381

WAR BY OTHER MEANS

WAR
BY
OTHER
MEANS

——

How the Pacifists of WWII
Changed America for Good

DANIEL AKST

Melville House
Brooklyn/London

First published in 2022 by Melville House.
Copyright © 2022 by Daniel Akst. All rights reserved.
First Melville House Printing: October 2022

Melville House Publishing
46 John Street
Brooklyn, NY 11201
and
Melville House UK
Suite 2000
16/18 Woodford Road
London E7 0HA

mhpbooks.com
@melvillehouse

ISBN: 978-1-61219-924-5
ISBN: 978-1-61219-925-2 (e-book)

Library of Congress Control Number: 2022944683

Designed by Patrice Sheridan

Printed in the United States of America
1 3 5 7 9 10 8 6 4 2

A catalog record for this book is available from the Library of Congress

For my wife and sons, proof that good things come in threes.

We who allow ourselves to become engaged in war need this testimony of the absolutist against us, lest we accept the warfare of the world as normative, lest we become callous to the horror of war, and lest we forget the ambiguity of our own actions and motives and the risk we run of achieving no permanent good from this momentary anarchy in which we are involved.

—Reinhold Niebuhr

CONTENTS

INTRODUCTION

THE FIRST TIME YOUNG David Dellinger made *The New York Times* was on November 3, 1932, under the headline "Yale Cub Harriers Pick Dellinger." The story, all of two sentences, reports that the former high school track star was elected captain of the university's freshman cross-country team. The doings of leading Yale men were news in those days, and although Dellinger was an enemy of hierarchy all his life, he was paradoxically a natural leader. Later, at New York's Union Theological Seminary, he was made president of his class. Eventually he would become famous as a towering and uncompromising figure in radical causes; Paul Berman, an insightful historian of the postwar Left, writes that, during Vietnam, Dellinger "became the single most important leader of the national antiwar movement." He became a great deal more famous as a member of the Chicago Seven, whose trial on charges of criminal conspiracy and inciting to riot arose from their antiwar protests during the 1968 Democratic National Convention. Dellinger sat through the proceedings with awkward dignity along with codefendants including Abbie Hoffman, Jerry Rubin, and Tom Hayden—all radical celebrities in those fraught times. But surely Dellinger, the oldest of the lot, was the only one entitled to a sense of déjà vu, because he had been through something similar so long before.[1]

In 1940, as he was about to begin his second year at Union, Dellinger was the de facto leader of an idealistic band of students who had decided not to register for the nation's first peacetime draft. Long before anyone might have dreamed of the Chicago Seven, newspapers across the country were reporting on the antiwar seminarians who would become known as the Union Eight. Despite considerable pressure from Henry Sloane Coffin— Union's president, who was known as "Uncle Henry" behind his back— these young pacifists refused to avail themselves of a provision in the new draft law that was included with precisely their sort in mind: "Regular or duly ordained ministers of religion, and students who are preparing for the ministry in theological or divinity schools . . . shall be exempt from training and service (but not from registration) under this Act."[2]

So determined were these resisters to remain untainted by the apparatus of war that they went to federal prison—a segregated prison, reflecting a segregated society—rather than violate their beliefs by filling out a piece of paper. "The war system is an evil part of our social order," the students wrote, "and we declare that we cannot cooperate with it in any way." Because their objections genuinely were religious, they probably would have been granted conscientious objector status even had they not been divinity students. "War is an evil," they wrote, "because it is in violation of the Way of Love as seen in God through Christ."[3] Reinhold Niebuhr, probably the nation's leading theologian and a Union professor they had looked up to, may have been their harshest critic. A reformed pacifist himself, and perhaps therefore imbued with the zeal of the convert, he met with the students individually to try and change their minds. Dellinger's hysterical father, in a hair-raising phone call, threatened suicide. But the young men were immovable, explaining: "We do not expect to stem the war forces today; but we are helping to build the movement that will conquer in the future."[4]

These words will seem impossibly idealistic today, much like the belief that freedom could be preserved from fascist military aggression by the sheer moral force of nonviolence. Yet to a great extent Dellinger and his fellow pacifists did conquer the future, even if he and many others left Christ behind. By 2004, when Dellinger died at the age of eighty-eight, Berman was able to put the late radical's activism into remarkable perspective. Dellinger, he said, "came of age in one of the tiniest currents of the American left—the Rev. A.J. Muste's movement for World War II pacifism, a movement based on radical Christian values and vaguely anarchist instincts. No rational person observing that movement during the 1940's would have predicted any success at all, and yet during the next two or three decades, Mr. Dellinger and his pacifist allies transformed whole areas of American life."[5]

That tiny current—which somehow became a tsunami of social change—has also given birth to this book, whose aim is not to make the case for absolute pacifism but to tell the story of its remarkable adherents during its greatest trial: the Second World War. No one can dispute the horrors of war, or that opponents of our nation's many military engagements were all too often right to challenge them as pointless, unjust, or both. But it will come as a surprise to most Americans that, even after Pearl Harbor, thousands in this country opposed World War II. That's the war we all seem to approve of—the quintessential "good" war during which Americans pulled together and sacrificed.

For the most part, they did, but it was a war thrust upon them despite their most strenuous efforts to avoid it. Before the outbreak of formal hostilities in Europe, polls showed that most Americans were firmly against U.S. involvement in yet another massive and bloody foreign conflict. Conditioned by the bitter disappointment of the Great War, which by the 1930s was widely seen as a waste and a scam, many Americans were determined not to be conned again, this time by a war erupting from an unjust peace. "You were supposed to be wised up about the War," said Mary McCarthy, explaining: "We were afraid of making a mistake, of being 'taken in.'"[6]

The evils of Nazism, visible early on only as the tip of a Satanic iceberg, competed in the public mind with those of Stalinism. The lies of the Great War had bred skepticism toward alleged German atrocities. People also worried that another foreign war would beget tyranny at home, for war always increases the power of the state, and tyranny in those days seemed to be in the air, spreading like a virus from nation to nation. American civil liberties had been trampled in connection with the last European war. This time, many feared, would be worse.

During the interwar period, moreover, the United States had developed perhaps the largest and best-organized pacifist movement in the world. Pacifism was part of the curriculum at some schools and firmly on the agenda of the mainline Protestant denominations that were such important institutions in the life of this churchgoing nation at the time. Liberal clergymen, including such celebrity ministers as the indefatigable Harry Emerson Fosdick, spoke out against war from their Sunday pulpits and via the popular new medium of radio, whence the gospel of pacifism reached a student by the name of Martin Luther King, Jr. Pacifism was well established on campuses thanks to a massive and diverse national student antiwar movement, with thousands pledging not to fight under any circumstances.

Even after the Nazi invasion of Poland, some people could find little basis for choosing between the growing array of combatants; alliances were shifting, and there were uncomfortable parallels between the imperialist Western powers and their enemies. Hitler's persecution of the Jews was widely condemned, even if the "final solution" was not yet apparent to outsiders. But why was it fine for Britain to occupy India and wrong for Germany to occupy Poland, or even France? Why not go to war with the Soviet Union, which invaded not just Poland but Finland and the Baltic States too? "If we see that Germany is winning we ought to help Russia," Harry Truman would suggest on the Senate floor, "and if Russia is winning we ought to help Germany."[7] But when Hitler's Panzers turned on Western Europe, more Americans began to side with the Allies and the mass pacifism of the interwar years began to dissolve. After Pearl Harbor, which surprised nearly everyone by bringing war to America from Asia, domestic opposition to entering the struggle collapsed.

Yet against all odds, and perhaps all reason, some Americans adhered so doggedly to the principle of nonviolence that they persisted in opposing the fight. About forty-three thousand men were granted conscientious objector status once the draft law of 1940 took effect effect, out of at least seventy-two thousand who applied.[8] Most were purely religious objectors, and some contributed to the war effort as combat medics or in other non-lethal roles. About twelve thousand, unwilling to cooperate in military activities, accepted assignment to a far-flung network of rural work camps run by the traditional peace churches in uneasy partnership with government.

A small number of resisters were radical pacifists whose opposition to war was—or would soon be—part of a vastly more ambitious reformist impulse. Not all these radicals were religious, and some who were grew less so. Some were granted CO status and some weren't, the haphazard local adjudication system inevitably producing widely disparate results. And some, like Dellinger, refused to seek that status. "*Extreme pacifist* is the best description I can think of," Christopher Isherwood wrote of them a few years after the war, "but it is unsatisfactory and vague; for the group combined several sorts of anarchists, individualists, religious and non-religious objectors. Some of them had refused even to register for the draft, holding that registration itself implies acceptance of the military machine."

Isherwood's description serves well enough. Of the roughly six thousand Americans who went to prison for refusing to cooperate with the war in any way, most were apolitical Jehovah's Witnesses whose confinement reflected the government's refusal to accept that everyone in the church was a minister. That left nearly two thousand absolute resisters, a small number that belies a large impact. For the most radical resisters, who emerged from the experience hardened against prison, poverty, and social disrepute, the war became a laboratory for developing the ideas and approaches they and others would employ, in the turbulent decades ahead, to bring about some of the most important social changes in this country since the end of slavery.

During the war, white and black pacifists attacked segregation with teamwork, negotiation, and sit-down strikes. They fought to reform mental health care at home, and to halt the bombing of civilians overseas. They protested the herding of Japanese-Americans into remote concentration camps. They railed, avant la lettre, against the military-industrial complex that was plainly on the horizon. Most of all, influenced by Gandhi, they transformed their pacifism from a philosophy of wartime refusal into an active nonviolent system for confronting and defeating injustice. Thus the title of this book; for the World War II pacifists, nonviolence was not merely a way of living or a matter of resistance. It was frankly aggressive, a way of actually fighting, and something religious pacifists in particular had historically avoided. In today's terms we might say these new pacifists sought to "weaponize" nonviolence by translating moral authority into power. In doing so they helped synthesize something new and distinctly modern from a blend of Gandhian nonviolence and Protestant resistance—something suitable to the political, cultural, and technological environment of their own country and culture. The elements were already there; Gandhi, after all, had been influenced by Jesus as well as by Thoreau, and Gandhi in turn had already influenced leaders of the nascent civil rights movement in this country. American pacifists, influenced as well by organized labor, worked during the war to develop a distinctive approach that amounted to nothing less than war by other means.

Practically speaking, there was little they could do to halt the terrible conflict of World War II. But, at the very least, they could call the world's democracies to conscience. When, in 1942, the Roosevelt administration interned 110,000 Japanese Americans, opponents of the war were among the few who cried foul. When the Allies, at the 1943 Casablanca conference, adopted a policy of "unconditional surrender," pacifists including Dellinger, Dorothy Day, and Dwight Macdonald called instead for a negotiated peace that might yet (they hoped) save some of Europe's Jews. Muste repeatedly urged FDR to raise immigration quotas for European Jewry before it was wiped out. And when the Allies intentionally bombed civilians, the nation's lonely remaining pacifists lost no time in decrying the immorality and hypocrisy of the action. One such unpopular protest, in 1944, made the front page of *The New York Times*.

All the while, war resisters were developing the techniques they would later use to far greater effect. It was during the war that they refined "direct action" as a means of protest—a media-conscious style of nonviolent confrontation suitable for revealing injustice to its perpetrators and their constituents. Locked up (during the war one in six federal inmates was a prisoner of conscience) or relegated to a remote archipelago of Civilian Public Service (CPS) camps, pacifists from different walks of life got to know each other in facilities that threw together city boys and farmers, Christians and communists, whites and blacks, naïfs and sophisticates in bubbling cauldrons of radicalism. Behind bars and in the dusty outposts where they worked on irrigation projects and the like, these young men argued, plotted, and educated one another, holding classes and publishing newsletters. Thus did federal efforts to manage the pacifists only radicalize them further, hardening them against social pressure and empowering them to school one another in the tactics of dissent. It was an extraordinary opportunity to hone the nonviolent techniques that would later propel the nation through a period of wrenching progress with far less bloodshed than might have been.

"The biggest single mistake the government made," said Roy Kepler, one of the more radical conscientious objectors, "was introducing us to each other."

Faced with a widely supported battle against fascism and a booming economy, pacifists had good reason to shift their focus from war to the injustices they saw at its root. The most egregious injustice of all, one connected with the colonialism that was a perennial casus belli in their minds, was America's treatment of its black citizens. During the war white and black pacifists founded the Congress of Racial Equality, an important civil rights organization that was sustained in its infancy by Muste's pacifist Fellowship of Reconciliation (FOR). The war resisters and civil rights activists Bayard Rustin and James Farmer were crucial human links between wartime radical pacifism and the civil rights struggles to come—struggles that succeeded in large part because they were nonviolent.

The ramifications rippled outward in all directions. Opposition to the war shattered America's once-thriving Socialist Party and discredited a healthy strain of noninterventionism in U.S. foreign policy. It encouraged progressives to turn from labor (which supported the war) toward racial justice, and it established the basis for decades of progressive antagonism toward American militarism. It fostered chronic suspicion of government power and pronouncements, and it gave birth to the tactics of nonviolent direct action that would figure so prominently in the years to come. In the history of progressive change in this country, resistance to the Second World War is the crucial missing link.

After the war, resisters brought their ideals and experience to bear in agitating for nuclear disarmament, ending colonialism, and overturning apartheid. Their dogged idealism, honed in lonely opposition to a popular war, fitted them to withstand years in the wilderness during the 1950s. Eventually, as part of a groundswell of change, some of them would become important figures in the civil rights movement, which in turn gave impetus to the women's movement and the movement for gay rights. World War II pacifists would play a leading role in burying the conscription they loathed, and help to drag America out of Vietnam. By now opposition to militarism is a staple of the American Left, even if wars large and small have continued to this day. More important, the pacifists of World War II helped make the country many of us take for granted: a nation that approves of gay marriage, grants women something approaching equality, and elected a black president named Barack Hussein Obama.

Another group of World War II opponents had an enduring impact as well, but mainly by their absence, much like an eldest son full of promise but killed in battle. These were the Americans who fell into the impossibly broad category of "isolationists," some avowedly and some unwillingly, and they present interesting parallels to their radical pacifist counterparts. In both groups, antiwar feeling arose from disillusionment with the Great War and concern for civil liberties, which both sides were certain would yield to tyranny in the event we were drawn into another European conflict. Both groups were largely Protestant and anti-imperialist, and both were more internationally minded than people give them credit for. In both groups, paradoxically, we can detect a yearning for a simpler and more intimate America, a locally oriented society thick with personal relations, mutual understanding, and a kind of love—a place already fading in 1940, and whose demise was in fact accelerated by the national war effort. All parties would have agreed with John Dewey, who wrote at the time: "The serious threat to our democracy is not the existence of foreign totalitarian states. It is the existence within our own personal attitudes and within our own institutions of conditions similar to those which have given a victory to external authority, discipline, uniformity and dependence upon The Leader in foreign countries. The battlefield is also accordingly here—within ourselves and our institutions."[9]

The isolationists and radical pacifists ultimately failed to deter American war-making, even if today's leftists and libertarians still live by Dewey's words. For a fleeting moment, before December 7, 1941, the two sides sometimes worked in wary tandem to form a kind of antiwar Peaceable Kingdom, finding ways to cooperate despite deep ideological differences. Imagine some noisy latter-day Edward Hicks painting of Norman Thomas, Herbert Hoover, H. L. Mencken, James Farmer, Paul Goodman, Dorothy Day, Charles Beard, Charles Lindbergh, A. J. Muste, and even Elijah Muhammad, all united in aim if not in outlook.

Following America's horrible "date which will live in infamy," former isolationists patriotically took up arms, but their prewar cause, tragically misunderstood by later generations, never recovered. As a result, America was left largely without the strong, establishment anti-interventionist voices it badly needed in the decades to come. Such voices might have curtailed more than half a century of ill-advised international adventures, from the overthrow of elected governments in Guatemala and Iran to such fiascos as the Bay of Pigs, Vietnam, Iraq, and Afghanistan.

World War II was, of course, the ultimate challenge to nonviolence. Given public opinion, how should pacifists conduct themselves? Was there any sense in protesting? What actions could a pacifist in good conscience undertake? And how could the menace of fascism be halted with nonviolence? There were as many answers to these questions as there were pacifists. For the most part, they saw opposition to war as a moral and religious imperative that was inviolable regardless of its consequences.

In studying the war's pacifist opponents, I found it impossible not to admire their radical antiauthoritarianism. Like the Pilgrims, our pacifists were dissenters, a word that has always had religious connotations, and their dogma was nonviolence. They sought not to vanquish their opponents, but to convert them—understandably, given that in the Christian tradition nobody is beyond redemption. Again and again these nonconformists showed not just moral but physical courage. They calmly withstood imprisonment, assault, forced feedings, and solitary confinement, insisting on the role of conscience despite the mortal threat posed by powerful enemies in a global war. They were wrong about one very big thing, it is true, but they were right about many others, as time would tell. In their own way, they fought for freedom just as their countrymen did, even if one might wish they had acknowledged their debt to the Americans who fought on the battlefield.

It's noteworthy that the American Civil Liberties Union (ACLU) arose from a precursor called the National Civil Liberties Bureau, which focused on protecting antiwar speech and conscientious objectors during the Great War. American pacifists in the Second World War were similarly concerned with liberty as well as peace, which was in keeping with the long antiauthoritarian history of Anglo-American pacifism. It's largely a religious tradition, and the churches most identified with nonviolence—the Quakers, for example—are descended from sixteenth- and seventeenth-century reformers who were skeptical toward authority and placed conscience above worldly power.

The pacifists who encountered a world at war starting in 1939 did likewise. They recoiled from violence but also from the pervasive power of mass society. They saw the state as "flawed, coercive and corrupt," in the words of one wise student of the era's radicals,[10] and a strong anarchist streak ran through many of the most ardent resisters, who naturally believed they were answering to a higher power. War, to them, was the very worst manifestation of an increasingly regimented, technological society that many people are reacting against still. They insisted that America live up to its values, no matter what was at stake. And, in keeping with their country's venerable reform tradition, they had faith—for the most part, Protestant faith (although some had Socialist faith). Foreshadowing evangelicals yet to come, they believed they were walking with Jesus, just as had their intellectual and political forebears, who crusaded to protect the Indians, end slavery, tamp down tippling, achieve women's suffrage, and otherwise bring American life more in line with divinity. Those impulses were largely quiescent when the new war broke out, by which time liberal Protestants were the establishment. Radical pacifism revived religious protest in America, turning its focus to all the work yet left undone.

This book ranges widely to offer an account of the war from the perspective of its opponents, but focuses on a handful of individuals who would go on to play an important part in the social and political changes to come. They include that consummate radical David Dellinger, the brilliant and charismatic Bayard Rustin, the compulsive dissident Dwight Macdonald, and the visionary Catholic anarchist Dorothy Day, as well as less-known but important antiwar figures such as James Farmer, A. J. Muste, Harry Emerson Fosdick, and George Houser. Consider this a snapshot in their pilgrimage as well as our own, an image filled with characters and events that speaks of their time but also contains clues to our own.

Through these individuals we'll see the modern progressive movement emerging. The resisters' loathing of hierarchy, their suspicion of the modern state, and their keen devotion to personal autonomy and moral hygiene would shape the character of the Left into the twenty-first century—and make it impossible for them to build enduring political organizations. The predilections of the Good War refuseniks are detectable in the rights revolution we now take for granted, and the near-pacifism that prevails among modern-day progressives. The COs' preference for consensus over authority can be found in the shape and governance of the internet, and their combination of moral outrage and organizational reticence was evident in Occupy Wall Street. Their emphasis on race, complicated by immigration, gender, and sexuality, has metastasized into an obsession. The essentially libertarian orientation of the resisters, who would have agreed with Milton Friedman that conscription was slavery; the religious roots of their ethics; and their wariness of central authority are all commonplace in significant precincts of today's political culture. This speaks partly to their influence, but also to their all-American political DNA. Their stress on personal conscience, to cite a single strand, goes all the way back to the Puritans.

PART ONE

BEFORE

CHAPTER 1

AND NOW, YOUTH!

DAVID DELLINGER AND HIS friend Don Benedict caught a ride from New York to Washington, D.C., for the Lincoln's Birthday weekend of 1940. Who knows where they stayed—on somebody's floor, probably. It was the Depression, and Dellinger in particular knew all about roughing it. Benedict was hoping to learn from him on that score. They were in Washington because the two of them were part of a youth movement whose eager vanguard had descended on the city to agitate for jobs, rights, peace, and what they saw as justice. Both had backgrounds in the important Christian student movement of the era, Dellinger at Yale and Benedict at Albion, a little Methodist college in Michigan, and both now were graduate students at Union Theological Seminary in New York. There Dellinger had quickly formed a close bond with Benedict and Meredith Dallas, also from Albion. Pacifism, like socialism, was in the air at Union, at least among students.

It was an exciting time, even if, like W. H. Auden, America's young, having lived through "a low dishonest decade," could feel the

> Waves of anger and fear
> Circulate over the bright
> And darkened lands of the earth,
> Obsessing our private lives[.][1]

The students who made their way to Washington that weekend had come of age in the Great Depression. America's collegians, once apathetic, were now far more conscious of injustice, chafing under the political constraints imposed by paternalistic faculty and administrators—and determined to stay out of war. "It was a time when frats, like the football team, were losing their glamor," wrote the playwright Arthur Miller, recalling his days at the University of Michigan (Class of 1938). "Instead my generation thirsted for another kind of action, and we took great pleasure in the sit-down strikes that burst loose in Flint and Detroit . . . We saw a new world coming every third morning."[2]

Many such Americans worried that war would undo whatever progress had been made by the New Deal, while undermining civil liberties. Stuart Chase, a popular economics writer and FDR associate whose 1932 book, *A New Deal*, provided ideas and a name for the White House program, argued that by avoiding war we might achieve "the abolition of poverty, unprecedented improvements in health and energy, a towering renaissance in the arts, an architecture and an engineering to challenge the gods." But if war were to come, he wrote, we would see "the liquidation of political democracy, of Congress, the Supreme Court, private enterprise, the banks, free press and free speech; the persecution of German-Americans and Italian-Americans, witch hunts, forced labor, fixed prices, rationing, astronomical debts, and the rest."[3]

Some wanted to save the country for socialism. "For the last four years America has taken the first awkward but nevertheless giant strides toward a new social order," the radical editor Alfred M. Bingham wrote. "If the march continues as it has begun . . . we may see a gradual but nonetheless swift elimination of our capitalist past . . . The only positive alternative to Fascism is a Socialist democracy." The liberal *New Republic* concurred, declaring: "You cannot defeat fascism by defeating fascist nations in war. You cannot end war by waging war. On the contrary, nothing is more likely than that the United States would go fascist through the very process of organizing to defeat the fascist nations."[4]

If Franklin Roosevelt's New Deal didn't go far enough, it had at least offered hope. But in foreign affairs even this scant comfort was absent. During the thirties students had seen the rise of Hitler, the fascist triumph in the Spanish Civil War, and a series of futile appeasement measures culminating in the Nazi invasion of Poland on September 1, 1939, which triggered war with Britain and France. As Dellinger, Benedict, and thousands like them arrived in Washington, tiny Finland was still fighting with unexpected ferocity to repel an invasion by the Soviet Union, which had cynically agreed with Germany to divide Europe between them. The Red Army even joined in the dismembering of Poland. On the other side of the world, China had been struggling since 1937 against a brutal Japanese invasion.

Hope springs eternal, but on the morning of Saturday, February 10, 1940, even the nasty weather augured ill. Washington was rainy and cold as a young woman on horseback—dressed as Joan of Arc—led a procession of idealistic young Americans along Constitution Avenue. Many were in fanciful costumes. The rich array included some in chain mail and others dressed as Puritans. A delegation from Kentucky rode mules. Signs and banners held aloft by the students that weekend bore antiwar slogans, including, LOANS FOR FARMS, NOT ARMS; JOBS NOT GUNS; and, in sardonic reference to the discredited crusade of the Great War, THE YANKS ARE NOT COMING.

The context of their march was the national struggle over what role America should play in the European war—a war that had happened despite the best efforts of well-meaning people the world over to avoid it by means of rhetoric, law, arms control, appeasement, and every other method short of actually fighting about it. Now that it was at hand, America's young were far more opposed to intervention than their elders, and this was a source of conflict on campus. At Harvard's graduation a few months later, class orator Tudor Gardiner reflected the attitudes of many students in calling aid for the Allies "fantastic nonsense" and urging a focus on "making this hemisphere impregnable." When Gardiner's predecessor by twenty-five years recalled, at a reunion event, that "We were not too proud to fight then and we are not too proud to fight now," recent graduates booed. But when commencement speaker Cordell Hull, FDR's secretary of state, called isolationism "dangerous folly," Harvard president James Bryant Conant nodded in support. Scenes like this would play out at campuses all across the country.[5]

The students who converged on Washington for the Lincoln's Birthday weekend brought with them their generation's disdain for war. Marching in a steady drizzle, they were bound, these tender youths, for the White

House, to which they had foolishly been invited by Eleanor Roosevelt—herself an active pacifist during the interwar years. "Almost six thousand young people marched," her biographer reports, "farmers and sharecroppers, workers and musicians, from high schools and colleges, black and white, Indians and Latinos, Christians and Jews, atheists and agnostics, freethinkers and dreamers, liberals and Communists."[6]

Dellinger and Benedict were part of this "extraordinary patchwork," the two seminarians having made the trip from New York by car with some other young people. Dellinger in particular was already being noticed, as he always seemed to be. Years later he would recall (clearly as part of this weekend) being invited by the First Lady to a White House tea in early 1940 with other student leaders who had, as he put it, organized a protest that she supported. Benedict's memoir recalls that the two of them went to Washington that same month and attended "a huge rally, with thousands massed around the White House" to hear remarks by the president and the First Lady. "Dave and I talked a lot about demonstrating," Benedict writes, adding: "Both of us knew the value of drama."

Indeed they did. It is no denigration to say that theater, of a political kind, was to be an important part of Dellinger's long career as an activist. That very weekend he and Benedict were part of the drama of the "Youth Congress Citizenship Institute," organized by the pioneering American Youth Congress (AYC) in an effort to rally the young against war, fascism, and racism. The AYC could claim to represent 4.5 million young people from religious, peace, civil rights, labor, and other organizations. It was founded by the redoubtable Viola Ilma, whose brief and passionate 1934 book, *And Now, Youth!*, was fated to be panned twice in *The New York Times*. She was all of twenty-three. "Miss Ilma tells, with all possible enthusiasm and conviction, how ready and eager the masses of youth are to march and fight in the cause of peace," an unnamed *Times* critic wrote. "But if tomorrow there should be war it would rush headlong to enlist."

A tireless promoter and the founder of a youth magazine, Ilma had established a warm correspondence with Eleanor Roosevelt. The connection and the book helped her launch the AYC in 1934, but before long she was tarred as a fascist and ousted by the communists and socialists who took over the organization. The AYC quickly assumed a more radical cast, and the communists in particular, who undermined so many well-intentioned organizations with their plotting and parliamentarianism, nonetheless stood for civil and worker rights when few others did. The AYC was an outfit in which women, Jews, and blacks had prominent public roles at a time when this was rare, and its positions reflected those of many young Americans radicalized by the Depression.

But the communists had wrestled the Institute's weekend agenda away from economic issues to foreign affairs, in particular staying out of the war and criticizing U.S. aid to Finland. This was in keeping with the Soviet line since the Molotov-Ribbentrop nonaggression pact the previous August had made keeping the peace with the Nazis a Russian priority. The First Lady, deceived (perhaps mainly by herself) about the role of communists in the organization, was thus condemned to sit tolerantly through strife-ridden weekend sessions blighted by the Finnish issue and vitriol against her husband—who, thanks to her efforts, was to address the students on the White House lawn that rainy Saturday morning. For good measure, the talk was to be aired on radio (and would make the front pages of newspapers).

For the White House, it made sense to pay attention to the young, many of whom would be just old enough to vote in the upcoming presidential election. Before the Depression, college students were solidly Republican, but as the thirties wore on and their social consciousness expanded, they swung increasingly to Roosevelt's Democrats. The AYC was both a cause and effect of this change and enjoyed the warm support of Eleanor Roosevelt, who over the several years of its existence had raised money for it, defended it in her newspaper columns, procured access to important public figures, and even scheduled face time with the president. For the big weekend event she had gone all out, prevailing on officials, hostesses, and her husband to accommodate the anticipated five thousand young people in every possible way. An army colonel named George S. Patton housed a bunch of the boys in a riding facility the First Lady had recently visited. She lined up buses; helped with costumes and flags, meals and teas; and arranged at least one of the latter at the White House—consistent with Dellinger's recollection.

The event in Washington was billed as "a monster lobby for jobs, peace, civil liberties, education and health," but it turned out to be the *Götterdämmerung* for the youth congress, and a landmark in the decline of America's vigorous interwar peace movement. Nothing could more effectively symbolize the movement's tender idealism, fair-weather pacifism, and ecclesiastical aura than an American college student dressed as the Maid of Orleans—a sainted military hero—on horseback, just months before France itself fell to an onslaught of modern mechanized warfare. Of course the American Joan of Arc, whoever she was, can be read as a symbol of hope for France because, in fact, the Yanks *were* coming, even if most of them didn't know it yet. On the other hand, hopes for peace were starting to look more like delusions, even to those who held them, and here the symbolism becomes even richer, for Joan embodies three powerful drivers of the era's American peace movement: She is young, she is female, and she is religious.

While Joan and her followers make their way to the White House, it's worth stepping back for a moment to take in the great breadth of the antiwar feeling that grew up in this country in the muddy wake of the Great War. Disillusionment with that conflict was widespread, setting in as soon as returning doughboys brought home the so-called Spanish flu. But the pandemic of 1918–19, which ultimately killed some 675,000 Americans, was only the beginning of the regret over a war soon widely seen as a waste of American lives, put over on the rest of us by people who stood to profit by it.

Official repudiation started with the rejection by Congress of the Versailles Treaty and Wilson's passion, the League of Nations. Within a decade the United States would reject freer international trade, immigration from Europe, and forgiveness of French and British war loans, all signs of our postwar turn against internationalism. Besides the flu, people blamed "the European War," as it was often pointedly called, for the Russian Revolution, Prohibition, the farm depression of the 1920s, the Great Depression that followed, and practically anything else that was bothering them. These miserable sequelae were easily recognized as a judgement earned by our rash overturn of America's cherished tradition of aloofness from the vicious quarrels of Europe—and by our hubris for thinking we could somehow end them.

Antiwar fiction by John Dos Passos, Ernest Hemingway, Dalton Trumbo, and especially Erich Maria Remarque (*All Quiet on the Western Front*) fed public disillusionment not just with the Great War but the idea of war itself. An outpouring of articles and nonfiction books began to suggest that the war had really been fought on behalf of greedy bankers and arms makers, and the real basis for it had been nothing more than profit. This locomotive of cynicism gathered steam after the crash of 1929 and the onset of the Depression, when business and finance fell into bad odor. In 1934, an exposé in Fortune and a Book of the Month Club selection called *Merchants of Death* lent urgency to the notion that a shadowy cabal of profiteers was behind the recent war. Building on this momentum, Dorothy Detzer, the skillful lobbyist for the Women's International League for Peace and Freedom (WILPF), persuaded a sympathetic Senator George Norris of Nebraska that Congress should investigate.

Thus was born the Senate's Special Committee on Investigation of the Munitions Industry, headed by the progressive Republican Senator Gerald P. Nye of North Dakota, who allowed Detzer to join his staff and help choose her colleagues (they included Stephen Rauschenbusch, son of the famous Social Gospel figure Walter Rauschenbusch, and Alger Hiss, who probably went on to become a Soviet spy in the U.S. State Department). Starting in 1934 the committee spent two years probing the likes of Remington, DuPont, and Bethlehem Steel and taking testimony from their executives. Public pronouncements from Nye bolstered belief in the war as a conspiracy. (A 1935 poll of college students found 89 percent favoring "government control" of the discredited munitions industry.) The committee's work also helped bring about the Congressional neutrality acts of the mid-1930s that both signaled and cemented America's hostility to further foreign entanglement. At the same time, internationally minded Americans like Detzer poured extraordinary efforts into world peace organizations and limiting naval fleets.

Given the economic crisis besetting the nation, it's unsurprising that Americans were more worried about antidemocratic extremism at home than abroad. "When people spoke of 'the fascist menace' in 1935," Frederick Lewis Allen writes, "most of them meant the menace of an American fascist movement, which they variously imagined as being led by Roosevelt, or by somebody like Huey Long, or perhaps by an army officer supported by big business. So general was the belief that America must hoe its own row and take preventive measures in advance so that it could not be seduced into hostilities, that, in a Gallup poll taken in the fall of 1935, no less than 75 percent of the voters thought Congress should get the approval of the people in a national vote before declaring war."[7]

FDR surely knew that even in April of 1937, 71 percent of those polled said yes when asked, "Do you think it was a mistake for the United States to enter the World War?"[8] As late as April of 1939, a remarkable 95 percent opposed intervention in any European war and 66 percent opposed giving material aid to either side.[9] FDR, the historian Richard W. Steele reports, "consciously tried to dissociate the current conflict from the last. In April 1942," by which time we were already fighting, "he asked the public for an alternative to the name 'World War II,' indicating that he preferred 'War of Survival.'"[10]

When Dellinger and Benedict reached the nation's capital that weekend, there were two major strains of antiwar activism circulating in the feverish body politic of the day. The first, known even to itself as isolationism, simply wanted to keep America out of other peoples' bloody conflicts; it advocated strength through preparedness and put faith in the vastness of the oceans to keep us safe. "Isolationism" has become a dirty word since its heyday in the thirties, when it came into common usage. But in fact it started life as a pejorative, one used by American expansionists in the late nineteenth century to tar the righteous killjoys who objected to burgeoning U.S. imperialism—and to some extent it retains this function, despite a long and admirable national tradition (until the Second World War) of both internationalism and unencumbrance in foreign policy. Although isolationists were smeared as bigots and ostriches, the pragmatic noninterventionism of the day made sense at the time and easily drew levelheaded adherents, at least until the Japanese attack on Pearl Harbor. The subsequent paucity of strong anti-interventionist voices, particularly on the right, would be missed in the decades to come. "They stood for so much that was moral, sensible, and *American*," in the words of historian Walter McDougall, "that their discredit left a hole in the nation's soul."[11]

The other major antiwar strain, the utopian one that paradoxically had the more enduring impact, was pacifist. Although grandiosely named and numerous, interwar peace organizations had tiny memberships and overlapping leaderships. Muste once joked that "anybody is on very dangerous ground when he suggests there is something I haven't joined at one time or another."[12] Yet, like today's Twitter-enabled progressives, they had an outsized impact. An umbrella group called the National Peace Conference, to cite a single example, by 1940 encompassed forty membership groups, some pacifist and others civic in nature but pacifist-friendly (from the Central Conference of American Rabbis to the Woman's Christian Temperance Union), with a total membership exceeding forty million. The political scientist John W. Masland estimated that an active core of less than one hundred full-time peace workers in Washington and New York, through a maze of these interlocking committees and organizations, could reach out to between 45 million and 60 million Americans in a country of 132 million.[13]

Antiwar feeling was widespread, and demonstrations were commonplace. In 1932, a mile-long motorcade delivered a petition for peace to President Herbert Hoover. In 1935, fifty thousand veterans marched in Washington for peace. Roy Kepler, who with his brother would refuse to fight in World War II, would recall the antiwar attitudes of schoolteachers when he was a boy in the Denver public schools. U.S. publishers issued seven full-length biographies of the great Quaker William Penn between 1929 and 1938, and that year a proposed constitutional amendment requiring a referendum before going to war (absent foreign invasion) reached the House floor. Gallup found 73 percent of Americans in favor. Roosevelt had all he could do to defeat the measure.

Campuses were hotbeds of pacifism, and student newspapers regularly inveighed against involvement in the new war. Cornell undergraduates sent the president a dummy tank with a plea to keep the nation out of the fighting. At Princeton, students organized Veterans of Future Wars to sarcastically demand veterans' bonuses *before* being killed in battle. The joke quickly went viral, in the argot of a later time, with chapters springing up on many campuses. In 1936, two hundred members of Columbia's mock-VFW marched down upper Broadway, followed by Barnard students dressed as nurses and widows—complete with dolls serving as war orphans. Vassar girls talked about forming an "Association of Gold Star Mothers of the Veterans of Future Wars" in advance of presumed casualties.

At the University of Minnesota, the experience of future CBS legend Eric Sevareid foreshadowed the antiwar student activism of the generation to come, albeit in a life made more tenuous by the Depression. In addition to attending classes and working at the student newspaper, Sevareid had to get up at 5:00 a.m. to toil in the campus post office. He needed the money. Conservative fraternities had long ruled the roost at Minnesota, but

Sevareid was part of a group of agitators calling themselves the Jacobins, who took their studies seriously, pressed for change, and had learned to hate the Great War. "We felt ashamed," he recalled in his memoir, "ashamed for our fathers and uncles."

> We were revolted by the stories of the mass hysteria of 1917, the beating of German saloonkeepers, the weird spy hunts, the stoning of pacifists, the arrests of conscientious objectors. As enlightened scholars, we considered that the professors of 1917 had degraded themselves and their sacred function by inventing preposterous theories about the essential depravity of the German race, the worthlessness of their art, and the hidden evil of their music. We refused to believe that war was the responsibility of Germany or any single country.[14]

The Jacobins managed to end compulsory military training at Minnesota and, along with a raucous throng of fellow students, embraced an American version of the Oxford Pledge, whose adoption in Britain had caused a sensation. On February 9, 1933, little more than a week after Hitler became Germany's chancellor, the venerable Oxford Union debating society voted 275 to 153 for the motion "that this House will in no circumstance fight for its King and Country." An American student named Dean Rusk, who would one day serve John Kennedy and Lyndon Johnson as secretary of state, happened to be present, and the event left a lasting impression on him. Just as the students of the thirties saw events through the lens of the Great War, Rusk's generation would see Vietnam through the lens of appeasement.[15] The Oxford Pledge soon jumped the pond and spread like measles among heavily pacifist students in the United States.

Antiwar students made further headlines with a strike against war on April 13, 1934, when 25,000 walked out, mostly in New York. The following year, when the strike went truly national, 175,000 walked out, demanding funding for "schools, not battleships" and an end to military training. By 1936, writes Robert Cohen, "some 500,000 students, almost half the national undergraduate population, participated in the event, rallying against both war and compulsory ROTC." Student strikers enjoyed the public support of Albert Einstein, who had dodged the draft as a teenager in Germany and later came to the U.S. in flight from the Nazis (for whom he was to make an exception to his lifelong pacifism).[16]

On strike day, some campuses held peace assemblies or cancelled classes—including Dellinger and Benedict's own Union Theological Seminary, where the president, Henry Sloane Coffin, testily dissented from the faculty declaration of a school holiday. Coffin, an intimate of FDR's soon-to-be secretary of war, Henry L. Stimson, pronounced himself "glad to share with students and professors in a collective demonstration against the iniquity and folly of War at any suitable time," but complained that what the students were doing hardly qualified as a strike. "If this is a 'student strike' . . . faculty cooperation should not be asked. A 'Strike' with the benevolent patronage of those nominally 'struck' against is a piece of infantilism unworthy of the intelligence of men considered fit candidates for the Christian ministry."[17]

That kind of rhetoric will seem quaint today, but the pacifism of the 1930s, like Coffin himself, was rooted in the Christian activism of the nineteenth century, when evangelical Protestants drove social reform movements for aid to the poor, abolitionism, temperance, health, and peace. Like those earlier efforts, interwar pacifism was essentially optimistic, internationalist, and embodied Protestant hopes for a better world through love, reason, and cooperation. During the thirties, pacifism probably surpassed even the Depression as the dominant social issue in American liberal Protestantism (whose prosperous congregations always had trouble appealing to the working classes) and for many churches became the foundation of what would now be called their social justice efforts. These efforts would succeed, possibly beyond the imaginings of those who launched them, as mainline Protestantism achieved (in the words of sociologist N. J. Demerath) "cultural victory" at the cost of "institutional defeat."[18]

The interwar peace movement even had its own folklore in the form of pacifist fables, much like Catholic stories of the saints, in this case exemplifying the power of nonviolence. Originally aimed at children, such stories began appearing for adult audiences around 1936, including biographies of heroic nonviolent figures and collections of stories about ordinary people who triumph over aggression by responding with love, understanding, and nonviolence. A number of these stories are about someone, usually a woman, dealing calmly with an intruder who is invariably deterred from mayhem by conscience. In other stories a community flummoxes invaders by responding with nonviolence. Some of these involve colonial Quakers coping with hostile Indians. In one notable tale, Nazi occupiers are "helpless" against a demonstration by unarmed schoolchildren in the Danish city of Aarhus.[19] In *Victories Without Violence*, a 1939 collection by the English pacifist A. Ruth Fry, the very first tale is about how nonresistance saved the Jews from extermination by the Babylonians in around 600 B.C.E. She was not the only Christian pacifist, on the brink of the Holocaust, to hold up as exemplary the Jewish tradition of nonviolence.

What were all these folks thinking? Wasn't it obvious that free people everywhere would have to take up arms against fascism? The protagonists of our story were not gifted with our hindsight, and it was far from clear at which point intervention should be undertaken, or of what kind. For much of the time, the so-called isolationists espoused the same views that many, if not most, Americans hold today, which is that we should stay out of wars unless attacked and deter potential enemies by keeping ourselves strong. Pacifists took the far more radical position that war was immoral under any circumstances—that a lesser evil is still an evil, and you can't choose it even if your survival depends on it. Their stance, which a philosopher might call Kantian, was for the most part religious rather than practical, and amounted to "Thou shalt not kill." But they also argued that the consequences of wars are invariably much more bad than good, something about which they are often right, and their judgements about possible consequences were heavily colored by their belief in the wrongness of killing. Convinced that good ends could not come from bad means, they would have agreed with John Dewey's insistence that "freedom and individuality for all can be attained only by means that accord with those ends."[20] Dewey, though not quite a pacifist, in 1930 enthusiastically supported a proposal to create a peace university named for Abraham Lincoln as a counterweight to West Point and Annapolis.[21] Regarding war as evil, the pacifists saw opposition to it as a sacred duty—something that is easier if you have a strong sense of the sacred, which many of them certainly did.

Although the student antiwar movement was significantly secular, pacifism and religion were well mixed on many campuses. Dellinger's radical nonviolence, for example, emerged at Yale's Christian Association. Benedict, like his roommate Meredith Dallas and their friend George

Houser at Union, was a product of the Methodist youth programs that were part of the period's efflorescent Student Christian Movement, whose conferences would help create a national network of pacifist and civil rights activists. Bayard Rustin came to pacifism in similar fashion through the Quakers, attending student programs run by the American Friends Service Committee.

Pacifism was pronounced in most of the mainline Protestant denominations, which exercised vastly more influence than they do today. "Thousands of clergymen and laymen had pledged themselves never to endorse or have anything to do with another war," the sociologist Ray H. Abrams reported. "Practically every Protestant church in America had passed resolutions in the thirties branding war as a 'sin;' and they would have nothing to do with sin . . . When the Federal Council of Churches in 1932 declared that the Church as an institution should neither sanction nor bless war," hardly any delegates dissented. Print-oriented middle-class Protestantism took advantage of the era's exploding middlebrow literary culture by promoting pacifism in an outpouring of books and periodicals, of which *The Christian Century* was perhaps the most ardently and consistently antiwar. And don't overlook the lecture circuit; in 1940, the eminent pacifist Kirby Page claimed, he covered seventeen thousand miles and gave as many as three speeches a day. Muste had ninety-eight speaking engagements that year.[22]

Prominent antiwar clergymen such as Fosdick, remorseful for their support of the Great War, vowed to oppose any repeat, and their voices were amplified a thousandfold by radio. Unlike later televangelists, liberal religious celebrities like Fosdick and Ralph Washington Sockman used the new medium to preach pacifism to the masses; their listeners included Martin Luther King, Jr., whose first sermon, delivered at the age of eighteen at his father's Ebenezer Baptist Church in Atlanta, was cribbed from one by Fosdick called "Life Is What You Make It."[23] Pacifism was a common theme in sermons and religious publications just as it was in the classrooms of Union Theological Seminary, America's leading training ground for liberal Protestant ministers. Pacifist clergy also preached on secular campuses, where antiwar feeling ran high. And then there was the influence of Gandhi, a pacifist using nonviolence as a lever to overturn British rule in India.

American pacifists heard about Gandhi and satyagraha (a searching and nonviolent way of resisting evil) from the Unitarian minister John Haynes Holmes in a famous 1921 lecture, "Who Is the Greatest Man in the World Today?" Holmes corresponded with the Mahatma for three decades until Gandhi's assassination. When I think of Gandhi, Holmes said in a sermon, "I think of Jesus. He lives his life; he speaks his word; he suffers, strives, and will someday nobly die, for his kingdom on earth." The analogy to Jesus came naturally to American pacifists, many of whom had been, were the children of, or at least at one time aspired to be, Protestant missionaries to Asia. But as Leilah C. Danielson astutely observes, seeing Gandhi as a latter-day Jesus was also a way of domesticating an extraordinary Hindu prophet on the part of well-intentioned (and well-fed) souls who looked down on Eastern religions. Imbued with the can-do spirit of the Social Gospel movement, they seemed to believe Buddhism and Hinduism lacked vigor. "American pacifists," writes peace historian Charles Chatfield, "endowed Mohandas K. Gandhi with a mystique born of their need for a political model and enhanced by distance."

Paradoxically, given their prejudices about Asian fatalism, Holmes and other religious pacifists were uncomfortable with what they regarded as the coercive nature of Gandhian resistance. But during the thirties, battered by the Depression and ever more conscious of the desperate plight of the downtrodden, pacifist activists began to agree with Reinhold Niebuhr that forms of nonviolent coercion such as protests, strikes, and boycotts were necessary to effect change. Satyagraha, precisely by going far beyond passive resistance, thus offered a lot for American Christians to like. It was nonviolent, stressed opposing evil and finding alternatives to it, sought a new harmony with opponents rather than vanquishing them, reflected strength rather than weakness, and emphasized correct living. Most of all, it was *active*.

Even before the thirties, African American intellectuals and activists had visited India to learn from the Mahatma at first hand, and Gandhi's nonviolent struggle was publicized by America's vigorous black press. Gandhi employed nonviolence against not just white colonial rule but India's caste system as well. Black Americans had little interest in fasting and voluntary poverty, but this was the sort of thing that appealed to American pacifists, many of them white, affluent, educated, and already conscious of "privilege." Emily Greene Balch, a leader of the WILPF, said the United States and other affluent countries would have to make "a timely and generous renunciation of privilege." Norman Thomas made a similar demand of his own "privileged class" in the interests of achieving peace.[24]

Richard Gregg's 1934 book *The Power of Non-Violence* was particularly effective at amplifying Gandhian thought in this country. Gregg had been a successful Boston lawyer, but after four years in India, including months on Gandhi's ashram, he came home a convert to nonviolence as a means toward justice. He also became a proselytizer. His influential book gave American pacifists a framework for using nonviolence to bring about social change, and so played a major role in transforming pacifists from resisters into activists.

Many of these activists regarded abolitionism as the forerunner of their reformist enterprise, so it was fitting that here they were, in 1940, rallying for righteous change on the weekend of Abraham Lincoln's birthday. By now the students have reached the White House, arriving an hour early to hear the president. They had to leave their banners and placards outside the gates, where the guards on duty counted 4,466 gaining admission to the South Lawn—no doubt including Dellinger and Benedict. They grew colder and wetter as they waited.

After a while the American Youth Congress's national chairman, Jack McMichael, a southern divinity student who had earlier spoken out against the violent abuse and disenfranchisement of blacks, took the microphone on the South Portico and led the students in singing "America the Beautiful." And then, at long last, he introduced the president, describing our troubled country as a place where Americans dream of "the land of the free and the home of the brave," but face the threat of bloodshed.

> Now war, which brings nothing but death and degradation to youth and profit and power to a few, reaches out for us. Are we to solve our youth problem by dressing it in uniform and shooting it full of holes? America should welcome and should not fear a young generation aware of its own problems, active in advancing the interests of the entire nation . . . They are here to discuss their

problems and to tell you, Mr. President, and the Congress, their needs and desires . . . I am happy to present to you, Mr. President, these American youth.

When FDR finally appeared, looking out with Eleanor over a sodden crowd dotted with umbrellas, he wore a strange smile—and gave them a blistering earful, dismissing as "unadulterated twaddle" their concerns about Finland and warning them against meddling in subjects "which you have not thought through and on which you cannot possibly have complete knowledge." Concerning their cherished Soviet Union, FDR said that in whatever hopes the Soviet "experiment" had begun, today it was "a dictatorship as absolute as any other dictatorship in the world." It was a shocking public rebuke to the students as well as the First Lady. The young compounded the fiasco by booing and hissing, creating a public relations nightmare in a nation that took a dim view of such a response to the president. Later that afternoon the First Lady had to sit still at an Institute plenary session, calming herself by knitting, while the fiery anti-interventionist John L. Lewis pandered to his student audience by heaping abuse on FDR. He would support Willkie in the coming election.[25]

Besides Dellinger, other future activists who stood in the rain for Roosevelt's "spanking," as some newspapers called it, included future Representative Bella Abzug of New York and the writer Joseph Lash, who would win the Pulitzer Prize for his biography of Eleanor Roosevelt and help found with her (and Niebuhr) the liberal but anti-communist Americans for Democratic Action. Woody Guthrie was on hand, too, to write the student movement's requiem. The folk singer, not yet a celebrity, arrived by riding the rails from Texas. Stunned by the president's public scolding of the idealistic youngsters, Guthrie wrote a song on the spot entitled, "Why Do You Stand There in the Rain?"[26]

It was raining mighty hard in that old Capitol yard
When the young folks gathered at the White House gate.
. . .
While they butcher and they kill, Uncle Sam foots the bill
With his own dear children standing in the rain.

Without money, Dellinger and Benedict made like Guthrie by riding the rails to get home—a first for Benedict but something Dellinger had been doing on and off for several years. After the excitement of the weekend they entered the railyard in darkness, careful to elude watchmen, and hunted for a train heading north. When they found one, they couldn't gain access to any of the boxcars, but finally climbed aboard an open coal car, the freezing wind whipping them as they picked up speed, the air thick with choking dust and smoke. Miserable as it was, they were moving too fast to get off. It was an omen, perhaps, of the nature of their journey to come.

CHAPTER 2

CLASS ACTS

DELLINGER'S AND BENEDICT'S JOURNEY was not the kind anyone could take first class. Opposing the Good War required courage, a tolerance for social disapproval and physical misery, and a willingness to endure poverty. Paradoxically, the inveterate radicals at the heart of this book—Dellinger, Rustin, Day, Macdonald, and others—were aristocrats of a kind, even if they came from nothing.

Macdonald (1906–1982), the product of Phillips Exeter and Yale, is the most obvious candidate for the tumbrels. Born in New York, he was a descendant on his father's side of New England's grand old Dwight family. (Among his dad's classmates at Yale was Henry Sloane Coffin, who would one day officiate at the elder Macdonald's funeral.) At Exeter, Dwight was a dandy, and with some other "frightful snobs" formed a club called the Hedonists with the motto, *Pour épater les bourgeois.* He spoke disdainfully of blacks, Jews, and women, and showed no signs of social conscience. At eighteen he felt moved to write to a young woman he'd just met to explain why he disliked her so much, patiently enumerating her shortcomings before adding: "And then too there was the fact that you are a Jew, and are rather obviously one, to make me react unfavorably. For I dislike rather violently the Jews as a race."[1]

But in the ways that mattered, Macdonald would change, turning sharply from the prejudices of his time and social class (and the idiocies of youth) to champion freedom and equality for blacks and women, immersing himself in New York's largely Jewish left-wing intellectual life, and helping launch the careers of some key Jewish writers. During the war he used some of his wife's money to start a radical antiwar magazine that quickly began punching far above its weight as a source of prescience and provocation. It talked about the rights of conscientious objectors as well as of Negroes and homosexuals, as they were called then, and railed against the bombing of civilians. Its pages were filled by the likes of Simone de Beauvoir, Paul Goodman, Clement Greenberg, Mary McCarthy, George Orwell, Marshall McLuhan, C. Wright Mills, Simone Weil, and especially by Dwight himself, as well as by readers who wrote in to argue with all of them. Orwell, though no fan of pacifists, was an admirer of both the magazine and its editor, who shared his willingness to (in Lionel Trilling's words about Hawthorne), "dissent from the orthodoxies of dissent."[2]

Orwell's perspective notwithstanding, *politics* (the name was lowercase) became an important forum for coverage of America's radical pacifists, whose cause Macdonald took up, after some initial hesitation, with fervor. After the war, though his political radicalism persisted in various Dwight-ish permutations, he returned to the role of conservative aesthete, in which his coruscating disdain for "middlebrow" in the arts beat with tireless futility against the leveling tides of philistinism that would soon wash away his fine distinctions. Macdonald's attacks on "Midcult," as he called bourgeois pap in books, movies, and culture generally (attacks leveled from his choice perches at midcult magazines) may have been a product of his insecurities. But they were also a reflection of his admirable intolerance for cant and for unearned moral superiority. And they had political implications because they reflected his fear and loathing of the barbarism and dehumanization he saw as a feature of modern mass society, with its "adultized children and infantile adults," a dehumanization that reached its apotheosis in war—in particular, in the atomic bombing of Hiroshima.

With his Mephistophelian Van Dyke, bellicose wit, and growing fondness for booze, Macdonald was no saint. But in the 1930s this instinctive elitist was a passionate advocate for the hoi polloi, opponent of Stalin and devotee of Trotsky—whom he criticized so persistently that the Mexican exile supposedly declared, "Every man has a right to be stupid, but comrade Macdonald abuses the privilege." The quip, if Trotsky made it, probably only egged Macdonald on. Dwight Garner later wrote that "he relished this kind of abuse. He liked the smell of napalm in the morning, and wore it like after-shave."

Macdonald was a troublemaker and dissident throughout his career, starting at Yale and then at *Fortune*, where he worked for several years until his Marxist critique of the steel industry in a draft article was cut to ribbons by editors before publication. (He had begun his draft with a quote from Lenin.) A critic of power and pomposity wherever he found them (including in himself), Macdonald was fanatically anti-authoritarian and eventually called himself, with some accuracy, "a conservative anarchist." Henry Adams's version of the term ("conservative Christian anarchist"), which he applied to himself, fits Day and Dellinger too, as well as a great many of those who more anonymously opposed the war, all agreeing with William James when he wrote to a friend,

> I am against bigness and greatness in all their forms. . . The bigger the unit you deal with, the hollower, the more brutal, the more mendacious is the life displayed. So I am against all big organizations as such, national ones first and foremost; against all big successes and big results; and in favor of the eternal forces of truth which always work in the individual and immediately unsuccessful way, under-dogs always, till history comes, after they are long dead, and puts them on the top.

In some sense—a sense they shared with many isolationists—they were all "rebels in defense of tradition," to borrow the title of Macdonald's biography by Michael Wreszin, for they recoiled from the depersonalization of mass society and big government. And they defended the long American tradition of staying out of foreign wars. In 1940 Macdonald was still at *Partisan Review*, but his antiwar views put him at odds with his fellow editors and set him to dreaming of his own magazine. This he would eventually publish as *politics*, a remarkable journal of ideas and culture that would criticize Allied military excesses, call attention to his country's moral failings, and publicize the activities of pacifists behind bars and elsewhere. "Damn it Dwight," wrote the young socialist Seymour Martin Lipset, "whether you realize it or not you are playing a reactionary role while editing the best magazine the left has ever had."

Dellinger (1915–2004), also seems an open-and-shut case of upper caste. His mother was a chilly socialite burdened with the prejudices of gentility, and his father, a Boston attorney, was a Republican friend of Calvin Coolidge. But Dellinger's gifts went far beyond the material advantages of growing up in comfortable circumstances. A brilliant student, he was also a track-and-field star and, like Macdonald, an instinctive enemy of authority, which was probably one reason he was accepted as a leader in so many radical contexts. Dellinger's enmity toward dominion would later focus on the modern coercive state as well as the power of private capital. Even Coolidge could see that he was destined to impress himself on the world. When Silent Cal made it to the White House, little David was brought to visit him there. The president rubbed the boy's head and said, "He's a smart one. He'll go places."[3]

The same sort of thing must have been said of young Bayard Rustin (1912–1987), who would become one of the most important figures in the coming civil rights movement. Born to a 16 year-old unwed mother and a father he know only "by sight and reputation," he was raised by his middle-class grandparents, who didn't tell him until he was a teenager who his real parents were. He told different stories about this sensitive subject all his life. Yet his grandparents were loving and encouraging, and they set an example, within the constraints of their time, for Rustin's future activism. As a lad he surely noticed that civil rights pioneers and intellectuals including W.E.B. DuBois, James Weldon Johnson and Mary McLeod Bethune stayed in their home when visiting the Philadelphia area. And from the age of 14 he knew he was gay, something that was for most of his life as taboo as was his color. Not for nothing were his collected writings published under the title, *Time on Two Crosses*. Despite his humble background, he too was an aristocrat of sorts, creating a dignified yet colorful persona for which he acquired a fancy accent and adjusted the facts of his past as if arranging conjured snapshots on a storyboard. Like Dellinger, he was an outstanding scholar-athlete. Rustin flourished at his integrated high school. Once, in Media, Pennsylvania, with the football team, he was refused service at a restaurant and vowed never again to accept discrimination. After graduation he refused to let race get in the way of relationships or prejudice suppress the blossoming of his many talents. On the contrary, he insisted on first-class citizenship as a gay black man at a time when neither category was socially acceptable, and throughout his life confronted a hostile world with unflinching courage. He left star-struck admirers in his wake wherever he went.

In his early twenties he embraced the Society of Friends, recognizing that the socially engaged Quakerism of his grandparents, which pervaded their community, was an ideal fit. West Chester, Pa., where Rustin grew up, was within the penumbra of Quaker Philadelphia. The local librarian who guided his youthful reading was a Quaker. He attended Cheyney State Teachers College (founded by Quakers) and was the only one of its students to participate in a large 1937 peace conference organized by the American Friends Service Committee, which gave him a chance to hobnob with peace-oriented students from all over, including from elite schools. That summer he attended an AFSC peace program in Auburn, N.Y., where his teachers included the indefatigable Quaker peace activist Frederick Libby, and where he met Syracuse University English professor Norman Whitney, a pacifist who was to be an important father figure to him. These experiences powerfully enlarged his consciousness, as Rustin himself said later: "I never would have come to certain social concerns had I missed the experience with the AFSC."

Handsome, brilliant, instinctively theatrical and of course black, Rustin was not the stereotypical Quaker. He was also a glorious singer, and in January 1940 appeared in the chorus of a short-lived musical called *John Henry*, a vehicle for the return of Paul Robeson to Broadway after an eight-year absence. Rustin, in New York by then, was nominally a student at City College, that hotbed of radicalism rhapsodized in memory as the poor man's Harvard. Like so many intellectuals who were dedicated to reform and disillusioned with capitalism, he was (briefly) a communist. (In the 1930s the Communist Party USA was one of the few white organizations that made the rights of black Americans a priority. It demonstrated as much by aggressively taking up the notorious case of the black teenagers falsely accused of raping two white women in Scottsboro, Ala. The Communist Party also opposed segregation in the armed forces.)

Even while a communist, Rustin attended Quaker meetings and sang in Harlem church choirs. But through his work for the party he gained experience as a traveling organizer by establishing cells on campuses all over New York State—experience that would help him take on a major role in supporting pacifist resisters during the war and in organizing the postwar civil rights movement. The nonviolence at the center of that movement is in significant part owing to Rustin, who until the mid-Sixties was among King's closest advisers.

Like Macdonald, Rustin was an aesthete. Over the course of his life he would collect art, walking canes, Renaissance musical instruments, and admirers of all sorts, including political leaders, art and antiques dealers, and the actress Liv Ullman, who called him, in complete admiration, "a poseur." He was renowned among friends and associates for his elocution, love of finery, and brazen self-invention. But in all of this so-called posing, Rustin was in fact true to himself, never swerving from the cause of nonviolence and justice for black Americans.[4]

Dorothy Day (1897–1980), for all her anarchism, was indisputably the autocrat of the chaotic Catholic Worker hospitality house she ran for New York's most wretched, and of the provocative and widely read newspaper that she edited and sold for a penny a copy. Unlike so many radicals of her generation, she was never a communist, nor even a socialist. It is character-istic of her that she never belonged to any party of any kind, or subscribed to any prefab ideology (unless you count Catholicism). Although her first jail stint was the result of a suffrage protest, she never cast a ballot in an election when women were finally permitted to vote. Her Catholic Worker network of hospitality houses fed and sheltered the destitute, yet she de-clined to seek official government designation as a not-for-profit, which would have made it easier to raise money. When the Catholic Worker or-ganization, with its national network of centers and volunteers, was riven by the paper's opposition to the Second World War, she issued a demand (unique in her long career) for participants to get with the pacifist program or get lost. She hated popular music, too, preferring opera, particularly Wagner. No wonder Dwight Macdonald was a fan. The historian John Lukacs, aghast at the applause for Henry Kissinger at the twenty-fifth an-niversary banquet for *National Review,* found himself thinking about the founder of the Catholic Worker movement:

> During that glamorous evening I thought: who was a truer con-servative, Dorothy Day or Henry Kissinger? Surely it was Doro-thy Day, whose respect for what was old and valid, whose dedica-

tion to the plain decencies and duties of human life rested on the
traditions of two millennia of Christianity, and who was a radical
only in the truthful sense of attempting to get to the roots of the
human predicament.

She grew up in working class neighborhoods but came of a literate family, her father finding work in various cities as a sportswriter with a focus on horse racing, his lifelong passion. His daughter's passion, aside
from works of mercy, was literature, and she read deeply all her life.
She started out as a writer, for years living the bohemian life of a hard-
drinking radical journalist, doing a little time in Hollywood, publishing a bad novel, and effortlessly attracting men, including playwright
Eugene O'Neill and novelist Mike Gold. The personalist vision that she
would develop—of a society knit together by mutual support, replete
with "the joy of doing good"—was strongly influenced by her childhood experience of the San Francisco earthquake of 1906, which struck
while she and her family were living in Oakland. "The flames and cloud
bank of smoke could be seen across the bay and all the next day the
refugees poured over by ferry and boat," she remembered, adding: "All
the neighbors joined my mother in serving the homeless. Every stick of
available clothes was given away." She was drawn to radicalism as much
as she was to God, and these passions (that word again) were mutually re-
inforcing.[5] David J. O'Brien, a leading scholar of the Church, has called
her with justification "the most significant, interesting, and influential
person in the history of American Catholicism."[6]

These were not the only aristocrats, broadly speaking, who turned
their backs on the Good War. Mayflower descendant Kingman Brewster,
a founder of the nation's largest isolationist group (before he became a naval aviator), would promote the leveling that was to come by opening up
Yale, as its president, to Jews, blacks, and even women, without ever shed-
ding his patrician manner or speech. Popular, silver-tongued A. J. Muste,
who opposed the war from beginning to end, inspired fierce loyalty in the
talented corps of aggressive labor organizers that he graduated as dean of
the Brookwood Labor College. Later, designated "The Number One U.S.
Pacifist" by *Time*, he would transform a timid antiwar organization into a
center of civil rights activism, leading Martin Luther King, Jr., to say that,

without him, "the American Negro might never have caught the meaning of non-violence."

The poet Robert Lowell, scion of one of Boston's most prominent families, was another antiwar aristocrat. He felt called upon to write to President Roosevelt personally to explain why he decided not to answer the nation's call to arms. (No pacifist, he socked Jean Stafford hard enough to break her nose while it was her misfortune to be his wife. Twice rejected for service because of bad eyesight, by September 1943 Allied bombing of German cities had soured him on a conflict that no longer seemed to meet Catholic standards for a just war.) The courageous radical pacifist Jim Peck, who like Lowell, Dellinger, Rustin, and many others in this story served time for resisting the draft, was an heir to the Peck & Peck retailing fortune (he was to give gobs of this money to the War Resisters League over the years). Although of Jewish background, he was raised Episcopalian and sent to Harvard. But he dropped out in 1933 to go to sea, write for union newspapers, and follow his radical instincts, spending the rest of his life as a union organizer and civil rights activist. Toward the end of the Depression, Peck came into an inheritance that enabled him to devote himself to radical causes without worrying about money, and during the war he was a columnist for *The Conscientious Objector*, probably the most important of the publications for COs.

Even run-of-the-mill resisters, while not aristocrats in the sense of Peck and Lowell, tended to be better educated than the men in the armed forces, and were quite a bit more likely to be artists, writers, and professors. Just among the prominent poets, we can count, in addition to Lowell, William Everson, Kenneth Patchen, and William Stafford among draft resisters. (e.e. cummings was a pacifist and Robinson Jeffers an isolationist, but neither was eligible for the draft. Delmore Schwartz ardently opposed the war and managed a deferment, but kept quiet because, as he told John Berryman, "my draft questionnaire is packed with lies." Ezra Pound, who recorded his anti-Semitic, anti-American screeds from Rome during the war, was too old, and anyway a traitor).

Yet if we take the trouble to situate our leading figures in the nobility, we must also acknowledge that they were democrats, regarding Americans as equal regardless of their race or bank balance and treating them for the most part as individuals. Day, Dellinger, and the others inhabited the Left, yet none had personalities compatible with collectivism and all instinctively recoiled from it despite flirtations with communism and love affairs with socialism. To some degree their objections were aesthetic; Dellinger and Macdonald remarked over the years on the excruciating rhetoric and suffocating dogma of Marxists. They saw government as a source of tyranny rather than a bulwark against it, an opinion powerfully underscored by the experience of incarceration. Just as they were small-*d* democrats, they were small-*p* protestants, if anyone can be such a thing, for dissent, protest, and conscience were at the center of their lives. Even Day, despite her ready submission to the authority of the Roman Catholic Church, determinedly went her own way, invoking Jesus and Catholic doctrine on her own authority on behalf of her own passionately held beliefs. Born a Protestant, she never really ceased to be one, even as an obedient Catholic.

Our protagonists had something else important in common: what William James called, in his classic *The Varieties of Religious Experience*, a conversion experience. James, it should be noted, signed up for a three-month enlistment in the Union Army at the outset of the Civil War, but he never actually served (unlike two of his brothers, who were psychologically damaged by combat). Later in life James called himself a pacifist and foresaw the growing destructiveness that technology would bring to armed conflict. In a famous paper called "The Moral Equivalent of War," published in 1910, he advocated peaceful national service for the young as a nonviolent way of cultivating discipline, loyalty, and love of country, while evening out some of society's inequalities. It was war by other means, to be fought against enemies within ourselves.

In keeping with his expansive view of spirituality, which he did not consider to require a traditional deity or religious organization, James took a broad view of the conversion experience. "To be converted, to be regenerated, to receive grace, to experience religion, to gain an assurance," he wrote, "are so many phrases which denote the process, gradual or sudden, by which a self hitherto divided, and consciously wrong, inferior and unhappy, becomes unified and consciously right superior and happy, in consequence of its firmer hold upon religious realities."[7]

Conversions needn't be overtly religious as long as there is the presence of some "ideal Power," James says. "In Christian saintliness this power is always personified as God. But abstract moral ideals, civic or patriotic utopias, or inner versions of holiness or right may also be felt as the true lords and enlargers of our life." To James, the "fruits of the religious condition" in a character (Christian or otherwise) are saintliness, whose consequences included asceticism, strength of soul, a concern with moral purity, and a great tenderness toward one's fellow humans. We'll see all of these in our radical pacifists, including in the many less-known resisters who endured prison and countless social and financial hardships in the cause. Nobody today knows the name Corbett Bishop, but this pacifist bookseller, the ultimate absolutist, rejected nourishment for a remarkable 426 days behind bars, where he was kept alive only by painful forced feedings.

Many of the pacifists at the heart of this book began their antiwar journey from religious premises and evolved in a more secular direction. Nonetheless, by James's broad standard, a riot of conversion experiences can be found among them. Some had two. Dellinger's life was marked by James's signs of saintliness—purity, asceticism, charity, fearlessness, strength of soul—from an early age, suggesting that conversion perhaps bestows its gifts not blindly but rather on those predestined for it. He was a track star in high school and college, and in those days much of his boundless determination was focused on running. Yet his idol was not some athlete, but Francis of Assisi. During his last two years as a high school miler, he lost only one race, and that was because he slowed down "to let a senior who'd never won a race catch up and pass me so that he could finish his career with a win." Was this senior grateful? Or did he resent such an act of ostentatious noblesse by the team's star? In any case, a rival from an opposing team sped past both of them to snare the victory. Dellinger brought Christian charity to track and field at Yale too; ahead of the pack in one race, he slowed to grasp the hand of a teammate just behind so they could share the victory against Harvard. To their coach, it was "a disgrace."[8]

Dellinger says that his conversion to nonviolence came after Georgia beat Yale in a football game at New Haven. This would have been in 1933 or 1934, when he was a sophomore or junior—Yale hasn't played Georgia on the gridiron since. Memory is faulty, and, like many of the exemplary stories of pacifism, this one is a little too pat. But if some of the details are off, the thrust is quite plausible and entirely in character. There was some postgame town and gown tension, and a fight over a piece of goalpost. Somebody blindsided Dellinger and, after a bit of sparring, he KO'd his assailant with a blow to the jaw, or so he says in his memoir. "When my victim fell, I dropped to my knees, lifted his head and inert upper body and cradled him until he came to . . . I walked him home—to be sure that he was all right and to convey more meaningfully my sadness, shame and love." When they reached their destination, his one-time antagonist gave him "a quick, shy hug" and walked rapidly away. Young David was not afraid of a fight, though he did his best, instinctively, to tamp down violence, if necessary holding an opponent at bay until tempers cooled. But now something had changed definitively. "I will always remember the spontaneous feeling of horror at striking human flesh," he would write later, "and the absolute nature of my knowledge that I would never again be able to hit anyone."[9]

CHAPTER 3

THE MAKING OF A RADICAL

I shall die, but that is all that I shall do for Death.
———EDNA ST. VINCENT MILLAY

WEARING AN OLD SUIT, David Dellinger joined the swollen ranks of the nation's indigent wanderers for the first time in the fall of 1937, when he was just twenty-two. He was to make several trips through this living underworld over the course of the next three years, riding the rails and begging when necessary, sleeping in hobo camps or Salvation Army outposts. A child of affluence conscious of the want on all sides in those dark days, he learned firsthand what it was like to live on one meal a day from a soup kitchen, and to be shunned by "respectable" people who feared you or blamed you for your plight. Companions would come and go, but hunger, filth, and contempt were constant sidekicks. He learned how to ride the rails, and he mastered the rigors and rituals of life on the road without money. Dorothy Day, who would one day deliver a baby for Dellinger's wife, leaves no doubt that ministering to the down-and-out meant living with the violence, stealing, rage, and booze that often came with unmoored men. Dellinger's encounters with the itinerant homeless, in his descriptions, were mainly lessons in the Christian communism he so devoutly believed in at the time—a bad time of hunger and hardship everywhere.

But Dellinger would have encountered a class of men on the move created mostly by the massive unemployment of the day rather than by their
own demons. Using the railroads, they traveled in search of what labor
and dignity they could find, and in their wanderings they followed well-
established customs of mutual aid. Dellinger, who would one day found
intentional communities, portrays the hobo encampments he visited as exemplary self-governing collectives: "Every new arrival was welcomed and
given his share the first night and morning, whether he arrived empty-
handed or not. After that, he was expected to take his turn in the daytime
search, provided he was well enough. Either that or take his chances at the
end of the line." He acknowledged romanticizing all this, yet insisted that
"the stew and coffee tasted better than any I had ever had before," and the
people he met "helped strengthen my faith in human nature."[1]

If you want to understand Dellinger, you have to understand all of
this—his passionate concern for those failed by capital and government, his
faith in people's ability to create functioning communities without external authority, his susceptibility to his own stories, and, most of all, his willingness to put himself on the line. His entire life was a turning away from
basic comforts—from respectability, financial security, and all the rest—in
devotion to the most extreme nonviolent radicalism. In his near-religious
devotion to change, he withstood poverty, family stress, prison, and beatings. And where necessary, as with the Second World War, he would ra-
tionalize his immense sacrifices by clinging to a highly stylized version of
reality. If the truth is a spectrum, like visible light, Dellinger saw a part of
that spectrum—but only a part—with unusual, almost painful clarity.

His time riding the rails and sleeping among the homeless helped
prepare him for the rigors of prison and even solitary confinement. The
things Dellinger saw and learned during his hobo forays were formative
parts of a pilgrim's progress toward the lifelong anarchism that was probably rooted in his nature. Certainly they were moving and appealing to
a budding young Christian radical who was, in some sense, slumming
from Yale. He had graduated in 1936 with a degree in economics and,
after an unsatisfactory year at Oxford, was back in New Haven, working
full-time at Dwight Hall, home of the Yale Christian Association, which
among other things helped to feed the hungry of New Haven and was,

essentially, the campus Social Gospel stronghold. "When I returned to Yale," he would write about the aftermath of each hobo foray, "I suffered for a week or two from the sores on my flesh left by lice and bedbugs. But my spirit had been cleansed."[2]

These were the twin pillars of Dellinger's evolving radicalism, one secular and built of experience in the world, the other religious and the product of his Christian faith. Together they rendered him incapable of the complacency required for a normal life. "I was radicalized by the Depression," he would tell an interviewer years later, "plus by the New Testament and the Acts of the Apostles where they sold all their worldly goods."[3]

David's freethinking communitarianism owed more to his father than his mother. Born August 22, 1915, in the conservative and (at the time) largely rural town of Wakefield, Massachusetts, near Boston, David was the oldest son of Marie Elizabeth Fiske Dellinger, a Natick socialite, and Raymond Pennington Dellinger, a southerner she had met while he was a law student at Yale.

Marie's father was a prosperous Boston insurance executive and her mother a lifelong member of the Daughters of the American Revolution. Status and propriety remained central concerns for her during David's upbringing, tempering one another in ways good and bad. She discouraged him from dating girls or making friends from the wrong side of the tracks, so to speak, but never used the kind of ethnic slurs that were common in those days to describe blacks, Italians, and other minorities. At bottom, she was a product of her milieu and content to perpetuate it through her family. Marie made it her particular mission to civilize Raymond. "When I was growing up and until he died, my mother was always teaching my father how to behave," David would write. "The right way was the way people from 'good families' in New England behaved."[4]

David's love for his father suffuses his memoir, which recalls the older man's unfailing kindness to waitresses. He would always accept whatever they brought, no matter how wrong or unwelcome. "Once a waitress spilled some tomato sauce on my mother's new dress. 'It was my fault,' he said. 'I bumped her arm.' . . . It wasn't just that he did things like that but that our eyes would meet and something very important happened—between us, and inside me." In a letter to a relative, David described Raymond as "a warm, generous, loving man whose example in those respects I have always tried to follow and had a lot to do with the kind of politics I came to espouse."[5]

As chairman of the Republican Committee in Wakefield and eventually for all of Middlesex County, it was natural that he should know Lieutenant Governor Coolidge, who occasionally came to dinner. During the Boston police strike, by which time Coolidge was governor, the elder Dellinger supported his hard-line stand against the cops and even volunteered for patrol duty in the city. The looting and violence that erupted after the police walked off the job, and the union's willingness to compromise public safety, only bolstered Raymond's conservatism. Yet he remained sympathetic to working people and encouraged his children to accept immigrants, Catholics, and blacks, quite in contrast with many of his neighbors and associates. And in his later years he would provide important financial support to David, his family, and his idealistic ventures. On visits to the extended Dellinger family in the South, young David saw no racism among his kin but noticed and abhorred segregation. On one trip he refused to eat in a roadside restaurant where the owner had ordered two black youths to stand nearby shooing flies from the Dellingers' table. Back home, his mother's sharp reprimand at his infatuation with a poor Irish girl in junior high school drove home the prejudice and elitism baked into his parents' world.

Raymond's religious impulses were in accord with his natural sympathies, something that could be said of David as well. Not content merely to belong to Wakefield's First Congregational Church, the elder Dellinger also taught a popular Sunday school class there. Both David's parents were strict teetotalers and, with their children, attended church every Sunday, although David considered the services "grim, negative and life-denying." But in junior high school he started reading the New Testament on his own and was captivated, particularly by the Sermon on the Mount. He was soon discussing the life-affirming version of Jesus he had discovered in the bible with his Catholic friend Paul Lazzaro, from whom he became inseparable. David moved away from organized religion, but remained deeply spiritual all his life—even as he and the American Left grew ever more secular. "It would be impossible," writes Andrew E. Hunt, his biographer, "to overstate the importance of Christianity in shaping young David Dellinger."

Dellinger's high school years were enviably successful in the classroom as well as on the playing field. In 1950, his hometown newspaper named him Wakefield's best athlete of the twentieth century. "He excels in track," said his senior class yearbook. "His specialty is the mile, but he proved his ability as a long distance runner by winning first place at the Harvard Interscholastic Crosscountry Meet last Fall over a field of one-hundred-eighty. Dave is, above all, a good sportsman and will be most valuable to Yale. He displayed his dramatic ability when he played the masculine lead in the Senior Play, and when he won a prize in the Senior Prize Speaking Contest."[6]

Dellinger ran because it came naturally to him, and for the sheer joy of it. Yet he couldn't reconcile himself to the special attention that came to him because of his gifts, or his tendency (in what seemed a frivolous pursuit) to throw himself into practice and competition to the limits of endurance and beyond—a tendency he would transfer soon enough to protest. In his memoir he regrets that he cared so much about winning, at his loss of perspective on what was truly important, at the vanity with which he reached for the sports section to read of his own exploits in the latest basketball or cross-country competition. Although he would mock the Spartan ideal of total dedication that his coaches tried to instill, it's hard to imagine how he could have spent the remainder of his life in such unswerving devotion to so many unpopular causes—a lifetime of poverty, assaults, imprisonment, and separation from his family—without the kind of physical and mental strength that serious athletics requires and develops.

Meanwhile, he was also a superb student, graduating high school with top honors just before he turned sixteen, in 1931. By then the Great Depression held American society in its grip and would leave a deep impression on nearly everyone, including young David. The Dellingers were fine, but on a family trip in 1929 he noticed the soup lines, and coverage of the crisis was appearing in even conservative newspapers. That year the stock market crashed. By 1932, when Dellinger entered Yale, one in four American workers was jobless, bank failures were common, and unrest was growing. People were frightened and even hungry. There was little of the social safety net we take for granted today. Business and government, it seemed, were silent partners in failure.

By the time of David's arrival, Yale had reversed the increasing egalitarianism it had pursued during the first part of the century to focus un-
abashedly on the sons of the northeastern WASP elite, filling its all-male
classes with graduates of prep schools and others whose kin had preceded
them. Roger Starr (class of 1939) recalled that "We lived a sybaritic life:
two men to the typical three-room suite in the residential colleges; one, to
a single room. Maids swept, and they made our beds. Porters laid fires in
the living room fireplaces, and waitresses served meals in the dining halls."[7]
Undergraduates mostly came from families that still had money. Geoffrey
Kabaservice notes that the Yale Daily News in those Depression years "carried ads for velvet-collared Chesterfield coats, new Packard automobiles,
New York custom tailors, and holiday vacations on the slopes of Sun Valley
and the beaches of Cuba. Every Friday the paper carried a Metropolitan
Weekend feature listing the entertainment at the big Manhattan hotels and
clubs like the Stork and '21.'"[8]

Dellinger's impressive academic performance got him into Yale's new
honors program, but he was still investing enormous time and energy in
track and field, where he was soon a star hoping to qualify for the 1936
Olympics in Berlin.[9] He also made friends, becoming especially close with
his roommate, a bright young Coloradan and future war resister named
David E. Swift, whose older brother Charlie would find himself in prison
with the Union Eight. Dellinger says in his memoir that he and David
Swift, both Phi Beta Kappa, "had a deep friendship," but that he did not
feel the first stirrings of sexual attraction for a man until he had been several months in prison. Nonetheless, the two Davids hugged and "used to
say that we loved each other (we did)." After graduation they would travel
together in Europe. In a draft of his memoir he describes what happened
when he tried to talk about his feelings with Swift, who was "shocked and
begged me, for my own sake, never to tell anyone else about it. People
wouldn't understand, he said."[10]

Dellinger's eventual wife, Elizabeth Peterson, with whom he had five
children, said of her husband that "he may've been interested in homosexual things because young men just clung to him so often. His most intimate
relationships were with young men." He wrote about his attraction to men
in his 1993 memoir, by which time the taboo surrounding homosexual
sex had lost much of its power. In 1951, however, when things were very

different, Dellinger was charged with a "sexual misdemeanor," as he put it in a letter to a friend thirty-five years later, a charge that haunted him for two decades—with good reason, for he later discovered, in declassified FBI records, that agents repeatedly tried (and failed) to get the media to publicize the incident.[11]

Notably, in his memoir he vaguely recounts a postwar sexual encounter with an unnamed man after the two of them, on a peace walk, had been confronted by hostile bystanders calling them "fags" and "commies." The episode that night in bed was "a fearful homosexual experiment" in which he was reassured by his experience of being hugged by his high school friend Paul Lazzaro when they shared a bed after a basketball game on the road. The unnamed lover from the peace walk, Dellinger reports, was later murdered by muggers in New York. It's impossible to encounter this tragic account without hearing complex echoes of the murder, also in New York, of Dellinger's brother Fiske, whose killer claimed Fiske had solicited sex from him. Dellinger later came to believe that everyone is to some extent bisexual, but that "most heterosexuals succumb to the homophobic pressures of society and shut off their bisexual impulses."[12]

At Yale he also formed an important friendship with Walt Rostow, a Jewish scholarship student from New Haven who would later be a key supporter of the Vietnam war in the Kennedy and Johnson administrations. Dellinger and Rostow spent hours talking about the issues of the day, and Rostow provided Marxist books and articles to his friend. "I think he helped radicalize me," Dellinger said, "though he also helped prevent me from turning into an orthodox Marxist communist" by dint of being such an insufferable ideologue.[13]

Dellinger's years at Yale were a crucial time of learning and maturation for him, political and otherwise. He had just turned seventeen when he arrived, and among its many preppies and scions he felt a bit of a rube, though his brains and athletic prowess must have given him some cachet. "I felt like a young, inexperienced small-town boy," he would write. Among those who made an impression on him were Robert Maynard Hutchins, the school's former law dean who, at just thirty years old, became president of the University of Chicago. Hutchins was anti-interventionist, but he was strongly internationalist in outlook and favored aid to Britain. He delivered the 1935 Storrs Lectures at Yale, which he used to put forward his passionate belief in the value of a traditional liberal education. "Hutchins," Dellinger would write, "presented a view of education that appealed to me and that I eventually concluded Yale didn't live up to."[14]

Dave also attended a reading by the charismatic antiwar poet Edna St. Vincent Millay, a literary celebrity of near-Byronic proportions, when she appeared at Sprague Hall in October of 1934. The overflow crowd was so large that some were seated onstage behind her; for at least one poem she turned around to read facing those stranded in back. She spoke informally, wandering the stage at times, soliciting criticism and even asking the audience what she ought to read next. Of special note were the poems from her forthcoming book, *Wine from These Grapes,* of which "the most striking," according to the *Yale Daily News,* "both in thought and expression," was the "Apostrophe to Man (On reflecting that the world is ready to go to war again)." In it, Millay rubs our faces in the perverse insistence on war despite the horrors of the last one: "Convert again into putrescent matter drawing flies / The hopeful bodies of the young." Dellinger had fallen in love with her poetry in high school, "and now I fell in love with her and her overflowing sexuality."

Meeting Robert Frost, Dellinger found him a bit of a blowhard. "I loved Frost's poetry but found him obsessed with his own importance. In the course of at least four dinners together, he always orated endlessly and was never able to listen to and exchange ideas with any of the four or five students present." He also met New Dealers, including Henry Wallace, FDR's agriculture secretary and later vice president, with whom he developed a friendship. And at Dwight Hall, Dellinger and his friends broke bread with a visiting Kirby Page, one of America's most prominent pacifists, whose career encompassed the ministry, the YMCA, the Great War, and the interwar peace movement. Through his writings as well as his editing of *The World Tomorrow,* a leading pacifist organ in the early thirties, he promoted the emergence of a politically active form of pacifism that young people like Dellinger were eager to embrace.[15]

During 1935 Dellinger's athletic career reached a peak—and then collapsed, in part because of the bulldog determination and indifference to pain that had helped him succeed in the first place. That spring he hurt his right leg in a meet at Harvard, but persisted in running anyway on sheer grit and some aggressive taping. In the Connecticut Championships, he won the mile, half mile, and two mile races, and he was chosen as Yale's team captain. His last race was at Princeton; he told his biographer, Andrew Hunt, that "the tape broke again, and I literally crawled across the finish line." That summer his bum leg took a further beating as a result of weeks spent with his roommate in Colorado, helping the Swifts build a log cabin in the Rockies. He got medical treatment back home in Massachusetts and still had the Olympics in his sights until finally, on a practice run, his right calf muscles ruptured. The surgeon who patched him back together told him his running days were over, and Dellinger briefly sank into despair—until he realized that a great weight had been lifted. No longer was he captive of his parents' expectations, or "a prisoner of my own myopic ambitions. Suddenly and unexpectedly," he wrote in his draft memoir, "I was free and the simplest things in life became enchanting again."[16]

Delivered from practices and pain, Dellinger shifted his focus to larger concerns. It's probably a measure of his standing and interests at Yale that, despite never taking a course with historian Harry Rudin, he developed a friendship with the Great War veteran, who impressed on young David the senselessness of that war's slaughter. During the 1935 Yale Anti-War Week, Rudin told students that "Young men take physical examinations to be killed. Senators, morons, and ministers remain at home to carry on," adding: "I don't know who won the last war."[17]

It was at Yale, to a great extent, where Dellinger developed a nonviolent political philosophy based on his readings of Gandhi, the sermons of John Haynes Holmes, and Richard Gregg's *The Power of Non-Violence*. At some point Dave started taking part in the annual strike against war held at college campuses nationwide, a manifestation of the national antiwar student movement. "I can't remember whether I began to observe the strike in my sophomore year at Yale or slightly later," Dellinger writes. "But for many years before the draft law was passed, many of my friends and I stayed away from classes on that day, holding a variety of public vigils, rallies, and demonstrations. And of course we did this in prison."[18]

More appealing than Yale's fraternities and drinking clubs, to Dellinger, was Dwight Hall. During his first week on campus, he spotted a sign there inviting students to join an effort to unionize Yale's nonacademic employees. His Irish maid and black janitor weren't interested, but the dean was, warning him that the campaign was organized by communists. Like many who were passionately committed to social change in the later thirties, Dellinger noticed that the communists "were by far the most energetic organizers of many of the struggles I supported, for racial and economic justice, industrial unionism, and even civil liberties."[19]

Besides, capitalism, in 1932, seemed a manifest failure. But Dellinger did not admire the mechanical rhetoric of communism (to which he'd been exposed by Rostow), nor the American party's subservience to Moscow. David's antiauthoritarian nature and instinctive anarchism made communism a terrible fit, although he did find it in himself years later to muster considerable sympathy for communist regimes in the developing world. At the time, however, the Stalinist show trials were too upsetting. "I was always less of a centralist I guess. I didn't believe in big state bureaucracy."[20]

Following their graduation in 1936, the two Davids embarked for Europe, at the conclusion of which Swift was to return to the States and Dellinger was to begin his studies at Oxford, where (like Rostow) he'd been awarded a fellowship. Word reached the Davids in mid-Atlantic via the ship's wireless: an attempted military coup was underway in Spain, where right-wing officers and troops loyal to them sought to overthrow the duly elected leftist government. Dellinger later spent some time in Spain and was sorely tempted to join the fight against Franco's fascists. He also spent a little time in Italy, in particular walking in the presumed footsteps of St. Francis in the Umbrian hill town of Assisi. Francis, it should be noted, fought in a war before renouncing violence, worldly possessions, and ties of kinship to serve the poor and preach the Gospels.

And then the budding Franciscan was off to Germany, where he was to be reunited with Swift. Dellinger made it to Berlin for the Olympics after all, even if he wasn't competing. He was shocked by the anti-Semitism he witnessed. At Yale he had encountered (by comparison) only a pale shadow of this ancient prejudice, but he probably didn't know the half of it. Yale was the first place Dellinger had knowingly met any Jews, and he wasn't likely to meet too many because the university, in response to its own "Jewish problem," stringently limited their numbers. (In this it was only reflecting common practice in a society where discrimination was widespread on elite campuses and beyond.) Dellinger happily associated with Jews. But not all his classmates felt that way. Jews were excluded from

Yale's selective fraternities and societies, and Nazi flags were part of the décor in some student rooms. Herbert Winer, a Jewish student arriving at Yale in 1938, reported that his freshman counselor, "somebody who was in a position of some authority," had hanging over his fireplace "a great, four by six foot, brightly colored German swastika flag. That was not exactly a neutral symbol, at that time, even before the war. And he didn't have it there as a joke."[21]

In Germany, Dellinger would later write, "I usually went to the Jewish residential area of whatever city I was in and stayed in a bed-and-breakfast home of a Jewish family. And I visited bookstore after bookstore to ask for a copy of the poems of Heinrich Heine, the German poet whose works had been banned because he was Jewish." (Heine converted to Lutheranism as a young man.) "I went to the bookstores as an act of protest but also in the hope of establishing personal contact with booksellers (people whose calling I admired)."[22]

Dellinger's Oxford fellowship was for two years, but he stayed for just one. While there, he dined regularly with Rostow, became a leading figure in a campus pacifist organization, and attended a talk by the philosopher and mathematician Bertrand Russell, who was also a pacifist. The Depression, Spain, Germany—all had a huge and lasting effect in making him the radical he was to become. But for now at least, he was a *Christian* radical. And so, instead of law school, he returned to New Haven and a full-time job at Yale's Christian Association. He would ride the rails, seek out the dispossessed, and do what he could for the cause of labor. "I managed to penetrate and leaflet in a variety of stores and other establishments where known union organizers were banned," he writes. "And in 1938 I spent a vacation from Yale working with the Steel Workers Organizing Committee in a number of risky nonviolent activities in a tightly controlled company town in New Jersey." He took part in demonstrations urging Washington to let more German Jews into the country. And at one point he was arrested for protesting segregation at a movie theater. As war approached, he attended antiwar rallies organized by United Mine Workers of America leader John L. Lewis. As he would all his life, David Dellinger was looking for trouble. And he thought everyone else should too.[23]

On a return visit to Germany in the spring and summer of 1937, he entered the country with his parents in a car they had brought over from the

States. "When we crossed the border, the uniformed Nazi guards gave us the Heil Hitler salute and pasted a swastika on our windshield. I objected, both vocally and by tearing it off in full view of the guards. The guards took no action in response, but my parents were upset. They pointed out that 'all the other Americans' accepted and displayed the swastika—and it was true." Dellinger connected with German anti-Nazis as a result of his friendship with one at Oxford, where he had spent the academic year, and carried messages from one to another under cover of his role as a tourist.[24] He couldn't help seeing parallels between the plight of German Jews (suffering but not yet bound for death camps) and that of American blacks, particularly in the South, where his father's family lived.

Back home, he laid his father's law school fantasy to rest and in May of 1939 visited the Union Theological Seminary in Manhattan, which he knew "had a reputation for activism and radicalism." That fall he enrolled. "I wasn't at all convinced that I was going to be a minister," he said years later. "I wanted to probe, I wanted to explore and study and understand more about the New Testament, about the early Christian church, the history of the radicals within." It's possible Dellinger already counted himself among them, but it was at Union that his time on the cross would begin.

CHAPTER 4

THE FOG OF WAR

DELLINGER'S ENROLLMENT AT SEMINARY in the fall of 1939 coincided with the onset of the deadliest conflict in the history of the world. Little more than two decades since the end of the "war to end all wars," the same combatants were at it again, this time in a global struggle that would come to be called the Second World War. By the time it was over some sixty million people had been killed, most of them civilians. Enabled by human ingenuity, the horrors reached new heights, culminating in genocide at industrial scale.

During the first months of 1940 it was still possible for Americans to believe they could stay out of this war, even if a certain amount of self-deception was required. Pacifism remained so commonly and easily espoused that even FDR claimed to be an adherent, notwithstanding his enthusiastic service as assistant secretary of the navy during the Great War. "I am a pacifist," he told the Pan-American Scientific Congress in Washington on May 10. "You, my fellow citizens of twenty-one American Republics, are pacifists too."

There was more, of course, as FDR subtly cajoled his Latin American listeners into hemispheric alliance. For on that very day, the president well knew, a glorious, cloudless spring day across Western Europe, Hitler had unleashed his Panzer divisions. In a matter of weeks the stunning Nazi *blitzkrieg*, a mechanized and highly coordinated new form of attack, had overrun the Low Countries, sweeping aside expectations for another conflict of static and bloody trench warfare. France and its vaunted army were quickly and shockingly crushed. Britain, after a miraculous rescue of its forces at Dunkirk, was fighting for its life in the skies and preparing for invasion on the ground. Thanks to the newly ubiquitous medium of radio (and a frenetic British propaganda campaign), England's courageous struggle hit home. From the broadcasts of Edward R. Murrow, bombs falling around him at the BBC's Broadcasting House, Americans heard that "London is burning."

The question was, what should we do about it? The onset of another war in Europe, Arthur Schlesinger, Jr., would recall, "ushered in the most savage national debate of my lifetime—more savage than the debate over communism in the late 1940s, more savage than the debate over McCarthyism in the early 1950s, more savage than the debate over Vietnam in the 1960s. The debate between interventionists and isolationists in 1940–41 had an inner fury that tore apart families, friends, churches, universities, and political parties."[1]

In today's public understanding of the war, shaped by hindsight, the villains and heroes are assumed to have been clear from the outset, and so were the actions that just nations and right-thinking people should have taken. But things were not that simple in the thirties. Certainly it was obvious that Hitler was awful. Even if the full extent of his malevolence was yet to be revealed, polling from the period shows that Americans disliked him and his treatment of the Jews and blamed Germany for the new war. Pacifists, despite their need to find blame on all sides, probably concurred. "I do not want to minimize the evil of a German victory," Muste said. "I recoil from every prospect of it."[2]

But it was not clear how the world should respond to the rise of this latest atrocious tyrant. Germany's erstwhile antagonists, all but shattered by the earlier conflict, might have interceded sooner. But neither their citizens or leaders wanted to risk another war. And Hitler's position in Germany, however unscrupulous his actions en route to it, sprang at least in part from the ballot box. Under the circumstances, when is it right to forcibly intervene in the affairs of foreign nations? Certainly adequate strength is a prerequisite. Early in Hitler's rise, his antagonists might have succeeded— though it's not quite clear by what means—but as Germany rapidly gained strength, the economic, political and military weakness of the European democracies grew apparent. Their generals lacked confidence that they could prevail in an offensive war, their armies were oriented defensively, and their voters, regretting the earlier war, were unlikely to back a politician seen as launching another one.

The Americans, who had tipped the balance in favor of the Allies in the last war, were decidedly uninterested in wading into another. Many were sympathetic to Britain and France. But others, including many voters of German, Irish, or Italian extraction, were much less so. The country's armed forces, meanwhile, were woefully ill-prepared. After the Great War, military spending was slashed, the army was shrunk, and war equipment was scrapped. Much of what remained was obsolete. European dictators were far away and invasion, from across the Atlantic, far-fetched. Besides, there were dangers across the Pacific to worry about. The Roosevelt administration understood that we were in no position to antagonize Japan. Britain's position in Asia was even weaker. At the very least, avoiding conflict was a way to gain time for rearmament.

Many voters and their representatives backed aid to the Allies (as did Roosevelt), but considered neutrality a better way to avoid being sucked into the latest wretched conflict. The Allies' appeasement of Hitler was repugnant to many Americans and was condemned by leading pacifists, though we may wonder what alternative they had in mind. FDR pronounced himself "not a bit upset" by the Munich agreement, but Detzer said that "anyone who knows the nature of fascism knows that fascism must expand and Hitler has obligingly laid out his plans for all to read in *Mein Kampf*." Muste summed up the pacifist view: "Those people are probably right who think the four-power deal at the expense of Czechoslovakia and other lands is unlikely to accomplish any good," he wrote. "They lapse into sentimentalism, however, if they think war would accomplish more."[3]

The failure of appeasement didn't mean that a more aggressive nonviolent posture would be any more effective. America's use of economic sanctions in 1941 would fail to deter Japanese aggression against China or, ultimately, against the United States. Among other American weaknesses was an economy battered by the Depression; many liberals and conservatives agreed that we had enough to worry about here at home, where joblessness combined with nativism to make refugees unwelcome. Conservatives in particular thought we ought to mind our own business.

Then there was the problem of colonialism. The freedom-loving Europeans who had taken up arms against German and Italian expansionism exercised hegemony over millions of foreigners and vast territories all over the world as a result of armed conquest. How could anyone justify Britain's rule over India, or France's over North Africa and Indochina, while criticizing Italy's invasion of Ethiopia, or even Germany's territorial ambitions in Europe? Muste put the dilemma succinctly: "If we should go to war to free Finland from Russia, why not go to war to free 350 millions in India from British rule?"[4]

Britain came in for particularly sharp attacks. In midwestern cities such as Chicago—strongholds of isolationism—posters blared: "Beware the British serpent!" Visiting British lecturers reported encountering surprising hostility on nationwide tours, partly as a result of Chamberlain's sellout of Czechoslovakia, but perhaps as well out of sheer resentment that we might be asked to fight the Germans once again on behalf of the world's greatest imperialist. Theodore Dreiser, in an isolationist book called *America Is Worth Saving*, complained in 1941 that Britain was no democracy and "now holds 500,000,000 of its world-scattered colonials as well as 29,000,000 of its natives in educationless, moneyless, and privelegeless bondage."

In October of that year, American newspapers carried an Associated Press interview with Gandhi in which he asserted that the United States "should think 50 times" before giving Britain additional war aid. "'She should ask what will happen to India, Asia and African possessions,' he said as he sat on the floor with legs crossed, spinning and surrounded by a circle of devoted followers. 'She should withdraw any help unless there are guarantees of human liberties. If America is true to her tradition, she should say what Abraham Lincoln would say. America would lose nothing by making stipulations concerning her war help.'"[5]

Charles Beard, one of America's most prominent historians, regretted his support for the Great War, and in 1917 resigned from Columbia's faculty when the university fired antiwar professors. By now he was convinced that U.S. foreign policy had taken a serious wrong turn with the Spanish-American War. In May 1940 he published a small book, *A Foreign Policy for America*, advocating a big, if ill-timed, idea: "Continental Americanism," which was essentially the vigorous anti-interventionist foreign policy he traced all the way back to the founders. Far from "isolationist," it favored trade, diplomacy, and cultural exchange, all with a focus on developing American civilization without getting entangled in foreign wars, moral crusades, or imperialism. Beard noted that "the creators of continental Americanism made no invidious discriminations on account of forms, ideologies, morals or religions," and thus when necessary "carried on business with despots, Tsars, Mohammed Sultans, and oriental tyrants, as well as with parliamentary Britain and republican France." (FDR, unimpressed, jotted in his copy: "40 years hard and continuous study has brought forth an inbred mouse.")[6]

The president aside, these were not just fringe concerns; they erupted in the halls of Congress. "Paint me a picture of the six years of persecution of the Jews, the Catholics, and the Protestants in Germany," Senator D. Worth Clark of Idaho dared. "Paint it as gory and bloody as you please, and I will paint you one ten times as brutal, ten times as savage, ten times as bloody in the 500 years of British destruction, pillage, rape and bloodshed in Ireland." Wisconsin Senator Robert LaFollette, Jr., denounced Britain's failure to defend victims of aggression, democratic and otherwise, in Ethiopia, Manchuria, Spain, and elsewhere, not to mention the betrayal of Czechoslovakia at Munich. Why should we come galloping to Britain's rescue? Senator Nye, in an attack on Britain that would fill ten pages in the *Congressional Record*, warned that we were in danger of allying ourselves with "the most aggressive aggressor the world has ever known . . . the very acme of reaction, imperialism and exploitation."[7]

Many American war skeptics saw the European conflict entirely through this lens, viewing the combatants as imperialist jackals fighting over maldistributed spoils. Norman Thomas and Representative Vito Marcantonio, the New Yorker who was probably the most radical member of Congress, held this view. But so did Joseph P. Kennedy, Sr., the conservative American ambassador to Britain whose defeatism so antagonized his beleagured hosts. On the other side of the world, a University of California student named Pauline Kael, whose early postwar film reviews would one day air on a radio station founded by pacifists, spoke for many people in 1939 when she called the conflict in Europe "a war of rival imperialisms for the economic and political domination of the world." The famous aviator Charles Lindbergh saw it more or less the same way, but with a racial twist, suggesting that Germany alone "can either dam the Asiatic hordes or form the spearhead of their penetration into Europe." A Gallup poll in the war's first month found that half of Americans saw it as a struggle for wealth and power rather than freedom or some other worthy end.[8]

What we would call "equivalence" was a persistent drumbeat from war opponents and went beyond European colonialism to encompass our own shortcomings. In fact, such egregious American practices as Jim Crow in the South were noticed by Hitler, Gandhi, and others. Nazi lawyers and scholars looked to America's race laws and practices—on miscegenation, for example, and disenfranchisement—as a basis for Germany's treatment of the Jews, and America's displacement of Native Americans as a precedent for German territorial expansion. Nazi propaganda made use of these issues, and Americans were not unaware of their sins. Dwight Macdonald had the nerve to bring this up even as American armies were fighting in Europe and the Pacific, but it was more often mentioned before we were in the war. On June 11, 1940, the day after Italy declared war on a staggering France, Robert Maynard Hutchins in his University of Chicago convocation address warned against giving ourselves too much moral credit. "How can there be a community between exploited and exploiters, between those who work and do not own and those who own and do not work, between our Negro fellow-citizens and those who have disfranchised them, between those who are weak and those who are strong? . . . We come much closer to Hitler than we may care to admit."[9]

With the benefit of hindsight, such talk of moral equivalence is embarrassing. But in fact pacifists were among the first to recognize the evils of Nazism—particularly in the context of Hitler's treatment of German Jews. As early as 1933 Holmes and Fosdick signed an appeal, which made the front page of The New York Times, to the people of Germany to halt these persecutions. Later that spring, at a massive rally at the old Madison Square Garden with his friend Rabbi Stephen Wise, Holmes minced no words in excoriating Hitler. "Be not deceived," he implored the crowd. "Whatever Hitler is doing or not doing at this moment, it is the will of this new Danton to destroy the Israel that for a thousand years has given the genius of its life to Germany."[10]

In 1935, just two years after Hitler took power in Germany, Dorothy Day and some members of her embryonic Catholic Worker movement went to Manhattan's West Side to picket the German liner Bremen, which sailed under the Nazi flag. One demonstrator, later said by Day to be a communist posing as a Catholic Worker, was shot by someone on the ship and a police melee followed on shore.) *The Catholic Worker* newspaper called for America to admit "all Jews who wish free access to American hospitality."[11]

Pacifists weren't blind to the failings of Stalin's Soviet Union, either. Fosdick, who hated and condemned Nazism, called the Soviet leader a tyrant "carved off the same piece of meat as Hitler."[12] Oswald Garrison Villard, the pacifist former editor of *The Nation*, suggested it would do little good to eliminate Nazism without somehow eliminating Soviet communism, too, since the two ideologies were "sisters under the skin."[13]

Many war opponents worried more about Stalin than Hitler. Shortly after the Nazi invasion of Poland, a conservative organization of antiwar women called the National Legion of Mothers of America rose up in Los Angeles with encouragement from newspaper publisher William Randolph Hearst, and quickly developed chapters around the country. It was likely quite large; in June 1940, when various resolutions were put to the membership for a vote, some two million women cast ballots. The group was led by Kathleen Norris, perhaps the best-selling novelist of her time—and a pacifist active on behalf of women's suffrage, prohibition, ending capital punishment, and aiding the poor. Norris worked to keep out the crackpots and fascists, repudiating Father Charles Coughlin, the anti-Semitic radio firebrand. But it was no use, and when she stepped down the organization splintered and succumbed to its most reactionary anti-communist, anti-Jewish, and anti-black elements.[14]

The organizers of the America First Committee had the same problem. Launched in September of 1940, the AFC started as a progressive campus organization at Yale. A group of law students, riveted by the war, started to spend evenings talking things over at the New Haven home of R. Douglas Stuart, Jr., who would soon emerge as their leader (with strong assistance from Kingman Brewster). Others in the group included Gerald R. Ford, who would one day be president; Potter Stewart, who would serve on the Supreme Court; and Sargent Shriver, who in 1938 had invited Dorothy Day to a communion breakfast on campus.[15] A devout Catholic, Shriver would launch the Peace Corps under John Kennedy, shape Lyndon Johnson's War on Poverty, and run for vice president on the ill-fated antiwar ticket of George McGovern in 1972. Like Brewster and Stuart, Shriver had been to

Nazi Germany and found it abhorrent. He ended up joining both America First and the Naval Reserve—conflicting roles that encapsulated his conflicted feelings about the war but also the essence of America First. The organization's stance, shared by most Americans, would be that we should stay out of the war if at all possible, and that military strength would deter potential enemies.

What started as a discussion group among Yale law students quickly blossomed into the largest antiwar organization in American history to that point. It was natural that Brewster got involved, since the organization attracted campus leaders at a number of universities, just as antiwar radicalism would do in the Vietnam era. "We were furious," he recalled, "at what seemed to be the false advertising, the dishonest huckstering of President Roosevelt's promise that we could enable the allies to win by providing aid 'short of war.'"[16]

Years later, as Yale's president, Brewster would guide it through the unrest of the sixties and seventies, incurring alumni ire for his liberal leanings in that role. In 1940, he had emerged as a nationally known leader among youthful anti-interventionists. He and the other young founders of America First were amateurs, but they were talented and well connected, and their effort took off like a rocket. At its peak, the organization probably had 800,000 to 850,000 members, an extraordinary number given its brief life in a much smaller and less networked America. The AFC held special appeal for Midwesterners (most members lived within three hundred miles of Chicago) and conservatives, but it drew Americans from all across the physical and political landscapes.[17]

Chicago quickly became the organization's headquarters. Thanks in part to Stuart's connections there (his father, a senior executive at Quaker Oats, would one day be CEO, a role Stuart too would eventually assume), the AFC racked up midwestern business types, including Jay Hormel and Philip Swift (meat) and Sterling Morton (salt). But America First wasn't just about businessmen or Plains politicians. Among the intellectuals, nonpacifist opposition to the war spanned the political spectrum. Gore Vidal established a prep school chapter at Exeter, and William F. Buckley, his eventual antagonist on national television, championed the organization at Millbrook. (Given a small sailboat, he named it *Sweet Isolation*.)[18] Other prominent anti-interventionists—some of them chary of actually joining the AFC—included Sinclair Lewis, Mary McCarthy, Edmund Wilson, Theodore Dreiser, H. L. Mencken, Louise Bogan, William Saroyan, Henry Miller and Edgar Lee Masters.

A key AFC asset—for a while at least—was Lindbergh, a figure lionized for making the first nonstop solo flight across the Atlantic. Lindbergh's writings, speeches, and radio addresses, many on behalf of America First and all of them aimed at keeping us out of war, brought an outpouring of support on all sides, from the reactionary Father Coughlin to the pacifist and socialist Norman Thomas. "We all knew you could fly straight," wrote the architect Frank Lloyd Wright, some of whose apprentices would be imprisoned for refusing military service. "Now we know you can think straight." Admirers such as Senator William E. Borah, the Idaho Republican who was instrumental in keeping the U.S. out of the League of Nations, even urged Lindbergh to run for president (Borah's lover, Alice Roosevelt Longworth, was at one point a member of the America First national committee).

From the start, America First was the subject of furious criticism. Robert Sherwood, Harold Ickes, and others in the Roosevelt camp attacked, but so did the press. *Time* said it was a group of "Jew-haters, Roosevelt-haters, England haters, Coughlinites, politicians, demagogues," and its sister publication *Life* said it was "emphatically anti-British, furtively anti-Semitic, and possibly pro-Nazi." A widely distributed interventionist pamphlet denounced America First as "a Nazi front," and *The New Republic* called it "the most powerful single potential fascist group in the country today." Theodor Seuss Geisel, having published only two children's books so far, was a cartoonist for New York's left-leaning daily *PM*, where he repeatedly and vividly skewered America First and Lindbergh with cartoons linking them to the Nazis and portraying them as complacent ostriches hiding from Hitler by burying their heads in the sand.

Lindbergh's fears about the war—that it would usher in a boundless expansion of government power at home, an enervating global American military empire abroad, and open Western nations to a great infusion of non-white immigrants—were shared by many isolationists who had roots in an agrarian landscape that was fast losing its centrality to American life, if not its hold on the national psyche. Often these Jeffersonian types were old stock Americans who longed for some prelapsarian landscape of generations rooted in place and small-town interpersonal relations, much of which was already gone or going if it ever truly existed. It's no wonder there was a strong strain of nativism in the movement, which drew anti-Semites like a light bulb on a summer porch. Many, like Mencken, participated in the usual mix of casual dislike, grudging respect and outright contempt common toward Jews in that era, but others went much further. Father Coughlin's publication *Social Justice* lauded America First, and many of the populist radio priest's followers joined. The isolationist historian Harry Elmer Barnes stopped speaking at America First meetings as it became more associated with anti-Semitism, but eventually indulged in Holocaust denial after the war, when a number of disgruntled and discredited isolationists descended into crankery. The journalist John T. Flynn, a leading figure in America First, became a Pearl Harbor conspiracy monger. Sears executive and former Gen. Robert E. Wood, who headed American First, would later support the witch-hunting Senator Joseph McCarthy.

The largely conservative nature of isolationism, as well as its emphasis on military preparedness, kept cooperation between pacifists and isolationists to a minimum, but the two groups met to some extent on the ground of peace and liberty. Across the board, these opponents of involvement in the new war recoiled from the coercive power of the state and the regimentation they feared war and technology must bring. All of them seemed to long for a more personal, more intimate America, and all feared foreign entanglement. But the pacifists embraced international organizations as a means of advancing the cause of peace, while the isolationists were more jealous of national sovereignty and seemed to recoil from foreign contamination. Pacifists and isolationists differed sharply on rearmament, but also on capitalism. Yet they shared cynicism toward the Great War, a conviction that the Versailles settlement had been a disaster, and a belief in the paradox that a global war against fascism would only mean tyranny at home. Everyday Americans largely agreed.

The AFC explicitly barred fascists and communists and kept out Coughlin and his movement's leaders. But it had plenty of Coughlinite members and soon became a magnet for anti-Semites and fascist sympathizers. Lindbergh didn't help himself or his cause on this front, ignoring pleas from supporters to condemn Nazism, and making no move to return a medal bestowed by Hermann Göring while the aviator was in

Germany. He finally did himself in with a 1941 speech in Des Moines that blamed the Jews, along with the British and FDR, for trying to get America into the war.

Condemnation was swift and widespread. Willkie called it "the most un-American talk made in my time by any person of national reputation." But Lindbergh also had his defenders, including Villard, Norris, and a young writer for *The Cornell Daily Sun* by the name of Kurt Vonnegut, Jr. "Charles A. Lindbergh is one helluva swell egg," he wrote, "and we're willing to fight for him in our own quaint way." Both Vidal and Buckley continued to defend him decades on. Brewster would later say he couldn't forgive FDR his treatment of Lindbergh, who was denied an official role when the war came despite his desire to fight (which he did unofficially as a civilian).

For some, the hypocrisy of his critics was just too much. A *Christian Century* editorial noted that "one hundred clubs and hotel foyers rang with a denouncement of Lindbergh on the morning after his Des Moines speech—clubs and hotels barring their doors to Jews." In Connecticut the chairman of the Stamford-Greenwich-Norwalk AFC chapter asserted that "smug citizens" who condemned Lindbergh based on a sentence or two "practice anti-Semitism every day of their lives." In his neck of the woods, he wrote, interventionists were members of "exclusive social clubs from which Jews are strictly barred. Pick at random any local newspaper report of the attendance at a Bundles for Britain party or a rummage sale for the RAF, and you'll find a very high percentage of names of wealthy snobs who would shun a Jew socially as they would a leper."[19]

America First tapped into the widespread isolationism that was among the nation's most powerful impulses in the thirties. In rejecting the League of Nations, imposing the Smoot-Hawley Tariff and redefining the war as a scam, America had returned to its long tradition of nonentanglement and unilateralism. FDR's hands-off "Good Neighbor" policy toward Latin America, welcomed south of the border, was much in the same vein. The Senate was dominated by isolationists, including Republicans whose populism meant that FDR could count on them to support his New Deal as long as he steered clear of intervention. Polls showed that Americans overwhelmingly opposed getting involved, and by 1940 the ranks of isolationists were swelled by defections from the pacifism that was once widespread but no

longer seemed credible. Right-wingers were especially eager to keep out
of war, but so were left-wingers. Nobody was more isolationist than the
communists; taking their cue from Moscow, which had made its peace with
Hitler, they loudly advocated keeping America out of war. This made for
some strange bedfellows, even if the romance was short-lived.

Antiwar music lovers on the right and the left, for example, both applauded *Songs for John Doe*, a scathing album issued in March of 1941 by a
pioneering folk group called the Almanac Singers. The Almanacs included
Pete Seeger, Lee Hays, and Millard Lampell; later Woody Guthrie would
join. Reflecting a change in communist orthodoxy (Seeger was a party
member), the previous anti-fascism of the Left was abandoned after the
Molotov-Ribbentrop agreement in favor of keeping America out of the
European conflict. Thus, the album earned praise from the *Daily Worker*
newspaper for attacking the prospect of American involvement in the war.

One song implied that the urge to war was yet another New Deal effort to eliminate surpluses, except instead of burying agricultural excess
the plan was to "Plow under, plow under, / Plow under every fourth
American boy." The Almanacs leveled equally savage musical denunciations at Roosevelt in "The Ballad of October 16th," whose lyrics bitterly
commemorated registration day for the new peacetime draft:

> Oh Franklin Roosevelt told the people how he felt.
> We damned near believed what he said;
> He said, "I hate war—and so does Eleanor,
> But we won't be safe till everybody's dead."

Eric Bernay, in his midtown Manhattan record store, The Music Room,
supposedly had so many requests for the record from America Firsters that
he kept it hidden in the bathroom. That may be, but the album probably
got more attention on the left. "After one performance before the League
of American Writers," Richard and JoAnne Reuss report in their history
of leftist folk music, "Theodore Dreiser jumped up, planted a kiss on the
cheek of a startled Lee Hays, and declared, 'If we had six more teams like
these boys, we could save America!'" A few months later, after Hitler's invasion of the Soviet Union, the album was withdrawn and the Almanacs
started singing a very different tune. The title song of their next, and last,

album, "Dear Mr. President," insisted that "Mr. President, we haven't always agreed in the past, I know," but the important thing now was "we got to lick Mr. Hitler."

Because 1940 was such a consequential year for the war, it was also a consequential year for those who opposed it. Thus, before the year was out, Dellinger and Benedict would both spend time in prison. Muste, the former Calvinist minister and Marxist labor organizer, would take the reins at the Fellowship of Reconciliation and push American pacifism far beyond mere refusal. That same year he would publish *Non-Violence in an Aggressive World*, a book in which two chapters would focus on "Pacifism as a Revolutionary Strategy." Day would testify before Congress against a peacetime draft, condemning the prospect of conscription in her newspaper, *The Catholic Worker*. Brewster, though still an undergraduate, would co-launch the nation's biggest antiwar organization. Macdonald was already laying the groundwork for starting his own magazine. Rustin, whose many talents included a fine singing voice, appeared on the Broadway stage, but mostly organized for the Young Communist League at City College—all the while retaining his interest, perhaps acquired from his caterer grandfather, in the very best pâté and cheeses. Norman Thomas would accept the Socialist Party's nomination for yet another hopeless presidential bid on condition that the party adopt an antiwar platform, which it did. But before all this, at the very start of the year, the nation's farsighted "peace churches"—the Mennonites, the Society of Friends, and the Society of the Brethren—laid out their vision for what conscientious objectors should be allowed to do instead of fighting. They put forth their view even though America wasn't in the war, because they could see conscription coming.

CHAPTER 5

FEELING THE DRAFT

AMERICANS HAVE MOSTLY COMPLIED with conscription when it came for them. Yet draft resistance is one of the most enduring and successful modes of civil disobedience in our history, and though resisters are often reviled in their own time, the judgement of history often falls in their favor. Conscientious objection, moreover, tends to go hand in hand with enlightened views on foreign policy, equality for minorities and women, the rights of workers, freedom of expression and other humane values. The Quakers, for example, worked hard to live in peace with the Indians. Draft resistance based on a moral objection to war has often had a religious basis, and for a long time government would acknowledge no other. But like society, morally premised resistance has grown ever more secular, not at all the sole province of the left, and deeply wary of the state. It's as much a part of the American tradition as violence, and both were in evidence before the country was born.

Probably the first recorded instance of draft resistance by a pacifist here was by Richard Keene in the province of Maryland in 1658. For refusing to be trained as a soldier he was fined "the sum of £6.15s. and was abused by the sheriff who drew his cutlass, and therewith made a pass at the breast of said Richard, and struck him on the shoulders, saying: 'You dog, I could find it in my heart to split your brains.'"

Keene was a Quaker, a Reformation splinter group that eschewed violence. A later and more prominent member of the Society of Friends,

Anthony Benezet (1713-1784), illustrates the early connection between pacifism and progressive social views. The French-born Philadelphian was a pacifist, abolitionist and vegetarian who worked to educate black children and build an international anti-slavery movement. He changed attitudes about Africa and pioneered mass advocacy techniques including the use of petitions, letter-writing campaigns and lobbying religious leaders. His influence, on both sides of the Atlantic, was large. He led both Benjamin Franklin and Benjamin Rush into actively opposing slavery.

The Friends who settled Pennsylvania embodied two characteristics that made pacifism possible: a religiously inspired unwillingness to take part in war, and a stubborn readiness to defy authority. The connection between these goes all the way back to Jesus, but was renewed by the earnest religious reformers of Europe's sixteenth and seventeenth centuries. The Quakers were among these zealots, who collectively revived early Christian pacifism in a way that would carry down to our own times. Members of these sects tended to emphasize personal religious values over worldly authority, leading them to reject the martial edicts of monarchs, clerics and lawmakers as the dictates of conscience required. Inevitably, these religious radicals faced persecution in Europe. Their departure for the New World is one reason modern conscientious objection may be said to have begun here.

Absent a standing army, every able-bodied freeman in the colonies (except for Pennsylvania) was considered part of a public militia subject to call-up as needed. But the arrival of Quakers and Anabaptist descendants such as the Amish, Mennonites and others set in motion a change. They rejected the power of civil authorities to compel military participation not from "obstinate humour or contempt of your authority [but] purely in obedience as we apprehend to the doctrine of our Beloved saviour & the discharge of a good conscience."

Resisters at first faced fines, jail and property confiscation. But members of these groups were valued and respected for their piety, industry and decency. The local authorities, religious Protestants themselves by modern standards, tended to be receptive to their claims of conscience. And the resisters often were immune to coercion, even on pain of death. Legal exemptions from military service started to arise, first in Massachusetts and eventually in all the colonies except Georgia. The struggle to balance the rights of objectors against the need to cope with a national emergency was thrown into high relief during the American Revolution. Most states exempted COs from bearing arms, but many imposed fines or taxes to fund the hiring of substitutes, and in some places resisters were harassed or whipped. In the First Congress, an amendment to the Bill of Rights guaranteeing the right of conscientious objection passed in the House but failed in the Senate. The issue would remain vexing for a long time to come.

The War of 1812 and the Mexican War were fought by volunteers. But the 1820s and 1830s saw the rise of something relatively new: a nonsectarian peace movement connected with eliminating slavery. Radical Christian pacifists such as William Lloyd Garrison, fired in part by the Second Great Awakening, forged a newly aggressive form of non-violent activism (in contrast to the quiet resistance of the Friends) on behalf of peace, abolitionism and universal suffrage. No less than Leo Tolstoy, himself a pacifist, praised Garrison as the first to lay down a nonviolent path of direct action to the future: "For the purpose of combating slavery, he advanced the principle of struggle against all the evil of the world," Tolstoy wrote, perceiving the magnitude of the great abolitionist's righteous ambitions. He added: "If at the time he did not attain the pacifist liberation of the slaves in America, he indicated the way of liberating men in general from the power of brute force."

Garrison's passionate commitment to equality of the races is one of several factors that made him an appealing antecedent for subsequent draft resisters, who often looked to abolitionism as the template for liberationist crusades. Civil rights was to be a focus and source of energy for pacifists and other reformers for the next 200 years, including for WWII resisters like the Union Eight. But Garrison is also an apt model (for better or worse) on account of his unbending refusal to compromise, his liberationist rhetoric and, toward the end of the antislavery struggle, his marginalization. In Garrison too, as in Henry David Thoreau, opposition to war and anarchism were entwined. In 1846 Thoreau famously spent a night in jail for refusing to pay taxes to a government that would countenance slavery and make war on Mexico (in the view of Thoreau and his fellow critics, a war that was nothing more than aggression to extend slavery). The result was "Civil Disobedience," his famous defense of conscience and call for action against injustice. Thoreau, it should be noted, was not a pacifist, at least when it came to ending slavery, and supported John Brown's raid on the Harper's Ferry armory. Anarchists meanwhile will be pleased to remind us that, when originally published, *Civil Disobedience* was entitled *Resistance to Civil Government*. In 1951 Muste sent *Civil Disobedience* to the IRS in lieu of a tax return.

The Civil War, a seminal event in so many ways, was a landmark for conscientious objectors as well, for it was a war of industrial scale fought by mass armies swollen with conscripts. There was serious draft resistance on both sides: many men bitterly resented being drafted, large numbers sympathized with the other side, and Civil War conscription rules were seen by many as unfair. (Men on both sides were allowed to purchase an exemption or pay for a substitute to fight in their place.) The Quakers in particular refused to contribute to the war effort in any way despite their active opposition to slavery, and pacifists on both sides suffered torture, imprisonment and even death. Eventually, though, North and South alike recognized that conscientious objectors were sincere, and that even draconian punishments would not move them. Ultimately most religious resisters were treated leniently.

Abolitionist Alfred H. Love, a pacifist who refused Civil War induction (his enrollment board, perhaps unwilling to create a martyr, exempted him for nearsightedness even though he wouldn't take an eye exam), took non-violence, draft resistance and the anti-slavery movement even further in the direction of social reform. Love founded the Universal Peace Union in 1866 and presided over it until his death in 1913, on the eve of the Great War. The UPU stood not just for peace and disarmament but the rest of the modern liberal agenda as well including women's suffrage, equality for blacks, Indian rights, prison reform, an end to capital punishment, and the creation of an international court. Love, who came of Quaker stock, was a Christian radical advocating literal obedience to the Sermon on the Mount. Like his political descendants during the Second World War and after, he had a sense of showmanship; at some UPU events, swords were quite literally beaten into plowshares, and he made extensive use of music, understanding that spectacle and song could move people powerfully.

After the outbreak of the Great War, American antiwar activists began to organize themselves to oppose it. In 1915 evangelist and YMCA leader John Mott brought the British Quaker Henry Hodgkin over to promote the new Fellowship of Reconciliation, a Christian pacifist organization he had launched at the University of Cambridge. From a meeting of 75 men and women in Garden City, N.Y., a new American peace organization was born. Through its unique blend of Christian nonviolence and social activism, the American version of the Fellowship of Reconciliation was to play a major role in shaping the antiwar movement, the struggle for African-American equality, the future of mainline Protestantism, the course of the American left and even the nature of protest, all far out of proportion to its modest size. It was also to prove itself a magnet for talent and a productive lab for exploring when and how to make a moral ruckus.

America had little tradition of secular pacifism before 1914, and religious opposition to war largely took the form of quiet resistance. Aside from the historic peace churches, old-line antiwar organizations like the American Peace Society and the Carnegie Endowment for International Peace were dominated by gentlemanly Brahmins who, in time of national crisis, were as likely to patriotically support the war effort as oppose it. All that changed on Aug. 29, 1914, soon after the outbreak of war in Europe, when 1,500 women in funeral attire marched silently down Fifth Avenue under the large white flag of peace, which featured a dove bearing an olive branch. It was an event that marked a transition in American pacifism, for it involved new leadership, a new outlook, and some participants already radicalized by their work on behalf of social and labor reforms and getting women the vote. Here peace was connected with a broader agenda of social change, and the women staged the kind of direct action more common among unions and suffragists. Men were excluded, and the march committee, headed by Fanny Garrison Villard, the great abolitionist's daughter, soon evolved into the Women's Peace Party and then the Women's International League for Peace and Freedom, the longest running women's organization of its kind. The marchers also wanted to emphasize the special role they believed women deserved, by reasons of instinct and temperament, in the cause of peace.

Because the Great War raged in Europe for nearly three years before America entered, there was ample time for antiwar feeling and activity to percolate here. Previous wars generated antipathy, but opposition to this one was more extensive and radical. So was the new pacifism. Instead of Quakers and Brahmins it was animated by Socialists, anarchists, activists, labor organizers, students, social workers, clergymen and professors. It also involved more women.

America's entry into the Great War was controversial. Opposition, encompassing as many as half of Americans, was especially strong among ethnic Irish, Germans and Scandinavians, anti-czarist Russians, socialists, and religious and secular activists engaged with the broad international peace movement. As in prior conflicts, the relatively small minority of religious pacifists paled against the legions who opposed America's entry into the war for political, ethnic, financial or other reasons. The historic peace churches, moreover, were now a minority among American pacifists. Secular opposition to the war and the draft arose in both major political parties, in women's groups, among organized labor, and in rural areas. There were complaints, even from Wilson's own Democrats, that conscription was tyranny. Anarchists, socialists and left-leaning intellectuals, including Emma Goldman, Crystal and Max Eastman and Randolph Bourne, were at the forefront of this opposition but found themselves stymied in the courts of law as well as public opinion. The Supreme Court unanimously upheld the power of Congress to raise armies, and government propaganda, joined to a campaign against antiwar speech, buoyed public support. (The postal authorities could stifle any publication deemed too radical by refusing to deliver it; that was how, in 1917, a brilliant antiwar political and cultural journal called *The Masses* succumbed during Dorothy Day's brief and happy time on staff.) Foreshadowing the debate to come in the next war, draft opponents disagreed on whether to oppose conscription outright, however futile the effort, or husband what good will they had among lawmakers to seek legal protections for objectors.

Woodrow Wilson happened to have a pacifist in the family: his son-in-law John Nevin Sayre. A leader in the new Fellowship of Reconciliation, Sayre appealed to the president to exempt conscientious objectors on the basis of conscience rather than church membership. But Wilson feared doing so would open the floodgates, so membership in a peace church was required, at first, and non-combatant service was mandatory. The government ignored pleas from Villard and other secular pacifists to keep COs out of the military altogether, and most were simply inducted. In fact, 80 percent of the 21,000 drafted COs gave up their objections, sometimes under duress, and served as soldiers; one of them was Alvin York, who became America's most famous hero of the conflict. Encouraged by its success in limiting COs, the government broadened eligibility to include all who opposed war in general, though noncombatant service was still required. Many were assigned to agricultural work, but 450 absolutists were court-martialed and sentenced to an average of 10 years, although most ended up serving less than five. Yet some, like the two Mennonite brothers who perished of pneumonia in federal prison (and were sent home in the uniforms they had shunned), lost their lives for their principles.

More broadly, the Great War was the occasion for wholesale government repression. Civil liberties were curtailed and war opponents persecuted. The war was followed by economic turmoil, strikes, race riots, bombings and other unrest during which the ambitious Attorney General, A. Mitchell Palmer, presided over a controversial series of arrests and deportations in 1919 and 1920 to root out communists, anarchists, union activists and other political undesirables. Part and parcel of this unconstitutional enterprise were torture and detention without charges. It's no coincidence that the National Civil Liberties Bureau, launched in 1917 to aid COs, was pushed by its founder, Roger Baldwin, to evolve into the more aggressive and broadly oriented American Civil Liberties Union in 1920. Baldwin himself, its first executive director, had served nine months in prison for refusing to be drafted.

Nobody wanted a repeat of the ugliness and abuse and trampling of civil liberties that had occurred during and after the Great War. If there had to be another draft, it would have to come with another way of dealing with conscientious objectors. This awareness, shared by policymakers and pacifists alike, resulted in a surprisingly fertile ground for dialog and compromise. Government planning for conscription went all the way back to the late 1920s. By the late 1930s a thoughtful career soldier named Lewis B. Hershey, carrying his lunch in a bag while crisscrossing the country by train, had patiently established the structure and cultivated the relationships that would make a decentralized American conscription system work.

The peace churches had also been working on the problem for a long time. Meetings and conferences going back to 1935 had wrestled with the problem of how to handle some future conscription; the consensus was for the churches to advocate some form of humanitarian service drawing on several historical experiences, including in Czarist Russia, where a Mennonite Forestry Service was established for conscientious objectors. These Mennonite men, working out of church-operated camps, were tasked with reforestation during tours of service equivalent in length to those of soldiers. The program, operated and paid for by the church, lasted 35 years. Armed with their research, in January of 1940, the Brethren, Mennonites and Quakers laid out for Roosevelt their broad vision for alternative wartime service under civilian auspices. That vision entailed freedom from military service and control. It included civilian boards to judge the sincerity of COs, and authorization for the peace churches to run CO service projects. The plan would turn out to be a strong reminder to be careful what you wish for.

———

AT A NEWS CONFERENCE as late as May 28, Roosevelt had reassured the press that "We are not talking about a draft system." Disingenuous though his comments may have been, a new draft in fact bubbled up from outside the administration thanks to the collection of aging toffs behind the "Plattsburg Movement," an aristocratic civilian collective which had trained young Americans as officers in the upstate town in preparation for the Great War. Despite a discouraging early response from the administration, they used their connections to get conscription legislation introduced in Congress on June 20. By this time the stars were aligned, for less than a week earlier Nazi troops had shocked the world by marching down the Champs-Élysées. Yet the so-called Burke-Wadsworth bill, named for its prime movers in Congress, prompted a national debate that was intense even by the standards of the ongoing contention over what role America should have in the war. "Because the draft touched nearly every American family," two historians wrote in a book-length account, "no measure during the months before Pearl Harbor—not even the Lend-Lease Act of March 1941—generated as much public controversy."[1]

During the summer of 1940, Congress was besieged as it was considering the bill. In the process the nation's lawmakers and news consumers were
given a vivid snapshot of the many subspecies of antiwar activists—religious, socialist, isolationist—that still roamed the landscape, even if their
numbers were declining and they could sense their own fall from favor. To
be sure, opponents of both the draft and the possibility of war still wielded
power in Congress; these included senators Burton Wheeler, Robert Taft,
Arthur Vandenberg, George Norris, and Hiram Johnson, to say nothing
of Hamilton Fish, the Republican congressman who represented FDR's
own bucolic Hudson Valley district. There were also eminent private citizens, including Hutchins and Beard, and all the pacifists on America's campuses and in its churches. There were women's groups, from the Woman's
Christian Temperance Union to the Women's International League for
Peace and Freedom. And then there were, in Arthur Schlesinger's words,
"pathetic people in back parlors who hated themselves or their lives," many
of them none too fond of the Jews. Some of these people, surely, took their
cue from Father Coughlin, who called the draft bill a "communist plot to
place every adult between the ages of 18 and 64 in the military . . . at the
mere nod of a Hitlerized president and his American Gestapo." Congress,
he asserted, was going to yield the nation's young manhood "to an international clique which . . . is prepared to sacrifice the Gentile world for retention of its control."[2]

The forces of Christian pacifism and antiwar socialism, meanwhile,
were on the wane. Frederick W. Libby no doubt felt the futility. The ir-
repressible Quaker, who headed the National Council for Prevention of
War, spent a $17 long-distance phone call (more than $300 today) trying
to persuade Hutchins to unite pacifists and isolationists in a new antiwar
crusade. The worldly son of a theology professor (and Presbyterian minister) at Oberlin, Hutchins was, in the words of an admiring aide, a leading isolationist until Pearl Harbor, "immediately afterward becoming the
prime contractor for the atomic bomb."[3] But the canny academic wonder
boy, still only forty-one, shrewdly steered clear of the campaign against
the draft. Americans wanted no part of war but sensed it was coming for
them, and the culturally potent pacifism of the interwar years had lost
much of its currency. [4]

Still, the antiwar forces put on a good show. The summer's hearings featured not just representatives of the nation's three main "peace churches"—the Mennonites, the Society of Friends, and the Society of the Brethren, all of whom were to play a big role in the handling of conscientious objectors—but also Fosdick, the renowned liberal pastor of New York's Riverside Church, who was so ashamed of his support for the Great War that he vowed never to support another. Like many pacifists, he recognized that there was little hope of defeating conscription but sought to ensure that the final legislation contained solid protections for conscientious objectors.

Also appearing was Villard, the "liberals' liberal," who managed to overcome a painful bout of kidney stones to give Congress a piece of his mind. Villard came by his dual callings of pacifism and journalism naturally, as the son of tireless civil rights activist Fanny Garrison Villard. Driven by her example, he helped found the National Association for the Advancement of Colored People (NAACP) and marched on New York's Fifth Avenue for women's suffrage. But he was also the grandson of the abolitionist publisher and pacifist William Lloyd Garrison. Garrison's war—the Civil War—prefigured the moral conundrum that pacifists would face in World War II. Was ending slavery worth fighting for? Was anything? Forced to choose between his hatred of war and his hatred of human bondage, Garrison never publicly supported "his" side in the military struggle, a stance that diminished his influence in the most important movement of his times. His grandson would undergo his own tortured odyssey from liberal icon to wilderness crank in connection with World War II, which he opposed to the bitter end.

There was also testimony that summer by an imposing figure from New York, a woman of considerable magnetism who used her appearance before the Senate Committee on Military Affairs to "put over some personalist propaganda," as she put it, referring to the potent cocktail of anarchism, pacifism, and Catholic social thought that was to have such a sizable impact on the sixties and beyond. Dorothy Day began by describing her monthly newspaper, *The Catholic Worker*, which she said had a circulation of 125,000, and for which she served as editor and publisher. She added that "we have started thirty-three headquarters throughout the United States," houses of hospitality that took care of the jobless. In New York, she said, the organization fed about a thousand people daily:

> We have never missed a day. We do this because we want to express the sense of personal responsibility, the idea that everyone must shoulder his burden; that nobody can appeal to the State for relief and help unless he has done everything he can for himself; unless we have made full use of our own possessions, our belongings, our homes; that we have expressed the idea of hospitality; that we have expressed the idea of Christian obligation one to another. We feel that this work is a true expression of our obligations as citizens, as people of America.[5]

Her charitable and patriotic bona fides established, she went on to speak against the bill, which she described as unnecessary, driven by unwarranted fear, and "against all of our traditions, American traditions." What's more, she said, the proposal made no provision for Catholic conscientious objectors, for the version under consideration limited CO status to members "of any well recognized religious sect whose creed or principles forbid its members to participate in war." That was no help to Catholics. Day warned that if Congress were to adopt an unjust draft law, it would be her duty to resist it, and she worried for her newspaper's future if it should oppose the government in this way. The law, she noted, "does more than hint at doing away with free speech, free press, free assembly, even free conscience. Anyone who counsels, aids, or abets another in evading conscription is liable to fine and imprisonment."

She cast the obligation to disobey an unjust law in religious terms and suggested that individual conscience answers only to a higher power "If we consider that there is an unjust law passed, we would consider it our duty not to follow that law." People are "subject to the State," she acknowledged, but must also answer to a higher power: "A person is a creature of body and soul and made in the image and likeness of God and is superior to the State."

Like so many who opposed the conscription bill, Day saw it as the spearpoint of tyranny. A few weeks later, J. Edgar Hoover's FBI opened a file on her. She would remain of interest to America's unruly domestic spying agency for much of her extraordinary life, by the end of which her file would run to more than five hundred pages.

Along these very lines, Norman Thomas, the Socialist Party's presidential candidate, told Congress that America's greatest danger was not "conquest by Hitler, but the adoption of Hitlerism in the name of democracy. Conscription, whatever may be the hopes and intentions of some of its present supporters, in a nation potentially as powerful and aggressive as ours, is a road leading straight to militarism, imperialism and ultimately to American fascism and war." Thomas's brother, Evan, had suffered badly at the hands of his jailers while a resister of the Great War, and the government's trampling of civil liberties during that conflict conditioned the response of many who opposed the next.

Prison was exactly what the peace churchmen—the Brethren, Friends, and Mennonites—were hoping to take off the table for conscientious objection in this new war. The proposed draft legislation initially repeated a key mistake from the Great War, which was assuming that COs would submit to noncombatant military service. Moreover, CO status was restricted to established antiwar protestors.

Having anticipated these events, peace church leaders were well organized to confront them, working in concert and hiring Paul Comly French, a Quaker former journalist, to lobby. Their fondest hope was that Congress might emulate Great Britain, which, despite its mortal peril, had the most liberal and comprehensive framework for objectors in the world. That included allowing penalty-free objection for any reason and, under certain circumstances, without any requirement to perform military or alternative service. Even during the Blitz, parliamentarians spoke up for COs in Britain, which stood out among European powers on this subject. At the onset of World War II virtually no continental countries had made provision for conscientious objectors, the exceptions being in Scandinavia and the Netherlands. The American churchmen hadn't a prayer, figuratively speaking, of a law as liberal as Britain's. But they won important victories nonetheless. Clergy and divinity students were exempted from service (but not registration). Also exempted in the final version was anyone who, "by reason of religious training and belief, is conscientiously opposed to participation in war in any form" as long as the claim was upheld by the local draft boards who made such determinations (subject to appeal). Individuals qualifying under this broadened exemption were to be assigned to noncombatant service or, if conscientiously opposed to that, "assigned to work of national importance under civilian direction."[6]

But what did that mean? How was this work to be accomplished? Where would it be performed, for what pay, and under whose supervision? That mysterious phrase—"work of national importance"—and the arrangements made to fulfill it, would one day come back to haunt the churchmen, the resisters, and almost everyone involved in American pacifism.

CHAPTER 6

CATHOLIC DYNAMITE

LOOKING BACK AT THAT fraught July of 1940, Dorothy Day considered her time in Washington speaking against the draft as "three very good days."[1] She was forty-two, seemingly a lifetime away from the hectic bohemianism of her youth—a tall, handsome, simply attired figure with bright eyes and the empathic gravitas of a nun. By then her radical Catholic Worker organization, however shambolic, was well established on the edge of catastrophe, where it would linger doggedly for years to come. Through it she devoted herself to living the Gospels in the most challenging possible way.

She traveled a lot in those days, both to do the work of *The Catholic Worker* as well as to escape from it. A terrible driver, Day crisscrossed the country on long, grueling bus journeys, visiting the growing network of Worker hospitality houses that sprang up in various cities among Catholics she had inspired. She also covered labor unrest for her newspaper and gave talks to various groups, especially students at the Catholic colleges where the paper was widely circulated and eagerly read.

These wanderings were a respite from the chaos and conflict at the lice-infested Catholic Worker house in lower Manhattan, where some 150 workers and "guests" lived and many times that number were fed mornings and evenings off of soup lines.[2] Vermin were everywhere; bedbugs were endemic, rats had the run of the basement. There was no place to bathe. The clientele, many of whom suffered addiction, mental illness, and traumatic backgrounds, were difficult, sometimes violent, and usually no help to themselves or the organization. Day was unable or unwilling to address the appalling conditions, which may have fulfilled some religious need for self-mortification. Catholic Worker ideals anyway dictated that overcrowding and squalor were signs that a hospitality house was working optimally by directing all its resources to helping the maximum number of people. One frequent visitor and supporter, speaking of an earlier hospitality house on Charles Street, called it "a madhouse." The latest one was little better.

Known to some Catholic Workers as "the Abbess," Day was somehow both anarchist and autocrat, a blend rarely conducive to good management. Tom Cornell, who was to spend nearly his entire adult life in the movement, used to say, "Dorothy wanted to be an anarchist but only if she got to be the anarch."[3] Accordingly, when she returned to New York the usual troubles were waiting for her. "I got home to face the situation of Bill," she says without much elaboration in her diary entry for July 22. The next day: "Today the telephone was turned off. Gas and electric next. No Mass, ankle an excuse. It does get very badly swollen at night and pains . . . Frank is filled with grievances against Joe and me. I am so often shocked at the positive venom in the majority around me against me and Joe [Zarrella, the newspaper's business manager]. He is called a young punk, a stooge, a yes man, and God knows what else." The next day still: "A scene occurs with recriminations because we are broke, accusing me of bad management, bad judgment, and I realize how the father of a family feels . . . Wrote editorial and conscription article." Her diary entry for the day began: "To be hated and scorned by one's very own—this is poverty. This is perfect joy."

Unlike so many radicals of her generation, Day was never a communist, nor even a socialist. She never belonged to any party of any kind, or subscribed to any prefabricated ideology, unless you count Catholicism. Although her first jail stint was the result of a protest on behalf of women's suffrage, when the vote was granted to women she never cast a ballot in an election. She followed Catholic doctrine on abortion, yet had had one herself. Her organization's national network of hospitality houses fed and sheltered the destitute, yet she declined to seek federal designation as a not-for-profit, which would have made it easier to raise money. She signed a petition calling for a constitutional amendment to guarantee a minimum wage and forty-hour workweek, yet opposed Social Security and a prospective "Holy Mother State" as a source of succor for the needy.[4]

Dorothy Day, it should be clear by now, was a bundle of contradictions, but she was consistent on at least one thing: her total opposition to war. It was she who had given a forum to antiwar thinkers in her newspaper, she who would alienate readers and followers—and drive away subscribers—with her unwavering pacifism, and she who would win back admirers for continuing to oppose war when, during Vietnam, it had grown more widely repugnant. The June 1940 issue of the *Worker* she called "a peace edition," and in it she restated her view of war.

> Many of our readers ask, "What is the stand of the CATHOLIC WORKER in regard to the present war?" They are thinking as they ask the question, of course, of the stand we took during the Spanish civil war. We repeat, that as in the Ethiopian war, the Spanish war, the Japanese and Chinese war, the Russian-Finnish war—so in the present war we stand unalterably opposed to war as a means of saving "Christianity," "civilization," "democracy." We do not believe that they can be saved by these means.[5]

In the event that America should be invaded, her stance was the same: "We say again that we are opposed to all but the use of nonviolent means to resist such an invader." Many readers, and many Catholic Workers around the country as well, simply could not accept this stance. But Day insisted on it so adamantly that in August 1940 she issued a rare ultimatum (to some, an "encyclical") to all parts of the Catholic Worker empire: "We know that there are those who are members of Catholic Workers groups throughout the country who do not stand with us on this issue," she wrote, adding that those unwilling to distribute the newspaper or who chose to actively hinder it must "disassociate themselves from the Catholic Worker movement." Thus began the splintering of the Catholic Workers over the war.[6]

———

DOROTHY WAS BORN IN 1897 in Brooklyn into a Protestant family that clung tenuously to one of the lowest rungs in the middle class. As a child she had three joyous years in Oakland, culminating in the earthquake that shook her family loose from California by flattening the printing plant that made possible her father's paycheck. The experience of this crisis, with its spontaneous mutual generosity, left a lasting impression on young Dorothy. Propelled by necessity, the Days moved to rather harsher environs in Chicago, where her father found work and she had the sort of old-fashioned free-range childhood that is rare in middle-class children nowadays.

None of the Day children were baptized, but her father (whose ashes were spread, at his request, at Florida's Hialeah racetrack) carried a bible with him, and Dorothy seems to have inherited his fondness for writing and risk-taking as well as for the Good Book. She was always drawn to spirituality and religious practice, even as a child going to church with friends or feeling the attraction of prayer when she observed it in others. When she was twelve, her parents allowed her to be baptized into her mother's Episcopalianism, fearing that without some harmless exposure to a chronic form of religion she might be drawn to the acute Catholicism all around her in the working-class precincts where the Days mostly dwelt. As her sporty and reactionary father explained, "Only Irish washerwomen and policemen are Roman Catholic."[7]

As a student at the University of Illinois, Dorothy was so concerned with the injustices of the world that politics filled the space that might otherwise have been taken up by religion—precisely the case, it sometimes seems, for so many Americans today. She found college so wanting that she never graduated, embarking instead on the adventurous life of a radical journalist and novelist. In New Orleans, working for the *Item*, she wrote about taxi dancers (women paid by men to dance with them) by posing as one. In New York she spent a few thrilling months at *The Masses*, a legendary journal during Max Eastman's reign that was shut down during the Great War by postal authorities. For *The Call*, a socialist newspaper, she interviewed Leon Trotsky and was assigned to cover a group of student antiwar activists headed to Washington in March 1917, just days before President Wilson asked Congress for a declaration of war against Germany. Day was sympathetic to the protesters, opposing the war (as did many of her friends) on the grounds that it was largely an economic contest of no benefit to the workers who would fight it.

The protesters' bus, with Day aboard, stopped at various towns along the way, where the students, handing out leaflets, were met with hostility or worse. In Baltimore, Catholic collegians, incensed at the "Jew radicals from New York," instigated a riot; Day came away with a cracked rib from a policeman's club. Later some of the group were arrested for obstructing the draft. One was the son of a Columbia University professor; his father, serving as a chaperone on the trip, was soon fired by the university. A climate of jingoism prevailed, and dissent from the march to war carried a high price. Not yet a pacifist, Day nonetheless made a strong connection with some of the students and later worked at an antiwar organization with one of them, known at the time as Charles Phillips, who described her in the remarkable memoir he published years later under the name Charles Shipman: "Raw-boned, square-jawed, white-faced, and flat-chested, she was yet compellingly sexy," he wrote. "And she had a rich offbeat infectious humor. She drew men. But she was so easily involved herself and so generous with herself (as with everything) that she was often hurt."[8]

Day and Phillips sometimes ate at a saloon near Columbia where "she chain-smoked and made friends with everybody in the place, especially the bums." Dorothy told great ribald stories, often on herself. "And she never failed to tell at least one obscene joke about nuns or priests or rabbis or the evangelist Billy Sunday. (She pronounced herself 'a dedicated atheist.')" Lunch was free when you bought a midday whiskey, but Dorothy was a capable drinker, and no matter how boisterous things got, "in less than an hour, she would be back at the office, sober and zealous."[9]

In November of 1917 she was back in Washington, this time with her friend Peggy Baird, who with her husband Malcolm Cowley would introduce Dorothy to Forster Batterham, who would become Day's lover. Now Baird cajoled her friend into putting herself on the line over an issue—voting rights for women—that Dorothy didn't much care about. Carrying a suffrage banner outside the White House, she was arrested twice and subjected to her first experience of incarceration. She reacted to her initial manhandling—by the male guards at the workhouse she'd been sent to—by biting one and kicking others in the shins. Tossed into a cell, she took part in a hunger strike—the women insisted they were political prisoners—and after six days of terrible weakness, lack of sleep, and nicotine withdrawal was taken to the workhouse hospital, where she listened to the desperate gagging of other women being force-fed, knowing her turn was coming. She derived some courage from Peggy, with whom she was able to exchange notes on toilet paper. Finally they agreed to eat, and soon after, under the pressure of bad publicity, the women were pardoned.

In years to come Day would be jailed many times. In 1922, she was jailed for several horrific days in Chicago, where she had recklessly followed Lionel Moise, an abusive lover with whom she had become obsessed. The Chicago police had taken her in with other women suspected of prostitution, and in the city jail she endured degrading searches and the violent headbanging of a drug addict ignored by guards as she screamed in pain. Day was rescued by her old friend Phillips, who had spotted her as she came out of court. He interceded with a friendly judge, but not before Dorothy had come to know the kindness and empathy of the other jailed women. To Robert Coles she described one, whom she called Mary-Ann, explaining how to get along with their jailers: "Never forget that they're in jail, too." When she was released, Phillips writes, "She had been almost unrecognizable getting out of the patrol car because her face was a mess of swellings and discolorations—left there, she said, by Lionel."[10]

This was Day's second stint in Chicago in pursuit of Moise, who had as many women as he could handle and handled them roughly. The first time Day pursued him there, probably in 1921, she was pregnant. Moise characteristically repudiated her and the baby, and she obtained a miserable and unhygienic abortion from a former lover of Emma Goldman's, who was known for the procedure in left-wing circles. With the aid of her mother and sister back in New York, she recovered from the ensuing medical complications but descended into despair, twice trying to take her own life. After some adventures in Europe and more writing, she returned to the States only to seek out Moise in Chicago again, with similar results. "She waited on him like a slave," Phillips writes. "When we visited her she was ironing his shirts. He had lots of women, and eventually he threw Dorothy out. She disappeared, and the next I heard of her she was an inspired Catholic."[11]

During all this time, as if hearing some insistent voice that wouldn't go away, she was drawn to something higher, something greater than herself and all the world. During a stint working as a nurse in Brooklyn, she sometimes attended morning mass at a Catholic church nearby, or knelt in the hospital's chapel. Big questions, questions of existence, nagged at her. Without telling her freethinking friends, almost all of them godless radicals, she would sneak into St. Joseph's Church, a simple Greek Revival structure on Sixth Avenue in Greenwich Village. Slipping in now and then for vespers, she found the piety of the Catholic worshippers there captivating.

She read *The Varieties of Religious Experience* in 1927, probably on the beach and within the rustic bungalow she had acquired in furthest Staten Island, along Raritan Bay, with the movie money she got for her novel *The Eleventh Virgin*. (It's possible she never knew that William James, while visiting at Stanford, had lived through the San Francisco earthquake that so affected her.) In that bungalow she spent the warm months each year, typing furiously to keep together body and soul as a writer. James's frank acceptance of human spirituality and its purposes must have been a balm after Batterham's unremitting hostility toward religion. He was perhaps equally hostile toward conventional family life, an issue that took on new urgency after the birth of their daughter, Tamar, on March 4, 1926. Day also surely noticed that James saw in spirituality a powerful critique of progress and affluence, that he illuminated the meaning of saintliness and asceticism, and that he recognized the pursuit of communion with the divine as a source of human strength.

In search of such communion, Dorothy walked up to a nun on the street to set in motion the process of her conversion to Catholicism, formalized by her baptism on December 29, 1927. A proper conversion experience is a caesura in the rhythm of living, unmistakably dividing before and after. Before bearing a child and embracing Catholicism, Day had lived a life replete with drink, lovers, and adventure, but also heartbreak, restlessness, and regret. Afterwards she led a life of singular devotion: to the poor, to peace, to God. She still read and wrote fervently, still cherished her loved ones. There was still her courage, only enlarged. Yet everything was changed.

———

THE RADICAL ENTERPRISE WE know as the Catholic Worker movement sprang from the prayers of a fervent young woman with a vocation, who quite explicitly appealed to God for help in fulfilling it. She issued this appeal at the end of her third and most consequential visit to Washington, in December of 1932. By now she had worked in Hollywood ("Life in this place broadens the fanny and narrows the mind"[12]), lived in New Orleans and Mexico (where she met the anticlerical artist Diego Rivera), briefly married a wealthy but feckless older man (with whom she encountered Marcel Duchamp in Paris), and finally divorced and resettled in New York. Now a mother and a devout Catholic, she had begun losing track of her old friends even as she was estranged from much of her family. She led a quieter life now, attending mass (the beginning of a lifelong habit) and caring for her daughter, but still writing, including for Catholic publications such as *Commonweal* and *America*. For the daily *Staten Island Advance* she drove around the still-rural island interviewing people for her gardening column.

It was *Commonweal* that dispatched her to Washington this time, once again to cover a protest—a communist-backed march of three thousand unemployed men, one of a series of such "hunger" marches around the country in response to the desperate conditions of the Depression. Day came down on the bus with her friend Mary Heaton Vorse, another radical journalist, with whom she shared a dollar-a-night room on Massachusetts Avenue. "The city was in a state bordering on hysteria," she wrote. Police, the National Guard, Marines, and armed volunteers from the American Legion were everywhere. For two days the tired, hungry marchers lived on the frigid streets until they were allowed to march down Pennsylvania Avenue demanding Congress act on relief. "Suddenly permission was given to the marchers to proceed," Day would write.

> On a bright sunny day the ragged horde triumphantly with banners flying, with lettered slogans mounted on sticks, paraded three thousand strong through the tree-flanked streets of Washington. I stood on the curb and watched them, joy and pride in the courage of this band of men and women mounting in my heart, and with it a bitterness too that since I was now a Catholic, with fundamental philosophical differences, I could not be out there with them. I could write, I could protest, to arouse the conscience, but where was the Catholic leadership in the gathering of bands of men and women together, for the actual works of mercy that the comrades had always made part of their technique in reaching the workers? How little, how puny my work had been since becoming a Catholic, I thought. How self-centered, how ingrown.[13]

Keyed up by what she had seen, she felt the need to pray. Mark the date: December 8, 1932, a Catholic holiday celebrating the sinless conception of Jesus' mother, Mary. "When the demonstration was over and I had finished writing my story," she writes, "I went to the national shrine at the Catholic University on the feast of the Immaculate Conception. There I offered up a special prayer, a prayer which came with tears and with anguish, that some way would open up for me to use what talents I possessed for my fellow workers, for the poor."[14]

Day was praying in what is officially called the National Shrine of the Immaculate Conception—not in the huge basilica, which was still under construction, but in the much more intimate Crypt Church, with its vaulted ceilings and mosaic tilework. Her scribblings had come to seem small next to the needs of the day. "As I knelt there," she wrote later in her not terribly reliable memoir, "I realized that after three years of Catholicism my only contact with active Catholics had been through articles I had written for one of the Catholic magazines. Those contacts had been brief, casual. I still did not know personally one Catholic layman."

The next day, probably, she took the bus home—an eight-hour trip in that era before the Interstate Highway System. When she returned to New York, eager to see her daughter, Tamar, a strange Frenchman awaited her. "The man introduced himself briefly: 'I am Peter Maurin.' He pronounced it Maw-rin, with an accent on the first syllable, deliberately anglicizing the word. 'George Shuster, editor of The Commonweal, told me to look you up. Also, a red-headed Irish Communist in Union Square told me to see you. He says we think alike.'"[15]

Here at last was the answer to her prayers in the form of a stocky, garrulous French peasant-philosopher and rebel against modernity who wanted people to consider what it truly meant to live in Christ. He called himself at times a Christian communist, but also "a radical of the right," his notion of the good life encapsulated by the medieval village. He wanted someone to start an ambitious new radical-Catholic enterprise—in particular, a publication—and he was an irresistible force, turning up continually, talking endlessly about spirituality, Christianity, and the salvation of souls. His clothes soiled, his body unwashed, his pockets stuffed with books and papers, he had the look of a Union Square soapbox orator sent over by central casting. In fact, he had been a Christian Brother, a soldier, a farm worker, a ditchdigger, a teacher of French, and—for a while at least—a libertine. That was how he contracted the syphilis that would contribute to his death sixteen years later. Born in something like a medieval village in France, on a farm that had been in his family for 1,500 years, he made his way to Canada and then to the United States. In 1926, he had a religious experience, never specified, that left him changed—surely a kind of conversion. That was when his serious studies began, and when he had a vision of a new society in which it was easier to be good. He imagined a movement, and a newspaper. He was always mysterious about his past, but his peripatetic life as an unskilled laborer, his self-directed reading, and his homely philosophizing—simultaneously revolutionary and reactionary—suggest an earlier and more religious Eric Hoffer.

Twenty years Day's senior and consumed by ideas in a way she was not, Maurin had nonetheless found in his new acquaintance an intellectual equal and a kindred spirit. His vast learning may have struck Dorothy (a tremendously serious reader herself) as a powerful contrast with his shabby appearance—and a reason to take this eccentric stranger seriously. Maritain, Mounier, Kropotkin, Veblen, Chesterton, economics, church history, and of course the Bible—Maurin had read all of it, and much more, and it fitted him for one of his most important tasks: serving as the conduit for a more formal personalism to reach Day, who was already an instinctive subscriber to this radically anti-modern, anti-material, anarchist-adjacent strain of liberationism. (In September 1936 she would explicitly state her newspaper's personalist point of view: "We are working for the Communitarian revolution to oppose both the rugged individualism of the capitalist era, and the collectivism of the Communist revolution . . . We are Personalists because we believe that man, a person, a creature of body and soul is greater than the State . . . We are Personalists because we believe in free will, and not in the economic determinism of the Communist philosophy.")

On this basis, in the depths of the Depression, Day was to promulgate a broad critique of American materialism, militarism, racism, and other ills. But again and again she emphasized personal responsibility, insisting that the Catholic faith required adherents to take action against injustice. Becoming too dependent on "Holy Mother State," as she called it, would curtail our freedom, undermine our religious obligation to one another, widen the gulf between helper and helped—and often fail to solve the problem. Maurin did not like FDR's New Deal, but Dorothy seemed to regard it as a necessary evil, a stopgap against the terrible suffering of the Depression until people could once again take responsibility for themselves and one another. "She wasn't, as people might think, a religious leftist," says theologian and activist Jim Wallis. "So Dorothy on theological matters, ecclesial matters, biblical matters, was quite conservative. And she was radical in her social, economic, political views because of her conservative faith."[16]

It was Maurin who seemed to reveal the path laid out by divine providence for her to address the suffering of the poor and the wrongs of the world. Maurin was the inspiration for the hospitality houses and the quixotic Catholic Worker farms as well. Probably inspired by Emmanuel Mounier's recently launched French journal *Esprit*, which took a Catholic personalist approach to the day's political and moral questions, Maurin wanted to launch a radical Catholic journal in New York, which was why Shuster sent him to a radical journalist named Dorothy Day.

The first issue of *The Catholic Worker* was published on May 1, 1933. It was timed to come out on May Day, and distribution began in Union Square, that hotbed of collectivist radicalism, where the *Catholic Worker* name must have been recognized as a reference (or critique) of the Communist Party's *Daily Worker*. The new paper sold then for the same price it sells for now: a penny (they had to charge *something*, because they needed paid circulation to obtain a favorable postal rate on mailed copies). Some people, of course, gave more. "What happens," Day explains, "is that our work of hospitality in the city and country is paid for also by our readers who send a dollar for a subscription or five dollars! Love is an exchange of gifts, St. Ignatius said."[17]

The newspaper's unequivocal Catholicism was surprising and even dismaying to some, but *The Catholic Worker*'s unwavering path between laissez-faire and collectivism was laid out at the highest levels of the church. In 1891, in an encyclical called *Rerum ovarum*, Pope Leo XIII set forth a vision of social justice based on the mutual obligations of capital and labor, a vision relying not on government intervention but on such Christian principles as compassion, generosity, and the essential dignity of every person. He defended private property, but only absent greed and if the fruits of enterprise are properly used. Four decades later, Pope Pius XI went further

in an encyclical of his own that advocated fair wages, trade unions, an own-
ership stake for workers, and a role for government when economic circumstances made it impossible for employers and employees to uphold their
obligations to one another.

Just two years after that, the first monthly edition of Dorothy Day's
new newspaper proclaimed the vitality of these ideas in a badly fallen
world. In a letter to readers, Day said the paper was "for those who think
that there is no hope for the future, no recognition of their plight," and
that it was published to let them know it was possible to be radical without
being atheist, "to call their attention to the fact that the Catholic Church
has a social program—to let them know that there are men of God who
are working not only for their spiritual, but for their material welfare."
The money, she said, had come from begging small contributions and the
editors' own scant funds, and the paper, and its frequency of publication,
depended on further donations. "There is no editorial office, no overhead
in the way of telephone or electricity, no salaries paid." But there was confidence, unspoken, that God would provide. And there was a need. "It's time
there was a Catholic paper printed for the unemployed."

From the beginning, it was Dorothy's newspaper, which she began
putting together at the kitchen table, empowered in part by her reading
of St. Teresa's *Book of the Foundations*. ("Teresa and three ducats can do everything.") And unlike so many halting first efforts, which only grow into
themselves later, this one seemed to spring, like Athena, fully grown from
its creator's brow and armored against injustice. Even at the beginning, the
newspaper had a strikingly distinctive look and feel, its muscular and somehow very Catholic typography anchored by gorgeous woodcuts marrying
the earthly and the ecclesiastical. From the outset there were articles about
child labor, strikes, poverty, Hoovervilles and, perhaps most consistently,
the plight of African Americans. *The Catholic Worker* was a largely white
Catholic organization over the years, but Dorothy recruited black writers,
reported on lynchings and black unemployment, and at the prodding of
a black reader included black figures in the paper's distinctive woodcuts.
She alienated Mayor Fiorello La Guardia by exposing ghastly conditions
at Harlem Hospital and the city's inadequate provisions for the homeless. *The Catholic Worker* never had a formal program or ideology except

for the personalism of its founders. The editor took inspiration from Peter Maurin's big ideas, but instinctively focused coverage on the urgent issues of the day, seen through the timeless teaching of the Gospels.

Peter wasn't happy with the first issue. He had imagined a journal at once more devotional and more cerebral, dealing with the ideas and philosophers he cared about so passionately. The premiere issue of the newspaper he had inspired even misspelled his name. Dorothy wrote:

> Much later, when I had a look at that first issue, I could see more clearly what bothered Peter. We had emphasized wages and hours while he was trying to talk about a philosophy of work. I had written of women in industry, children in industry, of sweatshops and strikes.
>
> "Strikes don't strike me!" Peter kept saying, stubbornly. It must have appeared to him that we were just urging the patching-up of the industrial system instead of trying to rebuild society itself with a philosophy so old it seemed like new. Even the name of the paper did not satisfy him. He would have preferred *Catholic Radical*, since he believed that radicals should, as their name implied, get at the roots of things.[18]

But even in that very first issue, there was room for some of Peter's free-verse "Easy Essays," which expressed his lofty ideas in down-to-earth form. An excerpt:

> Catholic scholars
> have taken the dynamite
> of the church;
> they have wrapped it up
> in nice phraseology,
> have placed it
> in an hermetically
> sealed container
> and sat on the lid.

It is about time
to take the lid off
and to make
the Catholic dynamite
dynamic.[19]

The newspaper was, and always would be, trouble. Outraged readers complained to the Archdiocese of New York about it, in a pattern that would go on for years, leading to periodic run-ins with church authorities. There was trouble with the civil authorities as well. When La Guardia sent a flunky to register his discontent, Day regaled her readers (and rubbed salt in the Little Flower's wounds) with a sardonic account in print. Many readers objected to the extensive coverage of discrimination against blacks, and Maurin raised hackles with his criticisms of the Church's conservative clergy. The newspaper criticized Mussolini's invasion of Ethiopia, thereby antagonizing many Italian American Catholics. It attacked Catholic Charities for accepting money from the Rockefeller Foundation (if you were in the market for indulgences, you shouldn't expect to buy them from the Catholic Workers). And Dorothy antagonized her beloved sister, Della, by criticizing the teaching of contraception in public schools. A serious Catholic now, Day was no longer an acolyte of Margaret Sanger—presaging the recent turn of even Planned Parenthood against its once-revered founder.[20]

From the beginning, *The Catholic Worker* was hostile to militarism. Early editions attacked the international arms race and criticized such related phenomena as German anti-Semitism. In October 1933, Day announced that Catholic Workers, as "representatives of Catholic pacifism," would attend a meeting of the communist-linked Congress Against War, and this spark, it has been suggested, ignited a meaningful Catholic pacifism in America. There were many other such sparks within the pages of Day's newspaper, which increasingly reflected her view that war was a forbidden abomination.

In October 1934 an unsigned article, "The Mystical Body of Christ," probably by Day herself, asserted that humans are all part of Christ and that war is a disease which weakens this collective body. In 1935, the paper condemned the use of poison gas in war and talked about conscientious objection. In March of that year *The Catholic Worker* published a curious little article by a radical priest named Paul Hanley Furfey, entitled "Christ and the Patriot," which took the form of a dialogue between Jesus and a nationalist defender of a just war. Again and again Jesus repeats, in different ways, that we must turn the other cheek and resist violence. "Publication of the dialogue," says Day biographer Jim Forest, "is the first clear indication in *The Catholic Worker* of Dorothy's conviction that following Jesus required the renunciation of hatred and killing." [21]

In May of 1936, on its third birthday, the newspaper came right out with it, publishing a dramatic editorial by Day called "Pacifism" that began: "The Catholic Worker is sincerely a *pacifist* paper." It takes heroism to be a pacifist, Day asserted, and those who would tread that road should study and prepare. "A pacifist even now," she wrote, "must be prepared for the opposition of the next mob who thinks violence is bravery." The editorial reflects Day's evolution; like her radical friends, she opposed the Great War because she imagined it was nothing more than a struggle over profits—or a scam to create them. Now, a Catholic since 1926, her objections to war were religious: "My absolute pacifism stems purely from the gospel." [22]

From here on, Forest reports, "the paper increasingly voiced this unfamiliar position, which many Catholics found shocking and possibly heretical." That this should be so is a measure of the great distance the Catholic church has traveled over time, for early Christians interpreted Christ's actions and teachings as prohibiting violence. "Put away your sword," he told Peter, "for whoever lives by the sword shall perish by the sword." Many persecuted Christians died without defending themselves (and some died for refusing military service). But over time, the increasingly established church made its peace with armed conflict, even launching holy wars. Woven into a network of fractious European monarchies across the continent, Roman Catholic religious authorities learned to go along with the home team. In America, perhaps to signal loyalty out of a desire for acceptance by a largely Protestant nation, Catholic clergy were especially ready to support the nation's wars, even if Irish, Italian, and other American Catholics sometimes felt the tug of allegiance to the old country.

The early church's pacifism long past, Catholic theologians over the centuries developed a doctrine of "just war" to provide a moral and intellectual framework, in the light of the Gospel, for when Catholics should fight. St. Augustine, for example, recognized that war was horrible but

sometimes necessary and "justified only by the injustice of the aggressor."
Thomas Aquinas laid out three criteria for a just war: it has to be waged by
a legitimate authority, the cause must be just, and it must be fought with the
right intentions (to advance good and prevent evil).[23]

The Catholic conception of the just war has evolved since then and is
expressed in the Catechism, which lays out four conditions:

— the damage inflicted by the aggressor on the nation or community of nations must be lasting, grave, and certain;
— all other means of putting an end to it must have been shown
  to be impractical or ineffective;
— there must be serious prospects of success;
— the use of arms must not produce evils and disorders graver
  than the evil to be eliminated. The power of modern means of
  destruction weighs very heavily in evaluating this condition.

THE CATECHISM GOES ON to say that authorities "have the right and duty
to impose on citizens the obligations necessary for national defense" but
should also "make equitable provision for those who for reasons of conscience refuse to bear arms; these are nonetheless obliged to serve the
human community in some other way." Nor does war mean anything
goes; civilians and prisoners should be respected and "the indiscriminate
destruction of whole cities or vast areas with their inhabitants is a crime
against God and man." In addition, "the legitimate defense of persons
and societies is not an exception to the prohibition against the murder
of the innocent."

Day and her newspaper departed radically from this ancient and pragmatic tradition. In the years leading up to the Second World War they
developed nothing less than a theology of Catholic pacifism. It's noteworthy that in the Great War there were only four Catholics among the nation's four-thousand-some-odd conscientious objectors. It was in the pages
of Dorothy Day's newspaper that pacifism in America became Catholic.
Furfey, for example, "urged abandonment of the 'Constantinian compromise' with the war-making state and a return to the eschatological pacifist
vision of the early saints and church fathers."[24] Other writers tackled the
problem as well, some with scholastic logic and others in more accessible

terms, as with stories about saints who bucked the state in the cause of non-violence. Saint Telemachus is said to have been stoned to death around 400 c.e. by spectators when he interrupted a fight to the death between Roman gladiators; his martyrdom is supposed to have contributed to the end of gladiatorial combat. Thus were theory and metaphor recruited in support of action. "The long, dogged insistence," wrote Dwight Macdonald, "of the Workers on practicing what other Christians preach has been a major factor in radicalizing many American Catholics."

In April 1934 *The Catholic Worker* carried a favorable review of a book called *The Church and War*, in which a German Dominican named Franziskus Stratmann (later jailed and exiled under Hitler) argued that modern war couldn't meet the church's "just war" standard. Day and other writers for the newspaper used and expanded on this argument over the years, contending that the horrors of modern combat (exemplified in the massive killing of the Great War) meant that wars could no longer meet the church's definition of "just." Some people even called themselves "just war pacifists." In December 1936 Day wrote: "The Catholic Worker does not condemn any and all war, but believes the conditions necessary for a 'just war' will not be fulfilled today."

Yet this was only a way station in her thinking on the subject, for she was moving toward a more spiritual pacifism grounded in Christ. By the time the Spanish Civil War was over, she had probably arrived there. Spain's ugly civil war began in 1936 with a military coup (supported by many conservatives, and Catholics) against the country's leftist Republican government. The insurgents were backed by fascist Italy and Germany; the Soviet Union supported the Republicans, who were riven by factionalism and, in the communists, afflicted with the sort of friends that make one doubt the need for enemies. The Republicans also had help from some sixty thousand foreigners, including nearly three thousand poorly trained American fighting men. Both sides in the bloody conflict committed atrocities, and while Franco's nationalists were probably worse, targets of Republican slaughter included Catholic religious figures (in keeping with a long history of anti-clerical violence by reformers against Spain's conservative Catholic establishment). Republicans in Spain massacred nearly 7,000 Catholic religious figures, including more than 4,000 priests, more than 2,000 monks, some 283 nuns, and 13 bishops. Churches were torched as well.[25]

American Catholics tended to support Franco. So they were outraged when *The Catholic Worker* took a neutral, pacifist stance, prompting furious readers to cancel their subscriptions in an episode that, like the Spanish Civil War itself, ominously prefigured what was to come. Bulk orders in some dioceses were cancelled as well, leading *The Catholic Worker* to cut its print run by tens of thousands from 190,000, its remarkable 1938 peak, and the newspaper was expelled from the Catholic Press Association. George Shuster's neutrality cost him his job at *Commonweal*. But Day refused to budge.

> We are not praying for victory for Franco in Spain, a victory won with the aid of Mussolini's son who gets a thrill out of bombing; with the aid of Mussolini who is opposing the Holy Father in his pronouncements on "racism"; with the aid of Hitler who persecutes the church in Germany. Nor are we praying for victory for the loyalists whose Anarchist, Communist and anti-God leaders are trying to destroy religion. We are praying for the Spanish people.[26]

By April 1939, after a million Spanish deaths, Franco's forces were victorious. In September the Nazis would invade Poland and World War II would begin, immediately revealing the inadequacy of pacifism in the circumstances. *The Catholic Worker* greeted the news with a dismaying front-page article entitled "We Are To Blame for New War in Europe," which said:

> *The Catholic Worker* considers the present conflict an unjust war. We believe that Hitler is no more personally responsible than is Chamberlain or Daladier or any other leader. The blame rests on the peoples of the entire world, for their materialism, their greed, their idolatrous nationalism, for their refusal to believe in a just peace, for their ruthless subjection of a noble country.

Not just generals but pacifists, too, are always fighting the last war, it seems. Day's ill-considered outburst (Are the Jews to blame along with everyone else? Could the Allies have tossed an extra country or two Hitler's way?) seems preposterous now, but in 1946 no less than Albert Camus, who put out an even riskier newspaper during the war than did Dorothy Day, would tell an audience at Columbia something quite similar:

We must call things by their right names and realize that we kill millions of men each time we permit ourselves to think certain thoughts. One does not reason badly because one is a murderer. One is a murderer if one reasons badly. It is thus that one can be a murderer without having actually killed anyone. And so it is we are all murderers to one degree or another.[27]

The scholar who moderated the event said "all of us in the huge hall were convinced, I think, of our common culpability." Echoes of this notion can be heard in our own day. But we are getting ahead of ourselves; we have a war to get through first. Less than a year after the Nazis invaded Poland, Congress would be arguing about whether to enact the nation's first peacetime draft. By this time *The Catholic Worker* had not only laid some moral and intellectual groundwork for Catholic pacifism, but it had worked to build active Catholic support for peace. On the road, Day herself increasingly spoke about the need to avoid war, and in 1937 a few Catholic Workers formed PAX, a peace group that organized small chapters nationwide, mustering perhaps 200 members. None of it would stop the war. But it would help to start one inside the Catholic Worker organization.[28]

CHAPTER 7

NOT QUITE EVERYBODY

ON OCTOBER 16, 1940, a Wednesday, every man in America between the ages of twenty-one and thirty-six had somewhere to be. That was the day they were all supposed to register for the nation's first peacetime draft, the result of the contentious Selective Training and Service Act that President Franklin D. Roosevelt had signed into law a month earlier.

Conscription, it seemed, might well encompass the entire pageant of the country's masculine life, at least judging by the account in the next day's newspapers. In suburban Detroit, Henry Ford II, whose grandfather was the famous carmaker, pacifist, and persecutor of the Jews, stood in line behind "a Filipino domestic." At a public school near New York's Madison Square Garden, the men waiting to register included "almost 200 cowhands from the Rodeo [who] turned up early in the morning, plus a platoon or two of midgets."[1] Two of the cowboys found time during their stay in New York to beat a British sailor to death, telling police as they confessed to the crime that he "had made improper proposals to them."[2]

Scions of New York's wealthiest families, including the Warburgs and Lehmans, signed up on the Upper East Side, while on West Fifty-fourth Street Winthrop Rockefeller, the son of John D. Rockefeller, Jr., was beset by autograph-seekers as he tried to register at a school. "Just a moment please," he was said to murmur politely. "The government wants my signature first." Two more Rockefellers enrolled in Westchester. On East Fifty-first Street, Francis Warren Pershing registered. He was the son of General John "Black Jack" Pershing, commander of American forces in the "war to end all wars," by now a bitterly sarcastic nickname for the conflict that had claimed 116,516 American lives (including some 45,000 who succumbed to influenza).

On the Lower East Side, meanwhile, "a solemn Mohammedan" requested two registration certificates because he had two names—and produced two Social Security cards to prove it. Perhaps remembering Nathan Hale, who supposedly said he regretted only having one life to give to his country, officials went along with this unusual willingness to be drafted twice. The sardonic musician Oscar Levant, listed by a registration official as having a "sallow" complexion, proposed "swarthy" and acquiesced finally to "ruddy." In Chinatown nearly one thousand men, many alerted by Chinese-language newspapers, thronged a registration station. Selective service officials in New York, seemingly ready for any eventuality, quickly dispatched two buses containing 28 interpreters and 30 additional registration personnel. (It's possible the cheerful tone of the *New York Times* coverage was influenced by Julius Ochs Adler, the paper's general manager, a mustachioed hero of the Great War who was part of a patriotic civilian cabal that helped get the new conscription law through Congress. But it's also unlikely; Adler was "scrupulous in not making the paper his own mouthpiece on military matters." In fact, publisher Arthur Hays Sulzberger leaned pacifist between the wars, like so many of his fellow Americans, though in 1940 he had decided to back conscription.)[3]

All kinds of men turned out not just in New York but, as the *Times* noted, all over America, "in town halls in Maine hamlets, in fire houses at Arizona train whistle stops and the crowded districts of the nation's large cities. Aliens and citizens, rich and poor; the cripple, the conscientious objector—all will take their places to be counted for the military training and service that Congress has voted."[4] Hunters and trappers emerged from the Louisiana bayous, having learned of the draft by word of mouth. A government tugboat plied the waters of the Delaware River to register men working on dredges, barges, and the like in the area of Wilmington. At Riverhead, on Long Island, fishermen and farmers turned out early, and forty members of the Shinnecock tribe registered. Joe Louis, who had needed just two minutes and four seconds to dispatch the Nazi champion Max Schmeling in 1938, signed up for America's segregated armed forces on the South Side of a segregated Chicago. Also in Chicago: America's second most famous polio victim, Fred B. Snite, Jr., who would spend most of eighteen years in an iron lung, was registered for the draft by his father. Snite, who managed to marry, have children, and play competitive bridge during those years, expressed regret that he couldn't make it to the registration office himself.[5] The young governor of Minnesota registered, as did eligible members of Congress including West Virginia's isolationist Senator Rush Holt, who called the whole thing "silly and unnecessary."

Celebrities trooped to their local registration boards in Southern California. These included Tyrone Power, Orson Welles, John Garfield, Henry Fonda, Cesar Romero, Artie Shaw, Eddie Albert, William Holden, and John Wayne. Not all of these men would fight, of course. Some wouldn't even be inducted. But other prominent young Americans would make the ultimate sacrifice. Rose Kennedy, innocent of her heartbreaking future, said from the family home in Bronxville, New York, that her eligible boys, Joe Junior and Jack, would register at Harvard and Stanford, respectively, where they were at school. The former, a future naval aviator, would not survive the war; the latter, who did so barely, would give his life to his country on a later occasion.

America was a large and variegated place back then, just as it is now, yet a very different one. Married women in newspapers typically were identified in terms of their husbands; a Mrs. Walter Graeme Ladd, for example, "the former Kate E. Macy," donated money for English ambulances. And the draft took only men, although Reika Schwanke of Austin, Minnesota, somehow managed to register by mistake. Learning that she would not be inducted, she said: "There ought to be some place for a woman in the army."

Times were still hard. Unemployment lingered at 15 percent, much improved from the Depression's nadir a few years earlier but brutal nonetheless despite years of earnest government flailing and misguided central bank policy. Newspapers, which everyone read in those days, were full of ads for old-fashioned brown things: suits and hats, large wooden radios, hard liquor. Fur coats were big, too, and of course smoking was ubiquitous. There was "religious news," including, on Saturdays, notices of the weekend's planned sermon topics.

TV, the internet, air conditioning, credit cards, universal driving and flying, and countless other features of modern life were rare or nonexistent. Telephones were a luxury. Most homes were heated with coal, and 45 percent lacked one or more of the plumbing features we take for granted: hot and cold running water, a flush toilet, and a tub or shower. The South remained mired in economic and segregationist torpor, from which poor blacks and poor whites alike fled north for jobs in the nation's awakening factories. A dusty outpost called Las Vegas, thanks to the new Hoover Dam nearby, had mushroomed into a metropolis of 8,422 souls per the 1940 census. Mount Rushmore, timeless though it may seem, was still being carved, and Joe DiMaggio roamed center field for the Yankees. The best-seller list for fiction included *For Whom the Bell Tolls*, *The Grapes of Wrath*, *How Green Was My Valley*, and *Mrs. Miniver*. The latter, about an endearing Briton coping stoically with the war, would become a popular film starring Greer Garson. During preproduction, in 1940, the script became more anti-Nazi with each revision, suggesting well enough the direction of public opinion.

Families were bigger. In Philadelphia, Rose Del Buono accompanied her five sons and her son-in-law to the registration office, vowing to fight alongside them to repel any invader. The seven sons of the Joynt family registered in Clear Lake, Iowa. The eight sons of Mr. and Mrs. Jay Brown signed up in Little Falls, New York. Franklin and Eleanor Roosevelt had five children, and they weren't exempt either. "Today's registration for training and service," the president said in an 8:00 a.m. radio address, "is the keystone in the arch of national defense." Accordingly, Franklin Delano Roosevelt, Jr., took time out from campaigning for his father to register in Indianapolis. Another Roosevelt boy, John, signed up near home in Nahant, Massachusetts. The anti-Roosevelt, antiwar *Chicago Tribune* carried photos of the other two Roosevelt sons, James and Elliott, looking entirely too satisfied with themselves under the headline, "They Didn't Register for the Draft." But the caption admitted that, as members of the armed forces reserves, they didn't have to.[6]

Registering all the eligible men on a single day—a mere two weeks after FDR signed the bill—emphasized the universality of the program, minimized opportunities for vacillation and procrastination, and overnight yielded a draft roll of 16.4 million men, practically all that were eligible. Over the course of the war, that number would grow to 34,506,923.

Even George Washington turned out on October 16; in Chicago's First Ward, a twenty-five-year-old "Negro porter" by that name waited an hour to be first in line. His eagerness belied the conflicting feelings that beset blacks on this occasion. Black enlistments were limited and low "Negro quotas" kept down the number of black draftees. Despite the dangers of military service, few things cut black Americans more deeply than not being permitted to fulfill this fundamental obligation of male citizenship on an equal footing. A 1940 editorial in *The Crisis*, published by the NAACP, was titled "For Manhood in National Defense," and said that "Of all the shabby dealings of America with a tenth of her citizens none is more shameful." Although registration cards featured several checkboxes for "race," including "White," "Oriental," and "Negro," only the latter was shunted into an inferior shadow army.

When Dwight Macdonald launched his new antiwar magazine, *politics*, in early 1944, it contained a regular department called "Free and Equal" to deal with race, which it called "the most dynamic social issue of today." The first entry was about Winfred Lynn, a Jamaica, New York, gardener who refused to be conscripted into a segregated army and challenged the draft on that basis in court. It wasn't as if he wouldn't fight; he even offered to serve in the Canadian army. The issue was discrimination. Macdonald summed up the context with his usual acuity:

> The manpower demands of this war have accelerated the "upgrading" of Negroes on the job, while the official ideology of a democratic war against Nazism has both stimulated the colored people to insist on equal treatment and made it awkward for the Whites to deny this to them . . . Nowhere do the colored people of America feel more keenly the contradiction between ideology and practice in this war than in the armed forces, where they are segregated by an agency of the Federal Government itself.[7]

This was a time, remember, when Jim Crow prevailed even in the nation's capital, and throughout the north racial discrimination was rampant. Shortly after Pearl Harbor, and long before Edward William

Brooke III became the first black senator from Massachusetts, he was a young army lieutenant in a segregated unit training at Fort Devens in Ayer, Mass., where in 1942 "the segregation was total." Clubs for officers and noncommissioned officers alike were closed to blacks, as were the PX, swimming pool, and tennis courts. "We were angry," he wrote later. "I felt a personal frustration and bitterness I had not known before in my life."[8]

It was even worse in other branches and locations. Military leaders believed white fighting men wouldn't live with blacks or accept their leadership. "Colored troops do very well under white officers," Stimson wrote privately, "but every time we try to lift them a little bit beyond where they can go, disaster and confusion follows . . . I hope for Heaven's sake they won't mix the white and the colored troops together in the same units for then we shall certainly have trouble."[9]

Raising a vast military from all parts of the country posed problems for the nation's racial caste system—problems that underscored the system's wretched contradictions. But change was in the air. Black leaders and newspapers agitated for black servicemen to be treated like their white counterparts, and the organs of black advocacy swelled with members and importance. The circulation of black newspapers, for example, which were rivalled in influence only by black churches, grew 40 percent from 1940 to 1945, exceeding 1.8 million weekly copies, most of them read by more than a single subscriber. The federal Office of War Information estimated that four million black Americans read such a newspaper each week—back when there were fourteen million black citizens in total, including children. Gunnar Myrdal, in his famous 1944 study of race in American life, suggested that the black press might have been "the greatest single power of the Negro community."[10]

Blacks had been moving north since the Great War, in flight from segregation and in pursuit of industrial jobs, resulting in growing affluence yet continuing discrimination. Many black Americans felt they'd made a mistake in lending unconditional support to the earlier war, after which they reaped only Jim Crow, humiliation, and mob violence. This time, faced with little progress at home or in the armed forces, many wanted to stay out. As more and more men were inducted during the war, several black men refused to be conscripted into segregated armed forces. But black newspapers, led at first by the large and influential *Pittsburgh Courier*, advocated a "Double V" strategy of victory at war to achieve victory over injustice at home. These newspapers were wary of wartime civil rights activism. When Lewis Jones of New York City chose prison over segregated service, the *Baltimore Afro-American* newspaper sent a reporter (accompanied by black psychologist Kenneth Clark) to talk him out of it. Jones remained adamant and thereby, the journalist wrote, had "divorced himself" from supportive whites and "alienated most colored people."[11] Blacks, *The Crisis* said in 1940 of the war effort to come, had much to gain "by keeping everlastingly at the fight."

Southern blacks, traditionally Republicans, were largely prevented from voting; during the war only about 5 percent of the black voting age population in the eleven southern states was registered. But in the North, black voters were becoming an important source of support for Roosevelt and the Democrats (even if, in doing so, they were joining an uneasy coalition that included the southern segregationists who wielded so much power against them in Congress). With a presidential election coming in November, FDR couldn't ignore the pressure to treat black recruits fairly. The growing awareness that things had to change was manifested in the new conscription law, which specified "that in the selection and training of men under this Act, and in the interpretation and execution of the provisions of this Act, there shall be no discrimination against any person on account of race or color."[12]

In practice, the armed forces would remain segregated for the duration. But the law's language reflected the declining legitimacy of discrimination, and the growing insistence of black Americans on their rights. This issue would persist throughout the war, and pacifists of both races would be at the forefront of the struggle for equality.

The exemption for conscientious objectors notwithstanding, draft opponents marked October 16 as a grim milestone. The Fellowship of Reconciliation, the National Council of Methodist Youth, and others called for a Day of National Humiliation, in the old-fashioned sense of abasement before God; Lincoln had proclaimed one in 1863, soon after the nation adopted its first federal draft (to provide troops for the Civil War). This time around, pacifist leaders called for fasting; money thus saved was to be donated to the Fellowship's fund for European food relief, "used in part to provide activity against the British-imposed food blockade of Germany, and in part to support European pacifists."

In Bloomington, Indiana, presidential hopeful Norman Thomas vowed that he and his Socialist Party (in truth, badly divided over the war) would work to repeal the new draft. Sounding themes that would prevail among war opponents for the duration of the conflict, he described October 16 as "a day of mourning for the death of the American way of life and the triumph of the principle which is the very lifeblood of the totalitarian state," and said the men chosen under the new law were mere "extras" who were "potentially of use in imperialist adventure."[13]

A similar theme was struck in a leaflet probably distributed in New York and sponsored by nine antiwar groups, including the War Resisters League (WRL), the Methodist youth council, and the Catholic Worker organization. It proclaimed October 16 "a day of national mourning" when "free men lose their freedom" and "war is brought nearer by the creation of a military state." It called for demonstrations against the new draft law, "which gives fascism its first major victory in America," and urged the wearing of black to "mourn the death of liberty."

It's unclear what color attendees were wearing at an antiwar gathering that very day at the Broadway Tabernacle Church on Broadway and West Fifty-sixth Street, an institution with a long history in abolitionism, women's rights, and the Social Gospel. But at the event, sponsored by the Fellowship of Reconciliation, some 450 men of draft age attended a morning service for conscientious objectors, where they listened to John Haynes Holmes tell them "not to hate or be bitter against those who will make it unpleasant for you."

Holmes had been at this a long time. In 1912, besotted with Rauschenbusch and the Social Gospel movement, he published a book called *The Revolutionary Function of the Modern Church* in which he called for "an indefinite extension of the field of religious activity" that would plunge American Protestantism into fighting poverty, crime and disease. Jesus himself, according to Holmes, was more than a prophet. He was "an instigator of social reform."[14]

As pastor of Manhattan's genteel Unitarian Church of the Messiah, Holmes enjoyed a kind of "religious celebrity" that is difficult to imagine today outside the subculture of the megachurches or away from the evangelical pulpits whose clerics have achieved renown (if not notoriety) in the wider world. And in those days, famed ministers often were liberals. Holmes was honorary chairman of the WRL and helped found the NAACP and the ACLU. He used his sermons to condemn gambling, firecrackers, free love, and other such quaint indulgences—but also to address the plight of the downtrodden with talks on unions and socialism. In 1917, when Holmes preached against American involvement in the Great War by saying, "If Christianity is right, then war is wrong, false, a lie," it made the front page of *The New York Times*—and nearly got him fired. Now he was back in the *Times* for opposing America's entry into yet another European conflict. "We have taken our stand," the paper quoted him as saying at the Broadway Tabernacle. "We do not believe in war."

After he spoke, his listeners took a pledge calling conscription "an overt step in the direction of war and dictatorship" and vowing to "put into practice methods of non-violent, direct action." True to their word, they did this right away. The Reverend Francis Hall of Newark, who had introduced Holmes to the crowd, formed some of the audience into a "parade" of about sixty men and ten women holding aloft signs, the first of which he carried himself. It said, "As conscientious objectors, we ask . . ." Subsequent protesters, confronting passersby with a series of provocative questions, carried signs asking, "Is conscription for defense?" and "Does anyone win at war?"

Conscientious objectors, the *Times* reported, "were distinguished on registration day by their organized activity and the smallness of their numbers." Nonetheless, protests erupted in New York and elsewhere. "As conscientious objectors marched in single file down Fifth Avenue from Fifty-fourth Street to Thirty-fourth Street and back again," the paper said, "they were taunted frequently and advised, 'Don't forget to register.' Occasionally some one offered 'a punch on the nose.' Nothing came of it." They also tried to hand out leaflets from the WRL and Fellowship of Reconciliation, but people wouldn't take them. Pearl Harbor was more than a year away, and already it seemed clear that their task wasn't going to be easy.

Some men registered their objections by not registering themselves. In Florida, sixty-five draft-age Seminole men failed to emerge from the Everglades on the appointed day, even though they would probably never be called to serve, according to the Superintendent of Indian Affairs, who noted that the tribe was still technically at war with the United States.[15] Some Hopi, in keeping with the tribe's pacifist tradition, refused to register as well. "Today my people, in common with the Indian race, stand in this so-called democracy branded in the movies, in most history books, and in the mind of the public generally as blood-thirsty savages with characteristics scarcely above that of the beast," Riley Sunrise, a Hopi who was to have a notable postwar career as an artist and actor, wrote to his draft board in 1940. "We bear humiliating poverty, suffering and degradation . . . I am not afraid to fight nor die . . . I merely object for the sake of the principle of Justice which is dearer to me than life."[16]

Some religious objectors refused to register too. The Reverend Allen Clay Lambert, a thirty-four-year-old Lutheran pastor in Sinking Valley, Pennsylvania, who was surely CO-eligible, told a reporter he would not register and would submit to arrest "even though I know I am treated unjustly as a free man of God." Near El Paso, Texas, twenty-two-year-old Frank Wagoner, a member of the Negro Civilian Conservation Corps, was arrested for refusing to register even though he, too, cited "religious reasons" that might have won him CO status if only he had registered.[17]

But many war resisters did register, since so often their objection was religious in nature. Bayard Rustin, for example, signed up in Manhattan, where he was living, and was called before his Harlem draft board soon after. A natural performer, he unfurled his argument for himself with characteristically affected eloquence, subjecting the local burghers who usually constituted such boards to an Oxonian recitation of his deep religious commitment to nonviolence. Raised a Quaker by his grandparents, the only war he wanted to fight was against the injustices visited on black Americans. The somewhat bewildered draft board went along, and for now at least, Rustin was free.[18]

In Seattle, young Gordon Hirabayashi, the son of Japanese immigrants, was active in the Student Christian Movement at the University of Washington and lived at the YMCA, a liberal institution where he nonetheless encountered prejudice. Hirabayashi didn't imagine that he would one day gain renown for resisting the curfew and relocation imposed on West Coast Japanese Americans during the war—and that his conviction would be vacated decades later by the Supreme Court. For now, his problem was the draft. In the summer of 1940, at a Columbia University program for future leaders of the Christian student movement, he attended seminars with current and future antiwar icons including Muste, Rustin, and the Thomas brothers (Evan and Norman). Already en route to becoming a Quaker, Hirabayashi registered on October 16 intending to request CO status when the time came. Lest there be any doubt of his intentions, he wrote on the front of the card, in the neat cursive script of the day: "I am a conscientious objector."

Jim Peck also wrote "conscientious objector" on his registration form. But he was no religious objector—if anything, he was a sacrilegious one— and his request was denied. As he expected, he ended up behind bars, where he would carry on his habitual hell-raising. He was held, starting in November 1942, at the new federal prison in Danbury, Connecticut, at the time a place full of short-timers little interested in making trouble, but one where, during the war, plenty of trouble would occur.

Lowell Naeve, a former pupil of Diego Rivera, was hornswoggled into registering. The twenty-three-year-old Naeve, who was to document his wartime resistance with his art, says in his memoir that he went to his Manhattan draft board on the appointed day and proclaimed himself unwilling to register or fight. "I don't believe in wars and killing people," he explained. The official he was dealing with took up a small card and asked Naeve's name and address, which Naeve provided as part of his desire to oppose the draft openly. The man "laboriously explained that the small card he was filling out for me was *not really* a registration, and that the *real* part of it would be sent to me later on."

It was indeed. When Naeve discovered he'd been registered against his will, he tore up his draft card "in small pieces, so it couldn't be returned to me, put it in an envelope, addressed the envelope to Mr. Stimson, Secretary of War, Washington, D.C." He enclosed a note that read: "Mr. Stimson: I wish in no way whatsoever to participate in the draft, as I feel it is the machinery to put the nation into war. I regret that I ever registered. I hereby return my draft card and wish to be classified as a non-registered objector to war. Sincerely, L. Naeve"[19]

There is no record of a response from Roosevelt's septuagenarian war chief, but some months later Naeve found himself behind bars at "West Street," the federal detention center on Eleventh Street near the Hudson

River that would process a parade of draft resisters before their transfer to federal prisons. The socialist draft resister Howard Schoenfeld described the conditions: "Prisoners are kept in steel cages. Built upward from the floor, each cage holds between ten and twenty human beings; sometimes more. In the corners in full view are open toilets without seats, shared equally by the diseased and undiseased, and the flies . . . Windows are opaque, fresh air at a minimum . . . Solitary confinement imposed on the flimsiest pretexts."[20]

While Naeve was at West Street, he encountered Louis Lepke (really Louis Buchalter), an episode that would become the basis of a famous poem by Robert Lowell called "Memories of West Street and Lepke." Lepke, Naeve writes in his memoir, eventually published by David Dellinger's Libertarian Press, "the short stolid-faced boss of Murder, Inc., motioned me over to his adjoining cell. In a curious, soft-spoken, considerate manner he asked: 'You're one of those fellows who's going to object to the war when it comes?' Somewhere in the conversation we got around to the fact that I was in jail because I refused to kill people. The Murder, Inc., boss, who was headed for the electric chair, said: 'It don't seem to me to make much sense that they put a man in jail for that.' We just looked at each other. There we were, both sitting in the same prison. The law covered both ends—one in for killing, the other in for refusing to kill."[21]

Some families were divided over the draft. Consider the Swift boys, from rural Colorado. Yale senior Charlie Swift refused to register and would spend time in prison at Danbury, where incarcerated resisters would soon be stirring up righteous trouble. Later, as a child psychiatrist, he would spend years building up mental health programs in Tanzania. His brother David, a graduate student at Yale Divinity School (and roommate of David Dellinger when both were undergraduates), chose to register, but with the intention of becoming a conscientious objector. Certified as such, he was first sent into the system of rural work camps run by the peace churches for just such individuals. After agitating for a more meaningful assignment, he became instrumental in putting COs to work in the nation's mental institutions, where there was a desperate shortage of male staff. Eventually he became an orderly at a mental hospital in Philadelphia. In 1961, by now a professor of religion, he was briefly jailed along with Freedom Riders protesting segregation in Montgomery, Alabama. The third Swift brother,

a career Marine, fought at Guadalcanal. All the Swifts supported one another and their disparate choices, but the pacifist brothers were predisposed
against war by their mother as well as by Dellinger. At Dwight Hall, their
friend William Lovell, the son of Presbyterian missionaries to China, influenced both Davids, and Charlie Swift as well, toward pacifism. After
graduation and some more time at Dwight, Lovell and Dellinger enrolled
at Manhattan's Union Theological Seminary, where they and a half dozen
of their friends would become famous.

On October 13, 1940, next to a piece about the death by auto of cow-
boy actor Tom Mix, a front-page article in *The New York Times* was head-
lined: "Divinity Students Face Jail on Draft." In it, the director of Selective
Service for the city heaped threats and condescension on a group of twenty
students from Union Theological Seminary who had announced they
would refuse to register. "The trouble with these young men," Colonel
Arthur V. McDermott said, "is that their intellectual conceit is exceeded
only by their immaturity of judgment. The law expressly exempts from
service theological students who have completed their first year of study."

The colonel could barely contain his astonishment at their temer-
ity. "These so-called young intellectuals have smugly decided that their
judgment and intelligence is so far superior to that of Congress and the
American people that they propose to disdain the requirements of the
law." Deriding their "smug complacency," he warned they would face up
to five years in prison and a $10,000 fine. He vowed to prosecute them
forthwith, voicing a hunch they would eventually come to their senses
and "be good little boys."

Little did he know how wrong he could possibly be. On October 17
the fellows were back on the front page. "First Draft Objectors Are Called
to Federal Inquiry Here Today," says the *Times* headline. The story jumps
to page twelve, where you'll find a striking photograph of the eight handsome young seminary students who ultimately refused to register, the
other twelve having thought better of their recalcitrance. The holdouts
look terrifically comfortable in their suits and ties, the standard attire for
men of their station in their era, and nothing at all like little boys. They also
seemed relaxed in their fateful decision, which was remarkable given what
they had been through in recent days—and what lay ahead.

Their names were Don Benedict, Joe Bevilacqua, Meredith Dallas, David Dellinger, George Houser, William Lovell, Howard Spragg, and Richard Wichlei. They came to Union filled not just with religious zeal but with a righteous need to work for social change against the injustices of the day. They were Christians, but also, to varying degrees, socialists. They were born during the horrors of the "war to end all wars," came of age in the Great Depression, and had seen Spain succumb to fascism and Europe consumed by yet another continental war. Closer to home, in America, they had noticed injustice everywhere. They were training for the clergy, but their vocation was activism.

They would pay a price for this, as would their loved ones. Already, on draft day, the seminarians' obduracy had meant anguish for Willa Louise Winter, an idealistic young Ohioan living on an ashram in Newark, New Jersey, where city clerk Harry Lichtenstein took it on himself to refuse her a license to marry Dallas, who also lived at the ashram. The clerk had done this, according to the *Times*, "because the prospective bridegroom was notoriously and publicly engaged in breaking the law." Just four days past her twenty-first birthday, Willa Winter wept.

CHAPTER 8

UNION MEN

EVERYONE WENT TO THE movies in 1940. The big films that year included *Boom Town*, *Rebecca*, *The Philadelphia Story*, and, aptly enough, *The Great Dictator*, but in those days moviegoers also got to see cartoons, a second feature, and newsreels that made the news of the day come alive on film. Thus a woman sitting in the darkness of a Florida theater one day gave out a little scream when her nephew appeared on-screen. She was George Houser's Aunt Emma, and this newsreel was the first she'd heard about his draft resistance even though he and his fellow dissenters had made headlines all over the country that fall.

They were not the only World War II draft resisters, but they may have been the first, and they are exemplars of the type who mattered most to history: the radical pacifists who would go on to play important roles in political and social change in the decades to come. This particular crop, who would come to be known as the Union Eight, quite ostentatiously rejected the state's authority to enlist them in any aspect of war, including even filling out a form, and practically right up until they were carted off to prison, nearly everyone tried to talk them out of it—including the jurist who had the duty of sentencing them.

On November 14, 1940, they showed up at the federal courthouse in lower Manhattan to find demonstrators and counterdemonstrators picketing outside. Insults were shouted, and someone spat in Benedict's face. In a hushed courtroom crowded with dismayed loved ones, Judge Samuel

Mandelbaum sentenced each of the seminarians to a year and a day in the new federal prison at Danbury, Connecticut. In truth he let them off easy, having made it plain that he was acting more in sorrow than in anger toward these "fine young men" who had already pleaded guilty. Having given them a last chance to get with the program, which they declined, he announced that he would keep the court term open, a legal maneuver that would enable them to register at any time and appeal for a reduction in sentence once they had changed their minds. They wouldn't.

———

IT WAS ONLY NATURAL that they had come to Union, by that time America's leading institution of liberal theology in every sense of the term. A major reason for its stature was the man students called Uncle Henry. Alumni in our story include Muste, Fosdick and both Thomas brothers even though Evan became a physician. Coffin came from money, but he cared about the less fortunate. After graduating from Union in 1900, he opened a mission church in the Bronx, where he delivered sermons upstairs from a meat market using a chopping block for a pulpit. Later he would revive the Madison Avenue Presbyterian Church, ministering both to the wealthy families west of the church and the poorer ones to the east. He averaged one hundred pastoral visits a month even while finding time to teach at Union and write books. Managing to be at once evangelical and liberal, he often preached the need to apply Christianity to the problems of the world.

Coffin and his alma mater were exemplars of the Social Gospel movement, which propelled religion in the direction of reform. Coming to prominence during the rapid industrialization that followed the Civil War, the movement was energized by the plight of immigrants massed into New York and other teeming cities at a time of dramatic inequality and little government support. Its preeminent spokesman was probably Walter Rauschenbusch, a Baptist minister spurred by the poverty and struggles he saw during eleven years ministering to German immigrants in New York to argue that Christianity requires not just personal salvation but a kind of social salvation based on equality, charity, and justice. (He also loathed militarism.) Social Gospel proponents advocated a variety of reforms, including better pay and working conditions and an end to child labor. "Rauschenbusch had done a great service for the Christian Church," Martin Luther King would one day write, adding that "any religion which professes to be concerned about the souls of men and is not concerned about the social and economic conditions that scar the soul is a spiritually moribund religion only waiting for the day to be buried."[1]

King's comments on the subject closely echoed those of Fosdick, one of Union's many stars. As Union's president, Coffin had an eye for talents who could shine far beyond the library and the classroom. In 1928, he brought aboard a clergyman named Reinhold Niebuhr who had made a name for himself in Detroit by sticking up for labor, attacking the paternalism of Henry Ford, and writing provocatively for the liberal *Christian Century*. By the time Coffin discovered him, he was a committed pacifist. Union's faculty approved his hiring by a single vote, and for several years the wealthy former missionary Sherwood Eddy, a ubiquitous figure in antiwar circles, paid Niebuhr's salary. Within a few years Union gave him an endowed chair and a bigger apartment to prevent Yale from luring him away.

In 1933, Coffin noticed the name of Paul Tillich on a list of professors driven from their positions in Germany. Niebuhr, who had warmly reviewed Tillich's most recent book (translated by Reinhold's brother, Richard, a theologian at Yale), personally conveyed Coffin's and Columbia's joint job offer to Tillich in Germany. In a reflection of the era's hard times, money was so tight at Union that the faculty voted themselves a 5 percent pay cut to cover Tillich's first-year stipend. At the age of forty-seven, he arrived with less than perfect English; when he asserted that "all faiths have gnosis," he seemed to be describing ecumenical olfaction. Nonetheless, within a decade he was one of America's best-known theologians.[2]

Coffin increased the number of black students at Union, and the number of women grew thanks to the founding of Union's School of Sacred Music (though he disliked the idea of women as theology students). At Union's Centennial Dinner at New York's Roosevelt Hotel in 1936, guests learned that the seminary was about to get its first female board member in Elizabeth Cutter Morrow, an author and educator soon to become acting president of Smith College. She was the widow of Dwight W. Morrow, a former Union director, and together they were the parents of the writer Anne Morrow Lindbergh, who had married the famous aviator Charles. Mother and daughter were to take very different views of the coming war.[3]

Coffin also brought in more international students—including Dietrich Bonhoeffer for 1930–31, an all too brief academic year in which his aristocratic nature and talent for friendship were both on full display. The twenty-four-year-old Berliner and future anti-Nazi theologian took courses with Niebuhr, heard sermons by Fosdick, and read John Dewey, William James, and J. B. Watson.[4] With A. Franklin Fisher, a black Union student from Birmingham, Alabama, he attended—and was overcome by—services at Harlem's Abyssinian Baptist Church, one of the nation's largest Protestant congregations. There the famous pastor Adam Clayton Powell, Sr., embraced him, allowing him to lead classes, help with youth and musical events, and even preach. Bonhoeffer was especially moved by the spirituals at Abyssinian and took recordings back to Germany. Fosdick's Riverside Church, and in fact most of American liberal Protestantism, seemed pallid and self-satisfied by comparison. "There is no theology here," he complained. "[The Union students] talk a blue streak without the slightest substantive foundation and with no evidence of any criteria . . . They are unfamiliar with even the most basic questions. They become intoxicated with liberal and humanistic phrases, laugh at the fundamentalists, and yet basically are not even up to their level."[5]

Bonhoeffer had no patience for what he saw as the frantic relevance of the church here. But it's an odd complaint from a pastor so disturbed by America's oppression of blacks. Niebuhr, who got Bonhoeffer to read W.E.B. Du Bois and other leading black thinkers, spent the summer of 1931 trying to stir up activism during a busy lecture tour of southern Negro colleges. Fosdick was a lifelong supporter of civil rights. Union graduates were working to organize black and white tenant farmers in the South. And some Union students, including (when their time came) Benedict, Dallas, and Dellinger, were working to alleviate black poverty in the North while they were at school. Among a largely indifferent white establishment, Union stood out for concern with what Gunnar Myrdal would call, in his 1944 book, "the American dilemma."

Union's proximity to Harlem and the weight of the Depression meant that suffering and injustice were never merely abstract. After the crash of 1929 the seminary's staff took pay cuts and enrollment fell. Some students couldn't afford enough to eat, and jobless young men were housed in the gym. Radicalism flourished under such circumstances. Coffin found himself under continual pressure from radical students and faculty on one side, and from more conservative trustees, alumni, and donors on the other. During the thirties, students advocating government action far beyond the New Deal protested around the city and, inevitably, turned their fire on Union, demanding raises for housekeepers, among other things. On the night of May 1, 1934, some of them ran up a red flag above the gate at Broadway and 121st Street. Other tests of free speech and civility cropped up, and some students evidently considered Uncle Henry, who provided safe haven for any number of dissident thinkers, a "fascist despot."[6]

Coffin could defend students too. At one point the rector of a local church sent a telegram to the governor of California, lauding the lynching of two kidnappers there. Union students picketed the following Sunday, and one was arrested in a scuffle with parishioners. Coffin rebuffed the Church's demands that the protesters be expelled, declaring that if the congregation wasn't going to fire a mature rector for doing a foolish thing, he wasn't going to expel youthful students on that basis. But his patience was wearing thin.

Throughout this era all parties lived with the hangover of the last war and threat of a new one. By 1940 Fosdick and Niebuhr in particular had developed very different perspectives on war. Both were powerful orators, prolific writers and liberal theologians of great courage who understood the distinction between taking the bible seriously and taking it literally, as Schlesinger put it. Both had mental health issues; as a young man, Fosdick had come close to cutting his own throat with his razor. Both had risen to celebrity status in ways no mainstream clergyman could hope to do today; Fosdick made the cover of *Time* in 1925 and 1930, Niebuhr in 1948—for the magazine's twenty-fifth anniversary issue.

And both had been vocal supporters of America's role in the Great War. Niebuhr, the son of an immigrant who left Germany to avoid military service, was even appointed as the German Evangelical Synod's main spokesman for the war, during which German Americans were at pains to demonstrate their loyalty. After the war Niebuhr turned pacifist and for a while was chairman of the Fellowship of Reconciliation. Disgusted by the punitive Versailles settlement and not far removed from his German background (he remained fluent), he made the shift after a visit to the Ruhr region, painfully occupied by the French and beset by hunger and poverty. "This is as good a time as any to make up my mind that I am done with the war business," he said."[7]

Fosdick trod a similar path to Damascus: "I saw war at firsthand, and went through the disillusionment of its aftermath, confronting with increasing agony the anti-Christian nature of war's causes, process and results. I could not dodge my conscience." Fosdick, moreover, was among the Protestant clerics vilified in the early 1930s by Ray Abrams in his book *Preachers Present Arms*, which castigated pastors for betraying their convictions by enlisting their pulpits in the service of war. And so he, too, became a pacifist, a position he would sustain throughout the war despite his prominent role as the pastor of the new Riverside Church, built for him by the philanthropist John D. Rockefeller, Jr., where among his other duties he ministered to and married hundreds of newly minted naval officers from the wartime midshipman's school at nearby Columbia University. In one especially productive day, he performed the ceremony twenty-seven times.[8]

Fuzzy-haired, round-faced Fosdick was an exemplar of that enviable long-ago figure, the optimistic liberal, resolute and of good cheer. America's greatest sermonizer, he pioneered pastoral counseling, and in his career one can observe the faintest outlines of the therapeutic Christianity to come. Horrified by the carnage of the trenches and his own support for it, he transcended the Social Gospel's prewar utopianism while refusing to follow Niebuhr down the path of "Christian realism" to violence.

Ironically, it was the angular, Germanic Niebuhr rather than Fosdick who, despite his influential thought and prolific writings, is best known today for that therapeutic staple, the Serenity Prayer. He wrote some version of it in the thirties, and if it's possible to clear away the accumulated treacle, there is a lot of wisdom in that little homily, which encapsulates a Niebuhrian vision too often seen as purely tragic. A version of the prayer popular today conveys something of his larger perspective: "God grant me the serenity to accept the things I cannot change; courage to change the things I can; and wisdom to know the difference."

Who but an optimist could ask for all that? Niebuhr's pacifism, like his pessimism, was complicated, and by the early thirties he had mostly abandoned it on theological, ethical, and practical grounds. As early as 1932, his book *Moral Man and Immoral Society* challenged liberal passivity in the face of injustice and insisted that man's fallen nature makes conflict inevitable—and the possibility of force essential. "Modern Christian and secular perfectionism, which places a premium upon non-participation in conflict, is a very sentimentalized version of the Christian faith," he would write later in the decade. By 1940 Niebuhr, who liked to say he taught applied Christianity at Union, could see clearly that any pacifist response to the Nazi onslaught was sheer fantasy, and he was arguing, publicly and prominently, for American intervention in Europe's new war.[9]

———

LIKE ALMOST EVERYONE ELSE in America during the summer of 1940, students at Union had known that the nation's first peacetime draft was coming, and they understood all too well their eligibility. Most intended to register. But a few were deeply troubled by this prospect, which they felt would make them complicit in the state's war-making, and they were troubled as well by the special provision available to excuse them from service. No one, they felt, should be barred from excusing himself from the immorality of war. So when they returned to Union's Gothic complex on Morningside Heights that September, what to do about the coming draft was a major topic. This was especially the case for Houser, Dellinger, Lovell, and some of their friends, all of them more interested in applying Christian principles against injustice in the world than in soaking up whatever Union had to offer in a classroom.

Houser in particular liked to visit Harlem and enjoy an affordable chicken dinner at Father Divine's Kingdom on West 126th Street. This was part of the famous black religious leader's ecumenical Peace Mission movement, which, however cultish, made racial integration central to its mission, and which was at or near its peak of prominence at the time. As an undergraduate at the University of Denver, Houser had dropped in on services at one of Father Divine's charismatic churches and surely found the movement's religious collectivism and emphasis on racial equality hugely appealing. Short, dapper and energetic, Houser would never become as famous as David Dellinger or Bayard Rustin, yet led a hugely impactful life. Aunt Emma's nephew would one day cofound and lead the Congress of Racial Equality and take part in America's first civil rights Freedom

Ride through the South. On the occasion of his ninety-ninth birthday, in 2015, the Fellowship of Reconciliation would call him "one of the most important yet least-heralded activists of the 20th century." The son of missionaries, Houser was born in 1916 and spent some of his early years in the Philippines, an experience that helped shape his later life. During high school in Berkeley, California, young George was part of a student group run by Trinity Methodist Church, where his father was minister, and was influenced toward pacifism and socialism by the Methodist summer institutes that were prominent features of a vigorous church youth movement during the 1930s. "I was a Christian pacifist," Houser would write. "I was a product of the idealism, optimism, and social activism of the 1930s. World War I was in the dim past for me, and it had failed miserably to save the world for democracy. It was unthinkable that the United States could be involved in another war."[10]

By 1940 he had already joined the Fellowship of Reconciliation, in doing so committing to "identify with those of every nation, race, gender and religion who are the victims of injustice and exploitation, and seek to develop resources of active nonviolence to transform such circumstances; and refuse to participate in any war or to sanction military preparations; work to abolish war and promote good will among races, nations and classes." And he joined the Young People's Socialist League (who sang, "Thomas is our leader—we shall not be moved."). "The first of many picket lines he was to join," writes his biographer, "was in support of A. Philip Randolph's Brotherhood of Sleeping Car Porters."[11]

In his second year, Houser lived in the legendary melting pot of the Lower East Side, near the site of his fieldwork, which was the Church of All Nations, a big brick place with a swimming pool and other facilities. There he worked with rowdy Italian youth gangs and lived with four other young men in a vermin-infested tenement as God's gift to the bedbugs. One day he went over to the Labor Temple on Second Avenue, where he heard A. J. Muste preach. Houser was captivated by the lanky Dutch Reformed minister, whose person seemed to combine Christ and social conscience. Houser was chosen to represent Methodist youth at the first meeting of the newly merged Methodist Church, held in Atlantic City in April, and shocked everybody there by challenging Representative Martin Dies of Texas, whose House Committee on Un-American Activities hunted for communists in liberal organizations. In his talk to the Methodists, Dies called for a return to the old-time religion. When it was Houser's turn to speak, he said, "Yes, let's get back to old time religion—to Amos and Hosea and Jeremiah," prophets who inveighed against corruption, injustice, inequality, and hypocrisy.[12]

Although the war was an increasingly salient issue for the Eight, everything in their backgrounds made them conscious of race as a source of egregious injustice in American life. Now Dallas was doing fieldwork in East Harlem. Dellinger, in addition to his work at Dwight Hall, had witnessed Jim Crow firsthand during visits to his father's family in the South. His fieldwork now was in a poor black area of Newark, New Jersey. The Eight were frustrated by the turn away from pacifism at Union, where many students and faculty, like most Americans, shifted to more of a traditional peace-through-strength stance as a result of developments in Europe. And they were all too conscious of the poverty and injustice practically right outside the door of their own institution.

It was probably Dellinger, with his confidence, seniority, and more radical instincts, who led some of the students out of the classroom and into the community. Despite his antipathy toward status and hierarchy, he was elected president of his class. He was older than most of the first-year students, was a graduate of Yale rather than a religious college in the hinterlands, had seen the Spanish Civil War up close, and had even visited Nazi Germany. He also had a year at Oxford under his belt, and a couple more working at Yale's Christian center. In his first year at Union he quickly formed a close bond with Benedict and Dallas, with whom he had classes, took meals, and lamented the turn of their most famous professor, Reinhold Niebuhr, away from pacifism. Don and Dal, as they were known, had been undergraduates at Albion College together and were both bound for the ministry. Dellinger, alienated from his parents, seemed to treat them as family, and late in 1939 they decided to move together to an impoverished section of nearby Harlem, a black neighborhood where they imagined their ramshackle apartment would function as a Gandhian ashram.

They were not alone in pursuing Protestant pacifism as a "way of life," far beyond merely eschewing violence. In Aurora, Ohio, a handful of Antioch College students gained attention for a cooperative farm called Ahimsa, named for the Indian religious doctrine of nonviolence, where they grew food and studied key pacifist texts including Gregg's *The Power of Non-Violence*. Emulating Gandhi, they also launched a small march to the sea, in this case to focus attention on European hunger. Ahimsa didn't last beyond 1942, but supporters included A. J. Muste and the British pacifist Muriel Lester. Ahimsa's founders, through a connection with a black church in Cleveland, would become involved in a small nonviolent protest that was to have large ramifications.

Closer to Union, Jay Holmes Smith and Ralph Templin, Methodist missionaries essentially expelled from India for siding with Gandhi, launched their Harlem Ashram on Fifth Avenue near 125th Street in the winter of 1940–41 (situated, incongruously, opposite a tavern called the Bucket of Blood). It soon became a center for pacifist absolutists, including those who refused to register. From the discussions in its dingy rooms arose the Non-Violent Direct Action Committee, whose commitment to direct action was evident in its name, and the Free India Committee, a group that included many prominent activists (such as Randolph), and which in 1943 frequently demonstrated at the British consulate in New York and embassy in Washington. The protesters were usually arrested. Ashram residents at various times included future civil rights luminaries James Farmer and Pauli Murray as well as Krishnalal Shridharani, whose *War Without Violence*, published in 1939, quickly became a Gandhian handbook for American pacifists. "Shridharani's book became our gospel, our bible," said Bayard Rustin, who lived nearby for a while and was a frequent visitor. The ashram only lasted until 1944, when it succumbed to financial and other issues, including perhaps an excess of piety. Farmer called the furniture "old, cheap and tasteless," and the meals "an inducement to fasting." He recalls Smith once violating the usual dinner etiquette by serving the soup to himself first, thereby giving him a chance to discreetly ladle a cockroach out of it before it became visible to the other diners.[13]

While it lasted, the Harlem Ashram was an important test bed for the Fellowship and its members to break out in new directions. Shridharani, three blacks, and seven whites lived there at the outset, around January of 1941, and a Fellowship of Reconciliation nonviolent direct action group began meeting there. Smith and John Swomley, Jr., soon launched a summer training school in "total pacifism," which they portrayed in familiar Christian terms, including as "a way of life, in which we seek to live out the implications of truth and non-violence in all our relationships," and "a goal for social reconstruction, a co-operative socio-economic order, approximating to the realization of the Kingdom of God on earth." But they added something of more recent vintage: "Non-violent action." They surveyed black Harlem residents about discrimination, and launched a campaign to desegregate New York's YMCAs. In a pamphlet about the ashram, they wrote: "We Live in Harlem because we regard the problem of racial justice as America's No. 1 problem in reconciliation."

Accordingly, in the fall of 1942 Smith led fourteen marchers on an "Interracial Pilgrimage" to dramatize the anti-lynching and anti–poll tax bills then before Congress. The group walked from New York to Washington, D.C., carrying signs condemning discrimination, and also met with townspeople en route. It was an idealistic bunch. For symbolic reasons they trod the Lincoln Highway, and they debated whether they could allow the police to protect them from the hostility they encountered along the way. The activist Ruth Reynolds marched until her feet bled, and still refused to stop. Finally, trailing blood on the sidewalks of Philadelphia, she was arrested just to get her into an ambulance. After emergency care, she rejoined the group and finished the march. Father Divine's followers fed them all in Wilmington. When they wearily trudged into Washington, their journey ended anticlimactically when a minor White House functionary accepted their petitions. The black civil rights lawyer Conrad Lynn reflected on his participation uneasily. Like most black Americans, he was no pacifist. Later he wrote that "the elevation of nonviolence and orderliness as means, often vitiated the desired end," making the march mostly a "catharsis for the white people who participated" while blacks got only "suppression of indignation and a lesson in humility."[14]

As is evident from outposts like the Harlem Ashram and Ahimsa, the boys from Union were part of a rich vein of radicals launching intentional communities in the forties, many of them interracial ashrams, utopian farming ventures, and Fellowship Houses founded to promulgate nonviolent change. The years ahead would produce many more. After the war Dellinger and his family would live on a cooperative farm in New Jersey with a few likeminded families, eventually naming the place Saint Francis Acres and "changing the deed to declare that the land belonged to God."[15]

Meanwhile he was looking for something more than a mere academic experience from his time at Union—and besides, "I didn't believe in a community that had no meaningful associations with its poor, radically oppressed neighbors." Benedict was under no illusions that by living among the poor the fellows could do them much good, but he could at least show whose side he was on and learn from dwelling among the dispossessed. "My quarrel was not with the school," he writes, "but with its tacit elitism. In the gospel there was no place for elitism."[16]

When they took their plan to Union's president, Coffin—who had already had his struggles with radical students during the Depression—was adamantly opposed. Union required some pastoral fieldwork of its students, but this was something else again, and he threatened to revoke whatever scholarship funds they were receiving if they moved off campus. Convinced he was bluffing, they went ahead anyway, quickly proving that he was. But many students were against it as well, for it fractured Union's relatively small class. Said Benedict: "It split the student body wide open, you know. Those that were seeing us as kind of self-righteous monks, you know, and others would say, 'No, it's a legitimate thing to do.'"[17]

When they "finally found a place wretched enough to please us," as Benedict wryly recalled, they learned firsthand what it was like to live in bedbug-infested quarters with virtually no heat and run a gauntlet of derelicts and prostitutes to get home at night. Residents of the neighborhood were understandably wary of these young white guys. But Dellinger got to know people through sports, "playing stickball, shooting pool, having beer, and listening to the ball game at the corner bar, hanging out on the stoop on a hot night," and doing other things that neighbors might naturally do together. As Spragg put it, "We wanted to go down there to find out what the real world was like."[18]

One or another of the seminarians might bring home a lost soul, who usually left fed and cleaned up. Benedict recalls encountering, one freezing night, "a large, hulking fellow, revoltingly dirty and frowzy, altogether a disgusting sight, steeped in the sour smell of vomit and the stench of alcohol." Benedict was ashamed that he at first recoiled from the man's entreaties, and so, with Dallas, brought him home, where they treated a nasty abrasion and provided clean pajamas. Spragg, who was senior class

president, was on hand and challenged them, arguing that they weren't going to do much good one drunk at a time and needed to address much larger
social issues to bring about any appreciable change. Spragg had played football at Tufts, yet he, too, was a pacifist, having read Niebuhr on this score,
and a Norman Thomas socialist as well. He was another of those shaped by
the Christian student activism of the day. For five straight summers he had
accepted difficult assignments for the Congregational Church home mission, including two organizing stints in Harlan County, Kentucky, for the
United Mine Workers.[19]

Another time Dallas brought home a couple of guys he'd met in a bar.
They were supposedly trying to get together a tap-dancing act and had no
place to stay. After a few days the dancers vanished with their hosts' type-
writers and clothes. Dellinger's flute was stolen at one point. Later he said
of the thief, "Painful as the loss was, I knew that I had been less wronged
by him than he by the society that provided me with a silver flute and him
with a drug habit." At Union there was a certain amount of ridicule for
what the fellows were doing. But there was admiration as well, and when
they held an open house, many students and faculty members showed up.
Some fellow students started volunteering in their spare time. And Dallas
got the chance to preach out in the community, including at Fosdick's
Riverside Church. Adam Clayton Powell's Abyssinian Baptist Church left
a particular impression. "I was up there in the pulpit," he recalled years
later, "and I could get that wave of energy from the congregation that happens in a black church. My God! That was powerful."[20]

Dellinger and company were dividing their time at this point between
Harlem and a black section of Newark, where he worked as a part-time
minister. They met the full panoply of local residents and did what they
could to help those in need, including distributing coats and blankets they
had collected, providing canned goods to food banks, serving hot meals at
church, and pitching in on community cleanup efforts. "We offered hospitality to anyone who came to our door, sharing whatever food and clothing we had as well as shelter," Dellinger would recall. "Frequently there
were more of us sleeping on the floor than in beds."[21] Along the way they
made friends with their counterparts at Dorothy Day's Catholic Worker
house in lower Manhattan, which was something of a model for their own

Gandhian cooperative effort. Dellinger's friendship with Day, a comrade in pacifist arms, would endure for decades to come.

By the summer of 1940 he was hired full-time at his church in Newark, and the other Union boys figured they could all get by on his salary at the modest living standard prevailing in the community. That would enable them to devote their time to community service. So they moved operations to Newark, calling their enterprise the Newark Christian Colony at first. "We rented a house and lived in Christian ashram style," Benedict remembered, "having prayers together; working at painting, washing windows, and various odd jobs; putting the earnings into a common pot. Each of us took a dollar a week to spend. We decided to attend classes half-time at Union."[22]

In truth, the seminary could not contain them. The center of their lives had shifted from the classroom to the community, and in a telling shift of nomenclature the Newark Christian Colony became the Newark Ashram. The other idealistic young people taking part included Willa Winter (Dal's fiancée) and Charlie Swift, whose brother David had been Dellinger's roommate at Yale. Bill Sutherland, a black pacifist from a bourgeois family in the Newark suburbs, also joined, he and Dellinger having met in the Christian student movement of the thirties. Willa's parents let her move into the ashram on condition that Jan Mitchell, a trusted friend from a leading local family, went with her. Jan's father told her that if the whole venture had anything to do with "colored people," she was to send him a telegram. He would then send one back reporting a phony family emergency that would provide a pretext for her escape. "Jan had been there only a day or two when she composed the telegram," reports Tony Dallas, Willa and Meredith's son. Charles Forman, later Jan's husband and a professor at Yale Divinity School explained: "The group was going to hear Dave Dellinger speak at a church that night. Jan planned to stop off at the Western Union on the way home. But Dave's speech completely turned her life around. She crumpled up the letter and became a strong member of the group." Willa Winter did likewise. Willa and Dal were married eventually, but not before they were turned down for a license in New York and Connecticut as well as New Jersey.[23]

———

IN THE FALL OF 1940, Houser was living on campus at Union, where classes had resumed after the summer off. During the night of October 9, Houser was awakened by Benedict, Dellinger, and Howard Spragg, who told him they were working on a statement announcing that they (and anyone who would go along) wouldn't register. Tall, handsome Meredith Dallas worked on the text as well. Although he was a quiet seminarian in 1940, theater would become his career, which he would spend at progressive Antioch College in Yellow Springs, Ohio. Union, to Dallas, underscored the so-cioeconomic gulf between himself and his fellow students. Dal, as he was called by all who knew him, would later tell an interviewer that he was "from a working background" and "didn't feel easy with that total intellec-tual aristocracy kind of feeling" which prevailed at Union. Before divinity school, he had never been to Manhattan.[24]

After Albion College, Dal and Benedict naturally became roommates at Union. They had Methodism and pacifism in common too. Benedict was from a middle-class family that struggled in the 1930s. The Benedicts had had to move in with relatives for a while, but his father got a decent job in time for him to attend college, where he was a popular fraternity man and athlete. In fact, he was a better athlete than student; his pitching skills, at both baseball and softball, were legendary. Albion had an annual day of contests between freshmen and sophomores, and in Benedict's first year, his reputation well established, he was kidnapped by opponents who wanted him out of the big softball game. Unable to find an open boxcar in which to leave their bound captive, they locked him in an abandoned slaughterhouse. The resourceful Benedict managed to escape, making his way back in time to strike out twenty players. His pitching would get him and his friends out of an even bigger jam soon enough.[25]

Benedict, Dallas, Dellinger, and Spragg were all veterans of Union's Social Action Committee, headed by Houser, so they were already official dissidents of a sort. A draft of their statement circulated, and twenty stu-dents signed. On October 12, with no little naïveté, the group sent copies to roughly fifteen hundred church and government officials, family mem-bers, and friends, *The Christian Century,* and of course the press. Entitled "A Christian Conviction on Conscription and Registration," its preface began with these words: "We are a group of students at Union Theological

Seminary. After much consideration and prayer, we have come to the conclusion that as Christians we should not cooperate with the government in any way in regard to the Selective Training and Service Act of 1940."

The result, today, would be called a firestorm. The students' refusal was covered in newspapers and on radio from coast to coast—and during the month between announcement and sentencing it provoked outrage from nearly every quarter. Editorials called the students un-American or demanded tough penalties. The resisters were shocked to find themselves held up as exemplars of unpatriotic villainy. Their families and acquaintances were shocked, too, or at the very least unsettled.

Dellinger's conservative father, who had once hoped his son would become a lawyer, now confronted a young man facing felony charges and bringing shame on the family. "The night I made my decision not to register I talked to my father on the phone," Dellinger writes. His friend Lovell was present during this conversation. "Now that a long-feared catastrophe was coming to a head, he told me that he would commit suicide unless I registered. I did my best to comfort and reassure him, but he said he would not hang up until I promised to register; if I hung up, he would kill himself immediately. We talked for what must have been an hour or more before the crisis passed."[26]

The students' anguished parents, interviewed by the local newspapers that nearly everyone read in those days, were forced to answer for their sons in their own communities. The Denver newspapers, for whom Houser was a hometown figure, put the story on the front page. George's father, a prominent minister in a city that had been a center of pacifism and social justice activism, braved death threats to defend his son, doing so from his pulpit at the Trinity Methodist Church, in a letter to the *Rocky Mountain News*, and in media interviews. George's mother, Ethel, beset by questions about him, prayed for the strength and guidance "to face this hard thing, whatever it is, with courage."

The fellows no doubt did the same, for it was sobering to be attacked on the front page of *The New York Times* the day after issuing your highminded statement, and to read, from a senior Selective Service official determined to throw the book at you, that you face as much as five years in prison and a $10,000 fine. They found themselves under immense pressure from hostile citizens who wrote and telegrammed, and from the school's administration. At an extraordinary special meeting, the entire faculty came up with a statement saying that the resisters were wrong to consider mere registration as a religious issue and that "no member of the faculty has advised any student to follow this course of action."

Coffin, who had seen more than enough of student radicalism at Union during his time as president, declined to expel the students, but he pulled out all the stops to dissuade them, including sending telegrams to their families. Spragg said later, "I never forgave Henry for that." The one sent to Houser's father said, "Your son George has signed a statement that he will not register next Wednesday under the Selective Service Act. The penalty for such offense may be five years in prison. I have been unable to deter him. Can you prevent this tragedy?"[27]

Among those who tried to talk the boys into registering was Niebuhr, who by now had abandoned his earlier pacifism for a powerfully tragic "Christian realism" that admitted of war's necessity at times. "I have every appreciation for the integrity of our eight young men," he wrote, "but I do not see how they can be helped when in effect they courted martyrdom in the hope that their situation would start a general movement in the country." Niebuhr told his correspondent he knew "some of these boys very intimately" and had talked with them at length. Their stand, he said, "goes beyond any valid pacifism."[28]

On the night of October 14, the twenty young resisters met for a serious reevaluation. "Our whole group spent hours rethinking, arguing, praying," Houser later related. In a diary entry for the seminary's student quarterly, *Union Review*, he wrote: "We have had the most real heart-searching and the most sincere consecration to what we conceive our Christian faith to be that any of us have ever known." Twelve of the original twenty decided to register, but at least some of them became conscientious objectors. "Eight of us reaffirmed our position. I remember the peace I felt after making this decision."[29]

Dellinger, who had participated in campus antiwar activities as an undergraduate at Yale, evidently took seriously the Union Eight's hope that their resistance would spark a national upsurge in draft refusal (in fact only a smattering of young men refused to register). He sent a telegram to the *Yale Daily News*, whose October 16 edition quoted from it: "Hope

Yale men who cannot take similar action will attack roots of war by giving up privileges and dedicating themselves to a world of real democracy and Christianity. Last generation of Yale men made great sacrifices in a war they thought would end war. Let this generation make equal sacrifices of security, or career, and even life in revolt against all war."

Dellinger concluded with words that might serve as his lifelong motto: "This is no time for compromise."[30]

But the student newspaper that very day carried an extraordinary composition to the contrary that was almost certainly the handiwork of the paper's anti-interventionist chairman, Kingman Brewster. The editorial, referring to the threat of five years in prison, $10,000 in fines, or both, said: "That is a drastic penalty, but it certainly deserves to be invoked in this case." It went on to make an argument that would arise more widely within the pacifist movement during the war, which was whether, to the most radical resisters, the enemy was war or government itself:

> In effect, these twenty students are taking the law into their own hands before taking their case to court. It is not even an heroic gesture. It is an exhibition of intellectual arrogance on the part of a group which places its private judgment above that of Congress. It is a group which, on the basis of a creed, places itself above the law . . . It is a worthy cause, and the right to espouse it must be preserved. But the role of conscientious objector centers on a refusal to participate in battle, not the obstruction or evasion of registration measures.

Confronted with all the bad press, Houser had a "mighty shaky hand" while shaving. "The emotion involved in the first experience of facing an unsympathetic army administrator or judge has caused me once again to think through the entire position . . . The awful thought cannot be escaped that maybe—just maybe—we are refusing to budge at the wrong point."[31]

On the night of October 15—registration eve—nearly the entire faculty and student body came together for a moving reconciliation service in Union's imposing James Chapel, with its dark wainscoting, English stained glass and high ceiling of exposed timbers. (The chapel would later be remodeled into the architectural equivalent of a tabula rasa, a neutrally colored, flexible multiuse space considered more suitable to our era.). Probably accompanied by the chapel's organ, the assembled community sang "Once to Every Man and Nation Comes the Moment to Decide," a hymn based on a poem called "The Present Crisis" by James Russell Lowell, an antislavery man of letters and the first editor of *The Atlantic Monthly*. (The tune, "Ebenezer," was by the Welsh composer Thomas John Williams.) Lowell's poem was written in protest of the Mexican American War, an expansionist adventure opposed by many intellectuals and abolitionists in part because it would expand the province of slavery. (The NAACP magazine, *The Crisis*, got its name from the poem.) Lowell's lines, Houser would write, were "never sung more meaningfully."[32]

The next day, the eight holdouts held a silent prayer session in their dormitory and then walked downstairs to the classroom designated for the seminarians to register for the draft. They handed their statement over to members of the draft board who were on hand, having appended it to clarify that, rather than evading conscription, they intended "to face it with all sincerity and try to make clear our reasons for not complying with it." The fellows were handed federal grand jury subpoenas on the spot.

Yet there was still time for the young men to change their minds—and everyone still seemed to be trying to get them to do so. Frantic Union officials wheeled out some pacifist heavyweights toward this end. The great civil libertarian Roger Baldwin, who headed the ACLU in those days, met with the students, as did Fosdick and Sockman, all of them well-known opponents of war. Houser would write later that "These meetings and others were not necessarily designed to urge us to change our position, but were a subtle pressure in that direction nonetheless."[33]

———

BACK TO THE FEDERAL courthouse on the morning of November 14, 1940. The intransigent eight, wearing their best suits, were thronged by reporters, photographers, and newsreel cameras when they showed up to face the judge. Having admitted their guilt, each addressed him in turn. Several apologized for all the trouble but said they had no choice. "We cannot in this apparently small matter fail to follow the teachings of Jesus," said Lovell.

None offered a more aggressive polemic than Dellinger, whose despairing parents were on hand. "War," he said, "is the systematic mass murder of our human brothers and the destruction of our treasures and is completely contrary to the best human intelligence and the teachings and life of Jesus and the deepest instincts of all men."

When they were led out of the courtroom, according to the *New York Herald Tribune*, some of their relatives and supporters burst into tears, but one man shouted, "Hitler has conquered again!" Afterwards the fellows were fingerprinted and driven off in handcuffs to the "West Street" detention center. Another pacifist who passed through West Street, Alfred Hassler, who would one day head the Fellowship of Reconciliation, recalled the place as a segregated institution where black inmates were shunted "into one of two specified dormitories no matter how crowded it may be, or how empty one of the others." Blacks and whites mixed as they walked into the dining room, but then were sent to separate parts of the room. Benedict got in the food line for blacks until he was dragged away by a guard. In fact, segregation prevailed throughout the federal prison system as a matter of entrenched—and officially enforced—practice.[34]

With some bitterness, Dellinger reports in his memoir that Niebuhr "preached a sermon in the Union chapel the day we were being carted off to jail, saying that his greatest failing as a teacher of Christian principles had been his inability to educate us on the realities of Christianity."[35]

CHAPTER 9

HARDBALL AND SOFTBALL
AT DANBURY

DAVID DELLINGER GOT INTO trouble the first time he had a chance to watch a movie at the federal prison in Danbury. The gym was filled with folding chairs and cheering inmates, as it was every Saturday night, and a projector was rolled to the back to show the picture. On this particular night in late 1940 or early 1941, Dellinger entered the gym talking with a black inmate and sat down next to him. A guard, spying a white man on the wrong side of the color line, came over and said, "This section is for 'colored' prisoners. You'll have to move." Dellinger refused and soon found himself in "the Hole," which is what inmates called solitary confinement: a five-by-eight concrete cell maintained in complete darkness day and night and containing only a toilet—the only place to sit aside from the cold concrete floor. At night inmates were given a blanket that was removed in the morning. Cold coffee and perhaps a bologna sandwich were brought in for nourishment. The rest of the time there was only silence, darkness, and discomfort. Humans are social animals attuned to diurnal cycles, and the Hole, for almost anyone, was an ordeal.

American draft resisters during the Second World War were not sent to Alcatraz or subjected to the kind of wholesale abuse (at Fort Leavenworth, for example) that occurred in the Great War. But some were mistreated, and incarceration was a trial for all—including federal prison administrators suddenly afflicted with inmates the likes of which they hadn't previously encountered. These young radicals were committed, educated, increasingly organized, and deeply hostile to official authority. Prison, to them, was the apotheosis of government power, and they were allergic to it. "In the Prison," COs Holley Cantine and Dachine Rainer wrote later, "the population is subjected to the type of control that State functionaries aspire to impose on the population 'at large.' The Prison represents absolute freedom of coercion."[1]

The process that brought them to prison selected for those who were most likely to defy authority on behalf of conscience. At Danbury, where the young men of the Union Eight found themselves confined after refusing to register for the draft, the resisters had particular disdain for the warden, a liberal criminologist named Edgar Gerlach, whom they regarded as a vain and hypocritical martinet. At one point he telegrammed Dellinger's parents in Wakefield, Massachusetts, with the news that their son was on the brink of a nervous breakdown. Worried, they rushed to Danbury, where Dave reassured them at length. Schoenfeld, an objector confined to Danbury at the time, charitably described Gerlach as "a man of about fifty, with a clean cut, intelligent face . . . a comparatively advanced outlook . . . and a keen feeling of sympathy for the underdog." Unfortunately, "his fate was to discover us unmanageable. We were a proud, stiff-necked lot who openly boasted we were the most radical men in the country."[2]

They may well have been, but prison would make them more so. Starting with the Union Eight and a handful of others, the federal prisons and church-run work camps of World War II were about to become crucibles of postwar radicalism. Here, a disparate collection of pacifist young men encountered one another and the unchecked power of the state at the same fateful time. The resulting chemical reaction further radicalized the resisters, instilled a lifelong distrust of government, and helped them and their supporters coalesce into a broader movement that went beyond pacifism to push for social change. It was in these facilities, in never-ending discussion, subversion, strikes, publicity, and some surprising triumphs, that American pacifism shifted from defense to offense.

Some COs even took pity on their jailers. Malcolm Parker, a colorful polymath who was incarcerated as a CO, later recalled "the well-nigh unbelievable tolerance and restraint shown toward us by the staff of the Federal

Correctional Institution at Sandstone, Minnesota, in the face of what at times amounted to extreme provocation . . . I just wonder if I would have acquitted myself equally well had I been in their shoes."[3]

For the most truculent resisters, though, the federal prisons were America writ large: regimented, violent, arbitrary, racist, hypocritical, and satisfied with itself. The food could be sickening, sometimes literally, and every man was required to eat everything on his plate. Almost every aspect of prison life was segregated by race. Although otherwise run along fairly liberal lines—smoking was allowed in the dining hall, inmates could put on shows, and recreational facilities were ample—solitary confinement was routinely imposed. At least things weren't as bad as they were elsewhere, according to Schoenfeld: "Wardens at other prisons allowed guards to beat and torture inmates of our type." Lowell Naeve, arriving at Danbury in the summer of 1941, found the experience an embarrassing reenactment of the mindless conformity performed daily on the outside: "We didn't want to get up, but we did. Why? We didn't know. We just got up."

The number of COs who felt a duty to rebel was small, but they had an outsized impact. In the federal prisons, a few hundred pacifists through sheer force of will managed to bring about lasting change, demonstrating that organized nonviolence could work against segregation and other noxious practices. More broadly, and perhaps more importantly, the camps and prisons that held war resisters became laboratories for the techniques of nonviolent protest suitable to the circumstances but transferrable to America at large. Prepared by Gandhi, Shridharani, and Gregg, and drawing on the experience of labor radicals and suffragists, resisters showed that nonviolent "direct action," whether deployed by an individual or, much better, as a collective, can produce important institutional change. It had to be done in the right way; you had to be able to withstand potentially brutal consequences, and you couldn't overlook public opinion, which could help you leverage small actions to achieve a large impact. CO John Hampton, who spent much of his stay at Sandstone in solitary confinement, stuffed the toilet with bits of his clothing and kept flushing until he'd flooded the whole block of punitive cells. Water for the entire prison had to be shut off to solve the problems caused by a single determined inmate.

Men like Hampton didn't fit the stereotype of the meek pacifist or cowardly draft dodger. The masculinity of resisters was routinely questioned in those days; people called them sissies, yellowbellies, and weaklings. When federal marshals arrested pacifist Alex Stach and took him back to Indiana for trial, he reported, "they figured I must be a sexual misfit of some kind. They wanted to know if I liked women . . . How can a conscientious objector be a man? He couldn't possibly be interested in sex." Stach's lengthy sentence included hard labor. COs were better educated and probably more intelligent than the average military recruit, not to mention more religious. Two social scientists who studied them found that "conscientious objectors, like women, have more interests in musical, artistic, and literary activities and in people than non-conscientious objectors, who as more representative men, prefer mechanical, scientific, physically strenuous and selling activities."[4]

Homosexuality, like other kinds of difference, was probably more tolerated among the COs than in other contexts, and what we now call gay men were almost certainly more salient among them if not more numerous. Christopher Isherwood recorded that "his friend and lover had upset the Quaker directors of the California CPS camp where he was stationed: 'the long and short of it is that Denny has simply been talking about his gay life in Paris and making them discontented.'" And at the arty Waldport, Oregon, CPS camp, William Everson wrote to his wife about watching a drag performance by "one of the camp homosexuals."[5]

Yet incarcerated war resisters managed to stake out their masculinity in a new, nonviolent way. They were tough when they entered the prison system, and tougher still when they came out. Some, like Dellinger, served two separate terms behind bars, while others spent the entire war in unpaid physical labor far from home, in locales that had no use for draft dodgers. These experiences strengthened the COs they didn't break. Inured to punishment and social disrepute, hardened resisters carried forward the lessons of their wartime incarceration into their later nonviolent battles, and the networks they formed would endure after their release.

————

FROM THE OUTSET, THE pacifist establishment focused on a legal carve-out for conscientious objectors and discouraged any efforts to obstruct or undermine war preparations. The historic peace churches chose to cooperate with the government by running the CPS camps. Muste discouraged resistance in camps and prisons and any active interference with the war effort. Gregg urged "voluntary restraint," arguing that "wise conduct" by pacifists would hasten the arrival of postwar liberties. But some in the younger generation saw things differently. William Clark, a CO who served time with the Union students, put the case plainly in *Fellowship*: "Now is the time for non-cooperation; for non-violent direct action."[6]

The Union Eight had not defied the federal government, popular opinion, and their own families to sit quietly in Danbury, which was considered even then a relatively comfortable prison for less violent offenders and short-timers. Dellinger, as he would in later prison stints, began plotting protests soon after arrival, which no doubt accounted for his movie contretemps. George Houser meanwhile started organizing the COs by circulating a list of suggestions for his comrades that combined political and spiritual aims:

1) We should be a force for as great a democracy as possible within this institution;

2) We should be thinking continually with one another of what we are going to do when we leave here, of our mission to build a better world, and to build a movement of vitality in the church; and

3) We should practice daily devotions, if possible at the same time.

During their initial month of quarantine, the warden tried to plumb their psyches. He asked Houser, a loving son if ever there was one, whether he hated his father. Recognizing the intellectual capacities of his new charges and perhaps seeking their approval, the warden foolishly challenged Houser to Ping-Pong matches. Houser, a superb player, trounced him and was soon spearheading the prison team. It was during this initial period, probably, that Gerlach learned of Benedict's extraordinary pitching skills. Sports were a big deal to the warden, and to the inmates too. The prison had a baseball diamond, with bleachers, and several of the athletic young pacifists, including Benedict, Dallas, Houser, and Dellinger, were soon members of the softball team, having played in a league at Columbia University before prison. Guards were instructed to lay off

Benedict and let him stop work early so he could practice. He quickly became the team's star.[7]

But Benedict, Dellinger, and their comrades weren't about to let sports get in the way of protest—and there was plenty to raise hell about, including arbitrary punishments, Jim Crow, restrictions on reading material, mail censorship, and more. The COs, in their various accounts of these events, agree that they had no trouble with the other inmates and sought to help them in every way they could. After the war one came to live with Dellinger and his colleagues in Newark. "We cast our lot in with theirs from the beginning," Schoenfeld recalls, "and all our group of ministers, divinity students, and socialists had been in solitary or restrictions at one time or another for protesting against the evil conditions under which they lived."[8]

The petty tyrannies and humiliations of prison life were a continual goad to men who considered themselves political prisoners. At various times the pacifists got in trouble for refusing to answer to their numbers rather than their names and for refusing to countenance guards calling black inmates "nigger." Houser, who used his typewriter access to write collective letters of protest against segregation to the warden and federal prison authorities, lost his cushy job in the chaplain's office for refusing to stand when Gerlach came in. Confronted by a warden who was alternately ingratiating and imperious, Houser told him: "Warden, I respect you as a man, but not as the warden." The warden's pet divinity student was soon reassigned to the filthy and suffocating business of cleaning out boilers in the furnace room until he took advantage of warming weather to get himself reassigned to the farm. There he worked outdoors with Charlie Swift. Houser and Swift formed a lifelong friendship roasting corn in the fields or, smuggling out some bread from breakfast, making delicious sandwiches of fresh tomatoes pulled from the vine and lettuce torn from the ground.

On April 12, 1941, the Union guys and eight other conscientious objectors gave notice that they would stop work in honor of international student peace day, which during the 1930s had been the basis of strikes on campuses nationwide. The stoppage was set for April 23. Warden Gerlach immediately tried to talk the fellows out of it, ostentatiously brushing off his knees as he entered the room because, he said, he had been praying for them. When that didn't work, he gathered all the prisoners in the yard and warned that a strike would undermine efforts to liberalize conditions at Danbury. "If they carry out this threat I will be forced to take away all yard privileges for inmates—also Ping-Pong, softball, movies, and library privileges." He also apparently accused the protesters of disloyalty, of being unpatriotic, of trying to take over the prison. One or two of the resisters shouted "It's a lie, warden," or words to that effect, and the other inmates supported the resisters. Schoenfeld's colorful account (he subsequently became a fantasy and science fiction writer) says the warden offered to allow the strike if it was confined to the COs, who refused and in fact had already invited everyone else.

James V. Bennett, superintendent of the Federal Bureau of Prisons, did not take any of this lightly. Recognizing that Dellinger was the ringleader and knowing that the COs were not the usual inmates susceptible to the usual punishments and rewards, he came up to Danbury personally to try and talk him out of it, warning (in Dellinger's recollection) that "the American prison system is the most authoritarian institution in the world, and if you don't straighten up and obey every order that it gives you, no matter what it is, the full weight of that system will come down on you."[9]

This description of the conversation might be taken with a grain of salt, for Bennett was hardly a knee-jerk disciplinarian. In 1929, as a young lawyer in the federal bureaucracy, he wrote a report to Congress detailing inadequacies and abuses at the three federal prisons then in existence—places where inmates wore striped outfits, were moved about chained together, and ate out of buckets. Guards were ill-trained political patronage hires. To do something about all this, the Bureau of Prisons was established in 1930 with Bennett in a senior role, and by 1937 he was in charge. From then until his retirement in 1964 he was a tireless advocate of humane incarceration focused on rehabilitation rather than punishment. Indeed, this unlikely CO nemesis was often accused of "coddling" inmates, a charge he rejected. "Society need have no concern about our prisons being made so attractive to the men they will want to return," he said. "Imprisonment, being shut out from life, is punishment enough. Our job is to return that man to society better fitted to adjust himself to it." Toward this goal, his innovations included job training, counseling, halfway houses, and an emphasis on maintaining inmate ties with family and community. He opened the nation's first prison without walls, and he hired reform-minded wardens.[10]

But Bennett had no more success deterring a Union Eight protest than did Henry Sloane Coffin at Union. Finally, on the day before the strike was to go into effect, the warden ordered the protesters pulled from their cells under cover of darkness. Schoenfeld: "Between the steel wire and the back wall was a small walk along which guards made their nightly rounds. In the dead of night I was aroused by a guard carrying a flashlight. He shook me awake. 'Get your clothes and follow me.'" Each of the troublemakers was called into the warden's private office, its thick rugs and modern furniture contrasting sharply with the starkly utilitarian surroundings the inmates were used to. The warden, at least according to Schoenfeld, was in evening attire, evidently having come from a social function, but had traded his coat for a smoking jacket, and they discussed the reasons for the strike. Then the men were hauled off into solitary confinement.

There wasn't enough Hole to accommodate all of them, so a new and more conventional cellblock was opened up for this purpose. The rooms were still tiny and dark, though not absolutely so, and the men were let out only for meals, which were consumed apart from the rest of the inmates both to punish the recalcitrant and to prevent the strike from spreading. Dellinger had already proved his toughness to himself in the Hole, yet began this period of isolation filled with anxiety after Bennett's threats. "I found myself going through a period of anguish such as I had never experienced before," he would write. "I felt absolutely certain that there was no way I could continue on my present path, not just inside prison but on the outside—if I got out—and manage to stay alive." His only companion, imagination, conjured only conflict with loved ones and excruciating physical torture.

Dellinger was and would remain a profoundly spiritual person, and it was here, in his latest round of isolation, that he went all the way through a second conversion experience, one quite in keeping with William James's expectations. His earlier such episode happened when he turned against violence after that football game at Yale. This second, prison-inspired conversion had begun in the Hole, a place he had worried would break him and from which he'd emerged blinking and reeking of body odor, showing few outward signs of the strange feelings of relief and security that had come over him in the darkness.

This time, those feelings came flooding back and carried him much further—to a kind of resurrection. "There is no way to describe it except to say that I died," he says in his memoir, adding: "Nothing that any human being could do to me could ever harm me. I had faced the worst, had decided to continue in the direction that life was taking me and suddenly, unaccountably, I was free. I had died and, if you will forgive the phrase, had gone to heaven."[11]

It was here, perhaps, that Dellinger developed the sense of invulnerability that would help him through countless terrifying episodes in the years ahead. But what got him out of solitary was softball. Several of those involved have left accounts of the events at Danbury in 1941, ranging from the prosaic to the level of a movie treatment, but they all point to the same thing: the warden wanted Benedict to pitch. In some versions it was the championship game, though it seems a bit early in the season for that. Schoenfeld's story, ready-made for Hollywood, has the pacifist ace protesting that he's in no shape to pitch. Levelheaded George Houser offers the most plausible account, observing that "I smile even today, more than a half-century later, when I reflect on how this event ended."[12]

Houser recalls that the fellows had been in solitary for two weeks when the Danbury nine, playing in a regional league, was getting beaten by a team from outside the prison. In the bottom of the fourth inning (the Danbury team presumably played all its games "at home"), inmates in the stands began to chant, "We want Benedict." Warden Gerlach, who in some ways tried to be one of the fellows, dispatched the captain of the guards to retrieve the prison's pitching star, who "answered the call and struck out the next nine batters who faced him" in the seven-inning game, enabling Danbury to come from behind for the victory. For Benedict, it was back to isolation.

Days later, the Danbury team had another game, and again the captain was sent to retrieve Benedict. "But this time," Houser says, "he refused to go unless all of us were let out." So the warden, perhaps glad for an excuse, released his star pitcher and all the strikers were allowed out to watch the game. "Again Benedict was the hero," Houser says, "pitching a one-hitter and winning the game."[13]

After the final pitch, pandemonium erupted as inmates thronged Benedict, hugging him, shaking his hand, and cheering. And then the strikers, Benedict and all, were trundled right back to solitary confinement, but at dinner, at least according to Houser, when all the other inmates were already seated in the mess hall, the warden ordered the strikers released for their first meal with the others in more than two weeks. "As we entered the hall the place broke out into wild applause and a standing ovation. How sweet it was." Schoenfeld portrays a kind of delirium: "Six hundred pairs of hands joined in and the crescendo became pandemonium . . . A mass catharsis of human misery was taking place before our eyes. Some of the men were weeping, others were laughing like madmen. It was like nothing I had ever seen before."[14]

For COs, it was a victory that went beyond the softball diamond, and there were bigger ones ahead. Meanwhile the Union fellows gained friends and admiration among the regular inmates by listening to them, taking their side against the authorities, and absorbing punishment without complaint. "Under their influence many an inmate, who had never known kindness or even decent treatment, before, discovered his own spiritual potential," Schoenfeld would write, adding of the religious COs: "They were the finest people I had ever known. Gathered up from everywhere they seemed to me to embody the conscience of America."[15]

Even the warden probably had a grudging respect for them. The one group that seemed immune to the divinity students was the communists. Dellinger, who had the job of collecting trash from all over the prison, recalled that a group of inmates from the furriers' union worked in the prison tailor shop and were always nice to him, providing hot coffee, rolls, a cigar, and other extras they had obtained. His antiwar stand made him a hero to the men, who were communists. "One day, I walked in as usual and they called me a 'fascist' and a 'coward,'" Dellinger writes. "When I tried to talk with them, two of them literally spat at me." At his next stop, Dellinger heard the news: Germany had invaded the Soviet Union, and American communists had swung behind war. Houser had a similar experience, finding himself snubbed by a furrier friend (in for conspiracy to obstruct justice) who said, "I'm against you guys now."[16]

But key parts of the pacifist establishment were in their corner. Muste and Evan Thomas had written a letter of support early on, and news of the group's strikes and protests against segregation and other injustices spread among COs and came to public attention through *The Christian Century*, *Fellowship* (published by the Fellowship of Reconciliation), *The Conscientious Objector* (from the War Resisters League), and other resister publications. The prison protests were also covered in black newspapers, including *The Pittsburgh Courier*. Whether you agreed with the COs or not (and even some pacifists disapproved of their tactics), their courage made great copy, and for supporters it was an inspiration.[17]

During the summer, as the divinity students approached the end of their time in prison, they had a visit—not altogether welcome, perhaps— from the Reverend Coffin, president of Union Theological Seminary. The seminary essentially wanted the young men to promise they would avoid any further activities that would bring the institution "similar publicity" to what they had brought last time around. Not surprisingly, they all refused. Dellinger, Dallas, and Benedict would return to the Newark Ashram and their work there among the poor. Others would enroll at Chicago Theological Seminary, whose pacifist president, Albert W. Palmer, would welcome them.

Houser would head for Chicago. In June of 1941 he'd written to Muste about the prospect of building a new mass nonviolent movement, especially targeting youth, with the goal of "opposing the war, of preserving as much democracy as possible here at home, and of working ultimately for a more socialist society." Muste told him no new organization was necessary, and that he was overestimating the number of young people who shared his aims. But he offered Houser a part-time job (doubling as his seminary field work) as a youth secretary. Houser leapt at the chance, not knowing it would be the beginning of a career in domestic civil rights and anti-colonialism in Africa. Meantime, an important new organization is exactly what he would launch.

Houser, Dellinger, and the other divinity students were released on September 3, 1941, after serving a little more than nine months. Astonishingly, they were granted seventy-two days off for good behavior (or, more likely, good riddance). They would emerge changed men, though Warden Gerlach remained pretty much the same. Houser, already feeling nostalgic, came to their final meeting with sympathy for him—until the warden thrust a card at him and asked him to sign. It turned out to be a draft card, the very thing he'd withstood prison to avoid inking. Every member of the Union Eight refused, despite Gerlach's warning that they could be subject to another prison term if they didn't sign. As Dellinger and others would find out, he wasn't kidding.

PART TWO

DURING

CHAPTER 10

THE WAR COMES HOME

It was a Sunday, clear and cold—the best kind of New York winter day—
and the Reverend Harry Emerson Fosdick had ascended to his study in the
tower of Manhattan's Riverside Church, where he was broadcasting his
popular weekly radio program to listeners all over the country. He'd been
traveling the Midwest, speaking against the war, and he worried that his
position at the church was growing tenuous because of his obdurate pacifism. His plan, if push came to shove, was to join the Quakers. Suddenly,
in mid-broadcast, he was told he "was off the air because the Japanese were
attacking Pearl Harbor."[1]

Fosdick had no way to know if he would ever get back on, for he recognized, as did so many shocked and furious Americans, that on December
7, 1941, the world had changed, even if his views would not. The Japanese
attack sank American opposition to the war right along with much of
America's legacy navy, reducing a once robust and diverse national movement to a small, stubborn core of radical resisters, their sympathizers, and
an embittered rump of unreconstructed isolationists who obstinately refused to endorse the conflict. All were pushed to the margins of national
life, but only the pacifists would thrive there.

We'll get to the margins, but first let us take note of the war opponents who eschewed them. After the shock of Pearl Harbor, what was left
of the prewar peace movement collapsed. Almost everyone signed up for
the war, in one sense or another, even those who had been most vocal about

staying out of it. "Perhaps no war has ever produced so many individuals," wrote two pacifist historians, "who at one time or another in their lives had vowed never to fight again, and then with the first trumpets found reasons as to why *this* war was different."[2]

Lindbergh, at home on Martha's Vineyard, heard the news when he casually turned on the radio. He'd been working on his next America First address, planned for December 10 in Boston. Anne Morrow Lindbergh would tell her diary: "If C. speaks again, they'll put him in prison." She needn't have worried. Charles abandoned his planned speech and was to make no significant public pronouncements for years to come once he put out a statement about Pearl Harbor. Now that war was upon us, he said, "we must meet it as united Americans regardless of our attitude in the past . . . Our country has been attacked by force of arms, and by force of arms we must retaliate."[3]

On December 11, coincidentally the day Hitler declared war on the United States, the leaders of America First met in Chicago and voted to dissolve the organization. "Our principles were right," they said. "Had they been followed, war could have been avoided." But acknowledging that war was here, America First said the goal now was victory and urged its followers "to give their full support to the war effort of the nation."[4]

The young founders of America First, including Brewster, Stuart, Shriver, Ford, and others, had never been pacifists, and they served without hesitation in the armed forces. Brewster had already joined the navy, where he would put his experience as a pilot to use in anti-submarine work. (Although stationed on the home front, four of the ten members of his naval aviation unit were killed in flying mishaps.) General Wood, having led America's largest antiwar group, now went back on active duty. Even Lindbergh saw action. Roosevelt refused to reinstate the commission he had resigned, but he was hired by Henry Ford and tested planes on combat missions in the Pacific theater.

Many former pacifists also supported the war. Einstein was so alarmed by Hitler that he had already set aside his faith in nonviolence, as Bertrand Russell had done in England. But Einstein went further: in 1939 he signed a letter to FDR (drafted by Leo Szilard with help from fellow physicists Edward Teller and Eugene Wigner) urging a crash program to develop an atomic bomb. The Manhattan Project arguably was launched on December

6, the day before the attack. He couldn't fail to notice that various physicists of his acquaintance were dropping out of circulation (Einstein himself was not a nuclear physicist and would have had a hard time getting a security clearance). Nonetheless, and much to his dismay, he was widely credited in the media as father to the bomb; the July 1, 1946, cover of *Time* shows him with a mushroom cloud in the background bearing the label "E=mc²." He later called signing the letter to FDR his one great mistake in life.

Norman Thomas, in Princeton on December 7 to retrieve the belongings of a son who had gone off to drive an ambulance in Britain, learned of the attack from a professor. Though too old to fight, America's leading Socialist backed the war effort. "After Pearl Harbor there was no political alternative," he wrote to friends. Pacifists were faced with a choice between circles of hell, he said, "but the lowest and worst circle of hell would have been that imposed by a Nazi victory."[5]

Protestant clergymen (like their congregants) were evolving away from pacifism even before Pearl Harbor, but after the attack they changed tunes almost as sharply as the Almanac Singers had done after Germany's invasion of the Soviet Union. Nineteen months after the Methodist church, America's biggest Protestant denomination, declared that it would never "officially support, endorse or participate in war," its bishops met and stated, "Our duty, as American citizens, is clear . . . The Methodists of America will loyally support our President and our nation." Other leading Protestant denominations lined up as well, as did Catholic and Jewish clergy. Even *The Christian Century,* the most consistently antiwar of the era's religious journals (unless you count *The Catholic Worker*), accepted the new American war as a "guilty necessity."

The shift of young pacifists was equally pronounced, as the *Times's* critic of Viola Ilma's book had predicted. ("Miss Ilma tells, with all possible enthusiasm and conviction, how ready and eager the masses of youth are to march and fight in the cause of peace. But if tomorrow there should be war it would rush headlong to enlist.") Some antiwar youths who changed positions ended up making the supreme sacrifice. Baby-faced Neal A. Scott, in his Davidson College commencement address of 1940, confidently told his classmates that the "Yanks are not coming" in this new war. Yet, after Pearl Harbor, he was one of the Yanks who went to war. He died in 1942 as a Navy ensign at the Battle of the Santa Cruz Islands.[6]

Many Americans who abandoned pacifism were particularly conscious of the evils of fascism, not least the Nazi persecution of the Jews. Although the full scale of the horrors to come wasn't known, the plight of European Jewry was clearly dire, and many people feared the worst. The Women's International League for Peace and Freedom hemorrhaged members because of Nazi oppression of minorities; a small, largely Jewish chapter in New York's Rockaways "was disdained by the neighborhood's Christians and anathema to its Jews."[7]

Pacifism, after Pearl Harbor, wasn't just out of fashion. It was closer to taboo. Schoolteachers who refused to sell "defense stamps" to children (to raise money for the war) could find themselves out of work. People who disapproved of the war learned to keep quiet about it, as Mencken did. COs reported various contretemps with angry citizens, and when Americans were asked, in a national poll, if COs should be allowed to persuade others to become COs, 87 percent answered no. Eighty percent said men shouldn't be allowed to choose whether to fight.[8]

Even the pacifists who persisted did little to actively oppose the war. In an article called "What Should Pacifists Do Now?" Albert Palmer argued that they should "avoid obstructionism in the war effort and avoid promoting division within the church by seeking to win converts to pacifism."[9] The National Council for Prevention of War similarly pledged not to obstruct the war effort. The WILPF did its best to uphold the pacifist ideal but sustained a huge loss of support, and Emily Balch, in touch with European members of the organization, couldn't find it in herself to oppose this war (even though she had opposed the last one). Other traditional bastions of pacifism, deeply involved in the Civilian Public Service camps, were in no position to actively resist.[10] Even young men of the traditional peace churches signed up to fight. Three out of five young Mennonite men were COs, but only one in eight eligible Brethren men. Among drafted Quakers, a remarkable three-fourths failed to claim CO status.[11]

George Houser put the problem succinctly by observing that pacifists lacked "the power to effectively resist the war on the one hand, nor to effectively resist fascism on the other."[12]

The secular War Resisters League, its most ardent radicalism still in the future, toned down its literature, halted demonstrations, and stopped soliciting new members, at least until 1943. And it pledged not to obstruct authorities "carrying out the will of the government" even as it stepped up aid to COs and affirmed its faith in pacifism. There were reasons for the organization's caution. The Espionage Act of 1917 remained on the books during World War II (as it still does, having been used in recent years against Edward Snowden for leaking secret government documents), and the government had used it aggressively in the past. The WRL, moreover, was of great interest to the FBI, which repeatedly investigated the group and even advocated its prosecution. To fend off such troubles, the League opened its files to the agency, including information on its members and on COs. FBI agents visited WRL offices at least 166 times during the war, usually about COs.[13]

Yet rather than the end of pacifism, the onset of the American war triggered something like a new beginning. Pacifism quickly became countercultural, a marker of dissent, and a viewpoint that, pushed to the margins, led adherents into a closer association with other pacifists. The CPS system, not to mention prison, brought them closer still. These institutions became schools for radicalism, giving war resisters a bitter taste of arbitrary government power—and the opportunity to teach, learn, and bond. As a result of all this, the nation's remaining active pacifists became a much smaller group of much more radical individuals, and the expansion of their agenda, set in motion before the Japanese attack, was accelerated. They and their agenda far outlived the war they opposed, and key aspects of their radicalism became mainstream.

David Dellinger, emerging from church in Newark when he got news of the Japanese attack, would remain among these antiwar holdouts. Bayard Rustin was equally unshaken in his antiwar convictions—as was James Farmer, then living in Chicago. Farmer's white friend Bernice Fisher, a fierce, young religious radical who raged against war and racial injustice, called on December 7 to say, "Jim, for God's sake turn on your radio! The Japanese have attacked Pearl Harbor! We're going to war!" The burning question for Bernice and Jim was whether the nonviolent antidiscrimination movement they had envisioned was over before it started. They agreed that, as Bernice put it, "We can't let it stop us!" The other burning question, of whether he would ever love her, was left unspoken.

Dorothy Day was in Elmira, New York, probably to give a talk, when she got the news of Pearl Harbor. She was just a month past her forty-fourth birthday, the weight of care beginning to accumulate along with the years. Yet she was still upright and imposing, still facing the world with her resolute jaw, her solemn reserve, and her prophetic message. The next issue of *The Catholic Worker* left no doubt where she stood. "We Continue Our Christian Pacifist Stand," the paper said in display type, and underneath she laid out her position, having sent the text in advance by mail to all the Catholic Worker houses: "We are at war, a declared war, with Japan, Germany and Italy. But still we can repeat Christ's words, each day, holding them close in our hearts, each month printing them in the paper."[14]

Unlike most Americans, Dwight Macdonald wasn't especially shocked by the attack on Pearl Harbor. Still enmeshed in Marxist dialectics, he saw the world war as a battle of imperialists, and feared it would lead to ever more dictatorial societies with ever more dehumanizing consequences. It seemed inconceivable anyone could win such an extensive and industrially driven conflict without highly centralized rule, not to mention the kind of nationalistic or revolutionary fervor that doesn't usually drive bourgeois democracies. More practically, Macdonald and his fellow editors at *Partisan Review* were at loggerheads over the war, with Dwight doggedly opposed while the others increasingly recognized that there was no alternative to crushing fascism on the battlefield—and that too much antiwar noise in wartime issues of *PR* might bring government suppression.[15]

That a hard core of pacifists would persist in publicly opposing the war even after December 7 became clear the very next day in Congress, when the president gave his famous "day of infamy" speech and requested a declaration of war against Japan. The Senate vote in favor was unanimous, but in the House a single stubborn legislator, Montana Republican Jeannette Rankin, voted no. A gifted politician, in 1916 Rankin had become the first woman elected to Congress. She gained the office on a platform advocating child welfare, Prohibition, and suffrage for women nationwide. The following year she was one of fifty in the House who voted no on war against Germany. Gerrymandering in Montana and her own labor radicalism cost her reelection, but voters sent her back to Washington in 1940 largely to oppose the new war, which she did in her usual energetic fashion. Although she was a pacifist inspired by the settlement house pioneer and peace activist Jane Addams (who won the Nobel Peace Prize in 1931) and the British sociologist Benjamin Kidd (who argued that women were both wellsprings of social change and naturally pacifist), Rankin campaigned for defense preparedness and accepted speaking engagements from America First. After Lindbergh's controversial Des Moines speech, she took up his argument that war would be a disaster for Jews and others already treated as second-class citizens. To her friend Mary Church Terrell, a black civil and women's rights activist, Rankin wrote that if FDR "takes us into war, the reaction that will come later against those groups who have supported him—the women, the colored people and the Jews—will be like the reaction in Germany, if not worse. For the protection of themselves, it seems to me that the colored people should take an open stand against war now."[16]

Rankin was already sixty-one on December 8 when, anticipating the Congressional vote on war, she decided to drop out of sight for a few hours. "I got in my car and disappeared. Nobody could reach me . . . I just drove around Washington and got madder and madder because there were soldiers everywhere I went." Finally, as somber House members convened for the vote, her friend and fellow Republican Everett Dirksen of Illinois tried to persuade her to vote "present" instead of "no." Others, too, pleaded with her to change her mind, but she went ahead anyway. Her vote against the resolution prompted a torrent of boos from colleagues and the galleries. Afterwards a mob of journalists chased her into a phone booth, where she was bombarded with popping flashbulbs until rescued by Capitol police. The vote ended her political career, brought a cascade of hate mail, and made her persona non grata to colleagues for the rest of her term, much of which she spent away from Washington. Unlike her previous antiwar vote, Rankin said, "This time I stood alone."[17]

It was easy for the rest of America's remaining pacifists to feel the same way. "Today we are a 'Remnant,'" wrote WILPF President Dorothy Medders Robinson to her membership not long after Pearl Harbor. "But we should never forget that every great idea at one time belonged to a Remnant."[18]

Remnants can have important advantages: depth of commitment, cohesion, and a willingness to innovate (since whatever's been tried hasn't worked). The tenacious few who make up a remnant may become alienated and inert, as a number of antiwar figures did in finding themselves reduced to fringe magazines or embittered silence. But the few remaining pacifists seemed to thrive on their new adversity. Freed of the timid mass who saw in the creed only passive resistance to violence, what was left of the movement was liberated to stride off in new directions and develop new tactics—even reconceive itself. It could do this from its newfound position at the margins, where change so often originates, and where a key figure in the transformation to come was already in residence, eager to foment a peaceful revolution.

———

ABRAHAM JOHANNES MUSTE WAS pushing sixty when he assumed leadership of the Fellowship of Reconciliation on April 1, 1940, and immediately set to work making the FOR the vehicle of a far larger pacifist purpose. Indeed, probably no one since Thoreau was more important in making nonviolence central to American protest and reform. After World War II, Muste would play an important role in promoting draft resistance, advocating for nuclear disarmament, opposing the Vietnam war, and advancing the cause of civil rights. As a young seminarian, Martin Luther King, Jr., had heard Muste lecture. "I wasn't a pacifist then," King recalled, "but the power of A.J.'s sincerity and his hardheaded ability to defend his position stayed with me through the years. Later, I got to know him better, and I would say unequivocally that the current emphasis on nonviolent direct action in the race relations field is due more to A.J. than to anyone else in the country."[19]

With his background in organized labor, Muste departed from traditional religious pacifism by insisting on a far more active and ambitious agenda for change, rejecting a longstanding pacifist view, strange to us today, that nonviolent actions such as protests and fasts were "coercive." With the help of some new young associates, he would recognize equality for blacks as the great domestic issue of his time. He was not an anarchist. But like Day, Dellinger, and Macdonald, he saw the government as a source of oppression rather than liberation, insisting on the same general, religiously grounded personalism they did. Starting with the notion that "human beings are of infinite worth," it followed (for Muste) that more than peace would be required for each to live his fullest life. "Our only valid objective is the transformation of society," he would write, "not the building of a shelter for the saints or a secular elite within a corrupt social order, which in effect is assumed to be beyond redemption." In another essay he added: "In a world built on violence, one must be a revolutionary before one can be a pacifist . . . a nonrevolutionary pacifist is a contradiction in terms, a monstrosity."[20]

Muste's biography recapitulates the evolution of the American Left over the course of his lifetime. Born in the Netherlands in 1885, he was a child when his family emigrated to Grand Rapids, Michigan, where he grew up in a strict, Dutch-speaking Calvinist congregation. Ordained a minister of the Dutch Reformed church, he accepted a lucrative position with a prosperous congregation in upper Manhattan. His parishioners at one point gave him a gift of Tolstoy's writings on religion and philosophy, which were no doubt critical of orthodoxy, and which no doubt pushed him to be likewise.

In truth, Muste was already drifting away from the old-time religion and Republican politics in which he'd been raised. In New York, in the years before the Great War, he was exposed to radical ideas, radical politics, and radical social ills. He heard William James lecture on pragmatism, befriended John Dewey, and got an additional degree at the Union Theological Seminary. He was also exposed to the harshest aspects of American industrial life, including the tremendous gulf between rich and poor, the terrible slums, the labor battles, and the Triangle Shirtwaist fire. He began to think of himself as a follower of Walter Rauschenbusch and the Social Gospel movement, which flourished on the heels of scientific discoveries that displaced Biblical notions of human origins and reoriented Christian churches on the basis of their social justice mission. In the 1912 presidential election he voted for the Socialist candidate Eugene V. Debs. But his evolution at this point was manifest most clearly in the domain of God, not of man, and mirrors the evolution of so many other Christian reformers, including Dellinger: "I passed definitely from what you might say was an Old Testament religion to a New Testament religion and from the idea that you begin with a body of doctrine to the idea that you begin with a life, a kind of life. And I was also moving away from the idea that you have a God of Judgement and so on to a concept of a God of love."[21]

That movement carried him away from Calvinism to a Congregational church in Newtonville, Massachusetts, near Boston, where he spent the Great War, read Christian and Quaker mystics, helped create a Boston chapter of the new Fellowship of Reconciliation (a group that originated in

England), and slowly turned against war—just in time for the United States to enter the fight. The blend of Social Gospel and mysticism brewing inside Muste made it inevitable that his religious evolution would become political. Both William James and the important Quaker Rufus Jones (also part of Muste's reading) saw mysticism as a process that unlocked the energy for changing the world by channeling religious impulses into reform. James in particular regarded religious experience as a way "to find the hot place of human initiative and endeavor, and to encourage the heroic, the strenuous, the vital, and the socially transformative."[22]

That is precisely what religious experience was for A. J. Muste. For a while he made the kinds of noises about the European war that were expected from a bourgeois pastor. In April 1917, on the second Sunday after America entered the war, he led a patriotic ceremony in the church auditorium, replete with Boy Scouts, flags galore, and praise for the Pilgrims, Washington, Lincoln, and America's glorious ideals and achievements. But he had already preached as a pacifist on the topic of "The Conscientious Objector," and soon matched actions to instincts by opposing the war outright, by which time the U.S. was already in it and dissent was little tolerated. The Mustes quickly became pariahs in Newtonville. When the son of a neighbor was killed in action, "his mother was not able to regard me as anything but a traitor after his death, and she asked that I not come to the funeral. Others stopped speaking to us on the street. There were telephone callers, some of whom suggested I be strung up on a pole."[23]

In Newtonville he had "a mystical experience of God" sanctioning his religious efforts on behalf of peace, and after leaving the ministry there he worked for the newly formed ACLU helping conscientious objectors. After the war, perhaps owing to his blue-collar immigrant background, he became a prominent figure in the labor movement. He led workers in the bloody 1919 Lawrence, Massachusetts, textile strike, ran the Amalgamated Textile Workers union, and eventually founded his own labor organization, the Conference for Progressive Labor Action (CPLA), whose members— popularly called Musteites—were known for their passionate devotion to workers, their belief in something like universal industrial unionism, and their hostility toward the more conservative American Federation of Labor. They battled for unemployment insurance and against union racketeering, but also antagonized the labor establishment.

Union struggles in those days were often desperate and even violent, with the power of the state sometimes brought to bear against workers. A textile strike in Marion, North Carolina, was met with gunfire by sheriff's deputies, leaving six workers dead in a labor action that ultimately failed. Muste, moved by the religious faith that had helped sustain the strikers, spoke at the funeral, likening the slain to Jesus and calling them "martyrs in the noblest cause in all the world. The cause for which they died is the cause of labor, the cause of justice and freedom for the plain people who do the work of the world and who bear its burdens."[24]

It was a far cry from life as minister to a bourgeois Protestant congregation; even in the North, Muste the labor leader was jailed, badly beaten, and for a while worked in the shadow of death. In Lawrence, on the brink of defeat, "the gaunt, raw-boned, 'Fool-for-Christ' Muste . . . won for the workers and thus began an association with labor unparalleled by that of any other cleric," writes the ecclesiastical historian Robert Moats Miller.[25] At the same time, he gained deep practical experience of organizing, strike tactics, public relations, managing fractious activists, and sustaining nonviolence in the face of brutality. Always somehow out of step, in the interwar years (when religious pacifism flourished) he drifted away from his faith and accepted the idea that struggle had to be violent, even if he never personally participated except to absorb blows. In 1932, he refused to sign a statement backing Gandhi's struggle for Indian independence, explaining that "I do not want to discredit the left-wing elements in India that believe in violence."[26]

Eventually Muste became a communist. His CPLA became the American Workers' Party and, after a merger with Trotskyists, the Workers' Party USA, which he headed. "The effort to apply Gandhian methods to American conditions had scarcely begun," he wrote later in explaining his turn from nonviolence to Marxist-Leninism. "Pacifism was mostly a middle-class and an individualistic phenomenon. The churches certainly were not giving illustrations of spiritual force, of true community." By contrast, communists and their allies were "banding people together for action . . . putting up a fight. Unless you were indifferent or despairing you lined up with them."[27]

By 1936 Muste was marginalized in his own increasingly radical labor movement and dispirited by the tactics rivals had used against him. He was already fifty-one when friends funded a desperately needed European vacation for him, during which he visited Trotsky in Norway. Confessing his disillusionment, he found himself beseeched by the great man not to desert the movement. Later, in Paris, Muste walked quite casually into the seventeenth-century Church of Saint Sulpice, where he "sat down on a bench near the front and looked at the cross." The church was under repair, he noticed. Unexpectedly, he heard a voice within tell him, "This is where you belong."[28]

Renewing his involvement in the Fellowship of Reconciliation in 1936, he took the helm four years later at an organization already going his way. Earlier in the decade, the FOR had been sharply divided over how broadly and aggressively it should act. Should it confine itself to opposing war? Should it try to address what many pacifists saw as the causes of war? Were there wider injustices that nonviolence could help to address? In 1933, most members wanted the FOR to "identify itself with the cause of the underprivileged," and half of them favored "the use of non-violent coercion in behalf of that cause." That same year the FOR's key official for the South argued that "to attempt to emancipate the mass of white and Negro workers in the South . . . only through the methods of goodwill, moral suasion, and education is to invite the continued exploitation, misery and suffering of generations yet unborn." The FOR, he asserted, needed to see itself as a "revolutionary movement," and by the end of 1935 the organization's leaders had vowed to work toward "building up techniques for non-violent resistance." *Fellowship* began to write approvingly of sit-down strikes. No wonder they hired Muste; he was everything they were trying to become.[29]

In his revealing sketches for an autobiography (never finished), Muste explores the congruence between communism and religion, both of which after all were revolutionary movements:

> It was on the Left—and here again the Communists cannot be excluded—that one found people who were truly "religious" in the sense that they were virtually completely committed, they were betting their lives on the cause they embraced. Often they gave up ordinary comforts, security, life itself, with a burning devotion which few Christians display toward the Christ whom they profess as Lord and incarnation of God.[30]

Even in his disillusionment, Muste saw that Lenin's idea of the Communist Party was in some sense a recreation of the one true church—a transnational millenarian organization determined to bring about the Kingdom of God. Only Christians, it was clear, could rival communists in their commitment. The most ardent members of both groups were convinced of the existing order's hopeless corruption. The Party held itself out as a kind of successor to the faith of Christ: it was the revolutionary instrument of destiny, if not God, claimed to have history on its side, and insisted on its own universality. Muste, like Dorothy Day, sought to enact a decentralized, personalist version of this vision—a congregational version, if you like—that stood against the false gods of capital and state and collectivism and, now, war.[31]

The Christian nature of this enterprise, which Muste (and Day, among others) stressed constantly, was a way to make sure that means aligned with ends, and a counterweight to the dehumanization of modern life. With their deep awareness of sin and distrust of the modern state, Muste and Day would have agreed with the ex-pacifist Niebuhr that it's too easy for people who are "completely innocent in their own esteem" to be "insufferable in their human contacts." Without reference to God, anything can be justified, and we end up like Dostoevsky's atheist Shigalyov in *Demons*: "Starting from unlimited freedom, I conclude with unlimited despotism."[32]

With Muste now in charge, the FOR in its polite way would become a more revolutionary enterprise—even if hardly anyone at the FOR, let alone Muste, wanted to overthrow an elected government or subvert the Constitution. On the contrary, Muste's experience had made him an ardent civil libertarian with a particular emphasis on free speech. He understood that pacifists and other dissidents depended on the Bill of Rights—as the FOR did in the issue of *Fellowship* published soon after Pearl Harbor, in which it refused to support the war or participate in war measures, vowing instead to focus on protecting civil liberties and the rights of COs and workers, seeking economic justice, aiding interned Japanese Americans, and urging peace by reason and conciliation. "As to our new enemies," another writer in the journal warned, "we are no Sir Galahad with heart so pure that we can cast the first stone or carry war into Japanese homes and cities in any such fashion as will be acceptable to God."[33]

Yet the FOR leadership pointedly disavowed "the position of any who seek to sabotage or obstruct the war measures of our Government," because associating itself with such measures wouldn't have accomplished much except perhaps to provoke the government into shutting the organization down.[34] In 1943, the FOR's leader went so far as to invite the FBI to a conference of peace groups, presumably to show that they were up to nothing subversive, only to have the agency respond that it was quite familiar with the groups and "would really prefer not to sit through the conference, thanks just the same."[35] That same year, Muste, who had written pamphlets arguing for nonviolent resistance to Jim Crow, held a symposium of Protestant liberals including Roger Baldwin, Richard Gregg, Reinhold Niebuhr, Kirby Page, Howard Thurman, and Oswald Garrison Villard on the question of whether civil disobedience was the answer to Jim Crow. Niebuhr argued for gradualism, but Muste argued that this degraded blacks and whites both. He believed that Christians should simply refuse to cooperate with Jim Crow and take the consequences.[36]

By blending civic moderation with radical pacifism, Muste was able to lead the FOR in a daring new direction. At the same time, America's entry into the war paradoxically gave this peace organization strength. For one thing, the nation's remaining pacifists felt a greater need to affiliate. Even the Reverend George Buttrick, president of the Federal Council of Churches and a man whose words FDR had read on the radio in support of a peacetime draft, joined the Fellowship of Reconciliation the day after Pearl Harbor. A severely wounded Great War veteran, Buttrick had succeeded Coffin as pastor of New York's tony Madison Avenue Presbyterian Church, where he officiated, in 1936, at the nuptials of Frederick Christ Trump and Mary Anne MacLeod, who would later give birth to a boy they called Donald.

In addition, belonging to the FOR was accepted by Selective Service as evidence of the religious objection required for CO status, which no doubt boosted membership. The group's annual revenue rose from $60,000 in 1941 to $100,000 in 1945, when membership reached a high approaching fifteen thousand (it had been just five thousand in 1938). By 1944 the organization had more than twenty paid staff and four hundred U.S. chapters plus nodes in 125 of the 133 CPS camps.[37]

Like most pacifists, Muste understood that there was little chance of ending or even disrupting the war effort. At the same time, he made Gandhian nonviolence central to the FOR—and was soon recognized as the leader of what was left of American pacifism, where his version of Christian nonviolence would shape American radicalism for decades to come. He took on this leadership role with the same confidence, pragmatism, and good cheer he seemed to bring to everything else since St. Sulpice. "Whether he's at a ball game or climbing over a fence into a missile base, he's always at peace within himself," said his son John. "He's the *happiest* man I've ever known. I can't believe a man can *be* that happy, but *he* is, he really is."[38]

Muste had a well-developed eye for talent, and the same week the Union Eight were released from the federal prison at Danbury, he announced some new young hires: James Farmer as race relations secretary, George Houser as youth secretary, and Bayard Rustin as secretary for student and general affairs. They would soon be joined on the staff by Glenn Smiley, and Muste brought on other talented young people as well, reproducing his energetic young Musteites in pacifist form. Rustin, Farmer, and the other acolytes revolved around their upbeat and encouraging boss like planets around the sun, soaking up warmth and energy but (perhaps more like plants) competing for the light as well.

Muste's appearance hardly projected Sun King; tall, painfully gaunt, and slightly stooped, he worked in a Spartan office at the FOR's headquarters on Broadway across from Columbia University, the desk piled with papers and the walls lined with books. Farmer colorfully describes him as having "a face furrowed with the trenches of many political battles. His eyes spat bullets but twinkled and wrinkled at the corners. He was a chain smoker, and his long skinny fingers trembled as he lighted each Pall Mall. The hair on the back of his fingers grew long and tangled like the eyebrows that hovered over a birdlike countenance with lean, sharp features, and arched upward when the wheels in the brain were turning."[39]

Those wheels spun furiously all the time, and, despite his ascetic appearance, his presence galvanized the group's headquarters, which pulsed with energy and enthusiasm when he was around. Muste confronted his idealistic young charges with his immense experience, listening to them patiently and then making an irresistible argument for his own point of view. "As with the Musteites of the 1930s," writes Leilah Danielson, "his leadership flowed out of his unique combination of charisma and organizational savvy, passion and evenhandedness, flair for action and adroit reasoning."[40] Muste and Rustin were almost naturally in accord at meetings, and usually got their way during these sessions. Said Swomley, who was officially (and uneasily) Rustin and Farmer's supervisor: "Muste looked upon Bayard as his own son."[41]

Soon after taking the helm at the FOR, Muste put his experience to work, emphasizing a sense of mission driven by spiritual fellowship but drawing on his Bolshevik background as well by repeatedly calling on pacifists to become committed revolutionaries with the kind of self-sacrificing discipline of Communist Party members or early Christians. "There are those among us—in a sense we are perhaps all included—who shrink from participating in steps toward building a Gandhian movement," Muste wrote, adding: "We think that making speeches about pacifism, even superficial and dull ones, or mailing leaflets discreetly, is necessarily virtuous, but that there is something queer and vaguely discreditable about carrying a placard in a poster-parade or picketing a factory or the White House, and that only people who are a little 'off' ever get thrown into jail."[42]

Starting in 1935, the FOR encouraged the formation of religiously inspired local "peace teams" for study and humanitarian service. Muste took things further, asking (in the October 1941 issue of *Fellowship*) that every FOR member "including all our officers, should immediately join or help to build a pacifist cell or team or group" for the study of nonviolence, for mutual support, and for action. This concept of the "cell" united communist and Christian doctrine in various minds throughout the thirties; Trotsky himself could see a certain similarity between the Jesuits and the Bolsheviks, even if he denigrated the comparison. Richard Niebuhr (like his brother Reinhold) had called for small knots of revolutionary-minded Christians to form cells to organize, proselytize, and transcend nationality, class, and capitalism. Cells were also a way for a visionary minority like Muste's Christian pacifists to sustain themselves against the pressure of an indifferent or hostile world. Richard Gregg (with whom Muste was in touch in 1940) published a pamphlet called *Training for Peace* that recommended the formation of cells with up to a dozen members dedicated to righteous living and pacifist study. He intended for these cells to withdraw from mass society and materialism, members binding themselves to one another by singing, folk dancing, and meditation as well as by their sense of purpose. Gregg, writes Joseph Kip Kosek, "came to believe that in Gandhi nonviolence had become more than an inner conviction; it was now a performance, part of a public moral dialogue intended to elicit sympathy from both opponents and disinterested observers." [43]

George Houser, having spent nearly a year in a very different kind of cell, was now an FOR staffer devoted to seeding these units of nonviolent study and change around the Chicago area (activities that were noted in his FBI file). Still a seminary student, he found time to crisscross the region distributing FOR literature and organizing mostly college students. "A small man," his close friend Farmer would write of him, "there was about him an aura of confidence and authority that made size unimportant." Houser developed guidelines calling for cells to pursue four broad categories of activity: spiritual growth, study, action, and organization. They would read Shridharani's *War Without Violence*, Gregg's *Power of Non-Violence,* and Gandhi's memoir. Within a few months he'd established roughly seventeen cells.

The most important one, launched in October of 1941, was a race-relations cell focused on discrimination in and around the University of Chicago. Houser oversaw the cell and Farmer was involved, but its leading lights were the energetic young Bernice Fisher, a white student at the University of Chicago Theological School, whose misfortune it was to fall in love with Farmer, and the white literature student James Robinson, an acolyte of Dorothy Day's Catholic Worker movement who would serve time in a CPS camp. There were about a dozen members, all pacifists, and they all believed, as Houser put it, that discrimination "must be challenged directly, without violence or hatred, yet without compromise." Meeting Saturday afternoons, they worked their way through *War Without Violence* chapter by chapter as a prelude to action. "All of us," Fisher said later, "were afire with the ideas of Gandhian non-violence."[44]

Small as that flame was, it was about to spread. Farmer in particular had much bigger things in mind. A superb speaker and writer who would someday be among the most important figures in the civil rights movement, he was the grandson of a slave and the son of a professor (and minister) at a black Methodist college in Texas, where young Jim was a precocious student. At Howard University, where he took a divinity degree, he came under the influence of FOR vice chairman Howard Thurman, a pacifist who had visited Gandhi in India and helped Farmer become "deeply versed in Christian pacifist thinking." His draft board, wanting to keep COs to a minimum, exempted him as a minister on the basis of his divinity studies.

Having taken discrimination for granted until he realized his own easy compliance with the evil customs of Jim Crow, Farmer began to wonder about their persistence. What if people simply stopped going along? The more he thought about it, the more unlikely it seemed that segregation could endure massive and determined nonviolent opposition, not just by blacks but by all right-thinking Americans. Unhindered by modesty at twenty-two, he hatched a plan to overturn America's race system.

He wrote it up in a memo to Muste dated February 19, 1942, and entitled "Provisional Plans for Brotherhood Mobilization." It called for organized nonviolent action to end discrimination. "If such an endeavor is not to degenerate into violence and chaos, pacifists must serve as its nucleus, its moving force." Yet it could not consist only of pacifists; on the contrary, it should encompass nonpacifists too, as well as blacks and whites, Christians and Jews, and anyone else "willing to commit themselves to a disciplined nonviolence" in working toward the goal. And what was that goal? "Not to make housing in ghettos more tolerable," he wrote in a second memo, "but to destroy residential segregation; not to make Jim Crow facilities the equal of others, but to abolish Jim Crow; not to make racial discrimination more bearable, but to wipe it out."[45]

In Chicago, Farmer typed up the initial memo from his handwritten version. Considering it too consequential to drop into a mailbox, he carried it down to the post office and sent it by special delivery airmail to Muste in New York. With all the grandiosity of youth, "I slammed the envelope down on the counter in front of the clerk as if I were, by that act, driving the first nail into the coffin of racism in America."[46]

CHAPTER 11

A CONGRESS FOR EQUALITY

IT WAS FITTING THAT on the spring day in 1942 when Houser and his friends Bernice Fisher and Homer Jack set out to demolish racial discrimination in America—seeking, in a sense, to invent or discover a new world—they drove to Columbus, Ohio in a borrowed car with an unusual paint job. WORLD PEACE CAR, it said. On one side of the vehicle, a hellish war scene was presided over by the devil, with a caption reading, WAR IS SATAN'S WAY. On the other, angels looked down at a pastoral scene. PEACE, the caption said, IS GOD'S WAY. Fisher was mortified: "Don't we have problems enough? Everyone'll think we're a bunch of kooks."[1]

Yet the car was an apt metaphor. Nonviolence, to these young idealists, was to be the vehicle for ending discrimination in America. Fisher quickly resigned herself to making the trip in a rolling billboard: "As Gertrude Stein would put it, 'a car is a car is a car.' As long as it will run."

Run it did, carrying them through midwestern farm country to a meeting of the Fellowship of Reconciliation's national council, where Farmer was to present his ideas for a large-scale nonviolent civil rights campaign. The council authorized a new organization along the lines Farmer envisioned, but as a kind of pilot project in Chicago. Something like the organization he had in mind, however, was already growing there among Houser's multiplying cells. Houser mentions it to Muste in July almost in passing, at the end of a long, ruminative letter about the nature of pacifism, among other things. "There is another development in our Chicago action

program about which you should know," he writes. "We are very interested in seeing Brotherhood Mobilization get started. While we are waiting, however, we have started our own committee working along the lines
which B.M. will be working. We call this group the Committee of Racial
Equality (C.O.R.E.). We do not call the group a pacifist group as such, but
we are committed to non-violence in all that we do."[2]

CORE sprang from the interaction of Farmer's ideas, the FOR's modest resources, and the race-relations cell on Chicago's South Side. The
members of Houser's Committee of Racial Equality had read and discussed
Farmer's memos to Muste about forming a national multiracial civil rights
organization, but on the ground they were already building one. To get
things going, in March of 1942 they targeted the popular and evocatively
named White City Roller Rink, a huge Gothic pile on the South Side.
Although situated in segregated Chicago's Black Belt, it nonetheless barred
blacks; whenever they sought admission they were told the place was a private club, or was having a private party. So one day a group of white activists got in line, bought tickets, and went inside. When Farmer got in line
he was told it was a private club and all skaters had membership cards. His
confederates certainly didn't, but the manager still wouldn't admit blacks.
In his memoir, Farmer claims implausibly that he was so frustrated he had
the manager, the ticket seller, and the ticket taker arrested, presumably for
violating Illinois civil rights law. Then, at an emergency meeting of the
Chicago cell, he took up a collection and used the money to bail them out.

That was far from the end of the White City saga, but meanwhile the
Chicago cell quickly drew new members. In April the pacifists and their
friends—men and women, whites and blacks, about fifty in all—met to
form "a permanent interracial group committed to the use of nonviolent
direct action opposing discrimination." In June they decided to call themselves the Chicago Committee of Racial Equality. Later "Committee" became "Congress," and the organization became far larger than Chicago.
But the acronym was the same: CORE, a nonviolent, interracial organization for combatting discrimination through direct action, and an early
pioneer of the tactics and ideas that would animate the civil rights movement of the sixties. CORE would grow into one of the most important
civil rights organizations in American history, and probably the one most
responsible for the nonviolent character of the coming struggle. For years

before a mass civil rights movement gained national attention, CORE had codified and practiced nonviolent tactics to pry open the doors of theaters, restaurants, housing and other places formerly closed to blacks. It was the organization's founding pacifists who, for better or worse, set the tone.[3]

CORE, it must be said, was an elite and predominantly white organization. The six individuals most responsible included South Side cell activists Fisher, Robinson, Farmer, and Houser. They were joined by the young biologist Homer Jack, who would become a Unitarian minister though he was the son of secular Jewish socialists, and black Chicagoan Joe Guinn, head of the local NAACP youth council, who would go to prison as a war resister. All were pacifists. CORE also had a substantially white leadership, which would one day be another source of resentment. Meanwhile, the group demonstrated the use of nonviolence to attack discrimination on various fronts, including at the University of Chicago hospital and medical school, and it kept after White City too.

The group also battled housing discrimination. Houser and some other war resisters had decided to save money and seek out more interesting environs by moving to a vermin-infested rental at 4257 Cottage Grove Avenue on Chicago's South Side. Cottage Grove was the eastern border of the segregated city's Black Belt, and the demarcation was sharp; one side of Cottage Grove (where the pacifists settled) was black, the other white. Despite a large increase in black population dating back to the early twentieth century—an influx sustained by the booming defense industry during the Second World War—blacks still encountered discrimination in housing, dining, and other aspects of life.

CORE then launched a second interracial Fellowship House east of Cottage Grove Avenue. The landlord threatened eviction, but some neighbors signed a letter of support; the landlord requested a delay, and the court case eventually was dropped. A mixed-race women's house was started as well. All these Fellowship Houses broke anti-black covenants in white South Side Chicago. CORE also showed that having black and white members could be a big advantage in desegregating housing and restaurants.

While those efforts were percolating, Robinson and Farmer trudged one day through sleet and snow to the nearby Jack Spratt Coffee House, where, far above the Mason-Dixon line, they encountered the hostility of Jim Crow ("You'll have to get out of here," the manager told Farmer. "We can't serve you.") and were quoted a price of a dollar for a doughnut that usually cost five cents. Illinois civil rights law barred such discrimination, and the FOR cell soon returned in force. In the case of Spratt's, there were tense waits and various forms of hostility. The activists proceeded to the next step in *War Without Violence*, which was negotiation—but that didn't work either, so it was time for direct action. After much planning, they struck in May of 1943. "We began what I believe to be the first organized civil rights sit-in in American history," Farmer later wrote. "A group of twenty-eight persons entered Jack Spratt in parties of two, three, and four. In each party, there was one black man or woman. With the discipline of peacefulness strictly observed, we occupied all available seating spaces at the counter and in booths." Other diners joined in, either refusing to eat or, when served, passing their food to blacks who were refused service. The management called the police, but the officers insisted that no laws were being violated; Farmer recalls that as the cops left, one of them winked at him. In the end, all were served, as they were on subsequent visits. In a small but gratifying victory for nonviolence, Spratt's had changed its policy.[4]

Farmer was exaggerating to suggest that this was the first organized civil rights sit-in. Just three weeks earlier the NAACP chapter at Howard University used the same technique successfully at an eatery near the school. (These lunch counter sit-ins would become much more frequent after 1960.) What's more, Farmer knew that Ahimsa farm activists and NAACP youth had used a similar nonviolent approach to integrate a public pool. And in 1940, Pauli Murray and a friend were arrested in Virginia when they challenged a bus driver's authority even as they complied with the letter of state segregation law. Murray, who had recently read *War Without Violence*, consciously used Gandhian techniques in that episode. The Harlem Ashram, where Murray had spent time, challenged segregation at New York's YMCAs. Randolph's March on Washington Movement (MOWM), by the mere threat of nonviolent protest, had won a federal ban on discrimination in defense employment. Other groups were also active in this period, using pickets, lawsuits, and boycotts. The latter had been used by black Americans in pursuit of their rights as early as the nineteenth century, but they usually arose in various times and places absent any particular ideological framework or overarching strategy.

CORE had both. It drew on Gandhi of course, but on much deeper American traditions. Gandhi, after all, was strongly influenced by Thoreau, who was in turn preceded by a national history of civil disobedience going back to the Boston Tea Party if not further. Hannah Arendt asserted that civil disobedience was "primarily American in origin and substance" and "quite in tune" with our oldest traditions. But Muste and other activists had a much more recent example to draw upon: organized labor. Folding arms and refusing to leave—basically, occupying private property—was a union strategy that went back to the early twentieth century in this country, when the revolutionary Wobblies (officially the Industrial Workers of the World) used it in industrial disputes. In the late 1930s hundreds of sit-down strikes helped unions make important gains, including such episodes as the historic 1937 strike in Flint, Michigan, that led General Motors to recognize the United Auto Workers. These occupation strikes were usually orderly and, where possible, nonviolent, with strikers sometimes policing themselves by means of rules, trials, and even penalties for transgressions. Such discipline helped enlist public opinion while (with luck) keeping the violence of the state at bay. It also preserved the capital equipment on which jobs depended and made easier the reconciliation needed to function going forward.[5]

Muste and the founders of CORE certainly knew about recent union strike tactics and civil rights activities. But they do not seem to have known about long-ago instances of nonviolent direct action undertaken by black Americans. Houser later said "we felt we were really plowing new ground. If other experiences had taken place, we had heard about them only from a distance. So when we got together and planned our strategy . . . we felt that this was something that we were doing for the first time."[6] CORE's religious sense of mission, fellowship, and insistence on nonviolence helped it and its strategy to catch on. So did Farmer and Rustin, who spent much of their time at this point traveling the country on behalf of the Fellowship—but on behalf of CORE as well. Both captivating figures, they spread the word about what the fledgling organization was up to in Chicago, drumming up enthusiasm wherever they went. The kinds of audiences they would have encountered were probably primed for their message, in addition to which the war had brought America's tragic racial regime into sharp relief.

Negroes, in the parlance of the day, were being asked to risk their lives overseas for rights and values that they knew from bitter experience were missing at home. Their loyalty and labors during the Great War had gone unrewarded (Randolph had foreseen the Great War wouldn't do them much good), and now that a new war was underway the segregated armed forces, particularly in the South, were an additional source of friction. In April 1941 a black soldier was found lynched in a wooded area of Fort Benning in Georgia. Conflicts between whites and blacks—soldiers, MPs, civilians, cops, state troopers—erupted at Fort Jackson, South Carolina, as well as in Alexandria, Louisiana; Fayetteville, North Carolina; Gurdon, Arkansas; and Tampa, Florida. Throughout 1941 and 1942, and into 1943, violence in such places was common. Some of these episodes progressed to gunfights in which members of the armed forces and local police died. Here and there full-blown riots broke out involving masses of troops, sometimes armed with rifles. In 1944, Lieutenant Jackie Robinson, who three years later would break the color line in major league baseball, was court-martialed in Texas after refusing to move to the rear of a bus. Already a well-known athlete, he was found not guilty. Boxers Joe Louis and Sugar Ray Robinson had their own ugly bus incident, in Alabama. In all three cases the black press got a hold of the story, but countless such episodes occurred without public attention.[7]

In the north, meanwhile, war work drew an army of newcomers from the South, blacks and whites both, where they and their animosities were shoehorned into overcrowded neighborhoods full of strangers. More than fifteen million civilians moved during the war, and housing was in desperately short supply. In 1942, 1.2 million families were doubled up in single-family dwellings, and by 1945, 5 million families lived in substandard housing, which might include a woodshed. Things were especially difficult for blacks; the population of Chicago's black area grew by 33 percent, while San Francisco's grew by 100 percent. In 1943, antagonism erupted into race riots in several cities; the one in Detroit was quelled only by six thousand National Guardsmen. Segregation persisted, and in some factories workers struck rather than work beside black colleagues or share bathrooms and locker rooms. Said one white striker at a Packard plant: "I'd rather see Hitler and Hirohito win the war than work beside a nigger on the assembly line."[8]

Yet over the course of the conflict such jobs were opening to blacks, who recognized the desperate struggle of the new war as a catalyst. There was a new optimism that change had to come, and a new willingness to fight for it. NAACP membership, to cite one example, grew from 50,556 in 1940 to nearly 450,000 in 1946. Gunnar Myrdal, in his famous study, *An American Dilemma*, which came out in 1944, predicted that "There is bound to be a redefinition of the Negro's status in America as a result of this War." Dwight Macdonald meanwhile argued presciently that the military, far from being a dangerous venue for integration, was actually the most promising one because of the ways it remade men and bound them in the comradeship of a new, shared identity. James Baldwin said that "the treatment accorded the Negro during the Second World War marks, for me, a turning point." Charles Silberman used the same phrase, citing the era as one in which "the seeds of the protest movements of the 1950s and 1960s were sown."[9]

It was clear to Rustin in his travels in late 1942 that "we shall have less and less opportunity to present the direct pacifist message in school, church, and club. However, these institutions are quite open to the presentation of non-violence as a solution to internal and domestic problems." He described meeting "with local Negro and Jewish leadership" as well as Quakers and FOR members in various places. Action committees sprang up in his wake to address "the almost universal rise of racial tension between negro and white, Jew and Gentile." Farmer reported the same positive reception for the message of peaceful change. "By and large," he wrote, "the pacifists with whom I have come in contact feel that in the light of present international and domestic circumstances, pacifism can make no greater contribution than that which it can make in the interracial field. They are clamoring for an action program."[10]

CORE (among others) was giving them one, even if embryonic. In January of 1943, white and black members of Syracuse CORE challenged discrimination at the Alhambra roller rink in that city. Staff members found various reasons not to accommodate them, but found they were admitted to a competing rink. In subsequent discussions with the Alhambra manager, this fact seemed to move him more than their moral arguments, and he agreed to admit skaters of all races. In March, CORE launched a campaign to end segregation at Denver theaters. One theater would give blacks a red ticket. Another gave them tickets stamped, "Good only in upper right balcony." At one theater CORE enlisted the aid of a black corporal in the army. In another case black and white women worked together (organizers found that women could break the color line with less likelihood of violence, and men were reluctant to drag them away).[11]

In April of 1943, Farmer and Gloster Current, executive secretary of the Detroit NAACP, along with Don Benedict of the Union Eight, who was living in the city by this time, tried to overturn discrimination at Greenfield's Cafeteria in Detroit, which despite the NAACP's legal efforts refused to serve blacks. They led an interracial group into the restaurant one Saturday near 6:00 p.m. and managed to tie the place in knots when the black participants simply stood there waiting to be served. They were, in a manner of speaking. But afterwards a busboy purposely and ostentatiously shattered a tray with their dishes. Swomley, who was present, identified himself as "a minister of the gospel" and called the eatery's hostility to blacks "shameful" at a time when thousands of Americans "are giving their lives supposedly in defense of democracy, and our brothers of a different race receive such treatment as this in our own country." Some diners applauded and some hooted, but after negotiations with the manager, black and white visiting testers were served without problem.[12]

By the middle of 1943 enough antidiscrimination cells had been seeded around the country that the members of Chicago CORE felt it was time to bring them together into some kind of organization or federation. In June about thirty representatives from committees in Baltimore, Columbus, Colorado Springs, Detroit, Indianapolis, New York City, Philadelphia, Syracuse, and locally in Chicago convened in the basement of the Woodlawn African Methodist Episcopal Church, whose pastor was a Chicago alderman. Over the course of the three-day meeting, the marquee speaker was Krishnalal Shridharani, whose work on nonviolent change they had been studying. He encouraged the assembled activists even as he urged them to work out an American version of Gandhian nonviolence—something they had already been doing by, for example, dispensing with Gandhian rituals of self-purification and fasting.

The big question at the meeting was the extent to which the local groups should be subsumed into a national organization. Fisher argued for this approach, but Muste had warned Farmer and Houser that funding and other problems made it unwise for CORE to leap into a centralized national structure. Th debate grew quite passionate. The Baltimore and Columbus groups, in particular, opposed centralization, and as a compromise the local groups would adopt CORE principles but didn't have to take the name or send any significant funds to headquarters. CORE's constitution said simply, "The purpose of the organization shall be to federate local interracial groups working to abolish the color line through direct non-violent action."

CORE's first leaders were Farmer and Fisher. The latter moved on, but Farmer would be associated with CORE for most of his career, in particular leading the much larger organization of the early 1960s when it played a central role in the civil rights campaigns of the time. "CORE under Mr. Farmer often served as the razor's edge of the movement," wrote Claude Sitton, who covered the struggle for *The New York Times*. "It was to CORE that the four Greensboro, N.C., students turned after staging the first in the series of sit-ins that swept the South in 1960. It was CORE that forced the issue of desegregation in interstate transportation with the Freedom Rides of 1961. It was CORE's James Chaney, Andrew Goodman and Michael Schwerner—one young black man and two white ones—who became the first fatalities of the Mississippi Freedom Summer of 1964."[13]

The Chicago conference also hashed out another controversial question: whether to bar communists. "Those were the days," Farmer would write, "when U.S. communists, acting under party discipline, frequently entered organizations, especially in the area of civil rights, with the express purpose of molding the organizations' policies into conformity with the goal of world revolution as seen by Stalin and, if possible, to capture control of the organization." Farmer, a democratic socialist (like so many pacifists), wanted them barred. He considered CORE, with its relaxed rules and loose structure, especially vulnerable and vowed that the communists would get control of the organization "over my dead body." After a battle and charges of "red-baiting," he got his way.[14]

Having CORE activists on hand from all over the country gave the Chicagoans a chance to do something they had been wanting to do for a long time, which was to desegregate a big, well-known Loop restaurant called Stoner's. Activists who visited to test its practices were kept waiting a long time and, when finally seated, were served (in Houser's words) "meat with eggshells scattered on it, or a plate of food salted so heavily that it could not be eaten, or a sandwich composed of lettuce and tomato cores picked out of the garbage can." Talks with management were unavailing, so CORE tried to mobilize public opinion by passing out leaflets for a solid week asking diners to protest discrimination in the restaurant.[15]

Stoner's had two hundred seats, meaning the Chicago chapter of CORE couldn't muster enough bodies to create a crisis in the place. But the June meeting provided the reinforcements needed for action, and Stoner's presented an ideal opportunity to get everybody fired up. Houser had planned a choreography of action nearly as elaborate as the plan for the D-Day landings, except without the shooting. (Farmer called it a "masterpiece of non-violent strategy.") Starting at 4:30 p.m. on the afternoon of June 12, 1943, white activists began filtering into the restaurant and were seated. At 5:15, Houser walked in with a black co-conspirator, finding, as expected, that they were ignored. Other patrons began to ask why they weren't seated until the owner (who knew Houser from past run-ins) cursed him out and gave him a nasty kick in the shin before seating him and his fellow activist. Additional interracial groups were kept waiting, and before long what had once been merely an all-white restaurant was now the scene of a captivating drama as diners buzzed about what was happening. The activists worked to elicit sympathy from white diners, some of whom had no idea the place discriminated. The police were summoned three times until, finally, they threatened to arrest the owner if he called them again. When he gave in, seating the CORE members even at tables he'd previously claimed were reserved, diners erupted in applause.[16]

CHAPTER 12

PEACE AGAINST PREJUDICE

MUSTE AND HIS FELLOWSHIP of Reconciliation had placed fighting discrimination against black Americans at the center of the pacifist agenda, and as
the persecution of European Jewry became more evident, pacifists took up
their cause, too, though with little success. *Fellowship* regularly published
appeals on behalf of European refugees. Muste more than once pleaded
with the White House on this score and called for more Jewish refugees to
be admitted. In September 1943 he warned that "unless something is done
soon virtually none of the Jews native to Poland and Germany and who are
still there or in other Axis-held territory will survive the winter.[1]

Jessie Wallace Hughan worried that the Nazis might actually try to
wipe out the Jews. A charter member of the FOR, in 1923 she founded
the War Resisters League, which would become the organizational home
for a variety of pacifists, socialists, anarchists, and others in pursuit of a
more secular radicalism. In 1942, she suggested the Allies offer Germany
an armistice in exchange for sparing the Jews. "It would be very terrible if
six months from now we should find that this threat has literally come to
pass without our making even a gesture to prevent it." In 1943, her worst
forebodings coming to pass, she wrote to the State Department asserting
that two million Jews had already been killed and two million more would
die absent a cessation of hostilities. "Victory will not save them," she wrote,
"for dead men cannot be liberated."[2]

Between the wars Jewish pacifism flourished, perhaps as never before, and it did so even after Hitler's rise during the thirties. Antiwar
feeling among the American rabbinate (as measured by surveys) rivaled
or even surpassed that of Protestant clergy, and lay organizations such as
the National Council of Jewish Women and the National Federation of
Temple Sisterhoods belonged to peace organizations. Various rabbinical
organizations stated their opposition to war, asserted that conscientious objection had a basis in Jewish tradition, and attempted to promulgate a new
Jewish pacifism where none had existed. The liberal Rabbi Wise, probably
America's most respected Jewish clergyman, said in 1931 that religious
leaders "committed a sin when they blessed war banners, and I for one will
never again commit that sin." Wise, who demonstrated his commitment to
the American cause in World War I by taking a job in a naval shipyard, took
up his pacifism again afterwards, insisting that "war never ends war. War
ends nothing but peace." [3]

But he (and many other Jews) turned against pacifism as the profundity
of the Nazi threat grew clearer. An Orthodox Jew named Moshe Kallner,
for instance, spent seventeen months in a CPS camp after fleeing Hitler's
Germany during the thirties. Then he joined the army, explaining himself
in a letter to Evan Thomas: "Although I detest war, conscription, the hypocrisy with which this war is being fought by the Allies, etc., still it seems
to me that conditions would be even worse under Hitler and despite the
dark future, which is being prepared by the Allies, I have to cooperate with
them because under Hitler there is no future at all."[4]

Prejudice against Jews flared noticeably in the early years of World War
II, when it was widely condemned, but it had been commonplace during
the interwar years. "Anti-Semitism permeated American society in the
1930s," John Strausbaugh reported.

Its expressions ranged from mild prejudice to acts of violence.
A 1938 Roper poll asked Americans, "What kinds of people do
you object to?" Jews topped the list at 35 percent. Even the sort of
powerful Jews in FDR's circle suffered frequent, insulting reminders that for all their success they were still, as the saying went,
"not quite our sort." Top universities and colleges strictly limited
Jewish admissions; country clubs and patriotic organizations in-

cluding New York's Union Club barred them; Gentile employers limited how many Jews they hired, if any; intermarriage was severely discouraged. Even Eleanor Roosevelt once sniffed about an acquaintance acting too "Jewy."[5]

Catholic anti-Semitism was particularly overt thanks in great part to Coughlin, who railed against Jews and communists in his weekly newspaper, *Social Justice*. Coughlin had an enormous following. In 1938, his newspaper serialized *The Protocols of the Elders of Zion*, a vicious fabrication purporting to reveal Jewish plans for a world takeover. Coughlin's crusade reached such proportions that it finally became a movement. Dorothy Day and Peter Maurin were rare Catholic voices against this tide of hatred, criticizing Coughlin in *The Catholic Worker* and elsewhere while calling for more Jews to be admitted into the United States. A headline across the top of the front page in the summer of 1939 demanded: "Let's Keep the Jews for Christ's Sake."[6]

In the spring of that year, Day joined a group of academics, priests, the editor of *Commonweal*, the film stars Don Ameche and Irene Dunne, and even Hollywood censor Joseph Breen, in forming the Committee of Catholics to Fight Anti-Semitism. Their eight-page newspaper, *The Voice*, with a circulation in the hundreds of thousands, was briefly a *Social Justice* antidote, condemning anti-Semitism as un-American and unworthy of Catholics. It even infiltrated and reported on meetings of the right wing Christian Front, a largely Irish Catholic Coughlinite group that terrorized Jews with seeming impunity. Violence increased with the outbreak of war in Europe; anti-Semitic gangs, overwhelmingly Irish American, assaulted Jews, harassed and robbed shopkeepers, and desecrated synagogues and cemeteries with few consequences in Boston and New York into the early forties. "Entire neighborhoods are being terrorized," *The Christian Century* warned.[7]

But within a few months the Committee of Catholics to Fight Anti-Semitism was pressured to change its name to the Committee of Catholics for Human Rights, and the focus shifted to include anti-Catholic bias. The leading figure in the group, Day's friend Emmanuel H. Chapman (a Jew who converted to Catholicism under the influence of Jacques Maritain), lost his Fordham University teaching post at the end of the 1942 school year.

The president of that Jesuit institution, Robert Gannon, called Chapman's activities "a source of annoyance and embarassment."[8]

All the while, there was Hitler. Jews were not numerous among American antiwar activists, but there were some, including Julius Eichel, who was to become editor of the newsletter *The Absolutist* and would have the distinction of being the only conscientious objector imprisoned in both world wars.[9] Rabbi Abraham Cronbach, an American pacifist who was to wear a yellow armband in solidarity with European Jews under Hitler, wrote as early as 1937: "Of all the outrages committed against the Jews by Hitler, none is more calamitous than this—he has banished from the hearts of many Jews the will to peace."[10]

Yet here, too, pacifism persisted, though it was not easy for Jewish pacifists to stay the course. For one thing, the Selective Service law required that conscientious objection be based on religious beliefs, and Judaism was widely considered not to offer such teachings, even though it was the Hebrew prophet Isaiah who foretold that when the Lord's judgement comes, his rebuke will be felt by many, "and they shall beat their swords into plowshares, and their spears into pruning hooks; nation shall not lift up sword against nation, neither shall they learn war any more." In 1940, moreover, the Committee on International Peace of the Central Conference of American Rabbis adopted a resolution saying Jewish tradition could support conscientious objection. And in 1943 a federal appeals court broadened the notion of a religious basis for objection to cover religious conscience even absent a deity. But draft board decisions on Jewish CO claims were all over the map, with many inferring from the Old Testament that a Jew couldn't be a pacifist.[11]

Jews have fought in wars all through history, including on behalf of Germany in the Great War. Yet there is no military tradition among religious Jews, and the Holocaust descended on a people who had long practiced nonviolence even if few were pacifists. The reasons were largely pragmatic. War had not served the Jews well in the ancient past, and now they were a small and stateless minority whose highest values had long been spiritual, ethical, and intellectual. They had learned to survive by avoiding conflict, placating their enemies, cultivating allies in powerful positions, and making themselves useful if not indispensable. Jewish victims of the Holocaust were ill-prepared to fight not just by tradition but circumstances, including the overwhelming power and cruelty of the Nazis. "Asked whether traditional Jewish non-violence was moral choice or simply expedience," writes Evelyn Wilcock, "one must answer both."[12]

Indeed, probably no group practiced nonviolence more tenaciously in the face of absolute terror than did Europe's wartime Jews. Armed resistance by the Jews was so obviously unavailing that at least one writer condemned it as a kind of suicide. And while some commentators have lamented that there was not more rebellion, others point to the Jews' tenacious upholding of core practices (religious, moral, artistic) as the most noble possible kind of resistance—in fact, a kind of heroism. Jews in the midst of an extermination campaign risked their lives to worship, to obtain access to ritual baths, to compose music, to pursue science, to teach, and to learn. Wilcock cites the assimilated Italian intellectual Primo Levi, an unbeliever. "In Auschwitz, exhausted and starving, he tried to convey to a young Frenchman walking to work at his side the significance of the canto of Ulysses in Dante's *Inferno*." Until the war, Levi had no experience at fighting. "It is indeed because of this that my career as a Partisan was so brief, painful, stupid and tragic: I had taken on a role that was not mine."[13]

American Jews fought. Some 550,000 served in the armed forces during the Second World War, their dog tags marked *H* for Hebrew unless, headed for the fight against Hitler, they preferred not to make their religion known. More than seven thousand died in action.[14] Jewish GIs encountered anti-Semitism throughout the armed forces, just as they did in civilian life, where they were excluded from many law firms, banks, housing developments, hotels, and country clubs. Job applications often asked about religion, and the *New York Post* was the rare newspaper that rejected ads from resorts and the like that excluded Jews.

Confronted with one of their own who refused to fight for reasons of conscience, American Jews were often angry and confused, much as Gentile families were, but with the added burden of anti-Semitic stereotypes about disloyalty and the knowledge of Nazi persecution. Nathaniel Hoffman, a Jewish pacifist from New York influenced by his membership in the War Resisters League, had to file an appeal to obtain CO status. He reported that his family was thoroughly embarrassed by his stand: "It was almost a total inability to understand how a Jewish person could not go along with what the country needed, or Jewish people needed, in terms of what Hitler was doing."[15]

Max Kampelman's pacifism had the support of his mother, who never got over the death of her beloved brother in the Austro-Hungarian army during the Great War. The son of Jewish immigrants from Romania who sent him to a yeshiva six days a week instead of to a public school, Max was nonetheless raised to love his country—this country. There was discrimination, sure, but it was nothing in the big picture, and he might have been speaking for all of American Jewry when he wrote: "We were Americans, democrats with a vengeance, able at last to become not what the state permitted, but what we individually were capable of accomplishing. We might be poor, but we had reached the promised land, and tomorrow would be better."[16]

Max enrolled at the Bronx campus of New York University when he was just sixteen. Through a Jewish student organization called the Menorah Society, where he was elected president, he met Cronbach and fellow rabbi Isidor Hoffman. From them he imbibed pacifism in a Talmudic vessel. Hoffman told him that the Shema Yisrael, the bedrock prayer of Judaism that proclaims, "Hear, O Israel: the Lord is our God, the Lord is One," means we are all God's children and our political system has to reflect that. Cronbach told of God's wrath when his angels rejoiced at the destruction of Egyptian forces in the Red Sea, allowing the Israelites' escape to freedom. "The Lord rebuked them, saying, 'My children are dying and yet you would rejoice?'"[17]

Max joined the War Resisters League, the Fellowship of Reconciliation, and the NAACP. He spent the life-changing summer of 1940 at a Quaker work camp in Reading, Pennsylvania, where he and other volunteers renovated a playground, painted run-down houses, and talked about Gandhi, pacifism, unions, race, and social justice. (For several years thereafter camp alumni reunited to spend New Year's Eve at Pendle Hill, a Quaker study center near Swarthmore, Pennsylvania, where Kampelman began a lifelong friendship with Rustin.) Bursting with energy, Max excelled at school even as he wrote a column for the student newspaper, manned the coat check at student dances, measured guys for rental tuxedos, and sold hosiery, ice cream, Fuller brushes, and New York Times subscriptions to keep body and soul together.[18]

In 1940, he enrolled at NYU Law School (he would pass the bar even before graduating) and began writing for The Conscientious Objector, where he was quickly listed on the masthead and given a column. His articles included a long piece about Dorothy Day, Peter Maurin, and the Catholic Workers' heroic efforts on behalf of the homeless and hungry. During a visit, Max was able to observe firsthand the "shell-shocked veterans of World War I, as they gathered for a hot meal." Years later Kampelman would reflect with dismay on how he had managed to write with "an inexplicable lack of outrage" about the murder of two million Jews and the many more in danger. The young columnist suggested that Palestine would be the best place for them and wrote no more about the subject.[19]

Many young Jewish pacifists weren't religiously observant and opposed the war on secular grounds similar to those of many Gentile pacifists, including an unwillingness to kill, a belief that war would do nothing to remedy the injustices (economic and otherwise) that supposedly underlay it, and a conviction that capitalism and imperialism were the true evils. They also believed that many more Jews could be saved by letting them into the United States than by armed conflict. Igal Roodenko, a gay Jewish radical who was to form an enduring friendship with Rustin, was granted conscientious objector status, but after some alternative service he refused further cooperation and spent the rest of the war in prison. Irving Howe, a future literary star but for now a naïve string bean fresh out of college, saw the war through the lens of international socialism as a battle between competing imperialist camps. In February of 1942 he took both Dwight Macdonald and Partisan Review to task for not coming out forthrightly against the war. Eventually he allowed himself to be drafted. Pacifist and social critic Paul Goodman, also Jewish, avoided conscription and even wrote a piece in Partisan Review advocating civil disobedience on the part of artists and intellectuals. "I made such a pain of myself they rejected me as not military material," he said. Kampelman was a conscientious objector and among perhaps 250 Jews sent to CPS camps or prison for refusing to be drafted.[20]

The Jewish journalist Milton Mayer, a University of Chicago dropout, went to work as Hutchins's chief aide in 1937 (and was even made a professor, notwithstanding his own lack of a degree). In 1939, the freethinking Mayer, thirty-one at the time, wrote a scathing antiwar essay in *The Saturday Evening Post* called "I Think I'll Sit This One Out," and in fact that's just what he did, despite what he called "my horror of 'the Berchtesgaden maniac.'" Mayer based his stance on a passionate amalgam of skepticism and idealism, but gives three specific (and widely shared) reasons for opposing the war: "I think it will destroy democracy. I think it will bring no peace. And I think it will degrade humanity."[21]

Rabbi Roland Gittelsohn, in his own words "a complete, convinced, literal, unreasonable, dogmatic, unchangeable pacifist" before the war, started to waver during the evacuation of British forces from Dunkirk. After Pearl Harbor he enlisted in the Navy and became the Marine Corps's first Jewish chaplain. In that capacity, at Iwo Jima, he delivered one of history's greatest battlefield eulogies. Cronbach and Hoffman, on the other hand, remained pacifists throughout and were involved in the founding of the tiny Jewish Peace Fellowship (JPF), which gave the small band of Jewish pacifists a chance to face their special challenges together, including the need to develop and demonstrate a Jewish basis for their opposition to war. The JPF soon had a voice on the National Service Board for Religious Objectors (the NSBRO was the council of peace churches running the CPS camps) and organized Jewry ponied up some money to help CPS Jews, who were mostly being supported by the Quakers. The group's first leader was a Nebraska rabbi and conscientious objector named Arthur Lelyveld.[22]

"With perfect principle and futility," his son Joseph would write years later, after retiring as executive editor of *The New York Times,* "the Jewish Peace Fellowship aligned itself after Dunkirk and the fall of France with the Fellowship for Reconciliation." In a touching memoir, the younger Lelyveld recalls his unique situation during his wartime boyhood: "Not only was I the only Jew in my Omaha classes, I was the only student who refrained from investing his nickels and dimes in 'war stamps' to support the war effort. Instead, I bought 'peace stamps' issued by the American Friends Service Committee to support conscientious objectors in work camps."[23]

Years later Rabbi Lelyveld would nearly lose his life in the cause of civil rights. Meanwhile the JPF argued in its newsletter, *Tidings,* that Jewish pacifists "must strive for the earliest possible settlement of this war as an early peace would not only make an end to the world-wide slaughter, but might also, by the stipulation of the rescue of the Jews as one of the armistice terms, prevent their extermination."[24]

Was the hope of an armistice, perhaps as part of a deal to rescue the Jews, realistic? What might such a negotiation have looked like? (As early as 1935 Rabbi Cronbach tried to get the American Friends Service Committee to sponsor a meeting of Jews and Nazis to "discuss their points of conflict and explore the possibilities of reconciliation.")[25] Would Hitler be allowed to keep France, or some vast swath of the Soviet Union, in exchange for some number of Jews? Would further concessions be required to save the Roma? How about homosexuals? What might Stalin, no fan of the Jews, have thought about all this? The Red Army, after all, was doing most of the fighting in Europe at the time. And what new genocide might the Nazis have cooked up to get their way once some Jews were safe? Pacifists deserve praise for raising the alarm when many others were too wary or indifferent to do so. The trouble was that there were few good nonviolent answers to the problems posed by fascism, genocide among them. The well-known rabbi Judah Magnes, a pacifist during the Great War, became an advocate of force in 1939 because, he said, "we do not know what else to do."[26]

Vocal concern for the Jews was part of the general shift among pacifists toward a broader reform agenda. The WRL, like the FOR, made a wartime priority of opposing discrimination. In mid-1942 it not only condemned prejudice against blacks and Jews but called for the government to restore the rights and property of Japanese Americans and repeal the Chinese Exclusion Act. In 1944, the WRL asked the GOP and Democratic national conventions to include in their platforms a resolution calling for the repeal of Jim Crow laws, an expansion of civil rights, and serious enforcement of antidiscrimination employment legislation. The League's own action plan called for it to "strive to end all exploitation and discrimination based on race, color or religion."[27]

Japanese Americans shipped off to concentration camps—a hard term, but apt—found pacifists to be among their few supporters. The ACLU declined to take up their case, and the Supreme Court upheld the constitutionality of the relocations. Earl Warren, later famous as a liberal justice of that court, was California's governor during the shameful roundup of his constituents, and he supported it. Even Muste doesn't seem to have grasped the full magnitude of the injustice, writing that while it was "all wrong to evacuate the Japanese from their homes, it does not follow . . . that we insist that the only thing to do is to put them all back where they came from." In July 1943 he visited the Manzanar and Tule Lake camps in California—but then wrote a letter commending officials of the War Relocation Authority on their humane treatment of the inmates. Later he referred to the authorities' "sound and liberal policy of relocation."[28] Many pacifists saw things differently, and perhaps at some level Muste did, too, as indicated by the July 1942 Issue of *Fellowship* (a publication he edited).

"The Government of the United States, merely by Executive order, has now rounded up, forced out of their homes, transported, and concentrated behind barbed wire and under armed guard 112,000 Japanese Americans, approximately 70,000 of whom are American citizens," reported Floyd Schmoe, a Quaker pacifist and Great War CO. Schmoe left the biology department of the University of Washington to devote himself to aiding these unjustly imprisoned Americans, and in particular to helping Gordon Hirabayashi, who refused to cooperate with internment and, when Japanese American men were declared eligible for the draft, refused that too. In later years Schmoe would recall being asked how he'd feel if his daughter married one of "them," only to reply quite calmly that she had done precisely that. ("Quaker Girl's Parents Okay Marriage to Jap-American," *The Seattle Times* reported on June 30, 1944.)[29]

In his *Fellowship* article Schmoe detailed the inmates' living conditions in roughly built "rabbit hutches," their lack of privacy, the inferior food, the pathetically low wages for work. He derided the excuse of "'protective custody' (Schutzhaft)," which he called "made in Germany." And he asked: "How could it accord with American justice that if a man were dangerous to his neighbors, they should be put into custody rather than he?" Schmoe told readers that armed guards "have orders to shoot anyone caught prowling about the fence at night *on the inside*." Predictably, the FBI took an interest in Schmoe's activities.[30]

Dorothy Day, in *The Catholic Worker*, was even more scathing. Under the headline "Grave Injustice Done Japanese On West Coast," she wrote: "I saw a bit of Germany on the west coast. I saw some of the concentration camps where the Japanese, men, women and children are being held before they are resettled in the Owens Valley or some other place barren, wind-swept, inaccessible." She went on to describe her visit to a transit camp for West Coast Japanese. "We drove around the detention camp for the Japanese at Portland, and it is a stockyard where cattle shows have been held which is being used to hold some thousands, until they are moved to a more permanent place."[31]

In 1942, at CPS camp number 21, tucked into the Columbia River Gorge near Cascade Locks, Oregon, the conscientious objectors in resi-dence put up the rare sustained protest against the federal policy of re-moving Japanese Americans from the West Coast and locking them up in internment camps. Or at least they fought the aspect of it they could hope to defeat. The men battled (nonviolently) to prevent the removal of one of their number, a pacifist and conscientious objector named George Yamada, who was the only Japanese American on hand. Most of the two hundred men at the camp fought fires, built and maintained trails, and did other conservation work in the nearby Mt. Hood National Forest. Yamada, born in 1918, had grown up on a farm in Nebraska, the son of a man who had emigrated from Japan in 1902 to avoid military service.

The family was Methodist, but Yamada stopped going to services when he was twelve because "I was not impressed by the social applica-tion in daily life of Christian teachings. From that age my interpretation of the Gospel of Christ was uncompromisingly pacifist, and I was deter-mined to carry out the pacifist premises of the Christian gospel as I per-ceived them." At nineteen, chafing under his father's authority, Yamada moved to San Francisco. There he worshipped at the Evangelical Reformed Church in the Nikkei community, where the new minister was a pacifist. At San Francisco State, one of his professors introduced him to a visiting A. J. Muste (who led the assembled in singing "God Bless America"). Yamada was certified a CO by his draft board and arrived at Cascade Locks two days before Pearl Harbor—in time to meet Bayard. He arrived in time to meet Bayard Rustin, who visited on a speaking tour for the Fellowship of Reconciliation. At Cascade Locks, Yamada read about Buddhism (his family's faith in Japan) in the *Encyclopedia Britannica* with the Hollywood heartthrob Lew Ayres, famous as Dr. Kildare, who had arrived in March of 1942. A vegetarian and free thinker, Ayres risked his career for his pacifist principles and stayed only six weeks. He would eventually serve as an army medic. He was, Yamada recalled, "a man unaffected by fame."[32]

When the War Relocation Authority demanded that Yamada be transferred to an internment camp, he protested, and the director at Cascade Locks, Reverend Mark Schrock, refused to comply. Yamada also had the support of the other men in camp. "Wow, that camp blew apart!" recalled Kermit Sheets, one of the COs. "Because here was a guy as isolated as you could be. We knew George, he was a conscientious objector, for crying out loud! He wasn't going to send messages to Japan that would make them shoot us! The whole thing was absolutely ridiculous. Then we had loads of meetings as to how we were going to handle it when they came for George. It got extremely tense, verging on the melodramatic . . . wondering how many people should lie down in front of the car that was to take him away."[33]

Letters from Cascade Locks to camps around the country enlisted support from COs at those as well, including invitations for Yamada to relocate to one in Massachusetts, and a readiness, on the part of men in an Ohio camp, "to follow your lead in non-violent direct action if necessary."[34] Muste also weighed in. Ultimately the authorities settled for pointlessly relocating Yamada to a Mennonite camp near Colorado Springs, Colorado, where he remained for three years. During that time he spent eight days in the county jail as part of a CORE project to desegregate a local theater, after which he was transferred to the camp for incorrigibles at Germfask, Michigan.

There is a thin line sometimes between anarchism and anarchy. Marooned on Michigan's rural Upper Peninsula adjacent to the Seney National Wildlife Refuge, the Germfask resisters demonstrated how easily radical protest can slide toward vanity and nihilism. At Germfask, some men simply refused to work while others drove foremen to distraction by doing everything slowly, partially, and wrong. Chopping down even a small tree would be a daylong project. When directed to clean out a truck platform, the men would spend the day sweeping out a portion. "We got to be experts at not working," recalled Roy Kepler of his time at Germfask. "We became experts at digging a hole that never got dug." The camp's director, sensing the futility of trying to make anyone work and no doubt aware that the war was coming to an end, didn't require anything, and in return the men tolerated their confinement. One sympathetic visitor was taken aback, just three months after the camp opened in 1944, to find "washrooms the filthiest anywhere, dining habits those of hogs, 75% of the men unshaven, unkempt and dirty, liquor being drunk in the dorms on Sunday morning at church time, almost no project work being done."[35]

Germfask might have muddled along in this way had not the campers thoroughly antagonized their rural neighbors, in part by giving the impression that they would, "attempt to date girls in the high school library, in churches and on the street." Things went from bad to worse when the press depicted a mutiny among idle COs lolling about on the U.P. while other American boys were fighting and dying overseas. *Time* ran an exposé of the "studied defiance" of the troublemakers, whom it called "guardhouse lawyers" for their skill at staying within the law while thwarting Selective Service officials. The magazine said these officials were "at their wit's end. The problem that vexed them: how to deal with a group of draft-age Americans who have refused to fight, who now decline to work, and spend most of their waking hours finding new and more ostentatious ways of thumbing their noses at all authority."[36]

Washington got involved, but nobody had any real answers—and meanwhile the camp descended into conflict and recrimination, with once-moderate COs siding with the worst antagonists. The camp's fourth director, a former serviceman only weeks on the job, resigned and called the CPS system "the re-establishment of slavery."[37]

When Kepler arrived on January 20, 1945, he recorded his impressions of a bunkhouse known as Tobacco Road, where he found a "Saturday night atmosphere of beer and mixed singing that was somehow pathetic and strained, a put-on performance to convince themselves they were Bohemian." He told all this to the War Resisters League in New York, where an official responded with the same sort of question Selective Service officials were asking, and that parents would ask a generation later about some new young radicals: "Are they heroes, valiantly fighting a vicious set-up? Are they high-spirited pranksters, gaining a relief that keeps them sane? Are they psychopaths, revealing symptoms that need treatment?"[38]

To the extent that Americans respected "conchies," it was because they stood on conscience. But many at Germfask belied the stereotype of devout war resisters too religious to kill. The crowded and smoky Tobacco Road dorm, so dubbed after Erskine Caldwell's 1932 novel of

backroads dissolution, featured late night poker games, a coffee pot going all the time, food lifted from the mess hall, and nude pinups all over
the walls. Some Germfask campers took their campaign against sainthood into the surrounding communities. Delivered to the nearby town
of Munising for a bit of leave, they disabled their vehicle by tampering
with the engine and then got drunk at the local bars, where one got into
a fight with a soldier outside.[39]

A campaign of vandalism and sabotage at Germfask included clog-
ging toilets, hiding light bulbs and silverware, and spreading an inch of
flour on a floor, the better to write obscenities on it in coffee grounds.
An even more embarrassing episode occurred on the night of January 30,
when some of the men broke into the kitchen and, in a time of national
food rationing, made a shambles of the place, dumping a hundred-pound
bag of beans, a three-gallon jar of mustard, seven quarts of orange and
lemon extract, and thirty pounds of baking powder. They smashed or removed bulbs and oven doors, and in the cooler blended stewed apricots
and prunes with steamed rice.[40]

"CPS service was very hard on a lot of people," the poet William
Stafford said years later. Stafford spent the war in four different CPS camps
and, in a village near one in Arkansas, came uncomfortably close to getting
lynched by a mob that formed one lazy Sunday as he read Leaves of Grass.
He remained ever after an unwavering opponent of war, and opposition to
violence became the main theme of his life's work. But he saw that many
men came away from the CPS experience cursed with an outsized sense of
grievance. "It turned some of them into professional gripers, people who
can't do without a losing fight with society; I mean, they go around looking for it. I sense that in a lot of young people as a result of the Vietnam
War experience. They cannot settle down to being positive and expecting-
good-from-their-society kind of citizens. They just feel they've been betrayed, and that they will be again."[41]

At Germfask, Yamada fell in with a militant group of resisters including the soon-to-become-notorious Corbett Bishop. After taking part in a
work slowdown, Yamada (with others) walked away from camp, earning
himself a prison sentence of three and a half years. At Ashland, Kentucky,
where he was sent off to do his time, he was reunited with Rustin.

Let's go back for a moment to the lakeside retreat in Columbus, Ohio, the one where Farmer presented his civil rights proposal. He would have preferred, afterwards, to avoid the boring FOR business that took up the next two days of council sessions, but he stayed for the music—"moving renditions of Negro spirituals" sung by Rustin. "He sang like an angel," Glenn Smiley, who had heard Rustin on other occasions, would later recall. Might this have been Farmer's first inkling that Rustin was a star who could outshine him in the eyes of their shared mentor? Farmer had noticed that he and Rustin were the only blacks at the Columbus meeting. In their role as key Muste lieutenants on race, it was inevitable that these two young pacifists would vie for his attention and approval even as they worked toward the same goal. Their aim wasn't to stop a war but rather to start one, and to fight it without firing a shot. They were both staunch pacifists and integrationists, but they were two very different men, with different talents and experiences. Both would become giants of the American civil rights movement. And in the competition for Muste's affection, both would end up losers.

CHAPTER 13

A ONE-MAN ARMY

PEACE COULD HAVE HAD no more captivating emissary during the war than the FOR's roving ambassador, Bayard Rustin, whose travels afforded him a panorama of pacifist struggles at a time when many conscientious objectors were quite literally in the wilderness. But he observed, as well, the movement's stubborn vitality—and its potential. Based in New York, where much of FOR headquarters was already in his thrall, Rustin none-theless spent a great deal of his time on the road. In December of 1942 he reported that "Since September I have traveled some seven thousand miles from coast to coast, in New England, and in the South. In all I have visited 24 states, presented our message to some five thousand people, counselled with numerous men in eight C.P.S. camps from San Dimas, California to Coshocton, Ohio. I visited the Japanese concentration camp at Manzanar. I spoke before a number of luncheon service clubs such as Kiwanis and Rotary, presented the principles of non-violence in a score of colleges and to many young people's groups and high school assemblies. I visited about fifty F.O.R local groups and cells."[1]

Rustin covered all this ground by train, bus, or hitchhiking. Impressive though his itinerary may be, it doesn't begin to capture the impact he had on people everywhere he went. The editors of *Fellowship* called Rustin, with some justification, "FOR's one-man nonviolent army."[2] He captivated audiences with his oratory, transported them with his heartrending tenor singing voice, rejected discrimination anywhere he encountered it, and withstood violence with disarming stoicism and dignity. Once, according to the pacifist Bronson Clark, Rustin was traveling through Texas on a train carrying seven German POWs who were being taken to the dining car for an early meal. On the way a woman stood and slapped one of the Germans across the face. When Rustin asked the military policeman in charge if he could speak with the Germans he was told it was against regulations. "But there is no regulation saying I cannot sing to them," Rustin persisted, and the MP admitted as much. "So Bayard sang, in German, Schubert's 'Serenade' followed by 'A Stranger in a Distant Land.'"[3]

Carolyn Lindquist, an undergraduate at Ohio Wesleyan University, said she would "never forget that man and his nonviolent approach to solving problems," adding that "he was one of the unsung heroes of my time." Her black classmate Wallace Nelson was converted to pacifism by his encounter with Rustin. "I was always yelling and getting dragged out of public places when I protested against racial discrimination. It was Bayard Rustin who explained and demonstrated to me the demeanor you should adopt . . . simply insist on your dignity and your rights as a human being." (As a draft resister, Nelson would spend time at a CPS camp and in prison, later becoming a tax resister and leading figure in CORE.) And a former student at the Oakwood School, a Friends institution in Poughkeepsie, New York, recalled Rustin giving a "marvelous speech" there about nonviolence. "He concluded by singing beautifully to us a program of black spirituals and Elizabethan songs. His voice had an extraordinary range."[4]

After he stayed overnight with a couple in Bismarck, North Dakota, they wrote to the FOR that he was "one of the finest spirits it has been our pleasure to know," and that "he made a profound impression." A woman in Colorado said "he had such charisma that you cannot imagine . . . we were enchanted." A Quaker activist drew attention to his "electrifying presence." Houser, who saw Rustin in action many times, said: "You would see people with tears coming out of their eyes." Caleb Foote, in charge of the FOR in the Bay Area (with time out for prison), said that Rustin "was always a huge hit" in California. The draft resister and lifelong antiwar activist Larry Gara called Rustin's personality "electric." He was "a sensation," Smiley told Rustin biographer John D'Emilio. "There was magic about Bayard." Smiley, who went on to become one of the closest associates of Reverend King, called Rustin "my guru" and the source of "practically everything that I knew at that time of importance about nonviolence."[5]

His ability to move effortlessly from speech to song captivated audiences. One of his FOR colleagues, Doris Grotewohl, called it "spellbinding." Another recalled going along with him to address an audience in Brooklyn and hearing him sing movingly from the balcony, in his fine tenor voice, "Sometimes I Feel Like a Motherless Child." He often sang that at pacifist gatherings, surely infusing it with his own sense of loneliness. The secret of Rustin's sexuality, which he neither hid nor discussed, would have separated him from others, as did his race in the world of white pacifism. His father, known to the young Bayard only as a local ne'er-do-well named Archie Hopkins, was another source of insecurity. Rustin traveled alone, and he traveled a lot. At a low point in the early 1950s, he spoke explicitly of his loneliness to the gay pacifist David McReynolds, who had first heard Bayard in the late 1940s and recalled, "I was absolutely hypnotized . . . He left such an impact on me that I spoke like him and used his gestures for a week or two afterwards."[6]

Rustin's travels during the war occurred at a time of intense patriotism, when young Americans were fighting all over the world and people on the home front supported the effort. As a result, not everybody welcomed a mannered black pacifist (in fact a gay former communist) lecturing on nonviolence in a pretentious accent. But indifference or hostility only stimulated his creativity in winning hearts and minds. The president of a Kiwanis chapter in rural North Dakota said Rustin couldn't give a talk because he was from the FOR (whose pacifist message presumably was unwelcome) but he could sing if he wanted. Rustin agreed as long as he could announce his songs, by which means he made clear his message—if it wasn't clear from his music, which included "It's Me, O Lord," "Lord, I Want to Be a Christian," and "Study War No More." The episode inspired him to propose that the FOR consider "musical lectures" with commentary or music presentations that carried the pacifist message. "Discussions after hearing Wagner's 'Ring' would lead to [the] idea that violence and greed are destroying, for finally the gold was returned to the Rhine maidens [where] it could do no more harm. Discussion of 'Tristan' could lead to the fact that sacrifice tied to truth is progress, that love is stronger than any force in human relations."[7]

Even when asked to address nonviolence in the context of labor disputes, marital woes, and other issues, Rustin reported, and even when specifically instructed not to address the war, audiences inevitably asked him "to present our views on the world struggle in light of the principles I had outlined." But in addition to talking of peace, he spoke passionately about discrimination—and in the view of biographer Jervis Anderson, "came to be recognized as probably the most militant civil rights advocate in the United States." Topics included "Racial Exploitation in America" and "Can Nonviolent Non-Cooperation Win Freedom for the American Negro?" Especially incendiary was his tendency to note the ways in which our own country and its allies, while condemning our enemies, were themselves guilty of some of the same moral failings. The Dayton, Ohio, *Journal*, reporting on a speech Rustin delivered at a local Baptist church in 1943, gives some sense of how provocative his message could be in a time of war:

> While he emphasized that he was not in sympathy with Germany, the speaker said Hitler has been more honest than President Roosevelt and Prime Minister Churchill. For instance, he explained that Hitler does not pretend friendship with the Jews on the one hand and punish them on the other . . . He said that Churchill does not intend to bring racial equality, but rather intends to retain the status quo. He stated that much is said about equality in this country, yet the government, even in the armed forces, is one of the worst offenders.[8]

Rustin was certainly aware of the ambivalence toward the war in black America, where segregation in the military and persistent discrimination on the home front had bred profound resentment. "Many Negroes have little faith in the present struggle," he reported in a FOR memo dated September 8, 1942. "I have heard many say they might as well die right here fighting for their rights as to die abroad for other people's. It is common to hear outright joy expressed at a Japanese military victory. For thousands of Negroes look upon successes of any colored people anywhere as their successes."

Dellinger, in his memoir, reports being taken with Benedict and Dallas to an all-black jazz club where the three of them were celebrated by patrons for having refused to fight. "The general bitterness," Myrdal reported, "is reflected in the stories that are circulating in the Negro communities: A young Negro, about to be inducted into the army, said, 'Just carve on my tombstone, Here lies a black man killed fighting a yellow man for the protection of a white man.'"[9]

Around the same time as *An American Dilemma* was published (the spring of 1944), the army weekly *Yank* published an anguished letter from Rupert Trimmingham, a black corporal who discovered that the country he was fighting for could treat its enemies better than its own soldiers.

> Here is a question that each Negro soldier is asking. What is the Negro soldier fighting for? On whose team are we playing? Myself and eight other soldiers were on our way from Camp Claiborne, La., to the hospital here at Fort Huachuca. We had to lay over until the next day for our train. On the next day we could not purchase a cup of coffee at any of the lunchrooms around there. As you know, Old Man Jim Crow rules. The only place where we could be served was at the lunchroom at the railroad station but of course we had to go into the kitchen. But that's not all; 11:30 A.M. about two dozen German prisoners of war, with two American guards, came to the station. They entered the lunchroom, sat at the tables, had their meals served, talked, smoked, in fact had quite a swell time. I stood on the outside looking on. And I could not help but ask myself these questions. Are these men sworn enemies at this country? Are they not taught to hate and destroy . . . all democratic governments? Are we not American soldiers sworn to fight for and die if need be for this our country? Then why are they treated better than we are?[10]

Americans knew this was wrong. *Yank* was inundated with mail from GIs, "almost all of whom were outraged by the treatment given the corporal," the editors wrote. The original Trimmingham letter even became the basis of a short story in *The New Yorker*. In a subsequent letter published on July 28, Trimmingham reported that he was heartened to receive 287 letters in response to his own, including 183 from whites in the armed forces, most from the Deep South. "It give me new hope to realize that there are doubtless thousands of whites who are willing to fight this Frankenstein that so many white people are keeping alive," Trimmingham wrote. He was one of 1.2 million blacks who served in the armed forces during the war in spite of their second-class status.[11]

While blacks were concerned first and foremost with discrimination at home, there was also rising consciousness of race and imperialism elsewhere. Rustin's memo goes on to say that "No situation in America has created so much interest among Negroes as the Gandhian proposals for India's freedom. In the face of this tension and conflict, our responsibility is to put the technique of nonviolent direct action into the hands of the black masses."[12]

Rustin encountered plenty of discrimination during his wanderings, and confronted it in an era when most people went along. "He had almost unbelievable courage," FOR member Ernest Bromley told D'Emilio. Anderson cites the experience of Wilfred Gamble, principal of an all-black school in Marion, Alabama, who would sometimes find a place for Rustin to stay (and thereby keep him out of conflicts with the owners of whites-only hostelries). "Bayard was always determined to test the segregation laws of the South," Gamble reported, whether in hotels or on buses, all of which were strictly segregated in the region. In April 1942 he found himself barred from the CPS camp in Magnolia, Arkansas, because, he told Muste, Negroes could not speak to the men or even visit.[13]

Segregation was common in the North too. At a Friends conference in the summer of 1942, Rustin refused to confine himself to the "Negro beach" of Cape May, New Jersey, or even the "conference beach," an interracial area established for conferees apart from the local Jim Crow regime. Soon after walking onto the white beach he was accosted by a lifeguard. "Rustin expressed concern for the difficult position in which the lifeguard found himself, but explained that it was against his principles to leave. He repeated this to the manager . . . Rusty kept the whole conversation on a friendly and even humorous basis, offering suggestions of methods by which they might succeed in removing him . . . Eventually the manager and lifeguards left, and Rusty and his friends went swimming." From then on Rustin used that same formerly segregated beach, and other black beachgoers soon followed.[14]

Another time, late one rainy night in Baltimore, he was unable to get a taxi at the train station, where he had just arrived, because of his color. "Bayard thereupon took his stand in the narrow driveway by which taxis leave the station and stood there, in the pouring rain, for ninety minutes, during which time traffic remained paralyzed." When threatened with arrest, he asserted that "the only charge that could be leveled against him was, 'He wanted a taxi.'" Drenched, he finally got one.[15]

Even among sympathetic whites, there were startling reminders of the racial score in America. At a church in Ohio Rustin seemed to be a no-show, and someone suggested, "Why don't we ask the Negro janitor sitting back there if he has seen the speaker in any part of the building?" In response, the "janitor" answered, "I am Bayard Rustin." He gave a great talk anyway. Another time, a young white pacifist in Washington, knowing that most hotels wouldn't accommodate Rustin, asked his parents to put him up. His father, a minister, readily agreed. But his mother said she'd stay with her sister: "I couldn't spend a night in the same house with a black person."[16]

One particular episode, in the spring of 1942, was sufficiently hair-raising that Rustin described it in *Fellowship*, and later in an interview with journalist Milton Viorst. The two accounts vary a bit, but basically Rustin was boarding a bus from Louisville to Nashville when a white infant grabbed his necktie "and the mother hit it and said, don't touch a nigger." When Rustin settled himself in the back of the bus, "next to me was a Negro couple who had a box with chicken in it and having the best time on earth. And I said, how many years are we going to let that child be misled by its mother—that if we sit in the back and are really having fun, then whites in a way have the right to say they like it in the back . . . I vowed then and there I was never going through the south again without either being arrested or thrown off the bus or protesting."[17]

Rustin promptly moved up to the white section, calmly explaining to the driver why he would not go back. The police arrived about thirteen miles north of Nashville and beat the daylights out of him in front of everyone else. Later he had to pass through a gauntlet of blows at the police station. Rustin as usual made no attempt to fight back; he just tried to explain to his tormentors the moral basis of his actions. Some of the bus passengers tried to get the police to stop and later, hearing accounts of the events from the police and Rustin himself, the assistant district attorney said: "You may go, Mr. Rustin." Bayard made a point of this hard-won honorific in his *Fellowship* essay, a reminder of the different world of that era, when even the most fundamental courtesies were denied to black Americans.[18]

The founding of CORE provided a conduit for young FOR staffers to channel their energies—and that of the pacifist movement—into civil rights during the war. Farmer, Houser, Foote, and Rustin all spent time on CORE, and Muste supported them even as he worried about pacifism taking a back seat. Farmer in particular was far more committed to civil rights than pacifism. A brilliant speaker and ideas man, he antagonized senior FOR leaders for inspiring more than organizing during his travels on behalf of the pacifist organization. Swomley, to whom Farmer and Rustin officially reported, complained that Farmer would sometimes not show up where he was supposed to during a speaking tour, and Muste repeatedly urged him to focus more on organizing. Houser described him as "a great platform speaker. A very good front man. Not a good administrator . . . He did what he did magnificently. But he was not the organizer."[19]

No one could fail to notice the contrast with Rustin, who managed not just to inspire people but to meld them into a movement, preaching nonviolent action against discrimination everywhere he went and leaving new CORE chapters in his wake. He spent a month in the Bay Area and cultivated a thriving chapter in that time, connecting with blacks and whites, college graduates, and shipyard workers. "All around here," Foote reported with enthusiasm, "are the results of what you have done." Rustin also catalyzed a CORE chapter at the University of Colorado, where he'd gone to teach nonviolent techniques. One student was so inspired she joined the staff of the FOR. Rustin succeeded despite his frankness with audiences about the difficulty and discipline that nonviolence must entail, especially the flavor he espoused, which shunned passive resistance in favor of action. Rather than withdrawal from conflict, nonviolence to the new pacifists meant a disciplined and courageous encounter with it.[20]

If Rustin saw it as his duty to "speak truth to power," that may have been because he minted the phrase. He attributed it to the Swarthmore economist Patrick Malin, who supposedly uttered the words at the 1942 Friends conference at Cape May. But Malin's speech didn't actually include that phrase, and it may well be that Rustin himself bequeathed us the standard usage in a letter dated August 15, 1942. He wrote it to his Friends meeting in New York in protest of a proposal to provide hospitality to soldiers. "The primary function of a religious society," he said, "is to 'speak the truth to power.' The truth is that war is wrong. It is then our duty to make war impossible . . . The greatest service we can render the men in the armed forces is to maintain our peace testimony and to expend our energies in developing a creative method of dealing non-violently with conflict . . . They need most to return and find the church which has not forsaken the principles of Christ."[21]

Rustin was no more equivocal about the CPS system. His travels took him to some of the camps, where he lectured and spoke with the men who found themselves marooned there. After the initial idealism surrounding these arrangements wore off, discontent spread fast. What had at first seemed the promise of humanitarian work under church supervision for perhaps a year turned into brute physical labor, some of it just make-work, during a confinement to remote facilities for the duration of the war (and then some). Although run by the peace churches, it quickly became clear that the armed forces ultimately called the shots. Chemist Don DeVault, for example, a former Stanford professor who had been engaged in penicillin research, was assigned for a while to digging ditches. One of the most troubling issues was the lack of pay, which the men had at first seen as evidence of their pacifist commitment, and which was built into the program in order to get Roosevelt on board. General Lewis Blaine Hershey implacably opposed any efforts to change this, though we should not assume that this politically astute general, always conscious of public opinion in a democracy, acted out of vindictiveness. Aside from what the men's families could provide, the peace churches bore the burden of keeping everyone fed and sheltered, but working for free inevitably bred resentment among COs, a third of whom had dependents. After years of Depression, many families struggled to stay afloat deprived of their male breadwinner, never mind contributing to his upkeep at CPS (required for those who could afford it). Wives often found paying jobs back home but faced antagonism over their husbands' refusal to serve in the armed forces. To earn a few dollars, some CPS men took outside work on local farms and the like if it was available, but the uncompensated drudgery that for many was at the heart of the experience could make it seem like something between indentured servitude and incarceration. At the same time, some came to see their tenure at the camps as a form of cooperation with the war system and thus a violation of their deepest principles. Even absent these issues, the nature of the inmates, if such they can be called, made many camps seething cauldrons of radicalism—especially the Quaker camps, which tended to draw fewer traditional religious resisters and more of those for whom pacifism was part of a broader political worldview, as it was for Rustin.[22]

On his visits to the camps their shortcomings were readily apparent, and Rustin appealed to the FOR leadership to do more for the men, advocating the establishment of an emergency fund to help COs and their families. In the camps, he reported, COs "are in need of clothing and in one camp the men actually do not have enough to eat. How much longer are we going to take care of these needs on a fumbling charity basis?" he wrote to Muste. Lloyd Frankenberg, writing in 1947 of his time at a Maryland camp, reported that for work the men wore "whatever old workclothes we could scrape up; some of us looked like ash-men, others more like Harlequin. On the road we were sometimes mistaken for POW's; but as we explained, POW's were paid." (German prisoners of war brought to the United States were by and large treated in accord with the Geneva Conventions. Often performing farm labor or conservation work, they were paid eighty cents or more daily, about the same as a U.S. army private. Many gained weight.)[23]

In the South, where the camps accommodated local practices of racial segregation, Rustin antagonized FOR traditionalists by attacking CPS in talks to FOR chapters, and by advising men in the camps to refuse cooperation. Muste, always an indefatigable correspondent, did what he could by mail to assuage the ire of those who wrote in to complain, insisting nonetheless that the organization was unalterably opposed to racial discrimination. The immorality of discrimination was by now widely understood, as Myrdal pointed out in 1944, even among those who practiced it. But it was widely practiced, and Muste's willingness to allow his brightest young talents to devote themselves to organizing in this area was remarkable. "I could do anything I wanted," Foote said of his CORE activities in San Francisco, "and A.J. would support me."[24]

Rustin probably thought the same, for Muste's growing regard for him was no secret to anyone. Both were former communists who came away from their experience of the party with a high regard for the dedication and skills required by movement-building, including the importance of nuts-and-bolts organizing. Rustin had been to Muste's home, and his boss was a natural candidate for surrogate father. They shared a passionate dedication to the cause of nonviolent social progress, and they had suffered beatings for their beliefs. Yet they differed in some crucial ways. Rustin was a sybarite and aesthete, a man of boundless sexual appetites, a font of self-invention and embellishment. Muste had evolved from the strict Calvinism of his youth. But he was still a straitlaced family man who loved baseball and other wholesome diversions. For a long time these differences remained in the background. Muste was not blind, but remained enchanted with his brilliant young protégé.

His confidence in Rustin grew even as his faith in Farmer ebbed. In 1943, he loaned both men to Randolph, the Pullman leader, who seemed determined to revive his March on Washington Movement along Gandhian lines with a program of mass nonviolent civil disobedience. Muste shared Rustin's excitement about this; on top of the obvious congruence between their goals, their chosen means, and those lately embraced by Randolph, Rustin had worked with the Pullman union leader previously, during the initial excitement over the MOWM. Randolph, in fact, was another mentor and father figure in Rustin's life. Farmer was more skeptical that the MOWM could get very far with nonviolent protest, although he, too, had much in common with Randolph, who was (like Farmer) an imposing figure, an accomplished orator, a socialist, and the son of a Methodist minister.

Already a major figure in black America as the organizer of the first successful black trade union, in January of 1941 Randolph took the daring step of calling for a massive blacks-only march on the nation's capital to protest discrimination in the armed forces and in hiring by defense contractors. FDR bought peace through an executive order barring job discrimination in defense factories as well as the federal government (but not segregation in the armed forces). Randolph's young supporters were disappointed when he called off the march in June, but black newspapers lionized him for wresting some measure of justice from a popular president.

The nucleus of his organization persisted for a while and held some large rallies marked by Gandhian rhetoric. In June of 1942 more than eighteen thousand supporters thronged Madison Square Garden in the largest of these meetings, which all together brought in nearly six hundred thousand new movement members in three months. The success of these rallies led to a national convention of sixty-six delegates from around the country, held in September 1942 in Detroit. Pauli Murray, then a Howard student, attended. Like CORE, the organization intended for branches to operate with considerable independence. A variety of resolutions were adopted, including support for the war against the Axis, condemnations of anti-Semitism and anti-Catholicism, and a rejection of communism. Significantly, the convention endorsed nonviolent civil disobedience to combat racial discrimination. That focus, as well as the movement's evolution into what appeared to be a more permanent national membership organization, alienated the more established National Urban League and NAACP. If Randolph's caution had brought criticism from the likes of Murray, his calls for civil disobedience brought denunciations from the increasingly powerful black press, which was committed to the Double V approach.[25]

This want of traditional allies may have been a factor in bringing Randolph's movement closer to the pacifists. When he announced plans for a grand conference in 1943 on the use of nonviolence to advance the rights of black Americans—including boycotts of transit and other public accommodations, schools, and other segregated venues—Dwight and Nancy Macdonald were in his corner to provide rhetorical firepower. Armed with Nancy's ample research on the appalling treatment of blacks in the armed forces, Dwight in early 1943 produced a blistering attack on military segregation and stupidity, entitled *The War's Greatest Scandal!: The Story of Jim Crow in Uniform*. He pulled no punches, noting that "a doctrine of 'White Supremacy' which is simply Hitler's 'Nordic Supremacy' in Cracker lingo has become the official policy of the American armed forces. Racialism is monstrous in Nazi Germany but O.K in the U.S. Army."[26]

Macdonald went on to note that the 1940 draft law contained a clause stating clearly that, in choosing and training recruits, "there shall be no discrimination against any person on account of race or color." How is it possible, Dwight asked, that Congress and the president stand by while military authorities are violating this provision? "It is possible," he explained, "because up to now the colored people have not put up any real fight" to enforce the antidiscrimination clause. "But the record shows that the Negro gets something from the Roosevelt administration only when he kicks up a fuss . . . the colored people of America, and their white friends, must begin *right now* to make a real fight on this issue."[27]

Dwight didn't agree with Randolph about everything; in particular he objected to the MOWM policy of admitting only blacks as members, for he objected to chauvinism of all kinds. When a periodical in London praised his disdainful take on American culture as the "spirited and witty" product of "a good American," he wrote in to object. "How do you know I am a 'good American'?" he demanded, demurring that "I don't know as I'd call myself a Good American. I'm certainly a Critical American, and I prefer your country." Not content with denial, he goes on to criticize the premise. "A Bad American, cynical and traitorous, might still make perfectly sound criticisms of his country."[28]

Macdonald was a good enough American to address a "Monster Mass Meeting" on "Jim Crow in Uniform," as the ads proclaimed, on the night of April 22, 1943, along with Randolph, Roy Wilkins (editor of *The Crisis* at the NAACP, which he would one day lead), ACLU lawyer Arthur Garfield Hays, who was handling the Winfred Lynn case, and Wilfred Kerr, co-chair of the Lynn Committee to Abolish Segregation in the Armed Forces. The Lynn case, involving a black man who refused to serve in a segregated army, was at the top of the agenda for the event, sponsored by the March on Washington Movement, at Harlem's renowned Golden Gate Ballroom. "It seems to me the time is ripe and overripe," Macdonald told the crowd, "for this country to decide whether it is pouring out blood and treasure to win a war for democracy or a Jim Crow war." He urged blacks to lead the way in this fight, insisting that many whites would follow, even if the enemies of equality inevitably accused civil rights campaigners "of working for Hitler, of sabotaging the war effort, of being defeatists and traitors and God knows what else." In response they could simply ask, "Is this a war for democracy or not?"[29]

The Macdonalds' pamphlet on "the war's greatest scandal" explicitly promoted the big upcoming MOWM conference in July. That meeting, to be held in Chicago, would be called "We Are Americans, Too," and Muste was only too happy to lend Rustin and a skeptical Farmer to work on it.

As with the communist organizing of his youth and his earlier travels with the FOR, Rustin gained valuable experience, in this case dealing with the disparate constituencies of his new tripartite role (FOR, CORE, and MOWM). At the event, Randolph included nonviolent action in his opening remarks and Rustin, characteristically, addressed the assembled throng movingly. He spoke of using nonviolence to defy segregation and federal authority, and described real-world experiences, largely his own, to provide inspiring examples. Then he asked his listeners to bow their heads and sang "It's Me, O Lord, Standing in the Need of Prayer."[30]

By the time it was over the convention had agreed to adopt "non-violent, good will direct action to be developed in specific areas of injustice in protest against employment, transportation discrimination, civil rights violations, armed forces segregation and constitutional injustices." At Rustin's suggestion, the delegates called for "institutes in various localities to educate people" on this new program of nonviolence. Rustin—a true believer, a born teacher, and a man unencumbered by family obligations—was just the man to make these happen.[31]

He had already been conducting such workshops all over the country outside the South, with various combinations of the FOR, CORE, and the American Friends Service Committee. (The small world of pacifist racial justice organizations in those days had a great deal of overlap.) These were usually weekend events, starting on Friday evening with a lecture on the nature of race and the lack of a scientific basis for it as a category. The next day Rustin would explain nonviolent direct action and there would be a discussion of local discrimination in Dayton or Detroit or wherever Rustin happened to find himself. This might be followed by a modest demonstration of Rustin's methods at a local eatery or cinema—an event that might seem tentative, even timid, today, but that was important and difficult for participants, and that portended bigger things. Rustin held these institutes in New York, St. Louis, San Francisco, and various places in between. One remarkable all-star session was held at New York's Grace Congregational Church in early April 1943. E. Franklin Frazier, a Howard University sociologist, talked about "What Science Has To Say About Race." Then Lillian Smith, a white southerner and lesbian who would create a sensation in 1944 with a novel about interracial love, called *Strange Fruit*, gave a talk entitled "The Race Situation Today—in the United States and Abroad." Farmer's speech was on nonviolent techniques. Randolph gave an address called "A Program for Today," and Muste talked about "The Spiritual Basis for Non-violence." Finally, Rustin led a symposium and then the closing Sunday worship service.[32]

Muste, Randolph, Farmer, and Rustin also appeared together for a nonviolent institute at Lincoln Congregational Church in Washington, D.C., in August. From this event a group of activists emerged and began holding Saturday evening meetings at Howard University. After an interracial meal and a discussion of nonviolent theory and tactics, they fanned out among retail establishments known to discriminate. In some places they succeeded; in others they kept plugging away. By October there were several neighborhood cells in Washington doing the same kind of work, hoping to change white attitudes while changing business policies through sit-downs and other nonviolent techniques. Rustin was committed to integration and worked hard to build an interracial movement, but he stressed that blacks must show the way and take the lead, for it was their freedom at stake.[33]

In the Midwest, Rustin drew on a strong labor tradition to preach nonviolent action on behalf of equality, but he also strove everywhere to enlist black churches. He used music, drama, and art in these houses of worship, but also brought Christian parables, hymns, and spiritual-singing into secular settings. Rustin would preach nonviolent action before any audience, including one entirely white, as he did in San Francisco during several weekends in October and November. He had been summoned to California to conduct training in nonviolent techniques for leaders, and as Rustin biographer Daniel Levine puts it, "there was much talk, discussion, and soul-searching, in preparation for very small actions." Eleven "saints or fools," all white, registered for the workshop, where on the first weekend they heard about the philosophy of nonviolence and the importance of changing attitudes. The next weekend, joined by blacks, they put to work some of what they learned by taking some very modest action against local businesses. In one success, the symbolism of which is striking, a black man named Edward Booker said a haberdashery called Hastings had not permitted him to try on a suit because of his race. The head of the FOR's San Francisco chapter, in talking with the store's manager, was told the policy had been ended. Hastings would henceforth allow black men to try on suits. As this episode suggests, the immediate results of Randolph's grand conference and its embrace of nonviolent civil disobedience were scant. But it was part of a larger process that would produce real change.[34]

By then Rustin had met Davis Platt, a young white man who became the most important of his many lovers during this period. Everyone was attracted to Rusty, as he was widely known. "Physically, sexually, he was the most compelling man I have ever seen, before or after," said Gay Morenus Hammerman, who encountered him in 1947. "He was tall, broad-shouldered, broad-chested, bronze, with sculptured features, strongly marked cheekbones, and very lively speaking eyes . . . the uncategorized, unclassifiable essence of manhood." Rustin's homosexuality was well known to the FOR's leaders. He had many lovers during his peripatetic years at the organization—mostly men, but some women, for both routinely fell under his spell. "Bayard fooled around a lot," said Milton Kramer, one of his pacifist friends. "He wasn't a monogamous person. He responded to life where it was." According to Farmer, who defended his rival to Muste and Swomley on this score, mothers around the country wrote to the FOR "complaining that Bayard had led their sons astray." Muste agreed that Rustin's private life was just that, but was wary of his protégé harming the cause by bringing the FOR into disrepute at a time when homosexuality was scandalous and, in many places, illegal. He insisted that Rustin restrain himself when representing the FOR, and Bayard agreed to do so.[35]

If there were any doubts—or perhaps hopes—among the women of the FOR about Rustin's sexuality, the advent of Platt resolved them. They met in June of 1943 when Rustin spoke at a conference at Bryn Mawr College. He was thirty-one and Platt was nineteen, "as beautiful in his blond beauty as Bayard was in his dark," in the recollection of Margaret Rohrer, an FOR secretary who would eventually have the task of sorting through Rustin's correspondence with gay men he had met during his travels. "The moment our eyes met it was electric," Platt recalled. Rustin came to his room that night, and Platt, who had left high school early to live on his own in Philadelphia, now had an easy basis for choosing between Harvard, Yale, and Columbia: the latter was right near Rustin's office, so he enrolled there. Predisposed toward the pacifist worldview,

Platt was soon part of the FOR circle, appearing regularly at the office and socializing after hours. "I never had any sense at all that Bayard felt any shame or guilt about his homosexuality," he told D'Emilio years later. "And that was rare in those days."[36]

By the standards of the day the FOR crowd was open-minded. But Muste, who understood Rustin's tremendous potential as a proselytizer for nonviolence among black Americans, worried that Bayard's life as a gay man could derail their shared aspirations in an intolerant society, to say nothing of what was still quite a Christian peace establishment. He tried to get Platt to leave Rustin and vice versa, not because of any moral disapproval of same-sex relationships, at least according to what Platt could perceive, but because "if Bayard continued this way it could destroy him and hurt the movement."[37]

It came close to doing both, thanks in part to Muste himself, who would prove all too ready, like his namesake Abraham, to sacrifice his cherished son. But first Rustin decided to sacrifice himself. In registering for the draft along with millions of other men in October of 1940, he had submitted the necessary paperwork to become a conscientious objector. He was, after all, a Quaker. But he would still eventually face the choice of serving in the armed forces as a noncombatant or going to a CPS camp, and by the time he got the notice to report for a physical, his thinking had changed. A bit more than three years had gone by, and Rustin had spent them involved in pacifist resistance. Any military service was out of the question, and the CPS camps were no longer adorned with utopian illusions. Unpaid and unhappy, the most radical CPS pacifists were conducting work stoppages and slowdowns if not walking out altogether, in effect choosing prison as the more honorable alternative. Rustin had seen all this firsthand.

He also knew that war resisters were creating turmoil in the federal prison system, where protests, strikes, and disobedience of all kinds were aimed at segregated institutions built and operated to sequester conventional criminals, who wanted to do their time as painlessly as possible and secure the earliest release. The war resisters were entirely different, and didn't respond in the usual way to the usual incentives. They conceived of themselves as a movement, and they kept up with one another. Rustin was in touch with the COs fighting for integration at Danbury, for example. His intentional failure to report for the physical led to his indictment.

He waived a trial, pleaded guilty, and was sentenced to three years. That term may have been the result of his antiwar activities; Jervis Anderson reports that federal authorities were present when, in New York's Greenwich Village, he encouraged young men to step up and burn their draft cards. At the end of February 1944 Rustin found himself following in the footsteps of the many other resisters who were sent to the U.S. detention center in lower Manhattan, in this case until his incarceration in Ashland, Kentucky. If federal prisons were the centers of pacifist resistance, Rustin intended to be at the heart of the maelstrom.

CHAPTER 14

THE CONSERVATIVE ANARCHISTS

THE GROWING FERMENT AMONG pacifists behind bars and in the CPS camps was covered by a small but vigorous pacifist press, much of it associated with antiwar organizations. But Dorothy Day and Dwight Macdonald, the conflict's two greatest antiwar editors, were independent of such groups—and of a great deal more. Macdonald might have been describing both of them when he called himself a "conservative anarchist," and their shared opposition to the Second World War placed them on parallel paths. Mutual admirers, they later would take part in many of the same protests against war, nuclear weapons, and racial injustice during the turbulent decades to come. Friends of labor and enemies of government overreach, they also shared a distaste for popular culture and a passion for uncompromising works of art. Both were great editors who, during World War II, published the nation's most important antiwar journals.

The war years took a toll on Dorothy, who then and afterward never wavered from her pacifism or her simple yet extravagant idealism. Aided by his wife's money, Dwight had an easier time, and indeed his worst troubles were years into the future. The war, for him, was a way station in a lifelong ideological pilgrimage. To his critics it might look more like a drunken stagger, but, like Day, he consistently opposed all the forces of dehumanization he saw gathering power in American life, including big business, big government, and mass culture. Even later, when he was no longer a pacifist, he still mostly opposed war. Dorothy and Dwight couldn't be farther apart on matters of the spirit, but on this much they were in accord.

———

UNLIKE THE NEWLY ENERGIZED Fellowship of Reconciliation, which saw its coffers bulge and membership numbers balloon, the Catholic Worker organization had a much harder time during the war. Day had already antagonized readers with her newspaper's unyielding pacifism, and Catholic Workers in particular with her demand, in August 1940, that those who couldn't support her antiwar stand depart the movement. Her pacifism divided houses in Milwaukee, Pittsburgh, and elsewhere. The houses in Chicago, Los Angeles, and Seattle opposed her, while those in Boston, Cleveland, and Detroit remained on her side. The overcrowded and chaotic New York house, meanwhile, teetered for want of funds, staff, and leadership.

Even as Dorothy had to worry about keeping the New York operation afloat, she also worried about the changes war would bring to American society. War, it was plain, created lots of jobs and upward pressure on wages, but would the economy—and the country—become more or less permanently militarized? The growth of the state didn't just threaten civil liberties, but it undermined what Dorothy saw as the sacred responsibilities each of us has for ourselves and one another, responsibilities that could not and should not be outsourced to the state. She thought government handouts bred corruption, complacency, even a love of luxury. And she condemned the "tremendous failure of man's sense of responsibility for what he is doing. You relinquish it to the state." David O'Brien has noted how important freedom was to Dorothy, since, after all, voluntary poverty and Catholic faith and her lifelong vocation were choices she had made freely and that were in their own ways liberating. Day, like several of our key pacifists, could easily take a place in any respectable libertarian pantheon. Although she was an avowed anarchist, "she preferred the words libertarian, decentralist, and personalist."[1]

She was all of those things, but especially the last. Not much invoked lately, personalism is underrated as an influence on American cultural and political life. Leaving undisturbed for now its long and tangled philosophical roots, the version of interest here is a Christian creed that insisted on the sacredness and inviolable dignity of each person, whose fulfillment is necessarily communal and thus unattainable by means of radical individualism or state collectivism. Personalism offered a way of navigating between what appeared to be the corpses of capitalism and communism at a time when the former was discredited by the Depression and the latter by Soviet tyranny. In the face of mass production, mass movements, and the increasingly massive state, personalism insisted that each of us, driven by love, had the power to change the world simply by changing ourselves. It was mushy and idealistic, and its emphasis on feeling over knowing or reasoning probably contributed to the runaway empathy of today's Left. But the term captures an impulse that exercised considerable moral force, and traces of it will crop up again and again in this story.

Martin Luther King was influenced powerfully by personalism, especially in graduate school at Boston University, then a center of personalist thought. "This personal idealism remains today my basic philosophical position," he would write in 1958. King saw segregation as evil because it was depersonalizing, scarring both victim and perpetrator, and the communitarian black church, with its personal God who endowed *all* his children with dignity, was to be the engine of liberation. Idealistic young people imbibed personalism through the Catholic Worker movement. But there was personalism even among the godless, who elevated humankind in the absence of a deity. "The personalism of the 1960s," James J. Farrell writes, "was a combination of Catholic social thought, communitarian anarchism, radical pacifism, and humanistic psychology."[2]

The radicalism of Day, Dellinger, Macdonald, Rustin, Muste, and others of their ilk looks more cohesive seen as an imaginative personalist enterprise. To a great extent they were tilting at windmills back then. But they also promulgated an enduring critique of materialism, militarism, racism, poverty, and government repression without erasing the moral and spiritual responsibilities we owe ourselves and others. And of course they were pacifists. From the perspective of personalism, which relies on the inviolability of persons, nothing could be worse than war.

Dorothy's unusual demand that Catholic Workers everywhere adhere to pacifism particularly rankled John Cogley, editor of a Chicago edition of *The Catholic Worker*, who would one day become executive editor of *Commonweal* and later religion editor of *The New York Times*. Day's edict, he said, "nestled like a bomb" in every Catholic Worker house, and detractors throughout the anarchists' empire that was the Catholic Worker movement decried her seemingly dictatorial methods. The "bomb" in the organization detonated when Pearl Harbor was attacked.[3]

Many men in the Catholic Worker movement answered the call to arms, while others went off to the CPS camps or even prison. Without them to do the work and provide some semblance of security, the number of hospitality houses shrank from thirty-two in 1941 to just ten by 1945. While several factors were at work, including the wartime manpower shortage and the end of the Depression, which created jobs for many former clients, the rift over pacifism undoubtedly played a big role—as it did in the astonishing collapse of *The Catholic Worker*'s circulation. It peaked at 190,000 in 1938, an amazing number to achieve in just five years. But the regular run was 160,000, declining to 130,000 toward the end of 1939 and to 50,500 in May 1945. Day had hoped to bring Cogley around to her point of view, or at least prevent a full-blown rift, by inviting him on a Catholic retreat of the kind that for a while helped to sustain her, even if these events were a burden to the other Catholic Workers and especially to Dorothy's daughter, Tamar. Day later noted that this retreat, over the Labor Day weekend of 1940, "was the last great get-together the Catholic Workers had before we were separated by war."[4]

Cogley probably would have agreed about that much. "The C.W. is gone," he wrote in early 1942. "Now there are a group of pacifists defending their positions by calling attention to their good works and another group of die-hards like myself who leave gracelessly. Peace! Peace! And there is no peace. Give my love to all there who want it." Like other young men in the Catholic Worker movement, Cogley entered the armed forces. (Dorothy wrote to him and the others while they served, and prayed for them as well.) Years later, in *Commonweal*, he was no more mellow on the subject, calling *The Catholic Worker*'s pacifist rhetoric "simplistic, evasive, and even sentimental." But even he gave credit to Day's radical pacifism for having "made it impossible for non-pacifists like me to accept violence unthinkingly."[5]

Day tried to do the same for those who would accept violence against foreign civilians, or the trampling of civil liberties at home, or any number of other abuses that neither war nor tradition could excuse. These included the sin of discrimination, which *The Catholic Worker* frequently wrote about—for example in calling for Catholic colleges to open up to black students and in publishing the poetry of Claude McKay, an important figure in the Harlem Renaissance, who became Catholic in 1944. "The paper is for Negro and white alike," Day wrote in introducing the fledgling *Catholic Worker* to a Catholic journal called *Interracial Review*. "On the masthead there is a white worker on one side and a Negro worker on the other, and in addition to handling the problems of the Negro race, we want to have Negro writers for our paper."[6]

Like Rustin, Dorothy was not afraid ask how we could draft young Americans to fight for freedom overseas when our own country subjected blacks to a permanent state of second-class citizenship, or herded good Americans who happened to be of Japanese heritage into concentration camps with such haste that they had to sell everything at fire sale prices. Pick a couple of wartime issues of *The Catholic Worker* at random and you get a sense of the paper's commitment, courage, and spirituality, even if, on the subject of war, you also sense a persistent detachment from reality. Take the November 1942 edition, whose front page highlights the moral dilemmas of war by means of a large headline urging, "Feed the Axis." While insisting "we're not ostriches," the article presses the question, "Who shall feed the big dictators' starving masses?" There are three articles of various kinds about anti-Semitism, two about the travails of Catholic COs at a CPS camp in New Hampshire, and one entitled "Free India! Americans Plead, British Silent," noting that Gandhi and other leaders of the Indian National Congress were behind bars. Another describes the plight of Japanese Americans "taken from their houses and jobs without trial or hearing and put in detention camps" even though most are U.S. citizens. It quotes FDR himself as saying, in a different context, that discrimination "engenders the very distrust and disunity on which our enemies are counting to defeat us . . . We must not let that happen here. We must remember that we are defending liberty, decency, justice."

When the conscription of women was bruited in Washington, Day wasted no time in declaring that she would never comply, not even to register, regardless of any noncombatant role that might be in play—even if women were drafted only to grow food. After all, she asked, "Why are so many farmers being drafted for military service, why are Mennonites in conscientious objector camps when there is such need for farm workers, to raise food for the world?" Anyway, she asserted, women would not be conscripted for farm labor. "No, women are wanted to work in factories throughout the land to make the bombers, the torpedoes, the explosives, the tools of war."[7]

Throughout the five-column newspaper are Ade Bethune's muscular woodcuts, which reimagine religious figures as real people and grace each page with an earthy brand of Catholic spirituality. (When Bethune turned up shyly one day to donate some clothes, she encountered Dorothy as "a big tall woman who looked as though she had been carved with an ax.")[8] And of course there is Dorothy's long "Day After Day" column, which reports that, thanks to an invitation to speak in Peoria, whose bishop paid her expenses, "I visited Davenport, Chicago, Milwaukee, Detroit, Carthagena, Cleveland, Toledo, Pittsburgh, Harrisburg, Easton and now home to get out the November issue. We were sorry to have missed the October issue, but there was not a cent around." Macdonald would later praise Day's plainspoken column, rechristened "On Pilgrimage" in 1946, as "an odd composite of Pascal's *Pensées* and Eleanor Roosevelt's 'My Day.'"[9]

Dorothy crisscrossed the country obsessively in spite of the crowded misery of wartime travel. In the March 1942 *Catholic Worker* she described taking a bus all night from Tampa to Tallahassee, where she arrived at 5:00 a.m. in fourteen-degree weather. She had to wait three hours until her connection while "every bit of floor space was taken by people sitting on their suitcases," and the room was alternately stifling and freezing depending on the opening of the door and the labors of the potbelly stove. During a steamy train trip in July, her coach was jammed with men in uniform and women with babies, one of which she held on her lap, surrounded by others, until "I soon began to smell of baby."

Having driven a painful wedge into her own organization, if such a word can be used for the ramshackle and truncated thing that was the Catholic Worker movement at that point, Dorothy felt the need to visit the remaining hospitality houses. But she also felt the need to escape the endless burden of her days, to get away from the lice and lack of privacy, the roaches and ingratitude and raving, and even, occasionally, the violence of the squalid "hospitality" house in New York. Kichi Harada, a Japanese American woman living in the house, was frequently berated for the crimes of her ancestral homeland. A former middle-class artist who had difficulty adjusting to her noisy, dirty surroundings on Mott Street, Harada had been given the Catholic name of St. Francis of Assisi, and she decided, shortly before Pearl Harbor, to give the others a feast on his name day. She bought things at the Chinese stores, laid them out to prepare the meal and then went upstairs to get an apron. That's when another woman, evidently drunk, "threw everything Kichi had bought on the floor, scattering it with a wide drunken sweep to the four corners of the kitchen floor, cursing out the 'dirty Jap' and her evident intent to poison us all." Despite Dorothy's rage, she calmed the drunk, sent her off to bed, and picked up everything "so that Kichi never knew how close to disaster her feast had come."[10]

In addition to the disorder of Dorothy's life on Mott Street, there was her foreboding about her teenage daughter's attachment to a Catholic Worker farm resident who was thirteen years her senior, given to drink, and none too fond of work. A disastrous marriage and nine children would result. At one point Dorothy took a leave by spending a few months mostly in a Dominican convent on Long Island, near her daughter's school and her mother's home, but it was hardly devoted to uninterrupted silence and prayer, for family and other matters frequently interceded, and she ultimately cut it short, concluding "that such a hermit's life for a woman was impossible."[11]

Or consider the May 1943 issue. There are stories on how a negotiated peace might save the Jews, and about starvation in the Warsaw Ghetto. There was the news that the COs Taylor and Murphy had ended their hunger strike, and a report on blacks in the Civilian Public Service system that began by describing how a black Catholic CO was refused a glass of water after his white associates had been served. "In fourteen years I've never served a nigger, and I ain't goin' to start now!" said the man behind the counter. The black CO later encountered the same man in church. An editorial meanwhile asked, "How can we love God and kill our brother?" And in furtherance of Day's project of elaborating a Catholic pacifism, there was a closely argued rebuttal, sprawling across two full pages, of the contention that Catholicism offered no basis for refusing to fight. "Catholics Can

Be Conscientious Objectors" was written by Father John Hugo, a frequent contributor to the paper whose demanding retreats had strongly affected Day. In the November 1944 issue he wrote at length on "The Immorality of Conscription." *The Catholic Worker* reprinted both articles and distributed them widely.

Day's first retreat led by Hugo, a weeklong affair, was in July of 1941, and she was moved to describe it in the very next issue of *The Catholic Worker*: "We spent this period in complete silence, the day beginning at six and ending at ten. For spiritual reading at meals, we had the entire life of St. Francis by Jorgensen, and there were five conferences a day. These were so stimulating that not a moment dragged."[12]

She was so impressed that she got Hugo to lead the second annual Catholic Worker retreat at its farm in Easton, Pennsylvania. Her association with the priest continued for four decades, culminating in 1981 with a homily he delivered at a Marquette University memorial mass after her death. A powerful preacher and pacifist and dedicated religious reformer, Father Hugo was not beloved by all. But the passionate and ascetic form of Catholicism that he preached was just the thing to help reignite, in Dorothy at least, the idealism of the Catholic Worker movement's founding, now buried in her daily life under crisis and disorganization. Father Hugo, who might have sprung full-blown from the Catholic Worker imagination, derided the middle-class complacency that many Catholics seemed to confuse with piety, demanding instead self-denial and a deeper commitment to the Gospels.[13]

He was also an important figure in the short-lived Catholic Detacher movement, whose adherents sought to separate themselves from militarism and materialism, and who tended to write for, or at least read, *The Catholic Worker*. The writer J. F. Powers was a part of the movement and was influenced toward conscientious objection by Hugo's writings in *The Catholic Worker*, for which he would write as well. Unable to win CO status, Powers attended one of Hugo's retreats in 1943 just before going to prison. He served thirteen months at Sandstone and in 1963 won the National Book Award for *Morte d'Urban*.

"Detachment," writes Katharine Powers, one of the writer's children, "is possibly the most forgotten strain in the nearly forgotten American Catholic countercultural religious and social ferment of the mid-twentieth century."[14] The established church, none too keen on the idea that the army of bourgeois Catholics supporting the institution were doing religion all wrong, took a dim view. But during its evanescent heyday such a movement, based on renouncing worldly goods and desires, held strong appeal for pacifists like Powers and Robert Lowell. And the movement's spirit lived on, channeled through the pages of Dorothy Day's newspaper, in a powerful antiwar strain of Catholicism that flourished during the Vietnam era. Its apotheosis came in the person of one-time Detacher Senator Eugene McCarthy, a peace candidate who made a respectable run at the Democratic nomination for president in 1968.

Dorothy Day was the ultimate detacher, and like Father Hugo she had her detractors as well as her fans—but she could take pride in both. In 1934, Jacques Maritain visited and found "so much good will, such generosity, such courage!"[15] And in 1943 Dorothy gave the customary tour to a couple of Kennedys and some companions. They "came to visit us at Mott Street," she reported.

> Because it is more comfortable to argue over food and drink, we all went over to the Muni, not the municipal shelter but an all-night restaurant on Canal Street, where they serve cheese blintzes and chav and borscht. We had coffee and cheesecake and talked until the small hours. I remember only that we talked of war and peace and of man and the state. I do not remember which of the Kennedy boys were there, but those who do remember tell me it was our President, John Kennedy, and his older brother Joseph, who lost his life in the war.[16]

J. Edgar Hoover knew far more about Jack Kennedy and Dorothy Day than they would ever know about each other. The future president had been under FBI surveillance for a while because of his love affair with a Danish beauty queen, journalist, and suspected spy for Germany. Dorothy meanwhile was a subject of never-ending interest to the bureau, which opened a file on her in December of 1940. The following April, Hoover had written that she should be considered for "custodial detention in the event of a national emergency." In the fall, agents interviewed the chancellor of the New York archdiocese—Monsignor James McIntyre, who for Dorothy embodied the church's authority, functioned as intermediary and shock absorber, and over the years became a sort of friend. McIntyre told the agents that there had been complaints about Day's newspaper, of course, but he insisted that she was neither communist nor threat to national security. [17]

That wasn't the end of it. In April of 1943, during a speaking engagement at Harvard, Day argued for pacifism and the rights of conscience against conscription. She also told the students she'd had letters from servicemen who regretted not listening to her before entering the armed forces. An FBI informant in the audience told the Bureau all about it and vowed to try and find out who had written those letters. He probably had little success, just like all the others. During the war, agents interviewed Catholic clergy about Dorothy all over the country and asked the Justice Department if the nation's sedition laws would allow her prosecution. But nobody ever came up with any evidence beyond what could be gleaned by reading her newspaper, and Hoover ultimately decided to leave her off the bureau's list of people to be immediately interned, instead classifying her among those only "somewhat dangerous."[18]

The FBI was interested in Dwight Macdonald, too, opening a file on him in 1942 that ultimately grew to more than seven hundred pages by the early 1970s. The bureau's interest would wax and wane depending on his activities and whether he wrote or commissioned anything critical of the publicity-conscious police agency. They sometimes called him McDonald or even McCarthy, and they thought he was a former communist even though he never joined the Party and heartily loathed it for embodying everything he stood against. (The FBI seemed to lack any sort of guide to the complicated taxonomy of leftists in that period.) For a while the agency snooped into Dwight's mail, copying some incoming letters for the file, and investigated his assistant. It's as if J. Edgar Hoover and his myrmidons were determined to prove that Macdonald's instinctive anarchism and chronic suspicion of state power were all too well founded. The irony is that, in spite of his knee-jerk protestations, Dwight Macdonald was a very good American indeed.

"From the 1940s to the early 1970s," John Rodden writes, "Macdonald was the best-known political and cultural critic to the general American public. His finest work makes him a worthy descendant of H.L. Mencken and Edmund Wilson." To his friend Lukacs he was not just an American, but "an American in the individualist tradition." Czesław Miłosz had something similar in mind when he called Macdonald, whom he regarded as a plausible successor to Thoreau, Whitman, and Melville, "a specific American type—the completely free man, capable of making decisions at all times about all things strictly according to his personal moral judgement." Edward Mendelson, rebuking those who would remember Macdonald only for "his extravagant style and his Quixotic enthusiasms," insisted on the importance of Dwight's belief in the "permanent truths of justice and injustice" and his sense that "aesthetics were inseparable from morality. People mistook him for a great entertainer rather than the most entertaining of the great prophets."[19]

Macdonald would appear to have had conversion experiences as easily as other people sneeze, although perhaps not quite as suddenly (even admirers have noted over the years that the catalog of his political stances would resemble the Kama Sutra in its variety and contortions). The journal *politics* would accordingly reflect its editor's evolution away from Marxism (a kind of religion, surely) toward a broader anarcho-pacifism that encompassed sexual liberation, civil liberties, civil rights, communal living, and other causes embraced by the post-Marxist Left. Meanwhile, Macdonald was powerfully gripped by the absolutists' idealistic opposition to war and determination not to choose the lesser of evils. He also had in common with the resisters a serious awareness of colonialism and racial injustice. This awareness on the antiwar left fueled the convenient fiction that America and its allies were no better than their enemies and perhaps just as responsible for the war, a form of narcissism that Macdonald indulged almost pathologically (and at a safe remove from the enemy). "Europe has its Hitlers," he wrote in an especially outrageous pronouncement, "but we have our Rotarians."[20]

Dwight wasn't always a pacifist, even if he was, for most of his life, opposed to war. He was propelled leftward as a young man by the multitalented Vassar graduate and debutante Nancy Gardiner Rodman, who came to their marriage equipped with the twin assets of a social conscience and a trust fund. She met the tall, witty journalist with the New York accent at the apartment of her brother, Selden, the energetic author and poet who coedited the socialist magazine *Common Sense*, and

Macdonald came to depend on her in a variety of important ways over the course of their marriage. It was Nancy who introduced him to Marx; his opposition to World War II, when war erupted, was largely Marxist and anti-imperialist, though it also depended on the proposition that "if we go in, we will go totalitarian ourselves." In the July 1941 issue of *Partisan Review*, where he was still struggling to manifest his opposition to a conflict that did not yet formally involve the United States, Dwight and Clement Greenberg published a puerile piece called "10 Propositions on the War." Number three was "The issue—not war but revolution." Number ten elaborates: "To win the war against fascism, we must work for the replacement of the present governments in England and the United States by workingclass [*sic*] governments committed to a program of democratic socialism. All support of whatever kind must be withheld from Churchill and Roosevelt."

Dwight also argued furiously against "lesser evil" logic, insisting, like many out-and-out pacifists at the time, that means must accord with ends, and the method of warfare couldn't produce a positive outcome. For an atheist like Macdonald to sustain the whole business without re-sort to religious faith also required him to find again and again that the Allies were, if not as culpable as their enemies, then close enough to jus-tify opposing the war.

Years later he as much as admitted he'd been wrong about all that. "I still don't think it was necessary," he insisted in a 1980 interview when he was pressed on the war. "I now think it was desirable because it shortened the sufferings of millions of people. If Hitler had won, even temporarily, it would have been a horrible thing. So, I should have been in favor of the allied democracy side of the war."[21]

He wasn't, except to the extent that he exemplified the freedoms his countrymen were fighting for—and was a rare, unusually articulate critic demanding that they live up to their ideals. "Isolation is provincial inanity," proposition number four says in the essay he wrote with Greenberg. But right up until Pearl Harbor, Macdonald's resistance to the war had much in common with the prudential anti-interventionism of the Old Right, whose traditionalism and abhorrence of government power were congruent with Macdonald's most enduring impulses.

On top of everything else, the fighting in Europe was an assault on the high culture he cherished. "One of the many things I cannot get accustomed to in this war," he wrote in a 1944 editorial, "is the fact that the most ancient, famous and beautiful buildings of Europe may be blasted to bits in a few hours at any time. Rome, Paris, Assisi, Florence, Ravenna, Carcassonne, Venice, Beauvais—who knows when they will join Warsaw, Bath, Coventry, Nuremberg, Frankfurt, Kiev, Cologne, Palermo, Naples, Rotterdam, Cracow, Tsarskoe Selo, London, and Berlin? It is like living in a house with a maniac who may rip up the pictures, burn the books, slash up the rugs and furniture at any moment."[22]

But what, exactly, was the alternative? Macdonald's politics, always ardently advocated, were an ever-evolving mess, but running underneath it all was a baseline of personalist idealism that connected him to Day, Muste, Rustin, King, and others he found sympatico, and that helps us see coherence in what might otherwise appear just a uniquely Dwight-ish tangle of moralism, anarchism, and aestheticism. Macdonald's central concern was the dehumanization he saw as the product of modern mass society and the technologies that enabled it. Armed force, immensely powerful governments, religious dogma, mass media, kitsch in the arts—all conspired to erase individuality and turn people into things, the worst possible crime to this radical individualist and compulsive dissident. This is the lens that enables us to make sense of his animosity to both nuclear weapons and abstract art, and you can see as well that while his soon-to-be-born little magazine would have exquisitely sensitive antennae for signals from the world of tomorrow, Dwight was nonetheless hostile to modernity and writing in a tradition of American dissent going back to Thoreau. Certainly Dwight's anti-interventionism, which proved far more durable than his Marxism, is easily traced all the way back to the earliest days of the republic. It's not for nothing that Michael Wreszin's biography of Macdonald was entitled, *A Rebel in Defense of Tradition.*

Partisan Review may have been America's biggest little magazine in all the ways that mattered, but it still wasn't big enough to hold the compulsively provocative Macdonald and his cautious editorial partners. So during the war he started planning a journal of his own. In October of 1943, having consulted the lawyer and constitutional scholar Milton Konvitz (who was later Ruth Bader Ginsburg's teacher and longtime correspondent),

Dwight learned that what he'd already written against the war for *Partisan Review* was "not less 'seditious' than the statements in the court record" of the government's successful 1941 prosecution of Trotskyists under the Smith Act. Despite the FBI's recent interest and the various provocations he and his forthcoming journal were about to commit, Washington sensibly stood aside.[23]

It was in 1944 that Macdonald launched the short-lived publication he called, at the suggestion of the radical sociologist C. Wright Mills, *politics*, always lowercased, whose influence would extend far beyond the five thousand subscribers it managed to accumulate at its peak. Under the headline "Why *politics*?" in the first issue, Dwight laid out the magazine's aims, which included teasing larger trends from the day-to-day noise of the news, bringing to the fore new, younger writers from a variety of disciplines, considering artistic works in various mediums "as social and historical phenomena," and, not least, "to create a center of consciousness on the Left, welcoming all varieties of radical thought."

One of these was pacifism. In the March 1944 issue, Dwight ran a potently condensed piece by the war resister Milton Mayer, reprinted from *The Progressive*, entitled, "How to Win the War," which it proposes to do by dropping leaflets on the Germans telling them to emancipate themselves from the tyranny under which they live "and join us in the brotherhood of man." In a prefatory comment, Macdonald, noting that "Mayer has been viciously smeared by Walter Winchell, "PM" and similar guardians of public morality," says he nonetheless doesn't think becoming a CO is the right choice because "it seems to me one can more effectively fight for one's ideas if one does not isolate one's self from one's fellow-men, and that the Army is a better place to learn, and teach, than either a C.O. camp or a jail."

Characteristically for *politics*, the July issue carried a well-argued and informative response by a conscientious objector named Don Calhoun, who argues that COs have hardly retreated into some cloister. "There is probably no situation in which a drafted man can place him self which brings him into closer identification with the elemental social struggle than in a prison," he writes. Nor are the war resisters indulging in mere moral vanity: "The potentiality present in conscientious objection is demonstrated by the utterly disproportionate nuisance value of our handful of C.O.'s . . . Today the conscientious objector, and the conscientious objector alone, stands out as the possible nucleus for the only movement which can shatter the confidence of the state in its ability to effectively make war *if and when it wishes.*"

Despite his confident ferocity in argument, Macdonald was always open to persuasion, not only changing his mind frequently but annotating his own work and even writing critically about it in letters to the editor under an assumed name—what we might today call sock puppetry. Long before social media, he meant it when he said that he wanted his journal to be a place to thrash things out. Calhoun's cogent missive, which cited a variety of CO protests in places like Danbury and Lewisburg and the reforms that resulted, struck a chord with an editor who was nothing if not open-minded. "Don Calhoun," Macdonald began his rejoinder in the same issue, "has made out a much stronger case for Conscientious Objection as a political anti-war tactic than I should have imagined possible."

Dwight doubts conscientious objection can influence large numbers of people or even that it bestows moral superiority if the CO is doing "work of national importance," because doing that work in itself contributes to the war effort if only by freeing up men who would otherwise have to per-form it. "The C.O. *does* have a moral advantage, however," Dwight says, "over the man who submits to being drafted: that of refusing to cooperate in the war effort to the extent the State commands him to—even though, in an ultimate sense, he can escape cooperation only by taking to the hills. At least he puts limits on his obedience, at least he confronts the State power with his own conditions, at least he makes an overt gesture of opposition to the war . . . His day-to-day actions and his long-range convictions, if they do not wholly coincide, are at least on speaking terms."

Calhoun was back in the October 1944 issue, responding to Macdonald's response, their exchange spirited but never spiteful and Macdonald, at least as judged by the journal he edited, palpably evolving toward the CO posi-tion. In the editions to come, the issue would be reported on, discussed, and debated time and again as Dwight began to see pacifism not as futile and self-deluding resistance but as the potential basis for many of the changes he was seeking.

There was a great deal more than pacifism to *politics*. In an essay in the very first issue, Macdonald laid out a distinction between high culture and popular culture that would become an obsession in his later years. And the publication's sometimes ponderous essays were leavened by briefer articles featuring the editor's famous slashing wit. Here's the entirety of a review laying waste to the latest volume by the prolific Mortimer Adler, entitled *How to Think About War and Peace*: "No one who wants to understand the meaning of this war, and the problems that will confront us afterwards, can afford to read this little book. It is true that, as Clifton P. Fadiman writes in his introduction, the book is by no means easy reading. But for all its dull writing, *How to Think about War and Peace* is superficial. Mr. Adler once wrote a book called *How to Read a Book*. He should now read one called *How to Write a Book*."[24]

But of greater interest here is the role of *politics* as a bridge from Old Left to New, and from pacifism to nonviolent protest. In the pages of Macdonald's journal we can see the death throes of Marxism as an animating force on the American left. Diehards sometimes complained about this, but Dwight and his little magazine were doing some of the hard work that needed to be done to get past the hulking corpse of that particular god in order to find a path forward. This occurred perhaps most explicitly in Macdonald's influential pair of "Root Is Man" essays, which radicals to come would find particularly resonant. Theodore Roszak contended that "it is a humanist Socialist text like Dwight Macdonald's eloquent *The Root Is Man* that one discerns behind a document like *The Port Huron Statement*," the seminal manifesto hammered out by members of Students for a Democratic Society in 1962. Staughton Lynd and Todd Gitlin, two leading Movement figures, made sense of what was going on in the sixties in part by rereading *politics*.[25] The late journalist and wag Nicholas von Hoffman, three quarters of a century afterward, remembered his excitement at receiving each issue when he was young. (He would later work as a community organizer for Saul Alinsky and eventually as a mordant columnist for *The Washington Post*.) Noam Chomsky began his famous 1967 essay "The Responsibility of Intellectuals" by recalling a similarly titled piece by Macdonald that he'd first read in *politics* while an undergraduate. The young Chomsky was influenced by the journal toward anarchism and against war, and two decades later found that Macdonald's "The Responsibility of Peoples" still held up.

Macdonald's journal was so forward-looking that, in retrospect, it seems to feature headlines from the future. With uncanny prescience it focused on the areas that would be of foremost concern in the decades ahead, and not just to radicals. These included American militarism and the unholy alliance between big business and the war-state; racial discrimination at home and imperialism abroad; the power of bigness in any of its forms; the alienation of individuals in the face of technology, bureaucracy, and mass society; and the role of women, gays, and others who deserved a better shake from society. Contributors who had an enduring impact included George Orwell, Daniel Bell, Simone Weil, Irving Kristol, C. Wright Mills, Marshall McLuhan, Mary McCarthy, Paul Goodman, Clement Greenberg, David Bazelon, Roy Wilkins, Nicola Chiaromonte, Bruno Bettelheim, Nathan Glazer, Meyer Schapiro, John Berryman, Harvey Swados, Simone de Beauvoir, Albert Camus, Jean-Paul Sartre, Georges Bataille, Lionel Abel, Albert Shanker, and A. J. Muste.

Further enduring influence was channeled through Irving Howe, Macdonald's fifteen-dollar-a-week editorial assistant at the magazine. Dwight gave him the pen name Theodore Dryden, a "ferret breeder in Staten Island," and helped loosen up his style. But Howe also gained insights that influenced his vision for what would become *Dissent*, a magazine he cofounded that was in some sense a *politics* successor in subject matter and influence. "Howe's work on *politics* certainly shaped his thinking about *Dissent*," recalled his former coeditor there, Mitchell Cohen, "especially the kind of writing he wanted."

Years later, intellectuals like Hannah Arendt (another former boss of Howe's, and a close friend of Dwight's in those days) would recall *politics* wistfully even as they marveled at its continuing relevance long after it closed. In her introduction to a 1968 reprint edition of *politics*, Arendt wrote that rereading all forty-two issues for the task banished any feelings of nostalgia, "for the simple reason that so many of its articles, comments, and factual reports read as though they were written today or yesterday or yesteryear, except that the concerns and perplexities of a little magazine with a peak circulation of not much more than 5,000 have become the daily bread of newspapers and periodicals with mass circulation."[26]

That's probably because the magazine so thoroughly reflected its idiosyncratic editor—which is to say that it was a bit of a mess. Dwight was a brilliant critic and nothing if not open-minded. But in the early years, at least, the problems he diagnosed always seemed to come down to class exploitation, much the way some chiropractors embrace the motto, "One disease, one cure." *Politics* was a journal of almost irresistible vitality and wit, yet the editor's astringent blend of overreach and pessimism were rarely absent from an edition. These were most clearly manifest in the wearying obsession with finding some plausible form of collectivism to succeed the hideous failures of those which had come before, so that in the words of Richard King, "Marxism hung over the journal like the ghost of a deceased and distant but influential relative whose effect lingered on after death." Exhausted utopianism dovetailed nicely with a disdain for all things American, including not just American intellectuals but the average middle-class people he seemed to regard as a species of sheep. Forget about organized labor (racist sellouts all too eager to support capitalism and war). Dwight didn't castigate only his own countrymen (by saying, for example, that "we have made ourselves the accomplice of the Maidenek butchers by refusing to admit more than a tiny trickle of the Jews of Europe"). He also tarred the Russians for their betrayal of the Polish resistance, to cite a single example, and lots of other people for lots of other things as well. Most of all, Dwight liked an argument, and *politics* was full of them. Readers today who follow his friendly advice for enjoying *The Catholic Worker* ("judicious skipping is necessary") will find that *politics* was more consistently compelling, and as social criticism it was invaluable.

We've already noted the magazine's tireless prosecution of Jim Crow. Discrimination in the armed forces was a particular target, allowing the editor to nick the twin birds of militarism and race with a single sarcastic stone. Broadly speaking, racial prejudice was one of the magazine's main preoccupations. When Myrdal's *An American Dilemma* was published, it was given a long and perceptive review by George S. Schuyler, the conservative black journalist whose satirical novel *Black No More* was first published in 1931 and remains in print.

Race and gender would someday preoccupy the American Left, but that was years away. Meanwhile, at a time when male radicals paid little attention to the subordinate role of women, Macdonald took notice. In a penetrating attack on "such synthetic folk-heroes as Superman, Judge Hardy, Sherlock Holmes, Tarzan and the Lone Ranger," all of them designed to "unite power with morals in a most attractive way," he found it telling "that they are all men. When the central figure of a modern folk saga is a woman, she is likely to be not a *heroine* but rather a *victim* . . . The superficiality of the modern 'emancipation' of women appears when we descend into these profound cultural depths. When heroines are admired, not sympathized with, then we can talk of 'emancipation.'" He also published an essay by Ethel Goldwater arguing that women needed work as well as a family, and that men would have to take on their fair share of housework and family responsibilities. A subsequent discussion of the article in the pages of *politics* included a long and radical contribution by Marshall McLuhan that blithely suggested polygamy as a potentially sensible alternative to monogamy.

In August 1944 Dwight ran a furious essay entitled "The Homosexual in Society," by the anarchist poet Robert Duncan. It was a courageous act for both men. Macdonald accepted the article with characteristic frankness: "You've written a really thoughtful and sincere piece here, and very well expressed (though your style is more rococo than my personal taste)." The essay served as Duncan's coming out, as a result of which a poem of his previously accepted for the *Kenyon Review* was rejected by its editor, John Crowe Ransom. Duncan had been dishonorably discharged from the U.S. Army in 1941 after his friend Anaïs Nin had urged him to be forthright about his sexuality, which would serve the additional purpose of freeing him from service in a coming war he opposed. "I say accept the homosexuality," she wrote, "live it proudly, declare it." He did so, returning to New York after his discharge to find that his former lover, the painter Robert De Niro, future father of the actor, had taken up with a woman.[27]

There were other signs in *politics* of the tsunami of personal and sexual liberation ahead, including reviews and critical essays on Wilhelm Reich, Erich Fromm, and Sigmund Freud, all of which were harbingers of a shift in the orientation of American radicalism away from economic issues and toward cultural ones. Another harbinger: Macdonald's editorial view that, as E. F. Schumacher would someday put it, "small is beautiful." *politics* seemed to foresee a nation tyrannized by bureaucracy and technology, anesthetized by affluence, and lobotomized by kitsch, a social critique that would be offered in years to come from both the left and the right. From today's perspective "The Root Is Man" in particular seems pregnant with the hopeful fetus of the sixties, somehow conceived in the despair of what has come before. Published in April 1946, it was written in the disillusioning wake of the Depression, the loss of faith in Marxism (or its Soviet incarnation), the horrors of Nazism and the global war, and the betrayal of the Allied bombing of civilians—most egregiously, in the use of atomic weapons against Japan.

In the essay, Macdonald says we might as well "reduce political action to a modest, unpretentious, personal level" and "begin at the bottom again, with small groups of individuals in various countries, grouped around certain principles and feelings they have in common." These would be something like families living in psychological, if not physical, proximity. They would advance pacifism ("a sine-qua-non of any Radical movement"), oppose coercion "by the State or by a revolutionary party," and they will prioritize today over tomorrow. "All ideologies which require the sacrifice of the present in favor of the future will be looked on with suspicion. People should be happy and should satisfy their spontaneous needs here and now. If people don't enjoy what they are doing, they shouldn't do it."

Finally, they will abandon thinking in class terms and "free themselves from the Marxian fetishism of the masses, preferring to be able to speak modest meaningful truths to a small audience rather than grandiose empty formulae to a big one. This also means, for the moment, turning to the intelligentsia as one's main supporters, collaborators and audience." And against the forces of technological "progress" and top-down organization, which seem bound to sweep all before them, Macdonald urges a counter-revolution of *feeling*: "We must emphasize the emotions, the imagination, the moral feelings, the primacy of the individual human being, must restore the balance that has been broken by the hypertrophy of science in the last two centuries." With its emphasis on what Maurice Isserman has called "expressive individualism," the privileging of today over tomorrow, the priority given to feeling oddly coupled with a grudging dependence on the intelligentsia, Dwight's essay is practically a roadmap for the evolution of the Left in the decades ahead.

CHAPTER 15

DÉJÀ VU FOR DELLINGER

WHEN DAVID DELLINGER LANDED back in prison in the summer of 1943, he was determined to join in the resistance percolating behind bars—resistance to segregation, censorship, and other manifestations of prison tyranny that seemed to replicate, in microcosm, the noxious tyrannies which pacifists observed in the larger society. It was a resistance Dellinger had to a great extent initiated, for he had led the Union Eight in refusing to register for the draft and had set the tone for their conduct during their stay at Danbury. The fire they ignited there, smoldering in the early months of the war, was about to become a conflagration.

Dellinger was sent this time to the federal prison at Lewisburg, Pennsylvania. Sentenced to two years, he'd been assigned by a sympathetic judge to the minimum-security farm camp operating outside the walls of the much harsher penitentiary. It was a chance to pass the time working among the crops and the dairy cows. But it was beyond him to content himself with the outdoorsy berth he'd been gifted, and he was odd man out among the Jehovah's Witnesses who were his coworkers on the farm. Soon after his arrival he'd learned of a strike inside the prison by about a dozen pacifists trying to end segregation there. So he went on strike himself, refusing to perform his assigned farm labors, and the government obligingly sent this experienced and determined radical inside. It was like the decision by the leading sage of Chelm, in Yiddish folklore a village of fools, to punish a wayward carp by drowning it.[1]

In the two years since his release from Danbury, where he had served his first term in prison, Dellinger had created a productive life for himself and a useful community institution in Newark. He, Dallas, and Benedict had revived their ashram and expanded its activities, which included bible study, lectures, dances, and food and clothing for the neighborhood poor. Betty helped start a hot lunch program at a local school. Commune residents demonstrated against racial discrimination by picketing segregated restaurants and the like in Newark, much as some of their Union Eight colleagues were doing in the Midwest, and gave talks at churches and civic groups in Newark and its suburbs. He and the others worked to avert violence between rival local gangs, whose members in those days were armed with knives. And he found time to run boys' clubs and coach baseball, football, and basketball teams.

Dellinger took neighborhood kids into Manhattan (in most cases for their first visit), where he connected with other pacifists including Dorothy Day and Jay Holmes Smith, whose Harlem ashram was something of a model for the Newark version. There was a flow of activists in the other direction as well; many came out to visit the New Jersey ashram, which despite its name was still quite Christian, with regular prayers and a kind of chapel, according to Dallas. Sunday services at Jube Memorial brought people from miles around. "The spiritual atmosphere was quite intense," writes Leilah Danielson, who interviewed some former ashram residents. "In addition to daily prayers and meditation, every Wednesday the Colony held a retreat during which members fasted."[2]

Betty and Dave also took Newark children to the country, where some of them saw their first cow. The Newark radicals eventually got hold of a small farm where Dellinger and friends installed a pacifist organic farmer they had served time with at Danbury. (Dave's parents kicked in some money, Benedict reports.) A couple of cows and two dozen chickens produced food for the ashram, and a vegetable garden yielded produce for their table as well as for sale at the co-op store they ran. The place was open to ashram-area residents for outings and vacations too.[3]

Boyish William P. Roberts Jr. was playing the piano there one evening in August of 1942 in what proved the culmination of a two-month idyll.

The son of Episcopalian missionaries to China, he had declared his intention not to register in a long letter to Attorney General Francis Biddle just two months earlier. To make the most of his remaining freedom, he then left Yale for the Newark ashram. "I had spent such a grand day," he wrote to his mother from jail.

> I helped clean up the house in Newark in the early morning, then hitch-hiked out to the farm. We spent most of the afternoon digging up potatoes way up in the fields. Then Dorothy and I stayed in the field in the tall grass and talked for a couple of beautiful hours, looking up to the white clouds and out to the hills. Then supper altogether, and after the dishes I went in to play the piano that is there—all out of tune and broken. I was playing when I was told the FBI was outside, wanting to see me. It seems so natural for this to happen—so much a part of the whole picture—that I went out to greet them with no resentment or worry in my heart. The time had come, that was all.[4]

Roberts's mother "was fully sympathetic and supportive," he wrote years later, "even though her husband, my father, was at the same time a prisoner of the Japanese in a Shanghai internment camp."[5]

Dellinger meanwhile continued to speak out against the war, riding the rails and hitchhiking as needed to reach whoever would listen. In delivering an antiwar speech to a Christian student conference in Ohio over the Christmas break of 1941–42, he had met lively, twenty-one-year-old Elizabeth Peterson, a minister's daughter known as Betty, whom he would quickly marry. Both were radical Christians with a demonstrated commitment to activism. And despite two brothers in the armed forces, Betty was a pacifist. "David was my ideal," she recalled years later. "He believed in voluntary poverty, which was something I was coming to after working in a migrant camp one summer. And he believed in communal living, which I felt was closer to the original idea of Christian living."[6]

She could not possibly have known what she was in for, yet despite years of trials their marriage would endure. It did so despite the burdens of five children, the lack of money, the notoriety, David's protracted absences, and infidelities by both parties. It endured even though, as Betty later told an interviewer, "I was not active in David's causes."[7] It even survived a period of separation late in life, when decades of accumulated grievances and rising feminist consciousness drove her to explore living apart. David, too, came to feminism as time went by, but in 1941 it wasn't a paramount concern. He was, with his fellow male radicals, the creature of an era when only a quarter of women worked outside the home, and ideas about gender roles were different.

It's not clear that Betty had any more feminist consciousness in those days than he did. She could not know the fullness of the future when she got married, and she knew relatively little about her fiancé when they were wed. She likely knew nothing of his bisexuality and was even ignorant of his family background: "He hid a lot from me before we got married. I didn't know he'd gone to Yale. I didn't know his family was very well off. I was mending his pants the day before we got married because there was a hole in the knee."[8]

But she knew he was a draft resister, and that his continued resistance meant another arrest was likely. He'd already told her how, hitchhiking west for his own wedding in Seattle, the police had arrested him in the Sierra Nevada mountains because they thought he had helped steal the car he was riding in. He was innocent, of course, but, worried about his lack of a draft card, decided to risk escaping through the window, which involved leaping onto a nearby fire escape. Still athletic, he managed to get away. Once married, he and Betty took a bus to Salt Lake City (in order to disguise their real transportation plans from her parents) and then hitchhiked the rest of the way across the country, including a stop in Chicago to visit Union Eight chums. They covered the last few miles on foot, suitcases in hand, arriving at the ashram exhausted. Betty had never been east of Detroit, never stayed in a hotel or motel, never hitchhiked. Years later she called the journey "traumatic."[9]

As a newlywed, she now had the communal living she would later say she had wished for. "It was quite a cultural shock," she said.[10] There was little privacy, and a bunch of people with whom to work out household chores such as cooking, cleaning, and maintaining the building, not to mention all the other exigencies of group living. But there was also teamwork on the ashram's outreach programs and cooperative store, among many other ventures. Dave for a while worked the graveyard shift five

nights a week at a big commercial bakery to bring in money. Dallas and
Benedict worked there, too (but the latter soon moved on to a similar
project in Detroit). Dellinger insisted on being paid in cash so as not to
contribute to the war effort through his taxes, a policy he would follow
for the rest of his working life.[11]

Life at the ashram wasn't easy for women, especially for Betty. "She
was the most fragile of the group," Henry Harvey, who lived at the ashram
at the time, observed in a 1988 interview. Harvey was a pacifist and Union
Theological alumnus whose mother was first cousin to the secretary of war,
Henry Stimson. Evidently young Harvey came from money; he and fellow
Union student Francis Hall had put up $1,000 each to buy the house, ac-
cording to Willa Winter. Told that Betty was still married to Dellinger after all those years, the elderly Harvey said with a laugh: "She's a lot tougher
than I thought."[12]

Betty's focus was homemaking, she would recall, and there was plenty
of it to do. Draft resisters slept on floors and sofas, antiwar meetings were
held, and supporters including Dorothy Day came out from the city. "We
were deluged with visitors," Dellinger writes, many of them staying for
days or weeks. Among residents, there was continual turnover. The ashram
was a well-known center for draft resisters and their supporters, and as the
war progressed the FBI hauled away one resister after another. Virtually all
the men present—and of course their loved ones—lived under the cloud
of future arrest. "Every man there was either on his way from prison or
on his way to prison," Betty recalled. "Every woman there was related to
one of these men and had that sense of never knowing when it was going
to happen . . . There was quite a bit of anxiety." Sutherland was arrested
at the ashram in July of 1942. Benedict was picked up in Detroit in 1943
and would serve a second, personally quite consequential prison term at
Danbury. Dallas, too, would be back in custody before long. "The FBI was
always floating around," he recalled years later. "It got so we could spot
them anywhere."[13]

Dave and Betty knew his time was coming, but he didn't lay low or
move far away. On the contrary. In the first few months of 1942, by which
time his father was chairman of the Boston United War Fund, Dellinger
had joined the War Resisters League in a move emblematic of his increasingly secular radicalism. He would be joined there by many of his fellow

war resisters, who were eventually to take over the place. Meanwhile he launched his own miniature antiwar organization, the People's Peace Now Committee, which conducted small public protests against the war that all parties were prosecuting with such terrible ferocity around the world. Prospects for peace seemed to grow worse in January of 1943, when FDR was flown secretly to a conference with Winston Churchill in Casablanca. After the meetings, Roosevelt made public a notion previously discussed among the Allies privately: that they would require from the Axis powers "unconditional surrender" in order to end the war. The news dismayed pacifists, who hoped that a negotiated end to the fighting might save countless lives. The People's Peace Now campaign held small protests in Newark and outside the Capitol in Washington. "Month after month the peoples of Europe and Asia are being shattered by mass bombing raids, deliberate starvation and total war," said a leaflet from Dellinger's group. In a poke to the eye of Selective Service authorities, the leaflet added: "Peaceful Americans have been conscripted to help commit these acts of destruction."[14]

On April 6, 1943, the twenty-sixth anniversary of U.S. entry into the previous world war, Betty and David attended a Peace Now protest in Washington, outside the Capitol, where they distributed leaflets saying that "Truth and Brotherhood will not be helped by Unconditional Surrender." The flyers predicted Hitler's overthrow by the German people and called for an end to anti-Semitism, Jim Crow, and colonial exploitation. (Police confiscated leaflets and signs but made no arrests.) Dellinger attended other antiwar events as well, each time putting himself further at risk. He and Betty, knowing what was ahead, decided quite deliberately to have a baby. Betty's first pregnancy ended in a miscarriage, but she managed to conceive again.

The whole time, her husband had been engaged in a tussle with his local draft board, which conscripted him just a month after his release from prison on the basis of the registration form completed on his behalf—and against his will—by Danbury's warden. After ignoring a series of official notices, Dellinger finally wrote back explaining his religious objections to war and pointing out that he'd already served a prison term for his stance. In 1942, his Newark draft board responded with a furious condemnation of conscientious objectors:

Citizenship should be taken from them regardless of their birthplace and, as soon as it is practicable, all such should be removed from the soil they refuse to defend . . . Cowards, slackers, and hypocrites, who hide behind so-called conscientious scruples, must be denied membership in a free society. We owe it to our fighting men.[15]

A.J. Muste rose to Dellinger's defense, writing to Hershey and Biddle to suggest the removal of the board members, whose words he feared could incite violence against COs, and who appeared either ignorant of the law or eager to flout it. "Unfortunately," Muste added, "a good many members of local boards throughout the country have expressed similar opinions regarding conscientious objectors." The difference is that those other unlucky COs didn't have organized pacifism, what little there was of it, in their corner. Dellinger's corner was not an easy one to inhabit, as Muste would soon learn.[16]

Later that summer the Dellingers risked arrest again at another antiwar event, attended by about thirty people, in downtown Newark, where they encountered no interference. But when they returned the next day for another protest, Dellinger reports, police confiscated their materials. And when they returned home to 37 Wright Street, federal agents waiting there arrested him, probably on July 7, 1943. In custody, he refused to pay bail—another lifelong practice, albeit with exceptions. "I usually refuse because I believe the amount of money that a person can command should not determine whether or not he or she stays in jail," he wrote later, describing defendants who can't make bail as "hostages" held "for a ransom that neither they nor their families or friends are able to pay." Betty, pregnant, went to see the judge, explained her husband's point of view, and Dave was soon free on his own recognizance. She picked him up in "a flamboyant new sports car" driven by their friend Louis McMillan, a naval lieutenant in uniform who nonetheless supported the Dellingers' work in Newark. Dellinger was borne away from jail by capital in concert with military power, but he still managed to enjoy the ride.[17]

Back at the ashram, knowing he was bound for prison, he sat down and typed out a long and aggressive apologia for his pacifism and his stance toward the apparatus of conscription. "I believe that all war is evil and useless," he wrote. "Even a so-called war of defense is evil in that it consists of

lies, hatred, self-righteousness, and the most destructive methods of violence that man can invent. These things corrupt even the most idealistic
supporters of the war." Although Jesus is invoked briefly, he steers clear
of the religious rhetoric that marked the earlier statement by the Union
Eight. As a critique of American society, Dellinger's manifesto scores on a
number of points. It even spares a sentence or two for the evils of the Soviet
Union, our newfound ally. But as a response to fascism it is a hodgepodge
of utopian ideals and crude absolutism, spiced with what we would today
call conspiracy theories. By junking our weapons, opening our borders,
and abolishing capitalism, he asserts, we would make it impossible for foreign dictators to raise armies. Any possible occupation could be resisted by
means of peaceful strikes and the embrace of invading soldiers as brothers
even as we refuse to cooperate in the persecution of Jews or Negroes. "Our
courageous, kindly, nonviolent resistance would undermine the morale of
the German invaders." The CPS system, meanwhile, is dismissed as "a de-
vice whereby persons who know the wrongness of war and conscription
tone down their opposition in return for the theoretical advantage of avoiding open prosecution and jail. For most pacifists it is a faithless sellout."[18]

When the Union Eight launched the first prison protests by resisters
during the war, they were breaking new ground. But by his second stint
behind bars, Dellinger would enter a network of prisons and CPS camps
seething with hordes of resisters energized by their grievances and by one
another, and inflicting increasingly canny protests on their minders. Some
150 Americans were incarcerated more than once for resisting World War II
conscription, among them Dellinger, Dallas, Benedict, and Naeve.[19] They
entered a federal prison system besieged by its own recalcitrant inmates—
that is, by war resisters. By this time there were more COs in prison, they
were emboldened by their numbers, and the hopefulness with which many
had embarked on conscientious objection had worn off. Dellinger was sent
to Lewisburg, Dallas to Ashland, and Benedict back to Danbury. Resisters
at all three—and other prisons as well—mounted powerful nonviolent resistance campaigns, ostensibly against the injustices visited on inmates, but
also, it seems, to demonstrate the illegitimacy of their incarceration. With
their rejection of the CPS system and their increasing radicalism, many incarcerated resisters were in no mood to acquiesce. And though the road was
rocky, they made a difference. "Objectors continually prodded their jailers

to raise prison practice to the standards of modern 'reformist' penology ostensibly already in effect," Sibley and Jacob report in their painstaking 1952 history of World War II COs, adding: "The net effect of the objectors' protests was a marked advancement of 'progressive' penal policies."[20]

The COs were galvanized by the actions of a few particularly militant absolutists whose unbending resistance lit up the small world of hardcore pacifists. It was Corbett Bishop who embodied the most extreme form of the radical pacifist's rejection of state authority.[21]

A southerner in his mid-thirties with some graduate school under his belt, Bishop had a bookstore in West New York, just across the Hudson from Manhattan, when the draft came. On the form for the CPS camps he gave his church as Disciples of Christ, but where it asked the name of the official head of the denomination, he put down "Jesus Christ," and for headquarters listed "Heaven." Bishop began the first of his many fasts three months after arriving at the Friends camp at Patapsco, Maryland, in March of 1942. A camp newspaper described him as a "tall, thin, bearded figure with strained features and penetrating eyes." He called off the fast after forty-four days (having shed forty-four pounds) and, accompanied by his mother and sister, was taken to a Baltimore hospital to recuperate.[22]

Transferred to the camp at West Campton, New Hampshire, he rose during mealtimes to assail the CPS system as a form of slavery, haranguing his fellow inmates in a booming voice. "A man had better starve than compromise for bread," he might say. Or he would quote the founder of the Christian ashram movement, E. Stanley Jones: "Let any one be saturated with the thought of the Sermon on the Mount and he will not only not try to argue a man into slavery, but he will not rest until every man is free, including himself." Not everyone appreciated this, of course; some saw vanity and attention-seeking. Yet in his unmistakable seriousness Bishop seemed to embody an ideal that many of the others admired and aspired to.

He was only just beginning. Combining ego and righteousness, he proclaimed in a February 11, 1943, letter "To the Citizens of the World" the start of a fast in sympathy with a twenty-one-day hunger strike launched by Gandhi to free India from British rule. Bishop sent copies of his letter to world leaders including Gandhi himself, Britain's King George VI, Hirohito, Stalin, Hitler, and others. Some of these missives were of course returned as "undeliverable." Bishop, undeterred by this or anything else, doggedly continued fasting on and off on various grounds throughout his time in CPS and prison. The Friends soon gave up on him, telling the government he ought to be discharged, but Selective Service officials foolishly shifted him to the government-run camp at Mancos, Colorado, where at one point he apparently urged his fellow pacifists not to look outside lest the natural beauty raise their morale and in effect blind them to their predicament. He resumed his dinner harangues, at which, the camp newspaper reported, "a noisy minority invariably applauds him, and sometimes the whole dining room claps and cheers." From Mancos he was shipped to Germfask, that final redoubt of troublemakers which was itself the most trouble of all. There, at the Alcatraz of CPS camps, he took to clanking about in a ball and chain as a symbol of his oppression.[23]

Over time, perhaps as a result of his long stints without food, Bishop mellowed, appearing less and less the crank and more and more the prophet, if not the saint, for his resistance was no less steadfast. Accordingly, he excited tremendous support in the small but passionate world of nonviolent activists. "Bishop's radical tactics electrified the pacifist community," one historian writes, "and they organized numerous protests on his behalf."[24]

Using a furlough that he was entitled to, Bishop left Germfask and devoted himself to agitating against the system, not bothering to return. Arrested repeatedly, he ended up in various federal prisons, where "he began a policy of complete non-cooperation, insisting that if the state laid hands upon his body, it must take total responsibility for it." Accordingly, he would not stand, dress, eat, or even rise from his cot to use the bathroom. FBI agents, during one legal proceeding, had to haul his limp body in and out of elevators and push him in a chair equipped with casters. When they struck something, he was thrown out and remained inert on the floor. In his various stints at large, he obeyed no parole conditions and openly advocated pacifism and resistance in meetings with religious gatherings. During his many fasts he was force-fed but continued to lose weight, becoming a bearded, wraith-like figure whose physical strength diminished without impairing his fortitude.

The last way station in his odyssey through the government's network of pacifist holding areas was the federal prison in Milan, Michigan. When Bishop was paroled there, the warden, accompanied by a physician, drove him all the way to the CO-founded Macedonia Cooperative Community, in Clarkesville, Georgia, where he was to recuperate. "Is the body free now?" Bishop asked when they got there. Answered in the affirmative, he stripped off his government-issue clothes and stood naked until someone from the community covered him with a coat.

Even that didn't end his story, for officially he had been paroled to Macedonia, but of course he acknowledged no such parole, just as he acknowledged no right of government to incarcerate him. On September 1, 1945, the day before Japan signed formal surrender documents, eight FBI agents found him in Berea, Ohio, at the home of Ashton Jones, whose antiwar automobile had so embarrassed Bernice Fisher. Back in prison in Milan, he resumed fasting and prison authorities resumed forced feeding until, in March of 1946, he was paroled without conditions and without ever having signed or agreed to anything. By the time of his release Bishop had persisted in 193 consecutive days of complete noncooperation and had fasted on and off for a total of 426 days.[25]

Probably an even greater cause célèbre in pacifist circles were COs Stanley Murphy and Louis Taylor. On October 16, 1942, the second anniversary of registration day for the nation's first peacetime draft, both men rejected the conscription system by walking out of the CPS camp in Big Flats, New York, near Elmira. Their planned departure wasn't exactly a secret, as described by *The Conscientious Objector,* a leading pacifist news source:

> Two nights before they left they read their statements to a camp council meeting, at which a number of the men wept openly. On the day they left the musicians of the camp brightened the farewell scene by striking up *Auld Lang Syne* and *For He's A Jolly Good Fellow.* A camper at Big Flats, who reported the walkout for *The Conscientious Objector* commented: "While the views expressed by these men may not be shared by the entire camp, all of the men admire them for taking the stand they did."[26]

In January of 1943 they were sentenced to two and a half years each at Danbury, where they refused to work, were put in solitary confinement, and began an epic hunger strike—one that endured for eighty-two days and, in the words of Evan Thomas, "served to wake up the pacifist movement." Forced feeding via stomach tube began on the seventeenth day, each man wrapped tightly in sheets to prevent him from inducing vomiting. Their strike was the subject of disagreement among fractious COs, but after a while their courage, the cruel and disingenuous actions of prison authorities, and a changing mood among resisters brought many more around to their side. "In the beginning I couldn't see any sense to the idea," said Naeve, "but the more I thought about it the more I became convinced that their hunger-strike was doing more for the men in jail than anything else. The extensive newspaper publicity given the strike had made people aware that war objectors were being sent to prison. It was stirring a few anti-war people to thinking that something ought to be done."[27]

On March 10 nearly three hundred FOR and WRL members met at New York's Labor Temple, discussed at length how to support Murphy and Taylor, and entrusted further action to committee. It suggested letter-writing, sent a delegation to pressure officials in Washington—and recommended that the WRL and FOR withdraw from the NSBRO, the organization running the CPS system. The WRL soon did so. Dellinger and two others on the committee wanted to go much further, calling on pacifists to descend on Washington, picket the Senate to stop the war, and launch protests in CPS camps and prisons. In a statement, the three lambasted pacifists "sitting in bourgeois parlors and wooded hills quibbling over how far our own compromise can go—whether to buy war bonds, conduct medical experiments for the military, or support the USO . . . Pacifism implies not alternative service or noncooperation, but a vigorous, unsparing attack on evil."[28]

In June, Murphy and Taylor ended their fast on the basis of a settlement with the Bureau of Prisons that involved paroling them to charitable organizations, but both sides seem to have had different understandings of their agreement. When it fell apart, the bureau dispatched them to a prison medical facility in Springfield, Missouri, a repository for men with severe mental health issues and an unwelcome destination for others. "Springfield," *The Conscientious Objector* editorialized, "has been used as a dumping ground for rambunctious COs and the strikers now at Lewisburg fear that fate." The newspaper also reported that some inmates there, with or without mental health issues, had been thrust into padded "strip cells" where they were left naked with the four walls, a hole in the floor for a bathroom, until they modified their attitude.

James V. Bennett, the director of prisons, at first denied the existence of such things, but through Murphy's mother the men began to get out reports to the contrary, as well as of inmates being abused so harshly that one died. "The brutalities described," according to a front-page article in the *New York World-Telegram* of February 9, 1944, "include beatings, poundings with fire hose, deprivation of food, torture with burning cigarettes, kicks and punches to the most vulnerable parts of the body and confinement for considerable periods in stripped stone cells, without heat or furnishings of any kind, and prisoners being kept nude and forced to sleep nude on bare concrete floors."[29]

Agitation among COs and their supporters reached such a pitch that Bennett reversed his earlier denials. He admitted that Murphy and Taylor had been thrown into strip cells but argued that it was considered "the best method of therapy," and besides that they had sought such treatment for publicity. There was an investigation by a panel of outsiders, the Springfield warden was removed, and Murphy and Taylor started getting better treatment.[30]

There was much more to come in the saga of Murphy and Taylor, which would continue right into 1945. The CO grapevine had extended its branches to every corner of the camps and prisons where COs found themselves, as well as to influential figures such as Baldwin, Day, Macdonald, Muste, and Norman Thomas. Dellinger of course was well aware of the men's dogged resistance when he started his sentence at Lewisburg, in August of 1943. Nor would it have taken him long to find out that around the same time, eighteen COs launched a historic work stoppage against segregation at his prison alma mater, Danbury.

Dellinger's stay at Lewisburg would complete his evolution from Christian socialist into a secular anarchist. Once he was transferred from the farm into the prison, he connected with his ashram friend Bill Sutherland, who had refused to report to a CPS camp and, in July 1942, was sentenced to four years. Familiar with the genteel racism of Newark's leafy white suburbs and a graduate of liberal Bates College, he was shocked to find the unvarnished segregation of the American South prevailing at Lewisburg.[31]

When a black CO in the farm camp was forced to eat in the kitchen because the table designated for blacks was full, eight pacifists refused to eat at a white table and began to sustain themselves only on what little they could buy at the commissary. Sutherland and four other pacifists in the walled prison embarked on a hunger strike in support. All the strikers were sent to the Hole until they resumed eating what they were served, after which they were moved to more conventional cells isolated from the rest of the inmates. At one point, taken for haircuts, the renegades discovered that Sutherland was getting his hair cut separately by a black barber. In the face of this latest Jim Crow indignity, they went limp. The barbers, laughing, struggled to cut their hair anyway.[32]

Most of the COs had a strong antiauthoritarian streak that was inflamed by their encounter with the unbridled power of the state behind bars. Lewisburg's warden, in a meeting with two striking inmates and their mothers, proclaimed that "When you came inside those gates, you left all your rights behind . . . I have absolute authority."[33] This wasn't far from the truth, and it was this reality that outraged imprisoned COs. Hunger strikes and work stoppages in such an environment are hard to sustain, and in August, when Dellinger arrived, the Lewisburg resistance had begun to go off the rails, having evolved into a poorly focused general strike against the prison system with no easy path to victory. All of this was obvious to Dellinger, who at roughly twenty-eight was already an experienced and tactically sophisticated radical activist. Lewisburg's was precisely the kind of absolutist strike, with "an unrealistic 'shopping list' of demands," that he had decided back at Danbury not to participate in. Better, he felt, to enlist support "when I was confronted by a specially obnoxious act or saw a concrete objective that I thought was potentially winnable." Others agreed, and the all-purpose strike was abandoned. Instead, on September 28, Dellinger, Paton Price, Jack Dixon, Bill Kuenning, and Thomas Woodman launched a hunger strike, which some days later was joined by Bill Lovett. Raised a Quaker, he was sentenced for refusing to register and was just twenty-one when sent to Lewisburg, where he became a Dellinger acolyte. The hunger strike he joined and sharply raised the stakes. It was aimed at ending two deeply resented prison practices: the use of the Hole to punish inmates, and the censorship of letters in both directions as well as incoming reading material. Prison authorities also capriciously withheld inmate mail, leaving them in the dark about their families. Opening letters and packages to inspect for plots or contraband was fine, but otherwise, the strikers argued, everything had to be delivered, and without heavy-handed censoring.[34]

Protesters at Lewisburg and Danbury traded exhortations and kept one another apprised of their doings through supporters on the outside, who fed information to what was by now a vigorous pacifist press. In November of 1943 readers of *The Absolutist* learned that "Igal Roodenko and Jack Smock at Mancos, Colo. CPS camp upon hearing of the Lewisburg fast decided on October 12th to join them in a sympathy fast . . . In addition, ten COs in the Federal Correctional Institution at Ashland, Ky., are engaged in an eight day hunger strike, ending November 7th, in support of the men at Lewisburg . . . At Danbury Correctional Institution the men in isolation are beginning to show physical effects of their long isolation."[35]

But Muste, to Dellinger's great consternation, didn't support the Lewisburg actions, which he felt were out of proportion to the wrong that provoked them. He wrote to Caroline Lovett, Bill's mother, that it was time to end the strike, and he got Baldwin to send emissaries to persuade the strikers to accept any reasonable settlement. On October 22, Lovett wrote home to tell his mother that after nearly two weeks without food he was feeling "pretty well, considering." In fact, though, the strikers were growing thinner and weaker; that same day, Paton Price collapsed on the way back to his cell and had to be removed on a stretcher. The warden, W. H. Hiatt, insisted the others come and see what they had reduced him to. Price, later a director and acting coach whose students included Kirk Douglas, Jason Robards, and Jean Seberg, winked at them. "I'm fine," he said. "Don't give up."[36]

The others ended up in the hospital too. Badly constipated from prison food and weeks without outside exercise, Dellinger's health was worsened by fasting, and he would one day blame this long spell of stopped bowels for nearly three decades of subsequent colitis. He soon began hallucinating, finding himself floating along the ceiling or outside among the trees and sky. Not long after, Hiatt came to his cell and reported that Betty was dying from pregnancy complications: "She sent a message telling you to go off the strike so that she can die in peace." The story wasn't implausible. In an account of the episode written in 1948, Dellinger said that at the time "my wife was nearing the end of a difficult pregnancy. The prison authorities knew this, and they also knew that she had been seriously ill in a previous pregnancy, which had ended in a miscarriage. For three weeks they kept all mail from me. Then the acting Warden came into my cell and told me that my wife was dying . . . Later the prison doctor came in and told me the same thing." Dellinger believed at first and was tortured by worry. But when Hiatt rejected his request to be taken to Betty, he began to back away from panic and embrace the growing hope that it was all a ruse. "It was not until many weeks later I found out for sure that she had not been ill at all, and had been writing me encouraging letters all the while."[37]

In early November, probably, the forced feeding began. Lovett wrote his mother reassuringly that "the doctors are all very considerate," but it must have been miserable. The strikers were strapped down and Dellinger, though emaciated, dizzy, and suffering cardiac pain, refused to open his mouth. As a result, the tube was shoved in through his nose while someone held his head. Forced feeding provides some nourishment but doesn't substitute for eating, and on December 1 his hunger strike reached its sixty-third day. On the sixty-fourth, on the matter of mail and censorship at least, the Bureau of Prisons more or less capitulated. Bennett drafted a memo, soon the basis of a new policy, that permitted mail inspection but barred the confiscation or censorship of reading material over opinions or ideas—political, religious, or otherwise. There was no change on solitary confinement, nor were reading rights guaranteed to prisoners who were being punished. But the strikers nonetheless had won a significant victory—a victory for nonviolence.[38]

For Dellinger and Lovett it was followed by a more private victory, and a close call that offers insight into David's thinking about violence and its uses. In his memoir he reports that Lovett appealed to him for help with three inmates from the prison's general population of felons, who intended to rape him and make him their "boy." They had a shiv and access to his cell with a key fabricated in the machine shop. Dellinger decided that he had to do something. As he tells the story, Lovett had been warned of the coming assault, so Dellinger, through the aid of a friendly bank robber, slipped out of his cell after lights out and parked himself outside of Lovett's. He had decided that if he couldn't deter the men with talk, he'd fight the biggest of them in an attempt to deter the others, and he had taped his bum wrist in preparation. In fact, four men turned up. It was a terrifying experience for Dellinger, at least as related, and surely for Lovett as well.

Dellinger engaged them, asked about their backgrounds and sentences, and reminded them that he and Lovett had endured hunger and forced feeding for weeks to fight for inmate rights. The men assumed Dellinger was there because Lovett was his "boy" and he wanted to keep him all to himself. Dave claimed that neither of them would "go in for that stuff," although years later he admitted to "falling in love" with an unidentified man in Lewisburg (he denied any sexual relationship). In any case, faced with Lovett's potential assailants, he made it clear that anybody who tried to harm Bill "would have to stick a shiv into me before they could stick it into Bill. You can imagine how relieved I was to find out that it's you guys and not someone who would do that."

Somehow, it worked, and they never bothered Lovett again. When Dellinger got back to his cell, the tension finally burst and, shaking, he wept uncontrollably. Would he really have used violence? It appears so, and he could have made an argument for the difference between this episode and war, as the great pacifist Jessie Wallace Hughan did in making room in her pacifism for self-defense (and even, potentially, the assassination of Adolf Hitler). In his memoir Dellinger granted that the "absolute knowledge" that he'd never fight again, gained when he knocked cold a young man after that football game in New Haven, wasn't so absolute after all. He didn't fight that day in prison. But evidently he would have in order to spare Lovett.[39]

On January 2, 1944, Betty Dellinger gave birth to their first child, Evan Patchen Dellinger, whose name reflected Dave's esteem for pacifists Evan Thomas and Kenneth Patchen. Life at the ashram, though less crowded, was a struggle, with money running low and the mainstays (in particular Betty's husband) missing. By the end of 1943 it would collapse, and in the spring she and baby Evan moved for a while to a boarding house run by black pacifists in Chester, Pennsylvania. While Dave was in prison she received crucial help from Esther Eichel, whose husband, Julius, served time as a resister in both wars. Dave had contributed articles to the newspaper Julius edited, *The Absolutist*, which strongly supported resisters. The contrast with Muste wasn't lost on Dellinger; in February he was as usual the ringleader of an insurrection, this time against the Fellowship of Reconciliation, when sixteen Lewisburg inmates fired off an angry letter of resignation from a group they criticized for supporting the CPS camps. They invited Muste to join them in resigning from the FOR to form a nonviolent revolutionary movement to change the postwar world. Muste was none too pleased, but this rift was not the end of his relationship with

Dellinger, and the two would cooperate closely after the war. Other radicals, too, much as they admired Dellinger's courageous and charismatic leadership, would come to resent the unique brand of nonviolent bellicosity that was a part of his unbending militancy.[40]

He had special reserves of truculence for prison authorities and withstood punitive work assignments and bouts of solitary confinement. At one point after the Lewisburg hunger strike was settled, he reports, the warden wasn't holding up his end of the deal on mail, and Dellinger declared he would stop eating again. That did the trick. He and others at Lewisburg embarked on a subsequent hunger strike over the handling of parole for conscientious objectors. By the time of his release, in April of 1945, Dellinger was worn out by his uncompromising time behind bars. He'd been given three months off his two-year sentence for good behavior, but it was probably his defiance and troublemaking—his bad behavior— that earned him early release by authorities who were heartily glad to see the back of him.

A battered body and some bruised radical egos were just a part of the price Dellinger paid for his absolutism. Certainly it took a toll on his marriage; Betty later acknowledged having several affairs while he was behind bars with men who "were all good friends and like brothers." Dave, meanwhile, whose time in prison was essentially elective, missed out on the first fourteen months of his newborn's life, although he managed one fleeting but cherished embrace of the boy. During a visit to Lewisburg, according to a plan they had formed when she arrived, Betty waited until near the end of her visit and then thrust the baby across the low partition and into her husband's arms—a thrilling moment he would remember for decades to come. As an irate guard hurried over, Dave quickly handed back the baby and allowed himself to be dragged away.[41]

CHAPTER 16

PLAYING BALL FOR KEEPS

DON BENEDICT, IN SOLITARY confinement, was going through the torments of hell—and because the lashes were inflicted by his own conscience, they could not have been more excruciating. Like Dellinger, Benedict was another of the unlucky resisters sentenced more than once for rejecting conscription, and on his return to Danbury he was greeted by the guards like an old pal. "Now we'll have a winning softball team," they said. But things were different this time. Benedict was different. The world had changed.

The federal prison at Danbury was probably the epicenter of CO protests when Benedict arrived. It was where arch-resisters Murphy and Taylor had refused to eat before being shipped off to Springfield, Missouri, but by then the protests had metastasized. Thanks to the presence of such militant secular pacifists as Jim Peck and Lowell Naeve, Danbury in late 1943 was the scene of a dogged work stoppage against segregation. Naeve had been so determined to support Murphy and Taylor's hunger strike that he proclaimed his own in sympathy on the steps of the federal courthouse in Manhattan. A newspaper photographer, alerted by the War Resisters League, took pictures, a crowd gathered, and Naeve was hauled off by police. Briefly sent to the prison psychiatric ward of Bellevue Hospital, he was force-fed in a straitjacket before being shipped off for his own second term at Danbury, where fractious radicals, while admiring Murphy and Taylor, had a hard time showing more than token support aside from smuggling countless cigarettes to them when they were in the prison hospital. The hunger strike had electrified radical pacifists elsewhere, but at Danbury COs weren't clear on what the two were demanding, or disagreed with the pair's goals or tactics. They disagreed about a lot of things. "After wearisome argument," says Peck, some COs skipped a Sunday dinner or two or even fasted the entire day, and some signed a letter in support of Murphy and Taylor to the FBI.

But it wasn't long until, after a lot more wearisome argument, other Danbury COs launched their own campaign of resistance, choosing leaders, picking battles—and winning. When Peck refused to work on anything, such as victory garden signs, having to do with the war, he landed in solitary for ten days. But when the CO leadership committee met with warden Myrl Alexander, a reform-minded official who would later head the Bureau of Prisons ("a very decent guy," Benedict called him later),[1] he acceded to their demand that COs be permitted to turn down any war-related work. True to his word, there was no punishment for COs who refused to sand worktables used in making gloves for the Navy.

Next, the overwhelmingly white COs decided to tackle segregated seating in the mess hall. Negotiations with the warden dragged on while he insisted that such changes take time (a familiar refrain to reformers on race): "It may take six months. It may take a year and it may take three years."[2]

The pacifists recognized foot-dragging when they saw it. Some white COs argued that they should simply defy Jim Crow by sitting at the black tables. But all knew that some white inmates heartily endorsed segregation, and the administration, if it wanted to make trouble, could muster their support. Trying to force mixed seating could provoke a fight that would give credence to the notion that desegregation was dangerous. So the COs settled on a work strike. There was of course the usual debate and dissent. Some objected to a strike as a form of violence. Others said the issue wasn't important enough compared to the release of COs. Many worried about transfer to a tougher prison, being locked in cells indefinitely, or ruining their parole prospects. As the strike date approached there was continual wrangling over the issue wherever the men congregated. In the end just eighteen of them—a mix of socialists, labor activists, religious types, and outright anarchists—launched the work stoppage. Five more joined once it got underway. Albon Man, a professorial socialist (later the editor of a Prentice Hall unit publishing tax and legal materials) was made chairman.

Too numerous for the Hole, the strikers were marched upstairs to an area set aside for them on the second floor of a building called Upper Hartford. As Naeve recalls it, "When we reached the top of the segregation stairs, there was a feeling—we were actually on strike. To the tune of Glory, Glory Hallelujah, some of the men began singing, shouting out— Sol-i-dar-i-ty For-ever, Sol-i-dar-i-ty Forever, THE UNION MAKES US STRONG. The song boomed out several times over the prison yard to notify the other prisoners a strike had begun. The authorities sent up a guard to stop the singing, but we paid no attention."[3]

Prison authorities intended to keep the strikers away from everyone else, keep them locked in cells almost all the time, and wait for the whole thing to pass. Food was brought in. Windows allowed the men to yell down to fellow inmates outside, exchanging news. "Each cell had a bed with locker attached below, a small iron table, an iron chair, a small wash bowl, a toilet bowl and a radiator," Jim Peck wrote later. "That left a space about two and a half feet wide in which to walk back and forth between the window and the door. We did it in four medium steps."[4]

At first the strikers were locked in without reading materials. The human distaste for monotony runs so strong that they launched a hunger strike over this, even refusing their daily forty-minute yard period. Without breaks for meals or outdoor exercise, time dragged even more heavily. The headache of hunger's first day only made things worse. On the third day they decided to eat and see how the authorities reacted. "Next day," Peck reports, "we got books, magazines and newspapers."

There was still the need to pass the time and keep up morale. Much of the time was spent reading, writing letters, and pacing their small spaces, but the strikers also responded in far more creative ways. Peck played chess with the striker in the cell next door—David Thoreau Wieck would go on to postwar prominence as an anarchist, to the extent such a thing was possible. Each had created a cardboard chess seat; they called out moves to one another through the ventilation ducts, which also served as a communications conduit for reaching inmates on another floor.

The three-quarter-inch space under each locked door was all the opening they needed for dialogue, conferences, and even something like a mail service. "These openings enabled us to conduct strike meetings and hold bull sessions by lying on the floor with our mouths at the slot," Peck reports. "Since the concrete was cold, we used to spread our blankets for a lengthy meeting."[5]

On the very first day of the strike, they devised a way of dispatching messages from cell to cell by propelling them under the doors. "Clipped around the radiator pipes, where the pipes entered the wall, were metal discs found in every private home with plumbing," Peck recalls. "Since they were thin enough to pass under the doors, we pulled them loose and attached eight-foot lengths of string. At first we built our strings from the loops on Bull Durham tobacco bags . . . Later we got hold of an old mop which supplied us for the duration."[6]

A message would be attached to one end of the string and then the metal radiator collar, at the other end, would be fired under the door into another cell. "The man in that cell would pull the string until the message came into his cell," says Peck. "By zigzagging the length of the hall we could reach every striker."[7]

They also found that, with a careful push, they could slide magazines back and forth across the corridor. But why stop there? With time on their hands and the burden of an education, the strikers naturally launched a newspaper, which they agreed to call *The Clink*. Naeve, who cooked up the idea, recalls that it started as a vehicle for cartoons, but soon strikers were contributing all kinds of things in an echo of the many publications produced by creative COs at the CPS camps. "It contained articles, drawings, poetry, numbered at times as many as twenty pages," he writes. "We whisked it from cell to cell." For paper, the COs washed the ink off copies of *Life* magazine. The men took turns editing editions, with special numbers devoted to Eugene V. Debs, opposition to the war, and an imaginary sympathy strike by guards. "Reading *The Clink*," Peck recalls, "became one of the best breaks in the routine."

Peck had written some songs on the outside and now wrote one in his cell called "Jimcrow must go!" The inmates sang it in the evening sometimes, accompanied by Naeve on a guitar he had somehow built.

When in a correctional clink
They teach you that colored guys stink
We say that this sham
Must take it on the lam—
Jimcrow must scram.

Whenever you go to eat grub
The Negroes you have got to snub
In teaching to hate
They rehabilitate—
Jimcrow must gate.

They say Hitler is wicked
To persecute race in his way
But when it's done in the U.S.
It's quite perfectly OK.

The blacks are as good as the whites
Why shouldn't they have equal rights
The warden says no
But we tell him it's so—
Jimcrow must go.

Yet Jim Crow persisted—here, as elsewhere, upheld even by barbers. The strikers voted not to cooperate with haircut segregation, growing increasingly shaggy over the course of seven weeks until the administration sent in a black barber and a white barber together. Naturally a white striker seated himself for the black barber and a black inmate for the white one. Soon the strikers were shorn—and in the matter of haircuts, at least, the color line at Danbury was broken.[8]

But as the strike ground on through fall and early winter, a larger victory against segregation remained elusive, and morale began to sag. As the seasons changed, the radiators began to bake the cells, which grew so hot that the men put their mattresses and blankets over them. At other times they shivered without any heat at all. What was the point? They wondered. Were they having any meaningful impact? Would anything ever change?

Some just wanted the strike to end, and there were the usual differences over tactics. Often minutiae threatened to consume them. In a discussion of whether to continue cleaning the hall between the cells and a recreation room they weren't even allowed to use, "they got beautifully snarled in technicalities. We even digressed to argue what constitutes a majority vote." They finally decided to stop the cleaning, but the job was given to a non-striking inmate and nothing else changed.[9]

Although disgusted by a lack of support from pacifist groups, they did have Julius Eichel and Evan Thomas in their corner, but more important, probably, was the press. Their public relations volunteer on the outside, the father of a striker, obtained no coverage because, they believed, he wanted parole for his son—who dropped out of the strike anyway. So they enlisted the energetic Ruth MacAdam, who was engaged to one of the strikers and who began to get some attention by taking the story to various newspapers. This also served to publicize the discrimination going on even in a supposedly enlightened federal prison in the North, where people were embarrassed by it. Gunnar Myrdal noted in 1944 that "Even the white man who defends discrimination frequently describes his motive as 'prejudice' and says that it is 'irrational.'" Of the beliefs in black inferiority that once sustained the nation's racial caste system, Myrdal added that most white people with a little education "have a hunch that they are wrong."[10]

Averse, perhaps, to the harsh glare of publicity, Warden Alexander agreed to mediation by Wieck's parents, who were labor and antiwar activists in their own right. This was a small but suggestive victory, for Alexander previously had insisted that the strike had to stop before any discussion of change. Now, however, starting on Thanksgiving, 1943, life for the strikers changed. Cells were kept open all day, yard time increased to ninety minutes, and the men were allowed to take meals together instead of locked up separately. When the inmates said they wouldn't eat that day unless they got turkey (meat had been limited to Sundays and Tuesdays), they were promised it would turn up, and it did. So they knew things were going their way. But they were shocked nonetheless when, on December 23, they were called into a meeting with the warden, who said calmly that "I just came up to tell you boys that starting February 1, the inmates may sit anywhere they please in the messhall [sic]. Are there any questions?"[11]

After 133 days, the strike was over. It was a remarkable victory and likely made Danbury the first federal prison to desegregate its dining hall. "It seems to me," Peck writes, "that the campaign against racial discrimination may be counted as one of the most important accomplishments of COs in World War 2."[12]

The success at Danbury reinvigorated strikes and protests at other federal prisons around the country. Unfortunately the spirit of Jim Crow continued to haunt the rest of the system, with COs endeavoring to exorcise it one institution at a time. James Bennett, who presided over a prison system that prided itself on its enlightened practices, wrote a kind of separate-but-equal memo to wardens in 1943 about "the efforts of some of the extremist conscientious objectors to force us to permit indiscriminate intermingling of the white and colored groups." Although not mandating desegregation—prison authorities were worried about racist whites, particularly in the South—he did ask that living conditions be made equal. "The colored men have the same opportunities for work, for vocational training and for recreation as do the whites . . . They ought to work on the same details. Particularly 'dirty' jobs or poor paying jobs should be equally divided."[13]

Nor did the end of official segregation at Danbury stop CO protests there. Which brings us back to Don Benedict.

————

AFTER HIS FIRST STINT in Danbury, Benedict spent some time at the Newark ashram. But when his parole ended and he could relocate, he headed for Detroit, where he had an offer to help a minister at the deteriorating Cass Avenue Methodist Church in a mixed-race neighborhood. Don hoped to use his Newark experience to reach out to the community and to bring the gospel to working people by laboring alongside them. Before long he'd repainted the inside of the shabby church, inspiring volunteers to join him as he worked. And with help from Union Eight alum Bill Lovell, he turned a trio of Detroit storefronts into a space for working with children, a grocery co-op and a headquarters for community activism. Don and Bill lived in the sprawling apartment upstairs with an Orthodox Jew, a Chinese chemistry student, and other like-minded fellows. But when Benedict sought the local bishop's approval to operate under Methodist auspices, he was told there was no provision for such a lay ministry—and since he wouldn't finish his work at the seminary he was to be dropped from the official rolls of the church. Furious, Benedict stalked out, but not before demanding, "What would John Wesley have thought of this?"[14]

Alienated from the church, Benedict directed his considerable energies to his burgeoning milk cooperative, which delivered affordable dairy products to local residents. He and Lovell, determined to advance racial justice and harmony, hoped the venture could help bring black and white working people together in Detroit. The city was under stress; it had seen a large influx of southerners, black and white alike, drawn by the prospect of well-paid jobs in Detroit's booming factories. Relocating whites often brought their racial attitudes with them. Blacks meanwhile encountered hostility from whites already in place as well as from southern white newcomers. And housing was scarce. Fights between white and black young men were common; finally, in June 1943, mass violence erupted. Moving about to the extent they could, what Benedict and Lovell saw was chaos, with smoke rising from fires and mobs overturning cars, setting blazes, and besetting their racial antagonists. Woodward Avenue, the dividing line between blacks and whites, was a battle zone. (Nine whites and twenty-five blacks were killed in the turmoil.) Bands of white men were out looking for blacks to assault. "I saw one gang chase a guy," Benedict recalled. "I think they probably killed him. They chased him back through an alley."[15]

Thinking about what he could do, "I began to think about the blacks in our neighborhood some of whom were in our milk coop. So, I went to the store and loaded up on groceries in our panel truck, and I pulled right into that black neighborhood because they had no way of getting food. They were all out on the porch listening to the radio."

The police, themselves targets, were unable to restore order. Nothing seemed to quell the violence until finally six thousand heavily armed federal troops were sent into the city. "Ironically," Benedict would write, "it was with great relief that I watched trucks rolling by with grim-faced soldiers in position behind machine guns, in patrol of city streets."[16]

These memories plagued him one particularly dark night during his time in solitary. He was in the Hole because he had joined a former United

Mine Workers organizer in launching a series of work strikes by sixteen pacifists. The idea was that one or two would stop work on each succeeding Wednesday, leaving prison authorities with no sense of how extensive the movement was. Benedict's turn came last, and into solitary he went. Once there, he thought not just about Detroit, but about its implications for non-violence. "From boyhood," he would write, "I had believed violence was wrong. Now I faced a direct contradiction. The mere demonstration of the power of force in the Detroit streets had stopped the riots. I had to face that fact. Here was the one case that disproved my convictions . . . My belief in pacifism as an absolute was shaken."[17]

Benedict already knew something about the events in Europe that we now call the Holocaust. Hitler's murderous treatment of Jews who fell un-der the Nazi shadow, not just in Germany but in Poland and other occu-pied countries, was widely if hesitantly reported in the American media long before the liberation of the concentration camps toward the end of the war. Newspapers all over the country carried increasingly alarming accounts of what soon came into focus as an organized extermination cam-paign, even though The New York Times and other papers usually buried the news inside. Individuals in the public arena, such as the writer Ben Hecht, did loudly raise alarms. And The New Republic, notably, gave its December 21, 1942, cover to an article entitled "The Massacre of the Jews," which described the Nazis' attempt to murder an entire people. The author was Varian Fry, an American recently ejected from Vichy France for his work in rescuing anti-Nazi refugees, including many prominent Jews. "There are some things so horrible that decent men and women find them impos-sible to believe," Fry wrote, "so monstrous that the civilized world recoils incredulous before them. The recent reports of the systematic extermina-tion of the Jews in Nazi Europe are of this order."[18]

People like Don Benedict paid closer attention to such news, which was featured more prominently in the kinds of publications they read. Internationally minded pacifists, moreover, were in touch with counter-parts in Britain, where the enormity of German crimes against the Jews was given far more prominence by the press. And perhaps some pacifists, such as Dellinger, were more inclined to believe these reports because they had visited Hitler's Germany before the war. All along, American pacifists were among the loudest voices drawing attention to the plight of Europe's Jews, condemning Nazi persecution of them, and urging Washington to admit more of them as refugees. The Quakers, in particular, through the American Friends Service Committee, did what they could to help, including finding American sponsors for Jews seeking to emigrate. For such efforts, the AFSC and its British counterpart shared the 1947 Nobel Peace Prize.

The staggering scale of the horror now tormented Benedict. Along with his experience of the riots in Detroit, the Nazi murder of the Jews called into question his choices on the war and his view of the world. "By the seventh night," he wrote, "I no longer felt I was in solitary because of this last work strike. I was there because of my entire past life, and the question that faced me was not whether I could continue in solitary for the term of my sentence but for the rest of my life."[19]

Benedict's sentence included a proviso allowing for parole should he change his mind about conscription—should he, in the parlance of the day, decide to "play ball." He was in prison as a matter of choice, and the question now was whether he had made the right one—not just for himself, but for the others he had talked into striking at Danbury, and in proclaiming his opposition to the war in the national press. How painful it must have been at that moment to be racked by such doubt. He appealed to God by means of a litany, repeated day and night, that oscillated between self-justification and self-doubt. "I have followed my conscience. *Lord hear me.* I have striven for perfection and I have become only self-righteous. *Lord hear me.*" He recited as well the fate of some of his young teammates. "Midge Miller, shortstop. *Shot down over Germany!* Lou Krueger, first base. *Killed at Anzio!*"

While in quarantine, at the start of his second stint at Danbury, his reading included Reinhold Niebuhr, his former professor and pacifist hero, whose latter-day emphasis on original sin and moral realism was sounding increasingly persuasive. Like Saul on the road to Damascus, Benedict suddenly could see, and what he saw made it ever more difficult to justify pacifism. "It suddenly began to make a difference to me who won the war," he would recall.

He was having a conversion experience, but it took him a while to realize in which direction salvation lay. The breakthrough came when finally, one night, he told the guard who came through for last count that he wanted to see the warden. Benedict didn't sleep during that "terrible night," and no doubt greeted the dawn in a state. When Warden Alexander sent for him the next morning, he must have been astonished to hear his prisoner of conscience say: "I think I'm ready to enlist in the army."

CHAPTER 17

WORK OF NATIONAL IMPORTANCE

WHILE RUSTIN, DELLINGER, BENEDICT, and others went to prison for their principles, the twelve thousand conscientious objectors consigned to the nation's sprawling network of Civilian Public Service camps had discontents of their own. The 1940 draft bill said that COs were to be given noncombat roles in the armed forces or, if those were objectionable, "assigned to work of national importance under civilian direction." The three peace churches that had pushed for such a provision—the Quakers, the Brethren, and the Mennonites—agreed to operate what eventually became 152 camps intended for that purpose, imagining wholesome Christian communes serving as safe havens for COs who might otherwise have suffered like their predecessors during the Great War.

The reality fell far short of these arcadian dreams. The result was growing discontent—and, eventually, outright rebellion—at the camps, where COs chafed at the lack of pay, the pointless (if strenuous) labor, and the realization that the military was ultimately in charge. COs stranded for years in these dusty outposts tended to radicalize one another. As the camps evolved into unexpected incubators of militancy, frustrated resisters turned their ire on the peace churches, the Fellowship of Reconciliation and others, opening a rift in American pacifism and eroding support for the CPS program on all sides.

Most COs in the CPS program cooperated, but a significant minority used slowdowns, work stoppages, hunger strikes, walkouts, letter-writing, and even sabotage to protest the system and its shortcomings. Some men became expert at avoiding work. At one point pacifist John Lewis circulated a mimeographed study of a work slowdown at the camp in Lapine, Oregon. (The most recalcitrant resisters, ejected from camps run by the peace churches, ended up at government-run camps such as Lapine and Germfask.) This "imaginative use of passive resistance" he heartily recommended as a nonviolent technique for combatting conscription and working toward social justice while staying out of prison. The CPS men also resorted to mass petitions. At one point eighteen hundred men, or about 20 percent of the CPS population at the time, signed one asking the president "to appoint a civilian board to place each man in suitable and useful work in the public welfare at regular wages." The White House rejected it.[1]

It's hard to take seriously the complaints of chemists and sociologists set to work digging drainage ditches when men of similar backgrounds were digging foxholes under fire or serving in action as turret gunners over enemy skies. And for all their bellyaching, many conscientious objectors in the CPS system actually did perform work of national importance.

In fact, COs performed amazing feats—and took real risks. They built roads and wilderness trails, cleared brush, fought fires, and performed a range of farm and conservation tasks ranging from inseminating cows to digging irrigation ditches. COs even ran experimental farms and fabricated farm equipment. Others grew seedlings, planted trees, cleaned up hurricane debris, maintained rural telephone lines, and battled blister rust in the nation's forests. COs laboriously created dams, reservoirs, fences, and diversion ditches to battle soil erosion. A CPS cartoonist invented Joe Beaver, a cartoon figure on posters designed to spread best practices in timber husbandry. A mechanically minded CO, observing the painstaking efforts required to estimate the yield of a forest, invented an instrument to do the job in a fraction of the time. Nearly three hundred CPS men served as "smokejumpers," sustaining Forest Service firefighting operations in Montana, Idaho, and Oregon while the regulars were off to war. The work was arduous and dangerous. A foreman in Norman Maclean's classic *Young Men and Fire* says of some Mennonite COs, "Them sons-of-bitches was the world's champion firefighters."

COs also attacked human underdevelopment, battling malnutrition and poor sanitation in the rural South, Puerto Rico, and the Virgin Islands. They tended the mentally ill and submitted themselves as guinea pigs for a variety of dangerous and sometimes excruciating experiments that probably wouldn't be considered ethical today. Thirty of them made the supreme sacrifice, some of them by drowning or heart failure, but others very much in the line of duty. Twenty-seven-year-old CO Warren Dugan, trained as an engineer and married just a year, was a technician working on polio at Yale University Hospital when he succumbed to the disease in what appeared to have been a laboratory accident. Earl Kepler, Jr., Roy's brother, suffered massive burns in early April of 1943 when a woodstove exploded in the cabin he was sharing in California's snowy San Gabriel Mountains. He died soon after. An additional 1,566 COs were discharged as disabled and hundreds more were injured. Few of those harmed received any compensation.

All in all, the men contributed nearly six million hours of labor to their countrymen, two-thirds of which fell under the broad category of "conservation of natural resources," even if any number of the tasks accomplished might not pass environmental muster by today's standards. Most of the work they performed was difficult and took them to places where COs were exposed to public vilification and their spouses might be shunned. Of course, hardly any of them faced enemy gunfire. This is probably a good place to note that between twenty-five thousand and fifty thousand American conscientious objectors served in the armed forces during the war (the precise number has never been determined). Several branches of the service, such as the Quartermaster Corps, were designated as noncombatant and therefore drew disproportionate numbers of COs, but this classification was narrowed to the Medical Corps early in 1943, and COs in this branch of the service have gained the most attention over the years as death-defying battlefield angels. The Hollywood actor Lew Ayres served as a medic and then a chaplain's assistant, though he wasn't in combat. Seventh-day Adventists were particularly prominent among medics, the church having trained young men as stretcher bearers and medic's assistants before Pearl Harbor. Orville Cox was cited for his bravery in saving the lives of infantrymen under Japanese machine-gun fire, and Desmond Doss became the first CO to win the Medal of Honor for his fearlessness in saving American soldiers on Okinawa. Cox and Doss were both Adventists.

The stresses of combat included agonizing moral dilemmas. The work of World War II COs came with moral dilemmas of its own for men who were determined not to contribute to the war effort. Were they, by their labor, freeing men to fight? Would the scientific research they made possible help the military in its prosecution of the war? In their work at hospitals, mental institutions, and juvenile facilities, was it permissible to use force? And were they being exploited by a system that treated their labor (to say nothing of their well-being) all too cavalierly, especially when it was unpaid? A full description of the work performed by the thousands of COs who passed through the CPS system could fill a volume of its own, if not several. The focus here will be on the areas that throw into sharpest relief the courage and conflicts inherent in their stance during the war.

———

BEFORE THE ATOM BOMB presented pacifists with an unprecedented new basis for shock and revulsion, conscientious objectors experienced both in their encounter with the nation's vast and Dickensian system of mental institutions. It was in this horrific netherworld of neglect and abuse that they made their most immediate and humane contribution to American life. The example of young Warren Sawyer is especially salient, for reasons that will soon become plain.[2]

Born in 1920, Sawyer grew up mostly in New York's Greenwich Village, a child of divorce radicalized by the Depression. Although he and two brothers had been Catholic altar boys, as a young man he became a Quaker. In the City of Brotherly Love he earned money for college by working as a copyboy at the Philadelphia *Bulletin*, where the newshounds kept whiskey bottles in their lockers and nipped from them all day. Willkie shook his hand on a visit during the 1940 presidential campaign. When the draft came, Sawyer was granted conscientious objector status even as his two brothers went into the armed forces. At the CPS camp in Marion, North Carolina, he fought fires and helped build a national park for a few months until he volunteered to work in a mental hospital under a program designed to provide such institutions with desperately needed manpower while offering COs more meaningful work. By the end of the war roughly three thousand of them had taken up the challenge.

Sawyer was twenty-three when he started at the Philadelphia State Hospital in September 1942, beginning a very different journey through wartime hell than most of his male co-generationists, a journey that would not end until January of 1946. While a student at a small college in Tennessee, he had worked at a sanitarium with patients suffering dementia or delirium tremens. But nothing prepared him for the Philadelphia institution popularly known as Byberry. In an interview sixty-six years later the experience remained vivid: "It was a shock, right off the bat."

Sawyer's letters to a couple of aunts in Aurora, New York, document what he saw. "This week," he wrote, "I am going over to Building A which is where 350 incontinent male patients are housed . . . Nearly all the patients on this ward are naked from morning to night. A worker-patient does nothing all day but continually mop the filth from the floor." Sawyer tells of a patient named Sidney who liked to fashion "gloves" for himself: "He'd just pick up feces and plaster his arms up to his elbows," Sawyer recalled, "as if he had a pair of long gloves that a person might wear to an opera, for example, but he did that every day, and that's one example."[3]

When state inspectors came around, patients might be provided with clothing, bedspreads, and shoes, only to have these precious items removed soon after. Clothing, blankets, medicines, and nearly everything else was in short supply. "The attendants in Building A wanted to take the patients outside for a walk today," he wrote. "But because they didn't have enough trousers, or even underpants for their charges, they were stymied. Had they drawn on the scant supply of these garments, then the patients who have visitors on the two regular weekly visiting days would have had nothing to wear for these occasions."

Patients posed a continual threat to themselves, as well as to one another. "A week ago," Sawyer wrote, "one of the patients in Building A was observed to have swallowed a spoon. He was taken to X ray where they discovered he already had three other spoons in his stomach."[4]

There was little in the way of treatment; Byberry, like so many other such facilities, was essentially custodial, and in the wards a climate of menace prevailed. "On Saturday," Sawyer writes, "a murder was narrowly averted on the violent ward. The situation there has reached a state of bedlam."

If the patients had any rights, they were routinely violated, something it was easier to do when the authorities controlled communication with the outside world. "There's a hospital rule," Warren wrote in another letter, "that all outgoing mail from patients must be censored by the nursing staff before it can be sent. If the nurse reviewing the letter disapproves of its contents, it's usually put into the trash. The tragedy is that if the patient's letter doesn't pass inspection, he or she is never told. Byberry is supposed to be a hospital where patients are to receive care and treatment, yet in many respects they are treated as if they were criminals."

The regular attendants were poorly trained, badly paid, and barely vetted. This was true of the COs as well, but rather than badly paid they were unpaid; Sawyer received a stipend of $2.50 a month for much of his time at Byberry. But the COs provided some much-needed continuity. Turnover among regular staff was frequent; working conditions were deplorable and many "bughousers," as attendants sometimes called themselves, drank and drifted from job to job. To the extent that order prevailed, it was maintained through violence and intimidation. Attendants wielded broomsticks, clubs, or rubber hoses full of buckshot, and beatings, some of them fatal, were common at public mental institutions. But things were dangerous for staff as well. A number of COs sustained broken jaws, cuts, and other injuries. The food was horrible, and sometimes patients were sealed in without supervision or hope of release in a fire. "Instead of installing locks on broken ward doors," Sawyer writes at one point, "all that the maintenance men can do to forestall patients from escaping is to nail the doors shut. Lights keep going out because of failures in the electrical system. And when that happens at night, especially on the ward with the violent-prone patients, and you're the only one on duty, which is usually the case, you've got a big, big problem."

COs nonetheless had success using patience and understanding rather than makeshift clubs. But they soon learned that even with the noblest intentions it was impossible to maintain safety and good order without physical interventions. William Ludlow, the grandson of a Presbyterian minister, was a young Princeton graduate who joined the Quakers and became active in the FOR. A CO, he spent some time in the CPS camp in Big Flats, New York, "chopping down trees in snows about two feet deep," before he and his wife, Wilma, went to work at the mental hospital in Williamsburg,

Virginia, the staff of which had been drained by the well-paid war work available at nearby Newport News. The couple were thrown into the maelstrom without training. "The first day was terribly scary," Bill recalled.

He soon recognized the necessity, for the good of the patients, of laying hands on them—and the crucial distinction between force and violence. "Force was restraining, but with concern and respect for the person you were restraining, whereas violence was what was recommended by the old bughouse attendant who told us, 'The first thing you do when they come in is you beat them up, and you won't have any more trouble with them.'"[5]

Wilma, a Drew University grad, was an attendant in the women's unit, and years later recollected that "when I resigned, it left 15 attendants, night and day, for 1,200 patients in the women's section." For a while, COs working at Williamsburg "were locked on the wards with the patients and without a key for 12-hour shifts." At one point the administration mandated a seventy-two-hour workweek with no days off, but the COs simply refused and adhered to the wearying schedule they already had. There were electroshock treatments but no talk or drug therapy, and COs at the facility were soon disabused of their most idealistic notions. "My childhood fantasies were of St. Francis kissing the leper sores," Wilma recalled. She had imagined she could calm the patients' "raging spirits," but instead found her own spirit ever more disturbed. She later spent twenty years as a mental health caseworker "expiating my guilt."

Some COs, under the strain of circumstances, did resort to violence here and there, but overall their track record was exemplary. "This is a perfect setting in which to demonstrate the superiority of pacifism over brute force in handling tense situations," Sawyer wrote. "If you can convey to patients that you're not afraid of them and respect them as individuals—even though you're shaking in your boots—they return your respect. A few attendants have had their jaws smashed, but they're usually the ones who approach troublesome patients with broom handles and other similar weapons. When patients sense that you feel safe and have the situation in command without the threat of force, they are much more amenable to following instructions. I've already broken up several fights using this technique, and it works."

Sawyer, the Ludlows, and other COs worked tirelessly to improve conditions at these hospitals and accomplished a great deal, even if only by

treating patients humanely. In some places they helped administer treatments, sometimes taking on life-and-death responsibilities. At Byberry,
COs who took over the hellish men's incontinent ward cleaned and repainted the entire building, changed how meals were provided to encourage patients to eat calmly rather than bolting food, helped end nakedness
by getting every person dressed every day, and spirited away dirty linens
once they were soiled, eventually all but banishing the stench of feces and
urine once characteristic of the place. Byberry COs also made efforts to
share best practices, launching a national newsletter called *The Attendant* to
publish suggestions and information from COs working at mental institutions all over the country.

Some places were a lot better than Byberry. At the Duke University
Hospital, which offered pleasant surroundings and individualized treatments in keeping with the state of knowledge at the time, COs could see for
themselves that it was possible to help mental patients rather than merely
warehousing them. A relatively new institution at Ypsilanti, Michigan,
meanwhile, had tennis courts, men's and women's gyms, movie equipment,
well-outfitted kitchens, a dairy, a bakery, twelve hundred acres of farm-
land, and a progressive superintendent. Yet at Williamsburg, "one attendant was solely responsible for 100 to 175 persons in a violent ward, where
at any moment a patient might swing a fist or a chair."[6]

Lack of staff, no matter how inadequately trained or supervised, remained a huge problem. In early 1941, Sawyer told his aunts, Byberry "had
approximately 1,000 employees. It had been designed to accommodate
a caseload of 2,500 patients, but could handle as many as 3,500 patients
if necessary. As of October 1942, its employee staff had dropped to 200,
while its walls bulged with 6,000 patients in residence."[7] At times a single
attendant might have to cope with an entire ward full of patients. Always
underfunded, hospitals were even more undermanned during the war because so many attendants entered the armed forces or found better-paying
work in the booming war economy.

Albert Maisel's explosive article in *Life*, "Bedlam, 1946," appeared
not long after Americans had seen horrifying newsreels of Nazi atrocities.
"U.S. Mental Hospitals Are a Shame and Disgrace," *Life* stated flatly below
the title. Photos secretly snapped at Byberry by a CO working there showed
forlorn patients wandering naked or lying unattended in filth, inevitably

calling to mind images of German concentration camps. Paragraph after paragraph of Maisel's unrelenting report hammered home the neglect and abuse inflicted on the mentally ill:

> Thousands spend their days—often for weeks at a stretch—locked in devices euphemistically called "restraints": thick leather handcuffs, great canvas camisoles, "muffs," "mitts," wristlets, locks and straps and restraining sheets. Hundreds are confined in "lodges"— bare, bedless rooms reeking with filth and feces—by day lit only through half-inch holes though steel-plated windows, by night merely black tombs in which the cries of the insane echo unheard from the peeling plaster of the walls.[8]

Maisel's stunning indictment was one of many that appeared as a result of the extraordinary efforts of COs who documented abuses and, when authorities refused to act, enlisted journalists to expose what was going on in Cleveland, Philadelphia, Poughkeepsie, and elsewhere. Among the headwinds COs faced was the hostility of authorities, veterans' groups, and citizens who considered them cowards or even traitors. Maisel's article started with a description of the very institution where Sawyer labored to improve the lives of his charges: "In Philadelphia the sovereign Commonwealth of Pennsylvania maintains a dilapidated, overcrowded, undermanned mental 'hospital' known as Byberry." Maisel characterized Byberry as representative of mental hospitals across the nation, where inmates were routinely subjected to starvation diets, nakedness, cold and filth. "Beatings and murders," he wrote, "are hardly the most significant of the indignities we have heaped upon most of the 400,000 guiltless patient-prisoners of over 180 state mental institutions."

As if caring for hundreds of severely mentally ill patients wasn't enough, Sawyer volunteered for "jaundice" experiments conducted at the University of Pennsylvania under the auspices of Dr. Joseph Stokes, Jr., a well-known infectious diseases researcher who, during a long career, would play a role in developing vaccines against measles, German measles, influenza, and mumps. With a government grant, Stokes was investigating hepatitis, at the time a mysterious disease that was a big problem for the army in its Mediterranean operations. Sawyer was one of nine Byberry

COs, including his friend and fellow Quaker Neil Hartman, who signed up to be injected with fully active hepatitis pathogens. Warren and Hartman at first developed only mild cases of the disease, but Hartman became seriously ill from a subsequent injection of hepatitis A, resulting in weeks of hospitalization. He also developed an infection from a liver biopsy. An army doctor had warned that the program could be "a risky thing" and "a person could die," but Sawyer recalled years later that he didn't take this very seriously. Some of his colleagues, he said, "had the idea of trying to prove that we were not afraid to die, like the service people in the army." Hartman told scholar Sydney Halpern that he wanted to demonstrate he wasn't a yellowbelly, as COs were often branded, but also to do something worthwhile. "My main motivation," Sawyer told her, "was just to be of service to mankind." [9]

———

THE "JAUNDICE" EXPERIMENTS MAY have been the darkest chapter of CO voluntarism. Warren, Neil, and the other COs at Byberry were young, healthy, and intelligent, but even they do not seem to have fully understood the risks. And the hepatitis experiments involved many others, including institutionalized children, from whom truly informed consent was not, and perhaps could not be, obtained. Long before his service as the nation's surgeon general, which lasted from 1982 to 1989, C. Everett Koop studied medicine at Penn and, as a resident there, was involved in these experiments. He came to regret it. Interviewed in a documentary about World War II COs, he explained that "I as a young surgeon was asked to do serial biopsies on their livers to see what the effect of the virus was in the production of the changes in the liver. And in that way, I got to know that a lot of these young men had no idea that the risk they were taking also included death. And some of those youngsters did die."[10]

The world has changed since then. Research institutions have created panels of scientists to review experiments to avoid just such episodes. These boards, Koop said, "would not permit the use of a live virus in human subjects unless they really understood what was going to happen to them. And I doubt that even if they knew what the risk was, that an

Internal Review Board in any academic institution would consent to that kind of experimental work."

All the same, COs wanted to participate and the risks only made them more eager. "We feel that what we are doing is of utmost importance to our country now, and later to all humanity," wrote CO George Nachtigall, who volunteered for research into the effects of hot climates. And Max Kampelman—remember Max, the law student from the Bronx?—signed up for some trying experiments as well because, like Sawyer, he felt it was an "opportunity to do significant service for mankind."[11]

Granted CO status despite his relatively secular pacifism, Max was first sent to the Quaker-run CPS camp on the site of a former Civilian Conservation Corps camp in Big Flats, New York, where he continued to write for *The Conscientious Objector* and joined others in pressing for more meaningful work. In 1943, an opportunity came along to serve as an attendant at a school for the "feeble-minded" on a farm in Pownal, Maine. It wasn't a bad place, as such places go, and Max did what he could to help, including taking his young charges into town on Saturday nights for a movie, an ice cream cone, and a walk around the village. "A hug, a touch," Kampelman would later write. "These were our most effective tools."[12]

Max, the consummate city boy, also learned to drive a tractor on the school's farm. But like so many of the CPS pacifists, he was eager to do more, so when a brochure arrived in search of volunteers for a starvation experiment at the University of Minnesota, he signed on. "Will You Starve That They Be Better Fed?" the brochure asked. But it appealed to self-interest as well as altruism, mentioning free tuition for classes and the presence on campus of a women's dorm for COs wanting to be "a guinea pig by day and a 'wolf' by night!" The program had far more takers than it could accommodate, a pattern that replicated itself when other researchers sought CPS volunteers. The idea for using COs in this way came from Britain, where the contributions of pacifist human guinea pigs drew the attention of *Fellowship*, later *Newsweek*, and finally of Paul Comly French, who headed the NSBRO and got Uncle Sam involved. By now (June of 1942), David Swift, Dellinger's former roommate at Yale, was working for the American Friends Service Committee on finding more significant work for COs. He brought in the Rockefeller Foundation.[13]

Overall, between five hundred and one thousand COs served as guinea pigs in medical and scientific experiments, some of which were arduous and even dangerous. Some studies involved being infected with typhus, malaria, pneumonia, or hepatitis. Other experiments were aimed at investigating frostbite, high-altitude conditions, poison gas, seawater, and temperature extremes. Bent Andresen, incarcerated in Pennsylvania for resisting the draft, took part in a project at Cornell University that required him to spend three months in a refrigerated room. Peter Watson and other COs rode a stationary bicycle in a room at the University of Rochester heated to 123 degrees to simulate desert fighting conditions. During each eight-hour shift (without food or drink) they would lose about 10 percent of their body weight.[14]

Nathaniel Hoffman, after a stint at a mental hospital in Connecticut, took part in a study of airsickness and seasickness at Wesleyan University for which he was strapped into an elevator that soared at high speed and descended likewise. He also volunteered for experiments in New Hampshire that involved withholding various nutrients. CPS men in Arkansas took part in a study that aimed "to investigate the value of dehydrated grass in mass feeding" as a way of alleviating postwar food shortages. At Harvard, CPS men took part in a study of hearing aids that might alleviate the problem of communicating in noisy aircraft. And scientists from Caltech kept a dozen men awake for 112 hours straight. "After 48 hours," *Time* reported, "they couldn't talk straight," and one tried to climb a set of imaginary stairs. But they played basketball pretty well even on the fourth day. And once tired, Benzedrine proved a useful pick-me-up."[15]

In New Hampshire, meanwhile, CPS men wore lice-infested clothing for three weeks at a time—all the while laboring at their normal road-work—as a part of an anti-typhus experiment. Typhus had become a big problem for American troops beset by lice in North Africa, but lice-killing formulations had ample peaceful purposes as well, and the New Hampshire experiments showed that pyrethrins were effective lousicides. The lice were gathered from the alcoholic ward of New York's Bellevue Hospital, allowed to feed on New York University students paid for this purpose, and then sustained on their journey from the city to the CPS camp by feeding on the Rockefeller researchers making the trip. The section of camp devoted to this was nicknamed "Camp Liceum," and unlike volunteers previously tried on the Bowery (New York's Skid Row in those days), the cooperation of COs "was remarkable. None gave up the experiment because of its discomforts. None complained, and we believe that none killed lice intentionally."[16]

The role of COs as guinea pigs in food experiments (especially reduced calorie diets) seems to have captured the most public attention, garnering coverage in major publications including *Life, Time,* and *Reader's Digest.* At Camp Magnolia in Arkansas, CPS men working on soil conservation also consumed dehydrated grass tips to see if they could substitute nutritionally for fruits and vegetables. In New Hampshire, men were fed diets variously low in vitamin C or protein. Elsewhere, COs were used in "life raft" studies. At Massachusetts General Hospital they drank varying amounts of seawater to assess its effect on shipwreck survivors. Other studies focused on what mix of protein, fat, and carbohydrates should go into nutrient bars that could be stashed in lifeboats to keep people alive while adrift at sea. Max Kampelman took part in the most famous such study of all.

It was the fall of 1944. Max had never been west of Reading, Pennsylvania, when he took the train out across the autumnal farmlands of the Midwest and up the Mississippi River to Minneapolis, where he was to be one of the thirty-six COs (out of more than four hundred applicants) accepted into an experiment to explore the effects of starvation on mind and body and develop recommendations for helping people recover. Because of the war, hunger was rampant in Europe; perhaps a million Soviet citizens had starved during the siege of Leningrad, Nazi concentration camps had begun to be liberated, and food was short in western Europe. The starvation study, driven by the encounters of Allied forces with hungry civilians, was headed by an ambitious young physiologist named Ancel Keys.

Already somewhat famous, not to say notorious, for his creation of the K ration for the armed forces, Keys had grown up in Berkeley, California, and as a child lived through the same epic San Francisco earthquake as had Dorothy Day and William James. He was a restless, adventurous young fellow with an uncle in Los Angeles named Lon Chaney, and by the time Keys came to the University of Minnesota, where he founded the Laboratory of Physiological Hygiene, he was already amply impressed with himself, having studied with a Nobel prizewinner in Denmark before stints at the University of Cambridge, Harvard, and the Mayo Clinic. Margaret Haney, a young chemist descended from Quakers, became his wife and lifelong colleague.[17]

Her imperious husband was to become America's most famous post-war nutritional scientist. Always controversial, he gave us the wildly wrong notion that dietary fats were to blame for the rampant heart disease of the last century, but he and Margaret were also early advocates, in a bestselling cookbook called *Eat Well and Stay Well*, for Americans to adopt a Mediterranean diet. During the war he was made a special assistant to the secretary of war and investigated a variety of topics for the military, including, of course, nutrition. The availability of CPS volunteers was a particular wartime boon; Keys used these eager guinea pigs in a variety of research projects—on cold and heat, thirst, and the effect of various vitamins including riboflavin and thiamine. In 1943, he kept half a dozen COs in bed for a month to see what that would do a person.[18]

Keys's starvation study began in November 1944 with three dozen men who were on average 25.5 years old, 152.7 pounds, and 5 feet 10 inches tall, all typical of American draftees at the time. But they were far more intelligent, scoring two standard deviations higher than the average inductee. Their average on the Thorndike CAVD, a kind of IQ test, exceeded that of master's degree candidates at Columbia Teachers College. In fact, all had some college and half had degrees. On the Minnesota Multiphasic Personality Inventory, recently developed by some of Keys's campus colleagues, the men were typical for guys their age even if they did skew a bit "feminine" because (Keys believed) of their interest in cultural activities.[19]

The volunteers were put on a standardized diet of thirty-two hundred calories per day for three months, followed by six months of around eighteen hundred calories a day. The menu, which approximated the starchy diet of underfed civilians in war-ravaged Europe, featured potatoes, turnips, rutabagas, macaroni, and dark bread. The men weren't just expected to go hungry. They also had to walk twenty-two miles a week, with the goal of expending roughly three thousand calories every day, and they had to keep a journal recording their thoughts, feelings, and dreams. They were also subjected to continual monitoring of weight, size, strength, and other vital metrics. Information was recorded from x-rays, blood samples, psychomotor assessments, measurements of intelligence, and personality evaluations. Treadmill tests were brutal, requiring them to sprint until collapse. After the starvation period there would be three months of recovery, during which the men were randomly assigned to one of four groups given different quantities of protein and vitamins.

It appears that neither Keys nor his guinea pigs had any idea of the ordeal in store for the men. Issued white shirts, blue pants, and sturdy shoes, they lived in the South Tower of the university's football stadium, and they began the project full of energy and ideals. Some took courses at the university while others volunteered at settlement houses or took advantage of local cultural offerings. One volunteered at the Minneapolis Symphony in exchange for free admission. Another played accordion and called square dances. But when the first three months were over, they began their descent into the hell of starvation.[20]

On the first day of reduced rations, they sat down to a breakfast of a small bowl of farina, a couple of pieces of toast, some fried potatoes, a little jello, a bit of jam, and a small glass of milk. Each man was supposed to lose 25 percent of his body weight by dropping around two and a half pounds per week, and each man's meals were adjusted depending on where he was in relation to these goals. "We were given our food along a cafeteria line," one participant recalled, "and if the guy ahead of you is given five slices of bread, that's pretty hard to conceal. And if you're only getting three, that's pretty touchy." Participants came to dread the Friday postings of the coming week's portions, because it was painful to learn that you were about to face a further cut in your already meager allocation.[21]

The men were diligent in sticking to the plan, but when one cheated a buddy system was instituted. Traveling in pairs was also helpful as their strength faded. In the photos taken for the spread in *Life*, published July 30, 1945, the guys were downright skeletal. One fellow was so weak he got stuck in a revolving door in a downtown department store because he lacked the strength to push it. Marshall Sutton, one of the COs, recalled packing up his meager dinner ration and taking his girlfriend to dinner at the most expensive restaurant in Minneapolis. "I wanted to take her to a restaurant just to enjoy seeing her eat . . . but when the waiter came up with the food she just couldn't do it. I was a bit disturbed by it, I'd spent all that money on a big meal and she just couldn't eat it."[22]

The men suffered body aches, hair loss, anemia, swollen feet, and ring-
ing ears. Yet Keys would marvel at the extraordinary resilience of the human body in the face of such deprivation. The much bigger issues, he found,
were psychological. His human guinea pigs grew edgy and depressed, ir-
ritable with one another but uncharacteristically passive in the face of authority. Some had to give up their university courses because they didn't
have the energy. One man remembered that, out doing his walking with a
buddy, they would look for driveways when crossing streets because it was
a way to avoid hoisting oneself back up on a curb. More than one of the
fellows collected recipes and cookbooks. Said Harold Blickenstaff: "I don't
know many other things in my life that I looked forward to being over
with any more than this experiment."[23]

Sex drives, like every other interest but one, vanished. "It is amazing
what hunger can do," Kampelman wrote years later. "It dampens sexual
appetites, essentially eliminates them. You focus on food. You daydream
about it. You read cookbooks and books on nutrition. You go to bed at
night thinking of food and wake up in the morning thinking of food. It is
boring, if virtually unavoidable. My night dreams, for example, were not
of sexual fantasies, but of candy bars . . . I never see a picture of famine victims without empathizing with the dehumanizing effects."[24]

The strain was terrible. One man scarfed down sundaes and the like on
the sly and even resorted to stealing and eating raw rutabagas. Two men
had to be taken to the psychiatric ward of the university hospital for a spell.
Overall, four men failed to finish the project. One was almost finished by
it. It happened during the recovery phase—in a sense the most important
part, because that was when researchers hoped they would learn the best
way to rehabilitate the hungry. But for some of the men this segment was
the hardest, especially if they were assigned to the group fed the sparest
diet. For a while many even continued losing weight, thanks to the declining fluid retention that had been among their many starvation symptoms.
The men had originally averaged 152.7 pounds, but after the starvation
period the figure was 115.6 pounds.[25]

One man finally cracked. It was Sam Legg, one of the leaders of the
volunteers, and one of the longest-serving CPS men. Legg and his assigned
buddy (who was not a participant in the experiment) had formed the habit

of visiting two elderly ladies who had befriended the men. When it was time to eat, Sam would customarily go outside and chop wood for the women. On this particular night, he barely had the strength to wield the ax when he stood up one of the logs he was to split and placed his left hand carefully on its flat surface. He had reserves enough to lift the ax in his right hand and, with one fateful moonlit swing, bring it down on his left, lopping off three fingers. Keys got the news from his wife when he got home that evening. "My God, Margaret," he said. "I am torturing them."[26]

Yet, a few days later, desperate not to be expelled, Legg rejoined the group and Keys let him stay. After that, like crocuses in spring, something beautiful popped up among the men: an organized protest. Todd Tucker, in his absorbing book on the subject, says it came in the form of a letter many of the men had signed. Tucker's description: "The paper demanded, after a lengthy preamble about freedom of choice and the rights of man, that the buddy system be abolished."

Keys was peeved at first, but his deputy, Josef Brozek, was delighted and explained why: "It is a good sign, yes? The men are getting feisty." Keys summarily rejected the request. Glad the men were coming back to life but worried that their physical recovery was so halting, he raised everyone's daily allocation by 800 calories—a huge increase that allowed for three meals a day and the beginning of the end of their starvation. Just two days later, Keys' deputy brought him another manifesto against the buddy system, this one with even more signatures and, as Tucker says, "even more inflamed with left-wing bombast about strikes and non-cooperation." The authoritarian Keys was inclined to reject this one, too, but Brozek warned that he would have to give in or face a general insurrection.[27]

"And once again, you seem to find this insubordination amusing," said Keys.

"Don't you see?" said Brozek. "It is the ultimate validation of your theories. Hungry people mindlessly follow orders. You feed them enough and right away they demand self-government."

Keys repealed the buddy system and the men were free to travel about alone. Brozek had persuaded him that the ones who had made it this far were tough, better fed now, and unlikely to cheat. For a bunch of pacifists with their ribs showing, it was yet another small triumph for nonviolence.

CHAPTER 18

DÉJÀ VU FOR RUSTIN

By EARLY MAY OF 1944, Bayard Rustin had been locked up in the "colored" section of the segregated federal prison at Ashland, Kentucky, for a couple of months, long enough to get his list of correspondents through the approval process. And so he poured his heart out in letters to Davis Platt—to the extent he could, knowing that every letter was read by a prison censor. Sometimes he seemed to be writing to the censor as much as to his lover. "Tyranny is no harsh term for deeds practiced here," Rustin wrote, resorting to the bible to add: "We are held slaves to a state which 'grinds the faces of the unfortunate in the dust.' One ought to resist the entire system! . . . Perhaps the time rapidly approaches where such behavior will be the only honorable thing."[1]

In truth he had embarked on such a course himself long ago, and he didn't stop when he was sent to prison. He was trouble even at the West Street intake center, confounding an interviewer trying to figure out whether, if sent to a facility with minimal security, Rustin would walk away. It sounded as if he might, and so he was sent to Ashland. It was a couple miles outside of town, in a pleasant country setting, and as prisons go it might have been worse. A medium-security facility housing men with no more than five years to serve, it had a farm, furniture-making operations, and all sorts of classes and activities. Prisoners moved about freely during the day, living in individual cells where they were allowed books, photos, and musical instruments (Platt would soon bring Rustin a mandolin). An inmate production of Gilbert and Sullivan was a particular hit. Ashland, like so many American institutions, was segregated even though the warden, Robert Hagerman, was a progressive administrator with a PhD and family in the Brethren. At the outset, at least, Rustin described him as "a good fellow."[2]

But Hagerman saw Rustin as trouble and appealed (without success) to Bennett to have him transferred, producing letters in which Rustin asked Grotewohl to get the word out to the media on segregation at the prison. Rustin, the warden wrote, "possesses in abundance the rare quality of leadership" and "this man will be a constant troublemaker." Rustin was indeed a special case, but Hagerman was having the same troubles as many of his counterparts elsewhere in the system. By the time Rustin arrived, on March 9, 1944, dissent was already in full flower all across the many facilities holding pacifist war resisters. Bayard was to do his part; years later he called his wartime incarceration "the most profound and important experience I've ever had." In the segregated cell block he heard from the other black inmates, many southerners, about the hardships they had experienced, writing to Platt that "pleasures pale into the distance as one is brought face to face with suffering of the intensity revealed in lives here." Prison for Rustin was a profoundly humbling experience, for in attempting to live freely behind bars he would make a crucial mistake and torture himself for it during the rest of his time in stir. It was a mistake that he was condemned to repeat, with far worse consequences, nearly a decade later in Pasadena.[3]

Rustin had been at Ashland only about a week when his thirty-second birthday rolled around on March 17. He was still in quarantine, routine for the beginning of any inmate's sentence, and without much to celebrate. No one on the list of correspondents he'd submitted to the prison authorities had yet been approved, but he and his grandmother had agreed before he arrived that at 1:00 p.m. that day they would read Psalm 56 ("Be gracious to me, O God, for men trample upon me"). While in quarantine, new inmates got the lowdown from the other guys through the ventilation system. Rustin in turn used it to give instruction on how to campaign against a hated guard and win the freedom of someone in solitary. Then, through the vent, he sang "Strange Fruit," Billie Holiday's song about lynching.

The warden quickly recognized that the small band of COs in the institution (fewer than a tenth of the 450 on hand) accepted Rustin as their leader,
and that he was "an extremely capable agitator."[4]

Prison authorities also understood that the pacifists were an educated
bunch with influential friends on the outside, including in the media, and
that it made sense to be flexible and show restraint in dealing with them.
In one case Bayard, arriving for a meal after the other inmates, ended up
at a table by himself in the segregated dining hall. There was also a white
inmate sitting by himself at another table. When a group of four black newcomers was brought in, there was no more room among the other black inmates. Segregation meant they couldn't sit with the lone white inmate. And
because they were under quarantine, they couldn't sit with Rustin. So he
was asked to vacate his table for them by squeezing in at another "colored"
table, which he refused to do on the grounds that he wouldn't cooperate
with segregation. When guards, threatening a stint in the Hole, tried to
drag him out, Rustin's fellow pacifists surrounded them and pointed out
that no form of coercion would make him relent. The guards finally put
him down, and after further discussions it was decided to let the whole
matter drop—and to avoid using force when an inmate couldn't in good
conscience comply with a guard's direction.[5]

Mail censorship was another bone of contention. COs mostly accepted
that letters had to be read for reasons of security, but bitterly resented that
some were never sent out, especially if they reflected unapproved political
views, or that some inbound mail was capriciously withheld. They also
wanted to stop the prison practice of blocking radical periodicals. Rustin,
for example, protested the confiscation of a monthly called *Equality*,
edited by James Farmer, vowing to have "hundreds of his friends and
dozens of organizations send him stuff by the pound" in order to bury
prison censorship in an avalanche of words. And Bronson Clark reported
that Rustin "has trouble getting letters out. Few of them are returned to
him . . . so one would assume they are piling up in Washington." Rustin
was of course undeterred, insisting: "I prefer to lose my privilege of writing—have material held up or sent to the FBI—before I should pusil-
lanimously or expediently write material . . . so harmless as to please the
limited minds that are selected to pass on it . . . I've decided to write what
I most feel and believe."[6]

One such letter was to Kessel Johnson, a friend in the army to whom Rustin wrote about what he hoped to accomplish in prison and beyond. During the war, Rustin said, he wanted to be "in that place where I can gain the best political experiences for the task we shall have at the end of the war. Negroes especially will have to struggle for economic and political freedom." In prison, where black inmates who just wanted to get through their time were ambivalent about his activities, "I am learning the many factors involved in organizing the underprivileged and the fearful."[7]

In October, Meredith Dallas, who had already served time as a member of the Union Eight, went on a hunger strike with other pacifists to protest mail censorship. Hagerman, having said all along that he would never engage in forced feeding, started talks with the inmates' committee. After twenty-seven days he announced an end to censorship of mail on political, religious, or social matters and that discussions of the institution, even critical ones, would be permitted in correspondence—an essential point for inmates, who otherwise would have few means of reporting abuses to the outside world. It was a another small victory for nonviolence.[8]

Rustin's reading flourished. Thanks in large part to the FOR's Doris Grotewohl, he was able to receive a variety of publications, including *Time*, *Life*, *Newsweek*, and *The New Yorker*, but also *The Christian Century*, *The Nation*, *The Progressive*, and Macdonald's *politics*. As for books, he got novels including Richard Wright's *Black Boy* and Lillian Smith's *Strange Fruit*, a particular favorite of his fellow inmates. He also got nonfiction including Erich Fromm's *Escape from Freedom* and, yes, William James's *Varieties of Religious Experience*.

In his correspondence with Platt and Grotewohl, both of whom were devoted to him, Rustin kept up on the outside world and gained emotional support. The burden of prison, to a free spirit like Bayard in particular, was the complete loss of autonomy. "What is oppressive about prison is that one is unable to be a human being," Rustin would say later. "He is unable to make a single decision about anything he thinks important. A bell rings, and you are permitted to take a shower. A bell rings, and you can go and eat."[9] This common experience of incarceration was exacerbated by Bayard's sense of being sidelined from the great struggle for black liberation. The war, meanwhile, ground on. When he and the other inmates heard FDR address the nation after the D-Day landings, Rustin wrote to

Platt that he "wept inwardly—somehow the more for God who must have been bewildered by it, by so many millions of his children asking for victory . . . yet all of them meaning something different." Rustin said that he, too, was doing a lot of praying lately.[10]

Grotewohl, who for a while dated Rustin and appears to have been in love with him, did what she could to cheer him up. Besides sending reading material, she brought mandolin strings when she visited, and in her evocative letters described performances she had attended at their old downtown stomping grounds, including the Village Vanguard. Elsewhere she heard the jazz trumpet player Muggsy Spanier and the charismatic baritone John Raitt, a conscientious objector who sometimes sang for his fellow pacifists. Raitt would become a Broadway star (starting with *Carousel* in 1945, in the role of Billy Bigelow) and the father of singer Bonnie Raitt.[11]

Grotewohl gave Bayard encouraging news of the movement—including a report from Pauli Murray about nonviolent sit-ins by Howard students at Washington, D.C., restaurants, at least one of which won the support of black GIs in uniform—and a quick agreement to serve black customers. Outside the Thompson's cafeteria outlet at Eleventh Street and Pennsylvania Avenue, just blocks from the White House, protesters marched with signs including: ARE YOU FOR HITLER'S WAY (RACIAL SUPREMACY) OR THE AMERICAN WAY (RACIAL EQUALITY)? According to Murray, "the local metropolitan press ignored our exploit."[12]

When Rustin arrived at Ashland, the pacifists there, like their brethren at other federal prisons, were working to end prison segregation, or at least chip away at it. In April, Bayard refused to sit in the designated black area during the weekly movie, apparently without consequences. And Hagerman went along with the inmates' request that he let blacks and whites mingle freely by leaving open the barrier that divided them. Rustin (who alone among blacks took advantage of this chance to mingle) used the open gate on Sundays to join white COs in listening to classical music on the radio. A white convict named Elam Huddleston—a heavyset former Kentucky state treasurer imprisoned on mail fraud charges—warned Rustin to stay away.[13]

The next time Huddleston saw Rustin among the whites, on a Sunday in early May, he made good his threat, grabbing a mop handle or some such and viciously assaulting Bayard with it. When other pacifists rushed to restrain the assailant, they caught some of Huddleston's blows. Rustin, with his characteristic self-possession, told them to stand aside, simply covering his head and absorbing the blows while the others stood by in horrified witness. Huddleston continued to beat Rustin until the stick shattered and the attacker, shaking from this eruption of his own brutality, gave up. But instead of dragging off the perpetrator, guards ordered Rustin back to his cell as if he were the assailant, and they locked the gate dividing the races. A few days later the warden apologized to Bayard because "We acted as though you had done something wrong." Hagerman said he appreciated Rustin's nonviolent response as well that of the COs, and reopened the barrier between blacks and whites. He was going to dispatch Huddleston to solitary for a spell, but the COs asked that he not be punished and Hagerman granted their request.[14]

"I have just finished reading the account of the demonstration of non-violence by our friends in Ashland a couple of Sundays ago," Muste wrote afterwards. "It is difficult to put into words the joy I feel over the fact that their spirits under severe testing remained pure and true. If they were the sons of my flesh, I could not feel more closely bound to these young men than I do." He called their nonviolent approach "the method which can break the barriers of race and caste."[15]

Rustin, who was left-handed, suffered a fractured left wrist in the altercation, which must have impaired for a while his correspondence with friends and lovers on the outside. "Perhaps this will force you to join a majority for a change," Grotewohl teased, "and become a right-handed man." Some of the other pacifists came away with bumps and bruises too. But their prestige soared among black inmates, who appreciated this rare example of whites putting themselves in harm's way to aid a black man in the South. Rustin, meanwhile, had set an example for all parties. "As you know," he wrote to Grotewohl, "there are many inmates here who are conditioned to believe that persons of my 'expression' (to quote Father Divine) should 'stay in their place.'"

Rustin hated prison but was far too energetic and creative to sulk. He formed a drama group and put on what the inmates regarded as a praiseworthy performance of Eugene O'Neill's *The Emperor Jones*. He started teaching classes of various kinds, including English and music, and asked friends to send collections of Negro spirituals as well as religious music by Palestrina and others. The guys preferred "weak and sentimental lyrics with the most sickly melodies," so he worked on elevating their tastes gradually. "And so we have a Bach chorale and several spirituals with great beauty and simplicity." For southern whites, Rustin wrote, "being taught by a Negro is for them a revolutionary situation."[16]

That was in some sense the least of it. On arrival at Ashland, Rustin astonished some inmates with his concluding act after a series of inmate skits. He sat on the edge of the stage and "sang Negro folk songs, a cappella, in a high, thin, sweet falsetto," pacifist Donald Wetzel recalled, adding: "I looked around, incredulous, at his friends. Surely they must have known. He sang in the voice of a woman."[17]

It had long been Rustin's policy to flout discriminatory rules in whatever context he happened to find himself, and perhaps this, along with his sexual appetites, led him to flaunt behavior that could not fail to bring him the unwanted attention of prison officials. Rustin is the subject of at least three insightful biographies, the most recent of which, by D'Emilio, has a particular focus on his homosexuality. "Sitting in a meeting soon after his release from quarantine, Rustin bent forward and gave Charlie Butcher an affectionate kiss on the neck," D'Emilio writes. Butcher would someday be the chief executive of his family's eponymous floor products company, which he would expand a hundredfold during his five decades at the helm and then sell to Johnson Wax. He gave employees $18 million of the proceeds. "As the weather warmed and inmates had more time in the yard, Rustin startled everyone with his displays of affection."[18]

In fact, he was openly sexual toward some inmates. Guards reported him caressing and walking arm in arm with other men and, with one man in particular, mooning around the place like a couple of young lovers. It was courageous behavior but also foolhardy, and if the inmates allowed it to pass, the administration was taking note. It was already clear that Rustin intended to foment rebellion, but even absent his political activities, administrators knew that sexual relationships in prisons could lead to trouble (as demonstrated when Dellinger averted the rape of Bill Lovett at Lewisburg), and to this day even consensual sex among federal inmates is prohibited. Nor were all of the COs comfortable with Rustin's brazenness. His behavior toward other men too neatly fit the preconceptions of prison authorities (and others) about conscientious objectors and homosexuals alike, for both were considered maladjusted, emotionally crippled, and of dubious masculinity. James V. Bennett, reflecting what may have passed for psychological sophistication in that era, claimed that COs were "frequently motivated by an over-protective home or a mother fixation, or by revolt against authority as typified in the home and transferred to society at large. They are problem children, whether at home, at school, or in prison." His armchair psychoanalyzing was far wide of the mark, but his insight into the resisters' goals was remarkably acute, for he sensed that their pacifism was "only a part of a program for changing the social, political, economic and cultural order of the world."[19]

Rustin, despite his incarceration, remained (in the argot of our own times) an extraordinarily confident gay black man, one who by and large refused to dissemble about who he was. In late June a visit from Platt delighted him, even as it raised eyebrows and inquiries among black and white inmates alike. (The authorities knew more because they had been reading Rustin's letters.) With Platt came the mandolin. Rustin quickly began learning to play from Robert Currier, a CO on his cell block who would later be principal violinist for the Rhode Island Philharmonic. Bayard promised to reward Platt for the cherished gift of this instrument "by doing some sixteenth-century ballads on it for you." Rustin was musically gifted, but not everyone appreciated his climb up the mandolin-learning curve. One inmate reported that the guys loved the Elizabethan songs he sang and played while learning, although it drove the guards crazy. But fellow CO Larry Gara insisted that "he drove us nuts. We had to lay down the law that he could practice only so many hours."[20]

Meanwhile, Rustin pressed the warden on segregation. There had already been progress, and the changes so far suggested that the inmates would accept an end to the practice. Sports were already integrated at the prison, and kitchen staffers of both races had begun taking meals together in full view of the others. Southern whites didn't seem to have a problem taking a class from Rustin, either. Citing these factors, he argued that the color line in dining, sleeping arrangements, and theater seating could be erased. And he warned that while "I have tried to give due consideration to existing circumstances and to the problems involved in racial change," he was nearing the end of his tether. "I am faced with an almost impossible situation at each meal time."[21]

Part of what made Rustin so remarkable was that while he had the soul of a poet, he could think and plan like an engineer when necessary—and better yet, he could put the two together. In a meeting with Hagerman he laid out an exquisitely conceived plan that proposed to make cell block E, where Rustin and other pacifists bunked, into a model of integration, with inmates from that block permitted to dine interracially and other inmates free to join them if they wished. Muste helped, visiting Rustin to discuss strategy and then meeting with Hagerman. Muste followed up by mail to argue the case for integration in writing. During their meeting Hagerman had evidently criticized Rustin for stirring up trouble among fellow inmates, but Muste argued that the other pacifists were just as concerned about desegregation and would be, absent Bayard. Muste also wrote at length to Randolph and to Roy Wilkins at the NAACP to fill them in on Rustin's efforts—and to drum up support for him.[22]

At Ashland Bayard demonstrated the talent for coalition building that would serve him and the cause of civil rights so well after the war. The COs had formed a negotiating committee to back him, and he would soon expand his base of support beyond the relatively small number of pacifists by getting the much more numerous Jehovah's Witnesses on his side. "That," said Gara, "scared the hell out of the prison authorities." Ever organized, Rustin carefully recorded each step in the campaign to purge Jim Crow. In August the prison started to allow interracial seating in church. Later that month Rustin met with Bennett when the prison chief came for a visit. He left the impression that he didn't intend to countenance much progress on racial separation, and soon after the prison doctor asked Rustin how he would respond to a transfer. Rustin vowed to fight it by going limp, not wearing clothes, and other such tactics. An interracial section in the theater got no black takers other than Rustin. Something similar was tried in the dining room, but Rustin and his supporters insisted the signs come down—after which, he reported, the desegregation effort was going well and according to plan.[23]

"He was at that time the most astute organizer I think we had," Alex Stach told an interviewer, "and maybe the best theoretician" or strategist in "nonviolent tactics." A peace activist and former student at the University of Minnesota, Stach walked away from a CPS camp in late 1942 or early 1943, after which he served four and a half years in prison.

An uncooperative inmate, Stach spent some of that time at hard labor, but more of it was spent at Ashland, where he learned some Russian from an exiled aristocrat and some Chinese from a former missionary and prisoner of the Japanese locked up in his home country for refusing to be drafted. Stach and Rustin held "something like college seminars during yard period" and Stach was elected to lead the inmate council that was to negotiate with the administration.[24]

Unfortunately Rustin's reckless displays of physical affection for men were soon confirmed as the visible manifestations of an active sex life behind bars—and the basis for formal charges of sexual misconduct. In August of 1944 two white inmates told a senior officer they had discovered Rustin performing oral sex on a black inmate (identified only as "Whitlock") behind a curtain in the prison auditorium. One of the witnesses had seen Rustin kissing Whitlock in the prison yard. Another inmate claimed to have seen Rustin performing oral sex in the machine shop. A fourth inmate described rejecting Rustin's advances when the latter slipped into his cell one night. And yet another inmate told of being solicited by Rustin, rejecting him, and being urged to "come up and see me some time." Perhaps worst of all for Rustin, Whitlock testified against him—reluctantly, it seems clear, but on the record and in Rustin's presence. Rustin lied shamelessly—no doubt reflecting his awareness of what it would mean if he were found guilty, his sense of betrayal, and more generally the impossible position in that time and place of men who loved men. He must have been desperate, for his deception required him in some sense to deny who he was, and it would only add to his shame and humiliation when he came clean later.[25]

For Bayard and his movement at Ashland, it was a catastrophe. At the proceeding, his impassioned and entirely fraudulent performance culminated in an attack on his accusers (whom he might understandably have expected to lie), and when he was ordered into administrative segregation he resisted furiously, wrapping himself around his chair, prying loose the hands of guards—and ultimately getting himself carried out of the room and into isolation for his pains. When Larry Gara found a way to ask him if the charges were true, he said no—causing half a dozen inmates to go on strike in Rustin's defense. His lie landed them all in administrative segregation. Relations between the pacifists and the prison administration, only recently cooperative and reasonably fruitful, were now poisoned, for believing Rustin meant that the administration must have smeared him to discredit the movement and its leader.

In a sense they *had* smeared him, by exploiting the undue opprobrium attaching to his sexuality. But Rustin had discredited himself as well: by failing to subordinate his appetites to his cause, and by lying about it. He had sacrificed his credibility with his jailers, who now felt empowered to subject him to stricter control and, ultimately, transfer. He had also disastrously betrayed his inmate followers. And he had broken faith with the one essential figure who had supported him and his desegregation campaign throughout. A. J. Muste learned what had happened from Hagerman and Bennett and then visited his protégé twice, in mounting frustration. Afterwards, on October 23, Ashland's chief medical officer, H. M. Janney, talked with Rustin at length, learning in this emotional encounter that Bayard's father was a virtual stranger, that his mother had four other children by four other men, and that while visiting her when he was fourteen years old he spent the night in bed beside a man with whom he had his first sexual experience. During this fraught session with Janney, Rustin (having spent six weeks in isolation and having faced Muste twice) cried, admitted sex with two of the inmates, and tearfully promised both to remain abstinent and to abandon his contempt for prison rules. Soon after, Rustin received a letter from his surrogate father, Muste, that must have been eviscerating.

> You have been guilty of gross misconduct, specially reprehensible in a person making the claims to leadership and in a sense moral superiority which you were making . . . You had deceived everybody, including your own comrades and most devoted friends . . . You were capable of making the "mistake" of thinking that you could be the leader in a revolution of the most basic and intricate kind at the same time that you were a weakling in an extreme degree and engaged in practices for which there was no justification, which a person with a tenth of your brains must have known would defeat your objective . . . You are still far from facing reality in yourself. In the self that has been and still is you, there is nothing to respect, and you must ruthlessly cast out *everything* in you which prevents you from facing that. Only so can your true self come to birth—through fire, anguish, complete and child-like humility.[26]

Muste could be a hard man, for a pacifist. But he'd been through hells of his own, and he could not have survived and persisted without iron in his spine. He was tough with Bayard, yet stood by him, concluding his letter by insisting that "my love for you and hope for you shines through" and then, perhaps feeling guilty about how stern he had been, sending a telegram: "You are in my thoughts and prayers. My admiration for your courage and estimate of your possibilities never greater. God is our refuge and strength."[27]

He and Rustin were soon reconciled—the older man believed in redemption as much as in sin. But as Rustin would someday learn, Muste's patience was not without end where his cause was concerned—and there was a stonier Muste still in store. It was Bayard's promiscuity, as much as anything, his seeming recklessness, and the risks to Rustin as well as their shared causes, that frustrated and infuriated Muste. For now though, Rustin found relief from his massive shame as well as the older man's crushing disapproval by facing up to what he had done and voicing remorse. Expressing his love for his mentor, he admitted that "I feared facing the reality of the ugly facts," called himself a "traitor" to their cause, and acknowledged that "it was my own weakness and stupidity that defeated the immediate campaign" when success was at hand. "I have misused the confidence the negroes here had in my leadership; I have caused them to question the moral basis of non-violence; I have hurt and let down my friends over the country and caused people like you and Doris to grieve."[28]

To Platt, who evidently demanded faithfulness from Rustin once he learned what was going on, and who would eventually leave him when he came to realize it would never be forthcoming, Bayard responded with this brutal self-appraisal: "I have betrayed you and the things for which we stand," he wrote, adding: "I failed, Davis, more miserably than you can imagine." For the time being, though, Platt was more than willing to forgive, if not forget. In the wake of Bayard's troubles they had forged a much more intimate relationship by mail. When Rustin got word that his beloved grandfather was near death outside of Philadelphia, he was allowed to visit twice, first in November of 1944 and again near the end of March the following year, both times accompanied by the same broad-minded guard. On the second occasion, Platt persuaded an uncle to get lost for a few hours and turn over his house—and Rustin's minder allowed his charge to stay with Platt unchaperoned. They made love and pledged themselves to one another, and despite any number of contretemps they would live together for a while after the war in New York. Yet on the way back to Ashland, Rustin and his minder had to change trains in Columbus, where they were met by Helen Winnemore, yet another of the white activists hopelessly taken with him. She declared her love and opened the possibility of a life together, of a turn away from the difficult path of loving men. Rustin agonized over the choice she presented to him. It was no easy thing to be a man who loved men in the 1940s, a time when expert and popular opinion alike said you were sick if not worse. Hagerman, Ashland's warden, said "a diagnosis of psychopathic personality, homosexuality" was clear. A psychiatrist sent by the Bureau of Prisons called him "a classical picture of a constitutional homo—the invert type, the high voice, the extravagant mannerisms, the tremendous conceit, the general unmanliness."[29]

Rustin, in fact, had been getting in trouble for his love of men almost all his life. It was likely the reason he left Cheyney State after just two and a half years, and without a degree, even though he was such a good student that he was valedictorian at his high school graduation in 1932. His homosexuality—or perhaps more accurately, society's response to it—would later cause him far more trouble still, for his arrest in Pasadena came close to ruining his life. Despite his earlier promises, Rustin now oscillated between sullen cooperation and furious resistance, and was emboldened by the arrival of some hardcore militant resisters (including George Yamada) from the CPS camp at Germfask, Michigan. Finally, in August of 1945, with the war ending, Rustin and some of the other troublemakers were transferred to the federal prison at Lewisburg, a maximum-security institution with hardened inmates. Not long after his arrival, Bayard was refusing to walk in a segregated line of inmates or eat at segregated tables. Soon he and the other the resisters were quarantined in the library from the rest of the inmate population. They could read anything they wanted, but they couldn't mingle or organize. "It was the simplest way," said Gara, who had worked his way down, so to speak, from the federal prison camp at Mill Pond (in West Virginia) to the medium-security institution at Ashland and finally to Lewisburg. "Get them out of the way. Out of sight." The idea, he added, was to let them "drive each other nuts. And we did."[30]

Rustin's prison ordeal would outlast the war. He was one of a number of COs whose sentences kept them locked up beyond the Axis surrender. Others remained stuck in CPS camps even as American troops were being demobilized. As the band of remaining Lewisburg pacifists got smaller, Rustin grew more recalcitrant and embittered. Grotewohl wrote to tell him he was needed at CORE, and Houser wrote to tell of conversations with Wilkins, Randolph, and others about prospects for an interracial mass movement. Bayard's grandmother appealed in person. And in March of 1946 Muste visited after Rustin had embarked on yet another hunger strike and was force-fed. While Bayard was engaged in what amounted to a private struggle, the dawn of the atomic age had plunged American pacifists into a crisis. The bomb was bigger than racism, and the very next day Rustin wrote to Bennett to explain a change of heart. Henceforth he would be a model prisoner in an effort to get out as soon as he could. He was in prison, he explained, "because I felt that conscription and racial segregation, embodied in the Selective Service Act were the greatest evils of our nation." But now, he continued, "I see the Atomic Bomb, its use and disposition, to be the truly urgent problems of our time, for as A.J. said yesterday 'why speak of equality of men when there may be no men unless men of goodwill devote themselves to stop what may become World War III.'"[31]

PART THREE

AFTER

CHAPTER 19

DOLDRUMS

AMERICA'S USE OF ATOMIC weapons against Japan signaled the dawning of a new era in which it would be vastly easier to kill people en masse, and pacifists were quick to express their horror even as others exulted at the implications for Allied victory. Dwight Macdonald, by now an out and out pacifist, rushed to his typewriter to create a last-minute addition to the August 1945 cover of *politics*. "This atrocious action," he wrote of the Hiroshima bombing, "places 'us', the defenders of civilization, on a moral level with 'them', the beasts of Maidanek."[1]

For Macdonald and the others, this was exactly what they had been predicting, and why they had doggedly opposed a war that would seem to surpass most in its justice and necessity. In the next issue of *politics*, Dwight addressed the various rationales for the bombings: that they shortened the war, that they saved lives on both sides, that the Japanese had started it, and that our enemy had mistreated prisoners and established a tone of savagery in the fighting. "The flimsiness of these justifications is apparent," he wrote. "*Any* atrocious action, absolutely *any* one, could be excused on such grounds."

Dorothy Day, in the September 1945 edition of *The Catholic Worker*, spoke in quiet fury of Truman's "jubilation" at the news of the mass killing we had perpetrated in Hiroshima. "That is, we hope we have killed them . . . The effect is hoped for, not known. It is to be hoped they are vaporized, our Japanese brothers—scattered, men, women and babies, to the four winds, over the seven seas. Perhaps we will breathe their dust into our nostrils, feel them in the fog of New York on our faces, feel them in the rain on the hills of Easton."

John Haynes Holmes called the atom bomb "the supreme atrocity of the ages . . . a crime which we would instantly have recognized as such had Germany and not our own country been guilty of the act." Harry Emerson Fosdick condemned the bombings in a radio sermon: "Saying that Japan was guilty and deserved it, gets us nowhere. The mothers and babies of Hiroshima and Nagasaki did not deserve it." *Commonweal* said of the bombings, "The name Hiroshima, the name Nagasaki, are names for American guilt and shame."

For David Dellinger the bombings were so ghastly that they were grounds for a "Declaration of War" that he published in a new journal, launched with other pacifists, called *Direct Action*. But the "war" he declared was intended to be nonviolent: "There must be strikes, sabotage, and seizure of public property now being held by private owners. There must be civil disobedience of laws which are contrary to human welfare. But there must also be an uncompromising practice of treating everyone, including the worst of our opponents, with the respect and decency that he merits as a fellow human being."[2]

The Allies had been bombing civilians in both Germany and Japan, something *Commonweal* called "indefensible morally," as early as 1942. Two years later the Fellowship of Reconciliation brought out an American edition of *Massacre by Bombing*, by the English pacifist Vera Brittain, with a foreword endorsed by twenty-eight Americans, mostly pacifist clergy, including Buttrick, Fosdick, Holmes, Page, Sockman, and Villard. They called on Christians "to examine themselves concerning their participation in this carnival of death" and face "the realities of what is being done in our name." Their appeal to halt this carnage made the front page of the March 6, 1944, *New York Times,* for all the good that did. The Allies would only intensify their campaign of killing from the air.

To be sure, one or another of what would become the Axis had engaged in terror bombing as early as the 1930s, and the last German rocket fell on London as late as March 27, 1945. By then the fortunes of war—and Allied bombers—had brought the tactic home to Germany and Japan in spades. The public and press in the U.S. and Britain supported these bombing campaigns both as payback and as a way of winning the war faster, even as the raids reached horrifying proportions in scale and severity. Enemy cities were soon flattened by Allied bombing; Hamburg was devastated with the equivalent of two Hiroshimas-worth of bombs, and one hundred thousand people were killed in a single day's firebombing of Tokyo. Even *Life* observed in 1945 that "The very concept of strategic bombing . . . led straight to Hiroshima."[3]

Pacifists had warned from the outset that war is a slippery slope, one that in this case led from Pearl Harbor to Hiroshima. The use of nuclear weapons against Japan had many consequences, among them a gradual change in attitudes toward war. The potentially genocidal nature of these new weapons, which would only grow in power and numbers in the decades ahead, seemed to vindicate the pacifist view that war was inadmissible. Even President Truman could see that. "We can't stand another global war," he told an audience at a county fair in Missouri. "We can't ever have another war, unless it is total war, and that means the end of our civilization as we know it."[4]

The advent and spread of nuclear weapons—and the concomitant threat of Armageddon—stoked a growing appetite for the two things the pacifists most wanted: peace and justice. To the pacifists, they were always connected. Just two months after Japan's surrender, A. J. Muste had predicted "an armaments race of fantastic proportions" if the atom bomb wasn't subject to some kind of international regulation. "If the war against the atomic bomb is lost, there is an end in our day and for generations to come of any progressive social program," he cautioned. "If it is won, the solution of other major issues in the realm of economics, government, race, etc. will be greatly simplified."[5]

Muste made a more extensive argument for pacifism in the nuclear era in his 1947 book *Not by Might*, in which he characterized atomic war as "sin of the most hideous kind," as much a crime as Dachau, and one that we should study "until it has burned its way into our consciousness and in doing so has burned away all illusions about war, including World War II." To Muste, technology had caused the moral imperative of nonviolence and the practical importance of averting Armageddon to coincide. The only hope of avoiding annihilation, he argued, was to avoid war, and the way to do that was to embrace radical pacifism. To Muste the new age of "atomic atrocity" made any notion of a "just war" morally incoherent and repudiated Niebuhr's Christian realism, for war could no longer be the lesser of two evils. What, after all, could be worse than a nuclear war? Growing stockpiles of ever more advanced nuclear weapons would only add force to his argument in the years to come. Meanwhile he advocated draft resistance, tax refusal, and, if necessary, martyrdom, for it was preferable "to have atomic bombs dropped on you than to drop them on others."[6]

Bayard Rustin, too, saw the advent of nuclear weapons as a transformative event, one that motivated him to comply with prison rules and obtain his release in order to work all the more strenuously for peace. Back with Muste's Fellowship of Reconciliation, he became "a traveling evangelist," as D'Emilio put it, "for a world without war and weaponry." Wherever he carried his optimistic message that peace is not just necessary but possible, people were captivated. Yet he was appearing mainly before youth camps and colleges sponsored by the peace churches, among the few venues in America at the time where his message would be compelling. At headquarters in New York, meanwhile, his stance was uncompromising, in keeping with many resisters who had been through prison. Disdaining the FOR's lobbying and coalition building—the kind of thing an older Rustin would embrace—he advocated outright resistance to a militarized state, and at meetings in New York, at least, openly urged the burning of draft cards. "If the Germans had begun to break laws when Hitler came to power," he argued, "they would not have ended up by putting Jews into furnaces."[7]

The nation's first draft card burnings, probably, took place on Lincoln's Birthday, February 12, 1947, during a protest in front of the White House. More occurred that night at New York's historic Labor Temple in an event organized by Houser, with Rustin as master of ceremonies. Speakers included Dellinger, Muste, and Macdonald. "We have decided to attack conscription," Dwight told the crowd, "by the simplest and most direct way possible: that is, by refusing . . . to recognize the authority of the state in this matter." The police and FBI were on hand to watch sixty-three young men commit their draft cards to destruction (for fire safety, incineration had to be outdoors). All told, draft cards were destroyed or mailed to the White House by four hundred to five hundred Americans that month.[8]

In the African American press, meanwhile, there was pride that black chemists and mathematicians—and thousands of other black

Americans—had been part of the Manhattan Project, but bitterness that most were confined to menial roles, lived in segregated housing at Oak Ridge, and hadn't even been given a school for their kids. Many black commentators noticed that the bomb hadn't been dropped on white people, and suggested the $2 billion it cost might better have been spent on ending racism and poverty. Figures such as Langston Hughes and Du Bois were sharply critical, as was the NAACP. Wilkins, editor of *The Crisis* at the time, asked in an editorial, "Who is bad and who is good? Who is barbarian and who is civilized? Who is fit to lead the world to peace and security, and by what token?"

Muste maintained close ties with Wilkins and other important civil rights figures and was receptive when Rustin argued, based on his travels and his personal passion, that "now the area of conflict is in the racial field." Muste had already brought Houser to New York to work on this, and understood that the issue was of the greatest importance to Rustin as well. Together, with Muste's support, Rustin and Houser would spend much of their time and energy on civil rights. In particular they traveled the country, holding interracial workshops, days or even weeks long, ideally leading to action. Participants were given some basic instruction about discrimination and nonviolence and then sent out into the community in interracial teams to test how various businesses treated blacks. In many cases they went further with direct action. In 1947, they undertook a monthlong program in Washington, which was still quite segregated even if it was the capital of the free world. Several businesses were integrated by the efforts, generating extensive news coverage. Rustin and Houser had hoped they were building a national movement, and while they didn't succeed in any strict sense of that term, their efforts from 1946 to 1954, in Rustin's view, "prepared for the 1960s revolution."[9]

The hard core of radical pacifists who had opposed the Second World War were well suited to the task of revitalizing and reorienting the American Left. But first they had to get through the early fifties, a deeply inhospitable time for self-styled pacifist revolutionaries. The peace movement just then was in tatters. The totalitarian face of the USSR was plain for all to see, the Nazis had been worse than anyone imagined, and prewar predictions that fascism would necessarily arise among the Allies had proved wildly wrong. Norman Thomas quit the War Resisters League.

Dwight Macdonald backed the Berlin airlift and the fight to defend South Korea. At a time of frenetic and pervasive anti-communism in the United States, moreover, much of the "peace" activity seemed to be coming from communist front organizations. On August 29, 1949, the Russians detonated a nuclear weapon, and just weeks later Mao Zedong declared the creation of the People's Republic of China. In 1950, communist North Korea invaded South Korea, quickly seizing most of the country, and Wisconsin Senator Joseph McCarthy began his anti-communist witch hunts.

The state of the American peace movement was made all too plain on a nice, warm Monday in New York, where a band of pacifists gathered in a meadow in Central Park to protest the bloody war in Korea on its first anniversary—June 25, 1951. Twenty-three-year-old Michael Harrington, a pacifist waiting to be called up as a medic (he would later be declared 4-F by an army doctor who diagnosed tuberculosis) was in the park representing the Catholic Worker organization when he encountered a well-dressed, middle-aged man with whom he was to work closely in the years ahead. Harrington later described Bayard Rustin in this first meeting as "a tall, intense Negro with more than a touch of a British accent, who asked coolly if we were going to get arrested." Michael listened "with frightened fascination while my new friends argued the pros and cons of defying the police" and was hugely relieved when they decided against it.

Only a hardy—if not foolhardy—few dared publicly criticize the fight on the Korean peninsula, which was conducted under the virtuous banner of the United Nations. The few on parade this day from Central Park to Midtown included some of the hardiest, but Harrington was mainly self-conscious. When the motley band marched single file through Times Square with signs condemning the war, he inwardly cringed. "I saw myself shuffling along in that pathetic little parade," he writes, "and I thought I looked like one of those cartoon figures with a placard announcing the end of the world."[10]

Their podium was a stepladder set up at Fortieth Street and Seventh Avenue. Harrington spoke first, and evidently his antiwar rhetoric did more than just warm up the audience, for when it was David Dellinger's turn to speak "a man came screaming through the curious crowd, yelling that we were Commies." Seizing a picket sign and tearing off the placard, he rushed toward the stepladder wielding it like a club. Rustin, by now an expert at such situations, flummoxed the attacker by calmly offering him a second sign, causing him to drop both. When he persisted in calling Dellinger a traitor, Dave replied that we're pacifists, not communists. Then come down, the man demanded, and prove you'll turn the other cheek. When Dellinger walked over to reason with him, the man punched him in the face and continued to assault him as he lay on the ground, leaving him with a broken jaw and, eventually, legally blind in his right eye. Dellinger was defended by some of the women who were present, and even tried to resume his address, but Rustin talked him out of it and delivered a moving speech in his place. On the other side of the world, the Korean War raged on.

Rustin's own Waterloo would not be long in coming. In 1952, still working and traveling for the Fellowship of Reconciliation, Bayard journeyed to West Africa, where active opposition to colonialism was erupting. Prewar arrangements were unraveling. In Africa, Rustin met with Kwame Nkrumah and Nnamdi Azikiwe, key figures in the birth of what became Ghana and Nigeria, respectively. Azikiwe even offered him a job. "Africa is afire," Rustin wrote. But he worried that without a commitment to nonviolence, "Africa may reach independence but miss freedom." Trading white exploitation for black exploitation "is highly possible unless a revolutionary method is used that can recognize evil everywhere it exists—even in the African community—and accepts good everywhere it exists—even from the European settlers."[11]

Back in the States, Rustin resumed his busy travel schedule, which in early 1953 took him to California, where he delivered a "sparkling lecture on world peace" at the old Pasadena Athletic Club in an event sponsored by the American Association of University Women. His charmed audience lingered to get in a word with the imposing lecturer after which, declining the offer of a ride, he set out alone, on foot, presumably for his hotel. But he doesn't seem to have gone there. Shortly before 3:00 a.m., still on the street, he encountered two young white men driving slowly by and waved them over, getting into their car. By the time a couple of cops came along, Rustin was sucking them off in the back seat. All three men were sentenced to sixty days behind bars.

Rustin was devastated and sent word to Muste, still a surrogate father, that he would resign. And Muste made it clear that the FOR was through with him. The Fellowship was a radical organization in some ways, but thoroughly straitlaced in others. It was still the 1950s, Muste himself had somewhat lofty views about sex, and the FOR was to add immeasurably to Rustin's pain. Although his Pasadena contretemps made the newspapers in Southern California, it wasn't prominently played or much noticed. That changed when the FOR released a detailed statement explaining that Rustin "was convicted on a 'morals charge' (homosexual)," circulating this embarrassing and condescending document (complete with perfunctory gratitude "for the many services he has rendered") throughout the pacifist world. "Thus ended," D'Emilio writes, "his dozen years of service to a Christian organization dedicated to peace and social justice."[12]

Rustin's arrest that night would have ramifications for the rest of his life. It is the reason some people today have no idea that he belongs in the civil rights pantheon with King, John Lewis, and other such luminaries. Because of the arrest, which gave King's enemies a weapon to use against the movement in the sixties, Rustin had to stay in the background, ably marshaling people and resources by using his great organizational gifts. It was Rustin, as a close adviser, who schooled King in nonviolent action and mass organization, thereby playing a crucial role in setting the incipient civil rights movement on a Gandhian path. In his later years, Bayard would expand his civil rights activism to include the rights of gay Americans.

Meanwhile, he would have to go through hell first. He would briefly lose his job, his reputation, and his place in the world. For Rustin, it must have been all the worse because it had happened before, at the Lewisburg federal prison. Rustin was so ashamed of his Pasadena arrest—and his sexuality—that he lied to a sympathetic therapist about it, claiming he'd been framed by police as a robber because he was carrying a great deal of money in small bills (in fact he was carrying $600 in cash and checks raised from donors at his lecture). The psychiatrist, Dr. Robert Ascher, continued seeing Rustin for free when the FOR (which had hoped for a cure) stopped paying the bills, and they discussed Bayard's attraction to men, which Ascher considered inalterable—a problem to be managed through good judgement.

To Ascher, Rustin was a man brimming with anger against his family and his society, and the therapist saw his patient's pacifism as a way of mastering himself. Ascher developed a great regard for Rustin and even tried to find him work. Himself a product of Quaker schools and the son of pacifists (at least until Hitler), the psychiatrist tried the Friends but they rebuffed him when they learned of Bayard's homosexuality. Bayard was black, a war resister, an ex-convict, and a former communist in the McCarthy era. He did not have a college degree. Labor unions wouldn't hire him. He worked very briefly with the committee defending the Rosenbergs, who were soon executed. Ascher found him some work in a brewery and then as a furniture mover. A social worker thought he could get something cleaning hospitals or as a butler.[13]

He was rescued from the purgatory of his sex conviction by the radical pacifists who had taken over the War Resisters League. Muste served on the WRL executive council and opposed hiring Bayard; he actually resigned over it. Houser, also on the board, abstained. But Rustin had the support of hardheaded radicals Jim Peck, Roy Finch, Ralph DiGia, and Igal Roodenko. They had variously worked with him on CORE, been arrested with him in the South, and done time in the same prisons. Strongly libertarian, they had no concern with the unwarranted sexual proprieties of the era. Perhaps most important of all was the support of Dellinger, whose uncompromising resistance during the war gave him great authority in radical circles. Despite the unforgiving climate of 1953, he wrote a remarkable letter to Finch arguing powerfully on Bayard's behalf. "I see no sense in trying to force on Bayard a Puritanical abstinence from the form of sex which apparently is natural to him," wrote Dellinger, who of course had himself had sexual experiences with men, "however unnatural it may be to some of the others who will be concerned with Bayard's position in the League."[14]

It may not have seemed like it at the time, but Rustin's Pasadena conviction and the palpably futile protest in Times Square, culminating in the vicious assault on Dellinger and little else, were signs of a bottom for the American peace movement in the postwar era. Probably few of the ardent radicals involved could have predicted the enormous role their brand of dissent was to play in the years ahead. But their fortunes were about to turn.

———

DOROTHY DAY WAS ON the road in the fall of 1952 when she started hearing that Dwight Macdonald's admiring two-part profile of her had appeared in *The New Yorker*. She was still peripatetic, and still glad to get away from her

troubles in New York even if it meant, as it so often did, a series of punish-
ing bus rides. "Traveling in a bus," she once said in a letter, "is like traveling with a slum always with you." There were other troubles; when she
got to Seattle she discovered that a prominent Republican in Washington
State had put it about that she was a communist, and most of her lecture
dates out there vanished. There was nonetheless the hope that Macdonald's
long and indulgent account of her and her movement might help sales of
her new memoir, *The Long Loneliness*. And at the very least, it was nice to
be appreciated. Macdonald had come downtown to see her for the piece,
meeting young Harrington in the process and needling him a bit in the article. But the connection between Michael and Dwight was to be important
for all parties and most everyone else, especially the poor, as we shall see.
Meanwhile Macdonald opened the first piece about the Abbess by saying,
"Many people think Dorothy Day is a saint and that she will someday be
canonized," demonstrating that such talk was in the air even then. Pope
John Paul II opened the case for her canonization in 2000, and when Pope
Francis addressed Congress fifteen years later, she was one of "four great
Americans" he saw fit to name in his speech.

"Like so many people," Harrington would recall, "Dwight fell in love
with Dorothy. Not in the passionate sense, but in admiration. So he did
something which . . . if the magazine had known about it at the time, it
would've blown a gasket! He gave Dorothy his manuscript before he turned
it in. I was right there when Dorothy was sanitizing her life."[15]

Poverty, obscurity, and futility had been the pacifist lot, but gradually people were starting to take notice. Day and her compatriots had been
wrong to think that we could somehow defeat fascism without fighting,
but the war was past and now here we were at loggerheads with our former
ally, the Soviet Union, the two of us locked in a wary nuclear standoff. The
sense was growing that backyard bomb shelters and air-raid drills would
be useless in any nuclear conflict. In 1950, the Stockholm Appeal called for
an end to nuclear weapons and was quickly signed by five hundred million
people around the world. In a variety of ways, nuclear weapons were becoming taboo, especially after the U.S. hydrogen bomb test in 1954.

If the atomic bomb, for many people, had made war unthinkable, the
radical pacifists of World War II offered a model of principled opposition

to what they had always seen as madness. Want to resist the draft? They knew just how to do it. Their insistence on nonviolence and readiness to support equality for marginalized groups of all kinds would make their views compatible with the emerging prominence of women among a new generation of progressives. Opposition to war had natural appeal on campus among students who came of age in the shadow of the nuclear threat, and especially to young men of draft age. The bombings of Hiroshima and Nagasaki meanwhile inspired a generation of antiwar scientists to avoid the guilty role of their elders in the Manhattan Project, and to try and prevent a catastrophic nuclear war. Some scientists were propelled further down the road of activism to tackle environmental protection, nuclear power (however unfortunately), the war in Vietnam, and climate change.

On issue after issue, as time went by, significant portions of society were coming around to the views that radical pacifists had long held—on the bombing of civilians, on the internment of Japanese Americans, on colonialism in Africa and Latin America, on civil rights (not just for black Americans but for others marginalized in different ways), and on Vietnam. In 1948, under pressure from Randolph, Rustin, and the black press, Truman signed an order directing the integration of the armed forces. In 1953, a gay man belonging to the Fellowship of Reconciliation, appalled by Rustin's arrest in Pasadena, organized a chapter of the fledgling Mattachine Society in the Bay Area, a region that would become a center of gay life in the decades to come. That same year, President Eisenhower concluded an armistice on the Korean peninsula, leaving the Cold War to continue but at least ending the hot one. The phrase "ban the bomb" began to appear. Communism, if not already discredited, would soon become so, a process accelerated by the death of Stalin, Khrushchev's secret speech denouncing him, and the 1956 Soviet invasion of Hungary. In December of 1954 the Senate finally found the guts to censure a weakened Senator Joseph McCarthy. On Easter Sunday of 1955 the founder of the War Resisters League, Jessie Wallace Hughan, suddenly died—as if to signal the passing of pacifism's old guard and the establishment of the more militant and expansive vision of nonviolence percolating since the war. Finally, on December 1, a black woman named Rosa Parks refused to give up her seat on a bus in segregated Montgomery, Alabama.

CHAPTER 20

MOVEMENT

NOT EVERYONE FELT IT yet, but an earthquake was beginning to shake the foundations of the racial caste system that had prevailed in the American South since the Civil War. These early tremors were coming from black Americans who, remembering the Double V strategy, felt it was time to put the second victory on the board. Voter registration campaigns, boycotts, and the growing strength of civil rights groups were starting to show. The NAACP had taken its challenge to school segregation all the way to the Supreme Court and came away, on May 17, 1954, with a unanimous opinion that separate was inherently unequal. The historic ruling in *Brown v. Board of Education* applied only to public schools but made clear that a new day was coming in the nation's race relations.

American pacifists would be there every step of the way. CORE, which had all but succumbed to infighting and inertia, was revived in the late fifties thanks to the energetic leadership and fundraising of James Robinson, who set the stage for James Farmer to take charge in 1961. Both were pacifists. Farmer would quickly make the group into a major force in the civil rights movement, in significant part by launching the Freedom Rides. These bus journeys challenging Jim Crow throughout the South in the face of arrests and violence reprised an earlier, more limited effort that served as a useful trial run. Blacks had been challenging Jim Crow on public transportation for several years when, in 1946, the Supreme Court said it was unconstitutional for Virginia to mandate segregation on interstate buses. CORE and the Fellowship of Reconciliation set out in 1947 to test Jim Crow practices on buses in the real world, and by doing so draw attention to the persistence of segregation. The Journey of Reconciliation, as it was known, would be made by sixteen men, eight white and eight black, including former war resisters Bayard Rustin, George Houser, Jim Peck, Conrad Lynn, Homer Jack, Wallace Nelson, and Igal Roodenko. Except for four of the blacks, everyone in the group was a pacifist. They were a courageous bunch, but things were still so bad in places like Mississippi and Alabama that they confined their trip to the upper South. Thurgood Marshall, then the NAACP's top lawyer, had warned that "a disobedience movement on the part of Negroes and their white allies, if employed in the [deep] South, would result in wholesale slaughter with no good achieved."[1]

The sixteen pacifists of the 1947 journey had some scary moments but lost no blood. Segregation, on the other hand, was encountered everywhere, along with ignorance of the Supreme Court ruling. For sitting in the wrong seats and refusing to move, the men were arrested repeatedly. The charges for the most part came to nothing except in Chapel Hill, North Carolina; as a result of an arrest there, Rustin and two others spent twenty-two days on a "chain gang" in 1949, though they do not appear to have actually been chained on this otherwise brutal road crew. Just weeks before, Rustin had been in India, speaking to audiences around the country and meeting at length with Prime Minister Jawaharlal Nehru, who had been incarcerated by the British under far better conditions. Bayard used what spare time he had while in stir to make a powerful study of the men and the milieu. He later published his report as a multipart series in the *New York Post*.[2]

Rustin by the early 1950s was America's foremost exponent of nonviolent protest, distilling through the filter of his experience the influences of Christianity, Gandhism, Marxism, the labor movement, and human nature into a lived philosophy of direct action. And he continued to influence a generation of future activists. At Hartford Seminary, for example, sometime between 1952 and 1955, the future congressman, UN ambassador, and mayor of Atlanta Andrew Young heard him speak on nonviolence and years later would remember being awed.[3]

In 1955, Rustin was still working for the War Resisters League, a group now in the hands of radical World War II resisters, when he became part of a small band of New York leftists bent on aiding southern black civil rights

activists by raising money and support among unions and other liberal organizations in the North. When the Montgomery bus boycott erupted in
Alabama, the ringleaders of the New York group, including Randolph and
Farmer, sent Rustin south. Bear in mind that, in 1956, they were sending
a black former communist with a fancy accent and clothes, who was also a
convicted sex offender and had spent more than two years behind bars as a
war resister. They could not have made a better choice.

In Montgomery, Rustin recognized the beginnings of a mass upris-
ing, one that he thought could propel black churches into a "social action
phase," galvanize the NAACP, and launch Martin Luther King, Jr., into
nationwide prominence. "No force on earth can stop this movement," he
wrote. "It has all the elements to touch the hearts of men." Pacifism and the
struggle for racial equality were natural partners. Both were still largely
Christian, and both could thrive in a liberal democracy with a free and
active press, a functioning judiciary, and a belief by all parties in some essential national decency. The movement, long in the making, that was ignited at Montgomery cried out for someone with Rustin's experience with
nonviolence. And the events in Alabama's capital would thrust him into
the thick of the revolution that he had been working toward all his life.
His role would be enormous, and his pacifism would be at the center of it,
because nonviolence was the most effective way forward for a minority so
egregiously oppressed in a country such as this one. Yet, as a result of his
past, in particular his conviction on a morals charge in Southern California,
his efforts would have to remain in the background. Just the year before,
fourteen well-known pacifists including Muste, Rustin, and Milton Mayer
produced a pamphlet called *Speak Truth to Power*. H. Larry Ingle, a prominent historian of Quakerism, called it "the most important pacifist statement ever composed in the United States," but notes that Rustin's name
was quietly left off.

King spoke passionately for nonviolence even before Rustin's arrival.
Yet the twenty-six-year-old minister had no real idea how to build a nonviolent movement. The forty-four-year-old Rustin, his personality in
so many ways a contrast with King's, would take on the role of advisor,
sounding board, ghostwriter, publicist, tactician, and strategist in helping the younger man build a movement, from a small city in Alabama,
that would change the entire country. D'Emilio has a strong case when he

writes that "Rustin was as responsible as anyone else for the insinuation of nonviolence into the very heart of what became the most powerful social movement in twentieth-century America."[4]

The Montgomery bus boycott was not free of violence, but the violence was perpetrated by the enemies of equality rather than the protesters. In fact, the year-long boycott was an important proving ground for nonviolent civil rights protest, a chance for activists to gain skills and experience, and a force that catapulted King and the movement to national attention. Toward the end of 1956, the Supreme Court upheld a lower court ruling that segregated buses were unconstitutional. By this time Rustin had had to withdraw, lest journalists discredit the boycott by exposing his past. The minister and former war resister Glenn Smiley took his place, and so on December 12, when the first bus with integrated seating left the Montgomery terminal, Bayard wasn't there. But King sat up front and, with Smiley right next to him, had a pacifist ready to hand.

Rustin was far from finished, and would be involved in every step of the march toward equality for black Americans during the main years of the civil rights movement. In addition to his work at CORE, he played an important role in conceiving and forming the Southern Christian Leadership Conference to coordinate the movement across the South. He also used his organizational talents on behalf of various marches and protests, including the huge 1963 March on Washington during which King delivered his powerful "I have a dream" speech. He just had to do it behind the scenes, for Roy Wilkins and others feared that his background could be used to undermine the project. Dellinger was on hand for the event, alongside a quarter of a million others. But he had a ringside seat thanks to a backstage pass given him by Rustin.

Their friendship would not long remain so close. Rustin was a lifelong pacifist but his priority was always civil rights, and in the sixties, having decided that the way forward was through the political process, he made a painful choice, adopting a loud silence about the Vietnam war and urging King to avoid coming out against it—advice King would eventually reject in a break that would afterward diminish Rustin's influence with him. On July 3, 1964, Rustin and Dellinger found themselves on the same flight from LaGuardia to Washington. Rustin was going to attend the president's signing of the Civil Rights Act, a landmark piece of legislation in the black struggle for equality. Dellinger was flying down for a peace rally and tried to get Rustin to attend that as well, but his old friend demurred. The following summer, on August 6, Rustin was back at the White House to witness LBJ's signing of the Voting Rights Act, another landmark bill for black Americans. But some of Rusty's former comrades in arms were outside, unwilling to let up momentarily even for the voting bill. Dellinger, Staughton Lynd, and Robert Parris Moses stood with hundreds of others in front of the White House to commemorate the twentieth anniversary of Hiroshima and protest American involvement in Vietnam. The war—and Dellinger's habitual absolutism—would drive a lasting wedge between him and Rustin.

By now Dellinger was an acknowledged radical heavyweight. After a decade spent banging his head against a wall of indifference, things started to change in the mid 1950s. Dellinger did his part by cutting back some of his more quixotic activities; in order to rescue his marriage and spend more time with the children, he stayed home at the little commune he and Betty had going at Glen Gardner in New Jersey's rural Hunterdon County, where the Dellingers frequently hosted Day, Muste, Rustin, and other pacifists. Dellinger had already protested to ban the bomb, picketed to save the Rosenbergs, and, with a small group of like-minded fellow pacifists, tried to bicycle across Europe and through the Iron Curtain to thaw the Cold War just a bit. But before all that, he'd learned the printing trade. He was always a writer, and by 1948 he'd set up Libertarian Press as a workers' cooperative. In addition to some commercial printing, it became a leading publisher of radical pacifist and anarchist literature. In the early 1950s Dellinger and some key pacifist associates got together and took the next step, one that would help to shape the radical agenda. What they did was to start a magazine.

Macdonald had folded *politics* in 1949, leaving something of a gap. In 1956, Dellinger and some fellow members of the Peacemakers organization, including Rustin and Muste (who first proposed a magazine) joined forces to launch *Liberation*, with financial backing from the WRL, which by now was controlled by prison-hardened radical pacifists. *Liberation* picked up where *politics* had left off. "They shared similar concerns and beliefs, referred to the same tradition of radical thought, and held similar expectations of American society," writes Cristina Scatamacchia, who studied the two magazines. "*Politics* and *Liberation* were products of disenchantment with the Old Left and harbingers of the New Left."[5]

Irving Howe and friends had founded the more introspective journal *Dissent* just two years earlier, in 1954, and the more radical *Liberation*, with its Christian pacifist orientation, was to rival it as the most influential of the era's leftist periodicals. Both strove to find a "third way" between liberalism and Marxism but in their first issue the editors of *Liberation* announced their determination to find a new nonviolent, non-Marxist revolutionary path away from state oppression and liberal incrementalism. The goals were to end war, poverty, and even the affliction of boredom, which the journal, during its era of greatest vitality, did its part in overcoming. An editorial in that first issue, "Tract for the Times," might as well be speaking of our own: "The decline of independent radicalism and the gradual falling into silence of prophetic and rebellious voices is an ominous feature of the mid-twentieth century. Anxiety and apprehension have invaded the air we breathe. Advances in science and technology, which should have been our greatest triumphs, leave us stunned and uncertain as to whether human life and history have meaning."

Liberation struggled until, in 1957, David McReynolds came along to take on the role of publisher (his title was editorial secretary) with energy and aplomb, putting the journal on a solid financial basis much as Robinson had done for CORE. Writers for *Liberation* over the years would include King, Brittain, Todd Gitlin, James Baldwin, Norman Mailer, Lewis Mumford, Bertrand Russell, Michael Harrington, Gary Snyder, and many others. Dellinger's work producing *Liberation* led to a full-blown reconciliation with Muste and brought him closer to other key pacifists as well, but it also cemented his role as a linchpin of American radicalism. And the magazine influenced young radicals, including Tom Hayden. "What I did in the fifties helped me play a role in the sixties movement," Dellinger said, reflecting on his life in an interview. "For many of us, the sixties came out of those earlier types of experiences in which we stood up for what we knew was right."[6]

In the early sixties Dellinger's role at *Liberation* placed him at the junction of several key movements, including the growing efforts of black Americans to secure full civil rights and the drive to limit or ban nuclear weapons. But none proved so captivating to him as Cuba. Like so many

on the American left, he strongly backed the revolution. He also founded
a couple of organizations to support it, and protested the Bay of Pigs invasion with a day-and-night vigil outside CIA headquarters. He had visited
Cuba shortly after Castro took power and wrote a series of articles about
the island and its history in *Liberation,* where he seemed to justify violence
in the cause of overthrowing the dictatorial Fulgencio Batista (only fifteen
years after rejecting violence in the struggle against Hitler). Dave's good
friend Dorothy Day reprinted one of his long articles on the topic in *The
Catholic Worker* under the headline "America's Lost Plantation." Both publications got strong pushback on the left. Roy Finch wrote a dissenting piece
in *Liberation* saying Cuba was "pretty well being taken over by totalitar-
ian-minded people." He soon resigned from the publication's board over
the issue. Later in 1961 Day would acknowledge that, in standing with the
poor, "we are often finding ourselves on the side of the persecutors of the
Church." She would soon visit the island and write her own rosy account.
This would not be the last time pacifists would stumble over the issue of
revolutionary violence in postcolonial societies. Their hardheaded skepticism, honed against American social and political failings, tended to melt
into credulous rapture in such environs.[7]

Dellinger's greatest impact in later life was on the movement against
the Vietnam war. On June 3, 1964, he gathered with a small group of like-
minded individuals outside the White House for his very first anti–Vietnam
War demonstration. There he encountered old friends A. J. Muste and
Ralph DiGia and met Daniel and Philip Berrigan, brothers and Catholic
priests who would take Day's Catholic opposition to war in a more aggressive direction. Dellinger also met Joan Baez; she sang folk songs at the rally
and Dellinger addressed the crowd.[8]

In the years ahead Dellinger would visit Vietnam repeatedly and fall
under the spell of Ho Chi Minh despite the North Vietnamese leader's
evident disregard for pacifism. Dave even used his ties to communist leaders in Vietnam to help the families of American POWs. By 1967 he was a
leader of the fractious but booming American antiwar movement, which
encompassed liberals, anarchists, socialists, communists, and others. The
death of Muste in February of that year, at age eighty-two, thrust Dellinger
into the role of America's premier pacifist and chairman of the National
Mobilization Committee to End the War in Vietnam, or just "the Mobe,"

as the umbrella organization was known. His rhetoric more aggressive than ever, Dellinger now pushed to make the organization more militant and impactful. The new motto, "from protest to resistance," signaled a shift in tactics and emphasis for the antiwar movement. A big march on Washington planned for October of 1967 aimed to combine "Gandhi and guerilla" and shut down the Pentagon. Dellinger had warned, "There will be no government building left unattacked."[9]

Some nonviolent war opponents decided not to take part. In fact, in June, McReynolds quit *Liberation* because it seemed to have abandoned its pacifist principles. But the Washington event came off on October 21 without catastrophe and became a landmark in the struggle against the war.

The massive demonstration on the National Mall was attended by perhaps one hundred thousand people, including a number of Catholic Workers. Some of the marchers engaged in civil disobedience, but few were violent. An exception came when Dellinger was crossing the stage to introduce the speakers. At that moment three members of the American Nazi Party dashed out to attack him but were hauled off by movement members. Macdonald was on hand, as was Mailer, whose book about the event would win a Pulitzer Prize. The best speaker was perhaps Dr. Benjamin Spock, the famous pediatrician. Dellinger spoke, too, although as usual not especially well. After a concert by Phil Ochs, perhaps a third or half of the larger crowd marched across the Potomac to the Pentagon, which provocateurs Abbie Hoffman and Jerry Rubin had vowed to levitate. Government forces at the Pentagon fended off the demonstrators, but the event had a major impact, and so Dellinger and colleagues decided to stage another at the Democratic National Convention in Chicago the following year.

There Dellinger did what he could to keep the protest nonviolent, but perhaps inevitably, given the volatile mix of various protest factions and Mayor Richard Daley's attitude and police force, ample violence erupted. Once a member of the Union Eight—well-scrubbed seminarians piously standing on pacifist principle—Dellinger was now a part of the Chicago Seven, which made a contemptuous circus of the trial and at one point draped the defense table in a Viet Cong flag. (The trial and subsequent legal proceedings ended with no defendants punished.) On display in Chicago were the two rogue branches of the direct action pioneered by radical pacifists of Dellinger's generation. One branch, as exemplified by the Yippies, amounted to cynical attention-seeking, while the other, embodied in the Weathermen, was a resort to violent protest. Perhaps either could seem plausible to someone who felt the emergency was serious enough.

U.S. involvement in Vietnam produced the nation's first mass movement against a war, even if most Americans supported the conflict for much of the time it raged. That movement sprang from seeds planted by Day, Dellinger, Muste, Macdonald, and the other antiwar activists of an earlier generation. That's one reason the movement was so disorganized; allergic to authority, the World War II generation of pacifists practiced something approaching radical egalitarianism. Dellinger in particular could drive friends and antagonists alike to distraction with his communitarian militance; people used to say he was a great person to get arrested with. Yet he was able to keep a madly disparate movement mostly going in the same direction—an extraordinary accomplishment under the circumstances. He founded no enduring organization nor propounded any coherent philosophy, and his passionate convictions could blind him to inconvenient facts—including the toll some of his decisions took on his family. But even his enemies could never doubt his commitment or his courage. "This was a generous, decent man, who took more than his fair share of the beatings life handed to the rebel," said McReynolds. "He never caved in. At the end, as at the beginning, he was on the side of the underdog."[10]

The mass nature of this new antiwar movement meant that it could hardly be more different from the radical pacifists' experience of World War II. On the other hand, there were some remarkable continuities, not least among them the presence of General Lewis B. Hershey at the head of the nation's conscription apparatus. There was another draft lottery, too, the first since the one in 1940. Many Americans objected this time around as well, so much so that draft cards regularly went up in flames and some young men fled the country. Kingman Brewster, by way of America First and the U.S. Navy, was now running Yale, whose radical chaplain was William Sloane Coffin, a reformed CIA man and nephew of Henry Sloane Coffin, the antagonist of the Union Eight a quarter of a century earlier. The younger Coffin spoke at the big Washington event, as did Robert Lowell. Jeannette Rankin, once reviled for her opposition to declaring war against Japan, was now revered among antiwar activists. In 1968, she led the Jeannette Rankin Brigade—five thousand mostly middle-aged women in black—who marched to Capitol Hill from Washington's Union Station. Time had demonstrated once again that what looks like moral vanity in one context can be unyielding righteousness in another.[11]

Rankin was a feminist and probably a lesbian, and the changing times could not have suited her more. Day was by contrast ill-suited to the sixties. She gave women opportunities at *The Catholic Worker* but had little interest in the new feminism, opposed abortion, and regarded homosexuality with distaste. Changes in the Church and its services dismayed her, and she recoiled from superficiality and vulgarity in the arts. She was far too religious, and far too much the individualist, to embrace either the sexual freedom or the political collectivism that were such prominent features of the counterculture. On the other hand, she had been living in a kind of counterculture for years. Nobody was more skeptical of government, business, or bigness. And she absolutely hated militarism and war.

Thus did Dorothy Day become America's greatest force for Catholic radicalism. Many of the men who had left the Catholic Worker movement for the armed forces during the war never came back. But afterwards, slowly, it began to rebuild itself, finding new adherents to work in the hospitality houses, new voices for the newspaper, and new readers to send the paper to. Catholic Worker houses, particularly in New York, were a training ground for youthful acolytes and future radicals, even if the places seemed less and less Catholic. On Friday nights in New York there was something akin to a salon, with everyone from street people to working stiffs to young intellectuals in attendance. Dellinger and Rustin spoke on politics, for example, and Dorothy herself once gave a talk on the Chinese revolution. Harrington did several; his first was about Martin Buber's essays on socialism. The writer Dan Wakefield recalled that what drew him to the Catholic Worker movement back then wasn't just "Dorothy Day's bohemian-literary past, or even her eloquence or daily dedication to the poor. It was all those things perhaps, but more, a real mystique that called to young people of the fifties and drew them from all across the country, offering in the midst of the grim poverty of the Bowery something that all the glittering affluence around us lacked—a spirit, a purpose, a way of transcending self through service."[12]

Newcomers like Wakefield were inspired by the Abbess's dedication to the poorest, her hostility to the establishment (aside from the Catholic Church), and her absolute rejection of war, which of course extended to nuclear weapons. On June 15, 1955, Dorothy and members of the Catholic Workers, the War Resisters League, and the Fellowship of Reconciliation gathered in Manhattan's City Hall Park as hundreds of sirens went off around the city in a civil defense drill against nuclear attack. The protesters were in purposeful violation of a New York State law requiring people to repair to one of the thousands of designated air-raid shelters around the state if any such drills became necessary. By 1955 drills were underway as part of a national campaign called Operation Alert. Day considered the idea not just useless, but horrifying, because it sought to normalize what should be unthinkable and, for New Yorkers, very likely unsurvivable. (In July Bertrand Russell and Albert Einstein would issue their famous manifesto asserting that a large nuclear war could render life on earth extinct.) Her eccentric admirer Ammon Hennacy, anarchist, tax resister, and perhaps, if you squint, proto-Yippie, had the idea for the protest and helpfully alerted J. Edgar Hoover. The media were given notice and turned out in force; the protesters made sure to hold their signs high enough for unobstructed photographs. Hennacy and Day were joined by A. J. Muste, Bayard Rustin, and Jim Peck, among others. Twenty-seven pacifists were arrested, held for an uncomfortable day in jail, and given suspended sentences. Protesters in other cities were ignored.[13]

It was the start of an annual ritual drawing a larger group of participants each time—and a manifestation of nonviolent direct action at its best. Year after year, when the sirens went off on the appointed day, the Catholic Workers and their friends gathered in City Hall Park, carrying solemn signs or just sitting and enjoying a spring day. The arrests brought news coverage far and wide, putting the issue before the public, and soon editorials followed. In 1957, when the protest was held in Washington Square, twelve demonstrators were sentenced to thirty days, and the four women among them, including the sixty-one-year-old Day, were subjected to strip searches that included rough vaginal insertions ostensibly to root out weapons or drugs. But the protests continued, year after year, gradually spreading to area colleges and even high schools. In 1960, more than one thousand people turned out, including a well-organized and well-groomed crowd of middle-class young mothers with small children in strollers, along with Day and Hennacy, but also McReynolds, Goodman, Macdonald, Mailer, and *Village Voice* writer Nat Hentoff, an ardent civil libertarian who would write a biography of Muste. For the first time, nonpacifists took part. The police made just a few selective arrests, carefully avoiding Day and her older companions, for by now the press had come around to the protesters' view of these exercises and Dorothy was becoming famous.[14]

She had been interviewed on television by Mike Wallace, written about in *Time*, and photographed by Richard Avedon. In 1972 a new book about her and her work, *A Harsh and Dreadful Love: Dorothy Day and the Catholic Worker Movement*, was reviewed with obvious admiration for its subject by W. H. Auden. When he read that the organization was fined $250 for building code violations, he walked up to her on the street one day and handed her a check for the full amount. (Auden's countryman Evelyn Waugh had taken a similar shine to her in 1948, arriving in Clare Boothe Luce's limousine to take Dorothy and colleagues to lunch. Waugh, like Day a convert to Catholicism, later donated money.) By the seventies the Left and the great mass of Americans had already parted ways over various social and political questions, and the new young Catholic Workers, many of them, seemed hardly Catholic at all if not outright hostile to the church. There was no mistaking at this point that Dorothy was more celebrated among intellectuals than among everyday Catholics, so many of whom had reached the middle class and the suburbs far beyond the Bowery. Like pacifism, voluntary poverty tends to be an elevated taste, and Day's evolving celebrity was an indicator of where the Left was headed in the coming century.[15]

A further cautionary tale was offered by the Catholic Worker farm along the Hudson River in Tivoli, New York. The chaos of New York's Catholic Worker hospitality houses during Dorothy's life was legendary, and the movement's anarchism combined with the worst excesses of the counterculture to toxic effect in the verdant setting of the group's farm upstate. The property, which included a historic mansion, was acquired with great optimism for $78,000 in 1964 just as a hurricane of social changes was gathering force. Over the next fifteen years Dorothy and the farm would be hammered by that storm as a collection of selfish, rude, and often drug-addled strangers came and went. Dorothy at one point was attacked there by a deranged former *Life* magazine photographer. Theft was rampant; even her cherished signed editions of Belloc and Maritain vanished, and someone given $200 to buy groceries took off in one of the movement's cars, never to return. Probably worse, for Dorothy, was that the era's new free love was on sordid display in sexual liaisons everywhere on the property. At Rose Hill, as the estate in Tivoli was known, freedom without responsibility had deteriorated into license, and the bad had begun to drive out the good. Anarchism, like pacifism, depends a lot on context. The Catholic Workers finally sold the place in 1978, and over time it returned to its earlier role as a country estate for the rich. The current owner is the abstract painter Brice Marden, whose works command astronomical prices. In 2018 *Town & Country* reported of the Mardens that "they recently bought their sixth home, in Marrakech."[16]

Rich in spirit if not in wealth, Dorothy drew to herself idealistic admirers, and it was through them that her social and political outlook—pacifist, personalist, wary of capitalism and government alike—was to be transmitted to the younger generation. They were of course the young disciples working in the kitchen or reading page proofs, and they would carry her influence far and wide, whether or not they were or remained pacifists. In 1962, to cite a single prominent example, Harrington came out with a book called *The Other America*, which shone a spotlight on the persistence of poverty amid plenty in this country. He'd experienced this other America working for Dorothy at the Catholic Worker organization. Macdonald, having met Harrington when researching his 1952 profile of Day, touted the book in the January 19, 1963, *New Yorker*. Dwight's essay was read by JFK thanks to the chairman of his Council of Economic Advisers, Walter Heller, who was asked to develop legislation for the problem. After Kennedy's assassination, LBJ enlisted Sargent Shriver, Kennedy's brother-in-law and Peace Corps director, to help launch the War on Poverty. Shriver, an admirer of Day's even back at Yale, would head the new Office of Economic Opportunity from 1965 to 1968, creating Head Start, the Job Corps, Volunteers in Service to America (VISTA), the Community Action Program, and Legal Services for the Poor. Harrington, meanwhile, would remain an influential figure on the American left for most of his life, during which Medicaid, the Earned Income Tax Credit, and food assistance (yes, government programs) would become mainstays of the poor.

Many other World War II pacifists had distinguished lives of service after the war, often involving social change. George Houser, although not well known, spent his life on efforts to advance the causes of peace and justice as a pioneer in racial equality, nonviolence, and anticolonialism. Meredith Dallas became an esteemed drama instructor at Antioch College and a mainstay of local theater. Paul Goodman made contributions in a variety of fields, including helping to popularize Gestalt therapy by coauthoring a book with Fritz Perls in 1951. In 1960, he analyzed the discontents of the young, when these issues were only distantly visible on the horizon, in *Growing Up Absurd*. Roy Kepler founded a beloved bookstore in what was to become Silicon Valley and helped nurture the first nonprofit Pacifica radio station. The whole concept, and the Pacifica Foundation behind it, was largely owing to fellow World War II resister Lew Hill.

Some prominent pacifists abandoned the cause. Macdonald supported American involvement in the Korean War before opposing the war in Vietnam. Dwight did seem to flip-flop, yet if you look closely a consistent ethical pattern is discernible. For the most part he opposed war, saw the government as a dangerous source of violence and tyranny, couldn't abide cant, stood for the individual, and most of all spoke his mind. When the inaugural Bollingen Prize for Poetry was awarded to Ezra Pound's *Pisan Cantos*, Dwight cheered on the front page of his journal. "Whether *The Pisan Cantos* is the best poetry published by an American last year or not, I am incompetent to judge," he wrote. "Nor is this the point considered here, which is rather that by some miracle the Bollingen judges were able to consider Mr. Pound the poet apart from Mr. Pound the fascist, Mr. Pound the antisemite, Mr. Pound the traitor, Mr. Pound the funny-money crank, and all the other Mr. Pounds whose existence has properly nothing to do with the question of whether Mr. Pound the poet had or had not written the best American poetry of 1948."[17]

Max Kampelman, after starving himself for science instead of fighting, gave up pacifism to become a Marine Corps reservist. Yet the thing for which he is best known today was important precisely because it helped keep the peace, and that was his work in negotiating nuclear arms limitation agreements with the Russians. In bestowing the Presidential Medal of Freedom on him in 1999, Bill Clinton observed drily that: "Max Kampelman was probably not the first young man to work his way through college who made ends meet by skipping meals."[18]

Don Benedict, after two prison terms for draft resisting, went into the army during the war, though he saw no combat. Pardoned by Truman in 1947, he became a minister of the United Church of Christ—and an outspoken opponent of police brutality. Bayard Rustin didn't formally abandon pacifism but, in devotion to the cause of civil rights, and convinced that politics was the best path forward for black Americans, he supported Lyndon Johnson and stayed apart from the struggle against the Vietnam War. (He supported a negotiated peace.) Jim Peck spotted him at a party in those days and stuck a finger into Rustin's chest, demanding: "How can you live with yourself?"[19]

Peck, conversely, remained in the thick of opposition to war even as he was cast out of the civil rights movement. "I worked for CORE, without remuneration, from the initial freedom ride (Journey of Reconciliation) in 1947 until 1965 when I was ousted because of my skin color," he complained in *Liberation*, reminding readers that "I was beaten almost to death on the first of the 1961 Freedom Rides." The headline on his essay was "Black Racism."[20]

Corbett Bishop's postwar sorrows went beyond any sense of betrayal. In 1961, he seems to have been living as a recluse near Hamilton, Alabama, in a complex of four structures containing thousands of books, and nearly every day he walked five miles into town. Late one night in May a nineteen-year-old driving past wrecked his car and woke Bishop with a request for help with an ankle injury. Bishop tried to help, of course, and for his pains the young man, apparently motivated by robbery, shot him and then broke his neck with a rifle stock. Bishop was 56 when he succumbed to the violence he had so strenuously opposed.

The Holocaust, when its enormity finally became known, casts a dark shadow over the pacifism of the Second World War, especially for Jewish pacifists. Contrary to the lovely stories of children with flowers conquering aggressors, the Nazis were not abashed or deterred by the nonviolence of European Jews. Some of Gandhi's rhetoric from the era rings particularly hollow, and serves only to underscore the limitations of pacifism in the face of a ruthless foe. In 1939, he said nonviolent resistance by "a single Jew standing up and refusing to bow to Hitler's decrees" might "melt Hitler's heart," and in 1946 he called Hitler's mass murder of the Jews "the greatest crime of our time. But the Jews should have offered themselves to the butcher's knife. They should have thrown themselves into the sea from cliffs. As it is, they succumbed anyway in their millions."[21]

Rabbi Abraham Cronbach opposed the war anyway. In 1954, he published a book called *Judaism for Today* that argued for a modern, humanistic sort of Judaism ("reverence for human personality—that can be our religion. That can be, for us, the meaning of God"), and reaffirmed his pacifism. By now he was fairly well known, for the year before he had officiated at the funeral of Julius and Ethel Rosenberg, whose conviction for spying resulted in the death penalty. Other Jews, traumatized by the Holocaust, took up arms in the cause of a Jewish homeland. In Judaism's long tradition of nonviolence they saw only powerlessness, shame, and death.

Rabbi Arthur Lelyveld, though a pacifist, left his pulpit during the war to barnstorm the country promoting Zionism, a controversial cause among American Jews until the enormity of the Holocaust became known. In 1967, if not sooner, Lelyveld was calling for a halt to the bombing of North Vietnam and a negotiated end to that war. His involvement with the civil rights movement, meanwhile, brought him up against violence in an episode that nearly cost him his life. In 1964, registering black voters in Hattiesburg, Mississippi, he was beaten with a tire iron and narrowly avoided being run over by his assailants. Covered in blood, he miraculously avoided brain damage.[22] Then came the disappearance of Michael Schwerner, James Chaney, and Andrew Goodman.

"In that summer of 1964," the rabbi's son Joseph would write, "when the bodies of the slain civil rights workers were finally retrieved from an earthen dam outside the town of Philadelphia, he became an obvious choice, not only as a friend of the family but as a wounded Mississippi veteran himself, to deliver a eulogy at Andrew Goodman's service."

Not one of these young people who are walking the streets of Hattiesburg or Camden or Laurel or Gulfport or Greenville, not one of them, and certainly neither Andy nor James nor Michael, would have us in resentment and vindictiveness add to the store of hatred in the world. They pledged themselves in the way of nonviolence. They learned how to receive blows, not how to inflict them . . . To assume the risk so knowingly and willingly is to rise above all that is craven, sordid, limiting.[23]

It was left to another rabbi and former pacifist, Navy Lieutenant (junior grade) Roland Gittelsohn, to deliver what amounted to a eulogy for the American dead of the Second World War. It was March of 1945, and seven thousand Marines had just died taking Iwo Jima. Gittelsohn served with the 5th Division, some of whom were captured by the AP's Joe Rosenthal in his iconic photo of the flag-raising atop Mount Suribachi. Gittelsohn was asked to prepare a sermon for the dedication of the division's cemetery, laid out in the shape of a cross at the base of the mountain. He had encountered anti-Semitism in the armed forces before, but he was heartsick to learn that some Protestant and Catholic chaplains objected to having a Jew deliver a sermon at a joint memorial service. Some even refused to attend. To spare the division chaplain further difficulties, Gittelsohn consented to a plan for a joint secular tribute from the commanding general followed by separate denominational services. The rabbi would read his sermon to the Jews.[24]

In the event, three Protestant chaplains showed up in solidarity, along with forty or fifty Jews, to hear Gittelsohn's moving eulogy for the dead and exhortation to the living. His words expressed the American purpose in the war and his solemn hopes for the aftermath so powerfully that men sent copies back home. *Time* published excerpts and Fredric March did a radio broadcast. It's still read—and it expresses the same ideals that a younger Gittelsohn or any other pacifist might have expressed concerning freedom, equality, security, and our obligations to one another.

Here lie men who loved America because their ancestors, generations ago, helped in her founding, and other men who loved her with equal passion because they themselves or their own fathers escaped from oppression to her blessed shores. Here lie officers and men, Negroes and whites, rich men and poor . . . together. Here are Protestants, Catholics, and Jews . . . together. Here no man prefers another because of his faith or despises him because of his color. Here there are no quotas of

how many from each group are admitted or allowed. Among these
men there is no discrimination. No prejudice. No hatred. Theirs is the
highest and purest democracy.

Without the bravery of the men on Iwo Jima, there would be little prospect
of fulfilling anyone's hopes for freedom and fairness in American society.
But it is no denigration of their terrible sacrifice to suggest that we need the
pacifists, too, just as we needed them during that long ago war. For the goal
is a democracy of the living rather than the dead, and if there is to be death
there had better be a good reason. When should we fight? "Never" may be
a utopian standard, but it is a lot better than "always" or "often." Even on
the rare occasions when a fight is necessary, pacifists have served the useful
purpose of demanding that we distinguish ourselves from our enemies by
more than just victory. "Those who choose the lesser evil," Hannah Arendt
reminds us, "forget very quickly that they chose evil."

EPILOGUE

Aᴍᴇʀɪᴄᴀ's Wᴏʀʟᴅ Wᴀʀ II pacifists are easy to dismiss as a tiny and quixotic band of outliers. But the contours and concerns of the American Left
to come are apparent in the story of these heterodox dissidents. Their actions and evolution during the war informed the ferment of the sixties and
therefore arguably all that followed. The radical pacifists form the pivot
on which the Left swung from labor and economic issues to the concerns
it considers central today. These include race and the rights of minorities
generally, individual liberty on matters such as abortion and gender, and
automatic opposition to militarism and war.

Yet the hard core of pacifists who opposed the Second World War were
far more complicated than mere proto-progressives. They were against racism and war, of course, but also capitalism and the power of the state. They
turned their backs on communism while accidentally detaching themselves
from the white working class and the industrial labor movement. They
were hardened dissidents, courageous and educated descendants of Thoreau
and Garrison, small in number, who took naturally to civil disobedience.
Nonviolent protest and disruptions—sit-ins at segregated restaurants, for
example—were ideal weapons for a determined minority in the television
age, and their influence on the protest movements that followed would be
large, if little noted.

About the war, of course, they were mistaken. There was no good alternative to fighting and no hope that nonviolent resistance would work.

In the event of invasion, in fact, any foreign occupier would probably have included our pacifists among the first to be shot. Overwrought predictions to the contrary, the war did not bring about tyranny at home beyond the usual surveillance and constraints that came with the territory and that were to a great extent unwound once we got through the Red Scare of the fifties. On the other hand: our Soviet allies, who did most of the fighting in Europe, turned out to be brutal despots, just as Fosdick and others had warned. And the war did spawn the sort of military-industrial complex that many had feared (and that Eisenhower afterwards named). What followed was a massive worldwide U.S. military footprint that endures to this day, and a series of wars, large and small, that were nearly all misguided. Pacifism, it turns out, is a pretty good response whenever we are faced with the choice of military action in circumstances short of foreign invasion.

Our Second World War pacifists were right about other things as well, including the horrible treatment of blacks at home, the internment of Japanese Americans, and the wrongness of bombing civilians in enemy cities, whether with conventional weapons or nuclear ones. They understood, in other words, how important it is not to let yourself turn into the very thing you are against. They followed their conscience, and they usefully insisted that the rest of us follow ours. Even Reinhold Niebuhr, who turned against pacifism before the war, recognized the great value of this witness. "We who allow ourselves to become engaged in war need this testimony of the absolutist against us," he wrote, "lest we accept the warfare of the world as normative, lest we become callous to the horror of war, and lest we forget the ambiguity of our own actions and motives and the risk we run of achieving no permanent good from this momentary anarchy in which we are involved."[1]

The WWII pacifists were well qualified, by experience and temperament, for the task of revitalizing and reorienting the American Left. They saw themselves as revolutionaries, and they were tough, having withstood violence, prison, poverty, and social opprobrium. They felt no need to conform to the dictates of what they saw as a corrupt economic system or a tyrannical government, and their critiques of these would resonate with a new generation increasingly alienated from the traditional structures and institutions of society. Nuclear arms, the U-2 incident, the Bay of Pigs, the Cold War, and Vietnam would bring mounting disillusionment with official pronouncements and only burnish the credibility of those who had warned all along that war would bring upon us that which we were fighting, that militarism would persist afterwards, and that we Americans have no monopoly on virtue.

Most of all, they refused to tolerate wrongs that most people took for granted. They were wrong about the war, but they acted out of conscience rather than cowardice, and their choices back then would fade into the nation's rearview mirror as serious new challenges arose and long-simmering injustices boiled over. The radical war resisters had been concerned with these for a long time, and their insistence on absolute nonviolence could lend protest an air of sanctity. Pacifism was a moral movement unstained by the bloody excesses of the past, and it transcended the cynicism and doctrinal obsessions that had traditionally mired the Left. Dellinger in particular would have credibility with young radicals. "Dave didn't spend a lot of time wondering," Tom Hayden said, "if he was a schachmanite or deutscherite or stalinoid or any of the categorical junk that made it hard for the old left to get down with the new."[2]

It didn't hurt that he was fanatically antiauthoritarian. All the World War II resisters were wary of authority, often including their own, and longed for direct democracy and communitarian social arrangements in contrast to the increasing consolidation, dehumanization, and remoteness of power in modern society. They cherished the specific humanity of each and every person, all of them made in the image of God and therefore morally exempt from the carnage of war. The hopelessness of mobilizing public opinion against the conflict they opposed helped cultivate in them an unfortunate preference for demonstrations over electoral politics. They never built an enduring political movement. And the radical individualism embedded in their ethos has a real dark side. But they, and the rest of us, were served brilliantly by their unwavering nonviolence, and their insistence that we must live up to our country's Christian and constitutional ideals.

They were, in fact, surprisingly religious by the secular standards of today's educated Americans. More than that, they were quite specifically Christian in outlook and motivation, a legacy that can be discerned easily in their descendants even if modern progressives are as likely to be Buddhists, Unitarians, or Wiccans if they have any religious faith or practice at all aside from politics. The Christian church, the Christian bible and Christian traditions have been the source of America's most powerful reform undertakings for most of two centuries, from abolitionism to temperance to the civil rights movement of the sixties. Enlightened reformers nowadays are instinctively hostile to anything Christian, but today's left strongly reflects the values and practices of the liberal Protestantism that drove their forbears.

Implicit in the pacifists' Christian libertarianism is the rather tragic notion that we are often our own worst enemies. Like their isolationist counterparts, the radical pacifists would have agreed with John Dewey on this score. "The serious threat to our democracy," he said in a book published in 1939, "is not the existence of foreign totalitarian states. It is the existence within our own personal attitudes and within our own institutions of conditions similar to those which have given a victory to external authority, discipline, uniformity and dependence upon The Leader in foreign countries. The battlefield is also accordingly here—within ourselves and our institutions."[3]

The genius of the pacifist project was that it never sought to destroy or overcome its antagonists. What it wanted was to bring people around to the cause of justice—and to do it without coercion. The pacifists retained their faith in humanity even after their religious faith had waned or at least evolved. During the war they mixed with men of all faiths and backgrounds, including godless radicals and run-of-the-mill criminals. Their allegiance to traditional churches was further undermined by the support of those institutions for the war, and especially by the role of the historic peace churches, who were seen by many resisters as serving the state at the Civilian Public Service camps. The resisters did not abandon the Gospels, but the gospel they would live was the Social Gospel and, perhaps predictably, the social and ethical dimensions of their creed would come to supersede its spiritual premises. Mainline Protestantism has withered even as the reformist impulses it once fostered run amok. The American left, in the fullness of its secular piety, is in the position of Jean Tarrou in *The Plague*, who explains that "what interests me is learning how to become a saint." "But you don't believe in God," his interlocutor objects, to which Tarrou replies, "Exactly!"

Our war resisters, thankfully, weren't saints, which is part of what makes them so interesting, and the only one plausibly headed for sainthood was disdainful of the whole enterprise. "That's the way people try to dismiss you," Dorothy Day told the *Chicago Tribune* in 1980, before any formal canonization process on her behalf had begun. "If you're a saint, then you must be impractical and utopian, and nobody has to pay any attention to you. That kind of talk makes me sick."

To pacifists, peace and justice are usually entwined, but what happens when they are in conflict? The story of America's World War II resisters forces us to consider the limits of pacifism. The end of conscription in 1973—brought down, in part, by an exploding number of objectors—may suggest that this question is largely of historical interest, but history implies quite the opposite. Since the end of the Second World War, conscientious objection has increased here and elsewhere (though it remains largely a Western phenomenon) thanks in great part to its secularization. In the United States, the Supreme Court has held that "ethical and moral beliefs" are just as legitimate a basis for objector status as the religious principles that were once required. The court (during Vietnam) refused to allow objection on a war-by-war basis, yet in many democracies the conscientious objector laws, liberal as they are, tend to be even more liberal in their application. Even Israel, with its universal military service, small population, and slim margin for error, has found a way, however informally, to accommodate objectors. The United States, if ever the question of conscription should arise anew, will have to do likewise. We'll never manage if we forget how we handled this during World War II.

THE END

JULY 25, 2022
TIVOLI, NY

ACKNOWLEDGEMENTS

WRITING ANY BOOK IS a struggle at times, but in keeping with the subject matter, this one was at least nonviolent. One reason was that so many people helped.

At the New York Public Library, which generously provided a workspace, Kate Cordes demonstrated through her good humor and archival wizardry why librarians are some of the most beloved people in the world. Counterparts at Yale's Sterling Memorial Library and the Swarthmore College Peace Collection were also unfailingly helpful.

My editors at the *Wall Street Journal*—Gary Rosen, Adam Kirsch, and Erich Eichman—were patient, flexible and supportive. This book couldn't have been written without their indulgence. The same goes for Daniel Gross and Jakob von Baeyer at *strategy+business*.

This book probably wouldn't exist without the hard work and encouragement of my agent, Todd Shuster, who has my undying gratitude. But a book needs a publisher, too, and I was fortunate to have the team at Melville House starting with Dennis Johnson, who saw the potential of the subject, and Ryan Harrington, who bought the proposal. Editors Athena Bryan and Mike Lindgren were paragons of patience, to say nothing of insight, and the book is vastly better for their efforts.

A number of busy scholars, writers and friends went out of their way to help, including Richard Aldous, Mitchell Cohen, Thomas Guglielmo, and Geoffrey Kabaservice. Fergus Bordewich, Benjamin Schwarz, and David

Smith offered useful early feedback. Louise Dewhirst and Bob Keeler provided excellent suggestions and corrections on the manuscript.

War By Other Means was inspired in significant part by Adam Hochschild's *To End All Wars,* a moving account of opposition to what was known as the Great War, and Adam provided some timely encouragement. But I was also inspired by my wonderful sons, David and Nick, athletic young men of the kind who have fought most of the world's wars. I offer this work in hopes that they can continue to live in peace along with everyone else.

Nobody made a bigger sacrifice for this book than the woman who brought them into this world, and for Louise no thank you could ever fully express my gratitude.

NOTES

Introduction

1 Kaufman, "David Dellinger, of Chicago 7, Dies at 88."

2 Hunt, *David Dellinger*, 40.

3 Polner and Woods, *We Who Dared to Say No to War*, 173.

4 Polner and Woods, 1753.

5 Kaufman, "David Dellinger, of Chicago 7, Dies at 88."

6 Brightman, *Writing Dangerously.*

7 McMeekin, *Stalin's War*, 351.

8 Lawrence Wittner, *Rebels Against War: The American Peace Movement, 1933-1983*, Revised edition (Philadelphia: Temple University Press, 1984), 41; Albert Keim, *The CPS Story: An Illustrated History of Civilian Public Service* (Intercourse, PA: Good Books, 2013), 8.

9 Dewey, *Freedom and Culture*, 49.

10 Gretchen Lemke-Santangelo, "The Radical Conscientious Objectors of World War II: Wartime Experience and Postwar Activism," *Radical History Review* 1989, no. 45 (September 21, 1989): 8, https://doi.org/10.1215/01636545-1989-45-5.

And Now, Youth!

1 Auden, "September 1, 1939."

2 Cohen, *When the Old Left Was Young*, xiii.

3 Jonas, *Isolationism in America 1935-1941*, 83, 268.

4 Jonas, 81.

5 Logevall, *JFK*, 262.

6 Cook, *Eleanor Roosevelt, Volume 3*, 206.

7 Allen, *Since Yesterday*, 322.

8 Allen, 2.

9 Overy and Wheatcroft, *The Road to War: Revised Edition*, 327.

10 Steele, "American Popular Opinion and the War Against Germany: The Issue of Negotiated Peace, 1942," 720.

11 McDougall, *Promised Land, Crusader State*, 151.

12 Hentoff, *Peace Agitator: The Story of A. J. Muste*, 177.

13 Chatfield, "Pacifists and Their Publics," 304; Ferrell, "The Peace Movement."

14 Sevareid, *Not So Wild a Dream: A Personal Story of Youth and War and the American Faith*, 62.

15 Cohen, *When the Old Left Was Young*, 79; Karnow, *Vietnam: A History*, 179.

16 Cohen, *When the Old Left Was Young*, 92, 152.

17 Handy, *A History of Union*, 197.

18 Orser, "World War II and the Pacifist Controversy in the Major Protestant Churches," 6.

19 Appelbaum, *Kingdom to Commune*, 163 ff.

20 Howlett and Cohan, *John Dewey, America's Peace-Minded Educator*, 192.

21 Howlett and Cohan, 172.

22 Abrams, "The Churches and the Clergy in World War II," 112; Appelbaum, *Kingdom to Commune*, 30, 31.

23 Branch, *Parting the Waters*, 66.

24 Danielson, "In My Extremity I Turned to Gandhi," 363ff.

25 Cook, *Eleanor Roosevelt, Volume 3*, 210 ff.

26 Cook, 209.

Class Acts

1 MacDonald, *A Moral Temper: The Letters of Dwight Macdonald*, 16.

2 Orwell's 1942 essay "Pacifism and the War," published in *Partisan Review*, has become one of the most famous statements against the refusal to fight. Trilling, *The Liberal Imagination*, 9.

3 Dellinger, *From Yale to Jail*, 13.

4 Anderson, *Bayard Rustin*, 347.

5 Day, *The Long Loneliness*, 21.

6 O'Brien, "Dorothy's Days: Letters from a Saint."

7 James, *The Varieties of Religious Experience: A Study in Human Nature*, 150.

8 Dellinger, 437.

9 Dellinger, *From Yale to Jail*, 40.

The Making of a Radical

1 Dellinger, 54.

2 Dellinger, 55.

3 Dellinger, David - Interview and Memoir, 8.

4 Hunt, *David Dellinger*, 11; Dellinger, *From Yale to Jail*, 16.

5 Hunt, *David Dellinger*, 11.

6 Hunt, *David Dellinger*, 18.

7 Hunt, *David Dellinger*, 20; Starr, "The Yale of My Day by Roger Starr '39."

8 McCullough III, "Town, Gown, and the Great Depression: Yale and New Haven During the Construction of Yale's Original Residential Colleges"; Kabaservice, *The Guardians*, 46.

9 Hunt, *David Dellinger*, 20ff.

10 Dellinger, *From Yale to Jail*, 453; Hunt, *David Dellinger*, 24.

11 Dellinger, *From Yale to Jail*, 454; Hunt, *David Dellinger*, 105.

12 Dellinger, *From Yale to Jail*, 454.

13 Hunt, *David Dellinger*, 20ff.

14 Dellinger, *From Yale to Jail*, 18.

15 Dellinger, Dellinger, David - Interview and Memoir.

16 Hunt, *David Dellinger*, 25–26.

17 "Student Co-Operation Needed for Pacifism."

18 Dellinger, *From Yale to Jail*, 35; Dellinger, "Why I Refused to Register in the October 1940 Draft and a Little of What It Led To," 179.

19 Dellinger, 34.

20 Dellinger, David - Interview and Memoir, 5.

21 Kabaservice, *The Guardians*, 66; Elkin, "Labor and the Left," 489.

22 Dellinger, *From Yale to Jail*, 75.
23 Gara and Gara, *A Few Small Candles*, 31. Dellinger, *From Yale to Jail*, 77.
24 Dellinger, 76.

The Fog of War

1 Schlesinger, "Back to the Womb?: Isolationism's Renewed Threat," 4.
2 Doenecke, *Storm on the Horizon*, 32.
3 Wittner, *Rebels Against War*, 18.
4 Robinson, *Abraham Went Out*, 257 n9.
5 Associated Press, "Gandhi Hopes British, Nazis Become Exhausted, End War."
6 Olson, *Those Angry Days*, 51; Jonas, *Isolationism in America 1935-1941*, 231; Philbin, "Charles Austin Beard: Liberal Foe of American Internationalism"; Clifford and Spencer, *The First Peacetime Draft*, 143.
7 Jonas, *Isolationism in America 1935-1941*, 228 ff.
8 Doenecke, *Storm on the Horizon*, 30.
9 Hutchins, "What Shall We Defend?"
10 "55,000 Here Stage Protest on Hitler Attacks on Jews; Nazis Order a New Boycott. Other Faiths Join in; Crowd Overflowing the Garden Hears Leaders Assail Persecution."
11 Forest, *All Is Grace*, 157ff.
12 Miller, *Harry Emerson Fosdick*, 488.
13 Doenecke, *Storm on the Horizon*, 41.
14 The right-wing mothers' movement is well covered in Jeansonne, *Women of the Far Right*.
15 Stossel, *Sarge*, 44.
16 Kabaservice, *The Guardians*, 72.
17 Cole, *America First: The Battle Against Intervention 1940-1941*, 48.
18 Kauffman, "Editor's Introduction," xxxiv.
19 Kauffman, "Editor's Introduction," xxxiii; Cole, *America First: The Battle Against Intervention 1940-1941*, 150.

Feeling the Draft

1 Clifford and Spencer, *The First Peacetime Draft*, 4.
2 Schlesinger, *The Politics of Upheaval*, 82; Clifford and Spencer, *The First Peacetime Draft*, 148–49.

3   Mayer, *Robert Maynard Hutchins*, 2.

4   Clifford and Spencer, *The First Peacetime Draft*, 88.

5   Compulsory Military Training and Service: Hearings Before the Committee on Military Affairs, United States Senate, Seventy-sixth Congress, Third Session, on S.4164, a Bill to Protect the Integrity and Institutions of the United States Through a System of Selective Compulsory Military Training and Service, 152-155.

6   Selective Training and Service Act (public Laws-Ch. 720-Sept. 16, 1940), 889.

Catholic Dynamite

1   Day, *The Duty of Delight*, 58.

2   Piehl, *Breaking Bread*, 96.

3   Troester, *Voices From the Catholic Worker*, 72.

4   Loughery and Randolph, *Dorothy Day*, 206.

5   Day, "Our Stand."

6   Day, *All the Way to Heaven*, 150.

7   Loughery and Randolph, *Dorothy Day*, 19.

8   Shipman, *It Had to Be Revolution*, 31.

9   Loughery and Randolph, *Dorothy Day*, 36ff.

10 Loughery and Randolph, 86; Shipman, *It Had to Be Revolution*, 144; Coles, 5.

11 Shipman, *It Had to Be Revolution*, 144.

12 Loughery and Randolph, *Dorothy Day*, 123.

13 Day, *The Long Loneliness*, 165.

14 Day, 166.

15 Day, 169.

16 Doblmeier, *Revolution of the Heart: The Dorothy Day Story*.

17 Day, *The Duty of Delight*, 432.

18 Day, "Loaves and Fishes," 22.

19 Wright, *Dorothy Day: An Introduction to Her Life and Thought*, 109.

20 Loughery and Randolph, *Dorothy Day*, 130ff.

21 Forest, *Love Is the Measure*, 98.

22 Miller, *Dorothy Day*, 313.

23 Wright, *Dorothy Day: An Introduction to Her Life and Thought*, 118.

24 Piehl, *Breaking Bread*, 194.

25 de la Cueva, "Religious Persecution, Anticlerical Tradition and Revolution," 355.
26 Day, "Explains CW Stand on Use of Force."
27 Greif, *The Age of the Crisis of Man*, 78.
28 Piehl, *Breaking Bread*, 193.

Not Quite Everybody
1   *New York Times*, Oct. 17, 1940.
2   "Two Cowboys Confess Killing Sailor in Hotel," 12.
3   Clifford and Spencer, *The First Peacetime Draft*, 258.
4   "16,000,000 TO ENROLL TODAY IN FIRST PEACETIME DRAFT."
5   *Philadelphia Inquirer*, Oct. 17, 1940, 7.
6   *Chicago Tribune*, Oct. 17, 1940, 5.
7   "Free and Equal."
8   Brooke, *Bridging the Divide*, 22.
9   Klein, *A Call to Arms: The Epic Story of How America Mobilized for World War II*, 119.
10 Finkle, "The Conservative Aims of Militant Rhetoric," 693–94. The 1940 Census counted 12.9 million blacks but is estimated to have missed 1.1 million.
11 Finkle, 709.
12 Selective Training and Service Act (public Laws-Ch. 720-Sept. 16, 1940), 887.
13 "Will Try to Kill Selective Service," 14.
14 Kosek, *Acts of Conscience*, 28.
15 "Seminoles Go in Hiding."
16 Kohn, *Jailed for Peace*, 58.
17 Philadelphia Inquirer, Oct. 17, 1940, 7.
18 Anderson, *Bayard Rustin*, 66.
19 Naeve and Wieck, *A Field of Broken Stones*, 7ff.
20 Schoenfeld, "U.S. Prisons–A Disgrace."
21 Wittner, *Rebels Against War*, 48; Naeve and Wieck, *A Field of Broken Stones*. Naeve's memoir was published in 1950 by Dellinger's Libertarian Press.

Union Men

1   King, "My Pilgrimage to Nonviolence."

2   Brown, *Niebuhr and His Age*, 51; Handy, *A History of Union*, 181–82.

3   Handy, *A History of Union Theological Seminary in New York*, 178, 193ff; Pace, "Anne Morrow Lindbergh, 94, Dies; Champion of Flight and Women's Concerns," Feb. 8, 2001.

4   Myers, "Faith and Theology."

5   Marsh, *Strange Glory*, 116; Bonhoeffer, *Barcelona, Berlin, New York*, 265.

6   Handy, *A History of Union*, 159 ff.

7   Niebuhr, *Reinhold Niebuhr*, 55.

8   Fosdick, *The Living of These Days,* 293, 301.

9   Niebuhr, *Christianity and Power Politics,* ix.

10 Houser, "Reflections of a Religious War Objector (Half a Century Later)"; Collins, *Ubuntu,* Chapter 1; Fox, "George Houser, Freedom Rides Pioneer and a Founder of CORE, Dies at 99."

11 Weisbrot, *Father Divine and the Struggle for Racial Equality*, 109ff; Collins, *Ubuntu*, 21.

12 Collins, *Ubuntu,* 22 ff.

13 Farmer, *Lay Bare the Heart*, 149 ff; Appelbaum, *Kingdom to Commune*, 150; Anderson, *Bayard Rustin*, 69–71.

14 Lynn, *There Is a Fountain,* Chapter Seven.

15 Dellinger, *From Yale to Jail*, 151.

16 Benedict, *Born Again Radical*, 24.

17 Benedict, Benedict, Donald - Interview and Memoir Part one.

18 Dellinger, *From Yale to Jail*, 63; Spragg, Spragg, Howard - Interview and Memoir, 13.

19 Benedict, *Born Again Radical*, 25.

20 Benedict, *Born Again Radical*, 26; Dellinger, *From Yale to Jail*, 459; Dallas, "Part 2."

21 Dellinger, *From Yale to Jail*, 66.

22 Benedict, *Born Again Radical*, 30.

23 Dallas, "Part 2."

24 Hunt, *David Dellinger*, 38; Dallas, Dallas, Meredith and Dallas, Willa - Interview and Memoir, 4.

25 Benedict, *Born Again Radical*, 20.

26 Dellinger, *From Yale to Jail*, 420.

27 Houser, "Reflections of a Religious War Objector (Half a Century Later)," 134.

28 Tracy, *Direct Action*, 2.

29 Houser, "Reflections of a Religious War Objector (Half a Century Later)," 134.

30 *Yale Daily News,* Oct. 16, 1940.

31 Collins, *Ubuntu.*

32 Houser, "Reflections of a Religious War Objector (Half a Century Later)," 135.

33 Hunt, *David Dellinger*, 45; Houser, "Reflections of a Religious War Objector (Half a Century Later)," 135.

34 Keve, *Prisons and the American Conscience*, 205.

35 Dellinger, *From Yale to Jail*, 63.

Hardball and Softball at Danbury

1 Cantine and Rainer, "Prison Etiquette: The Convict's Compendium of Useful Information", introduction.

2 Hunt, *David Dellinger*, 56; Schoenfeld, "The Danbury Story," 334.

3 Brock, *These Strange Criminals*, 337.

4 Rogne, "The Greatest Generation Revisited," 15; Stewart-Winter, "Not a Soldier, Not a Slacker: Conscientious Objectors and Male Citizenship in the United States during the Second World War," 529.

5 Stewart-Winter, "Not a Soldier, Not a Slacker: Conscientious Objectors and Male Citizenship in the United States during the Second World War," 529.

6 Isserman, *If I Had a Hammer: The Death of the Old Left and the Birth of the New Left*, 132; Clark, "Just Out of Danbury."

7 Jackson, Jackson, Walter - Interview and Memoir, 8.

8 Schoenfeld, "The Danbury Story," 1966, 336.

9 Dellinger, *From Yale to Jail*, 94.

10 Smith, "James V. Bennett Dies."

11 Dellinger, 95.

12 Houser, "Reflections of a Religious War Objector (Half a Century Later)," 145.

13 Houser, "Reflections of a Religious War Objector (Half a Century Later)," 145.

14 Schoenfeld, "The Danbury Story," 26.

15 Schoenfeld, "The Danbury Story," 2001.

16 Dellinger, *From Yale to Jail*, 97; Houser, "Reflections of a Religious War Objector (Half a Century Later)," 147.

17 Collins, *Ubuntu*, 40.

The War Comes Home

1 Fosdick, *The Living of These Days,* 295.

2 Wittner, *Rebels Against War*, 34.

3 Berg, *Lindbergh*, 457.

4 Cole, *America First: The Battle Against Intervention 1940-1941*, 195.

5 Wittner, *Rebels Against War*, 37.

6 Clifford and Spencer, *The First Peacetime Draft*, 138.

7 Wittner, *Rebels Against War*, 44.

8 Crespi, "Public Opinion toward Conscientious Objectors."

9 Orser, "World War II and the Pacifist Controversy in the Major Protestant Churches," 9.

10 Chatfield, *For Peace and Justice*, 326.

11 Wittner, *Rebels Against War*, 45.

12 Wittner, *Rebels Against War*, 62.

13 Bennett, *Radical Pacifism*, 74–75.

14 Day, "Our Country Passes from Undeclared War to Declared War; We Continue Our Christian Pacifist Stand."

15 Wreszin, *A Rebel in Defense of Tradition*, 103; Greenberg et al., "A Statement by the Editors."

16 Lopach and Luckowski, *Jeannette Rankin*, 182.

17 Wittner, *Rebels Against War*, 35.

18 Wittner, *Rebels Against War*, 42.

19 Hentoff, *Peace Agitator: The Story of A. J. Muste*, 18.

20 Muste, *Essays of A.J. Muste*, 87, 181.

21 Robinson, *Abraham Went Out*, 14.

22 Danielson, *American Gandhi*, 49.

23 Robinson, *Abraham Went Out*, 21; Hentoff, *Peace Agitator: The Story of A. J. Muste*, 44.

24 Danielson, *American Gandhi*, 136.

25 Hentoff, *Peace Agitator: The Story of A. J. Muste*, 55.

26 Robinson, *Abraham Went Out*, 45.

27 Danielson, "In My Extremity I Turned to Gandhi," 373.

28 Danielson, *American Gandhi*, 200; Muste, *Essays of A.J. Muste*, 210.

29 Danielson, *American Gandhi*, 212, 380.

30 Muste, *Essays of A.J. Muste*, 135.

31 Muste, 210–11.

32 Niebuhr, *The Irony of American History*, 42.

33 Sayre, "Japan Attacks Us."

34 "The Course Before Us."

35 Robinson, *Abraham Went Out*, 259.

36 Danielson, Mollin, and Rossinow, *The Religious Left in Modern America*, 110; Danielson, *American Gandhi*, 225.

37 Wittner, *Rebels Against War*, 54; Chatfield, *For Peace and Justice*, 327. The War Resisters League also grew. With fewer than 900 paying members in 1939, it exceeded 2,300 in 1945. Annual revenue went from $5,000 to $20,000.

38 Robinson, *Abraham Went Out*, 64.

39 Farmer, *Lay Bare the Heart*, 85.

40 Danielson, *American Gandhi*, 219.

41 Anderson, *Bayard Rustin*, 74.

42 Muste, "Some Fellowship Objectives."

43 Trotsky, *Their Morals and Ours*; McCarter, *Young Radicals*, 57; Kosek, *Acts of Conscience*, 163, Kosek, *Richard Gregg, Mohandas Gandhi, and the Strategy of Nonviolence,* 1325.

44 August Meier and Elliott M. Rudwick, *CORE, a Study in the Civil Rights Movement*, 1942-1968 (Oxford University Press, 1973), 6–7.

45 Farmer, *Lay Bare the Heart*.

46 Farmer, 89.

A Congress for Equality

1 Farmer, 99.

2 Houser, "Letter to A.J. Muste," July 13, 1942.

3 This book's account of CORE owes much to Meier and Rudwick, *CORE, a Study in the Civil Rights Movement, 1942-1968.*

4   Farmer, *Lay Bare the Heart*, 90ff.

5   Perry, *Civil Disobedience* Background on American civil disobedience is from Perry's excellent book.

6   Collins, *Ubuntu* Chapter Three.

7   Lee, *Employment of Negro Troops* Chapter XII Harvest of Disorder; Vernon, "Jim Crow, Meet Lieutenant Robinson."

8   Adams, *The Best War Ever*, 119.

9   Dalfiume, "The 'Forgotten Years' of the Negro Revolution," 99; Dalfiume, "Military Segregation and the 1940 Presidential Election," 90.

10 Rustin, "Field Worker--Bayard Rustin"; D'Emilio, *Lost Prophet*, 51.

11 Houser, *Erasing the Color Line (Booklet)*.

12 Houser.

13 Severo, "James Farmer, Civil Rights Giant In the 50's and 60's, Is Dead at 79."

14 Farmer, *Lay Bare the Heart*, 153–54.

15 Meier and Rudwick, *CORE, a Study in the Civil Rights Movement, 1942-1968*, 13.

16 Collins, *Ubuntu,* Chapter Three.

Peace Against Prejudice

1   Robinson, *Abraham Went Out*, 89.

2   Wittner, *Rebels Against War*, 40.

3   Wilcock, *Pacifism and the Jews*. Chapter 6; Wittner, *Rebels Against War*, 3.

4   Young, "Facing a Test of Faith," 34.

5   Strausbaugh, *Victory City*, 35.

6   Miller, *Dorothy Day*, 319.

7   Norwood, "Marauding Youth and the Christian Front."

8   Loughery and Randolph, *Dorothy Day*, 196,197.

9   Tracy, *Direct Action*, 20.

10 Wilcock, *Pacifism and the Jews*, 126, 130.

11 Wilcock, *Pacifism and the Jews*, 139.

12 Wilcock, *Pacifism and the Jews*, 161.

13 Wilcock, *Pacifism and the Jews*, 160–61.

14 Young, 36.

15 Frazer and O'Sullivan, *We Have Just Begun to Not Fight*, 1981.

16 Kampelman, *Entering New Worlds*, 10.

17 Kampelman, *Entering New Worlds*, 27.

18 Kampelman, *Entering New Worlds*, 31 ff; Tucker, *The Great Starvation Experiment*, 48–49.

19 Kampelman, *Entering New Worlds*, 45–46.

20 Whitfield, *A Critical American*, 45; Young, "Facing a Test of Faith."

21 Ingle, "Milton Mayer, Quaker Hedgehog"; Mayer, "I Think I'll Sit This One Out."

22 Young, "Facing a Test of Faith"; Stillman, "About the Jewish Peace Fellowship."

23 Lelyveld, *Omaha Blues: A Memory Loop*, 25.

24 Young, "Facing a Test of Faith," 36.

25 Wilcock, *Pacifism and the Jews*, 126.

26 Wittner, *Rebels Against War*, 16.

27 Bennett, *Radical Pacifism*, 125–26.

28 Robinson, *Abraham Went Out*, 88.

29 Schmoe, "America's Protective Custody."

30 Schmoe, "America's Protective Custody."

31 Day, "Grave Injustice Done Japanese On West Coast."

32 Yamada, "My Story of World War II," 194ff.

33 Davis and Kovac, "Confrontation at the Locks."

34 Davis and Kovac, 498.

35 Hurwitz and Simpson, *Against the Tide* for Kepler quote; Sibley and Jacob, *Conscription of Conscience*, 253.

36 "U.S. At War."

37 Sibley and Jacob, *Conscription of Conscience*. Chapter XI.

38 Doyle, *Radical Chapters*, 37 ff offers an excellent account of Germfask through Kepler's eyes.

39 Doyle, *Radical Chapters*, 37 ff.

40 Doyle, *Radical Chapters*, 37 ff.

41 Frazer and O'Sullivan, *We Have Just Begun to Not Fight*, 233.

A One-Man Army

1 Rustin, "Field Worker--Bayard Rustin."

2 Farmer, *Lay Bare the Heart*, 110.

3 Clark, "Prison Memoir," 14.

4 Anderson, *Bayard Rustin*, 89.

5 D'Emilio, *Lost Prophet*, 47–48, 108.

6 D'Emilio, 126.

7 Rustin, "Field Worker--Bayard Rustin."

8 Anderson, *Bayard Rustin*, 82–83.

9 Myrdal, *An American Dilemma: The Negro Problem and Modern Democracy*, 1006.

10 Trimmingham, "Mail Call: Democracy?"

11 Trimmingham, "Mail Call: Democracy? II."

12 Rustin, "Report of Youth Secretary--Bayard Rustin."

13 Levine, *Bayard Rustin and the Civil Rights Movement*, 32.

14 "Non-Violence vs. Jim Crow--II."

15 "Non-Violence vs. Jim Crow--II."

16 Anderson, *Bayard Rustin*, 90.

17 Rustin, "The Negro and Non-Violence"; D'Emilio, *Lost Prophet*, 46.

18 D'Emilio, *Lost Prophet*, 46; Rustin, "Non-Violence vs. Jim Crow."

19 D'Emilio, *Lost Prophet*, 62.

20 D'Emilio, 55.

21 Rustin, *I Must Resist*, 2–4.

22 Frazer and O'Sullivan, *Oral History Series*. Introduction.

23 Rustin, "Report of Youth Secretary—Bayard Rustin"; Frankenberg, "Conscience Free"; Thompson, *Men in German Uniform*, 79.

24 Rustin, "Report of Youth Secretary—Bayard Rustin"; D'Emilio, *Lost Prophet*, 49, 55.

25 Lucander, *Winning the War for Democracy*. Chapter 2; Anderson, *Bayard Rustin*, 85.

26 Macdonald and Macdonald, *The War's Greatest Scandal! The Story of Jim Crow in Uniform*, 4.

27 Macdonald and Macdonald, *The War's Greatest Scandal! The Story of Jim Crow in Uniform*, 4.

28 MacDonald, *A Moral Temper: The Letters of Dwight Macdonald*, 280.

29 Wreszin, *A Rebel in Defense of Tradition*, 116; "Advertisement for Monster Mass Meeting"; "Arthur G. Hays to Speak for Lynn at Mass Meeting"; "Tells Why Race Must Fight War Dep't Jim Crow."

30 D'Emilio, *Lost Prophet*, 60–61.

31   Siracusa, *Nonviolence before King*, 122.

32   Levine, *Bayard Rustin and the Civil Rights Movement*, 35–36.

33   Lucander, *Winning the War for Democracy* Chapter Four.

34   Levine, *Bayard Rustin and the Civil Rights Movement*, 36–37.

35   Anderson, *Bayard Rustin*, 158ff.

36   D'Emilio, *Lost Prophet*, 70–71.

37   D'Emilio, 71.

The Conservative Anarchists

1   O'Connor, *The Moral Vision of Dorothy Day: A Feminist Perspective*, 79.

2   Farrell, *The Spirit of the Sixties: The Making of Postwar Radicalism* Chapter One.

3   Mel Piehl, *Breaking Bread: The Catholic Worker and the Origin of Catholic Radicalism in America*, 2nd edition (Tuscaloosa: University Alabama Press, 2006), 196.

4   Piehl, *Breaking Bread* 109, 197; Mize, "We Are Still Pacifists," 465 ff.

5   Miller, *Dorothy Day*, 344; Piehl, *Breaking Bread*, 172.

6   Day, *All the Way to Heaven*, 69.

7   Day, "If Conscription Comes For Women."

8   Troester, *Voices From the Catholic Worker*, 72.

9   Macdonald, "Revisiting Dorothy Day."

10   Day, "For These Dear Dead."

11   Loughery and Randolph, *Dorothy Day* Chapter 12; Day, *The Duty of Delight*, 90.

12   Day, "Day After Day."

13   Peters, "John Hugo and an American Catholic Theology of Nature and Grace," Introduction.

14   Powers, *Suitable Accommodations,* xvii.

15   Piehl, *Breaking Bread*, 75.

16   Day, "Loaves and Fishes," 165. "Chav" here is probably schav, a cold sorrel and egg soup.

17   Loughery and Randolph, *Dorothy Day*, 212, 219.

18   Loughery and Randolph, *Dorothy Day*, 212, 219.

19   Rodden, "Memorial for a Revolutionist: Dwight Macdonald, 'A Critical American,'" 94; Mendelson, *Moral Agents*, 48.

20   Wreszin, *A Rebel in Defense of Tradition*, 64.

21 Macdonald and Wreszin, *Interviews with Dwight Macdonald*, 160.

22 Macdonald, *The Memoirs of a Revolutionist*, 118.

23 Whitfield, *A Critical American*, 44.

24 Macdonald, "How to Think About War and Peace."

25 Wreszin, *A Rebel in Defense of Tradition*, 373.

26 Howe, *A Margin of Hope*, 115 ff; Arendt, "He's All Dwight."

27 Jarnot, *Robert Duncan, the Ambassador from Venus*, Chapter 12.

Déjà Vu for Dellinger

1 Hunt, *David Dellinger*, 75.

2 Danielson, "'It Is a Day of Judgment': The Peacemakers, Religion, and Radicalism in Cold War America," 222.

3 Danielson, "'It Is a Day of Judgment': The Peacemakers, Religion, and Radicalism in Cold War America," 222; Dellinger, *From Yale to Jail*, 107.

4 Roberts Jr., "Prison and Butterfly Wings," 154–55.

5 Roberts Jr., "Prison and Butterfly Wings," 152.

6 Hunt, 62 ff; Dellinger, *From Yale to Jail*, 101 ff.

7 Dellinger, Elizabeth Dellinger Interview, 13.

8 Hunt, *David Dellinger*, 68.

9 Dellinger, *From Yale to Jail*, 105–6.

10 Dellinger, Elizabeth Dellinger Interview, 3.

11 Dellinger, *From Yale to Jail*, 107.

12 Harvey, Henry Harvey Memoir, 14; Dallas, Dallas, Meredith and Dallas, Willa - Interview and Memoir, 35.

13 Hunt, *David Dellinger*. Chapter Four; Dallas, Dallas, Meredith and Dallas, Willa - Interview and Memoir.

14 Hunt, *David Dellinger*. Chapter Four; Dallek, *Franklin D. Roosevelt: A Political Life*, 500 ff.

15 Muste, "Letter to Francis Biddle from A.J. Muste," June 17, 1942.

16 Muste.

17 Hunt, *David Dellinger*, 71; Dellinger, *From Yale to Jail*, 115–18.

18 Dellinger, *Revolutionary Nonviolence*, 13–14.

19 Sibley and Jacob, *Conscription of Conscience*, 542; Cooney, Michalowski, and Jezer, *The Power of the People*, 103.

20 Sibley and Jacob, *Conscription of Conscience*, 477.

21 This account of Bishop's exploits is drawn primarily from Sibley and Jacob, *Conscription of Conscience*, 401ff; Tracy, *Direct Action*, 42–43; Wittner, *Rebels Against War*, 89–90; Doyle, *Radical Chapters,* 38-39.

22 "Bishop Ends 44 Days."

23 Bishop's saga is largely drawn from Sibley and Jacob, *Conscription of Conscience*; Tracy, *Direct Action*; Wittner, *Rebels Against War*.

24 Casey, "From Religious Outsiders to Insiders," 469.

25 Sibley and Jacob, *Conscription of Conscience*, 409.

26 Cooney, Michalowski, and Jezer, *The Power of the People*, 102.

27 Wittner, *Rebels Against War*, 86; Naeve and Wieck, *A Field of Broken Stones,* Chapter 15.

28 Bennett, *Radical Pacifism*, 89 ff.

29 Quoted in Peck, *We Who Would Not Kill*, 94.

30 Sibley and Jacob, *Conscription of Conscience*, 412 ff.

31 Hunt, *David Dellinger*, 86; Bennett, *Radical Pacifism*, 119–20.

32 Bennett, 120. The Lewisburg strike is also treated by Dellinger, Hunt, Sibley, Tracy and others. Accounts differ but Bennett's appears to offer the most coherent and extensive version.

33 Bennett, 120.

34 Sibley and Jacob, *Conscription of Conscience*, 375; Dellinger, *From Yale to Jail*, 120.

35 Tracy, *Direct Action*, 20.

36 Hunt, *David Dellinger*, 77–78.

37 Dellinger, *From Yale to Jail*, 121; Tracy, *Direct Action*, 19.

38 Dellinger, 78–79.

39 Dellinger, 132–37.

40 Hunt, *David Dellinger*. Chapter 4.

41 Hunt, *David Dellinger*, 80; Dellinger, *From Yale to Jail*, 122.

Playing Ball for Keeps

1 Benedict, Benedict, Donald - Interview and Memoir, 72.

2 Peck, *We Who Would Not Kill*, 102.

3 Naeve and Wieck, *A Field of Broken Stones* Chapter 17.

4 Peck, *We Who Would Not Kill*, 108–13.

5 Peck, 113–17.

6 Peck, 114.

7 Peck, 115.

8 Peck, 122.

9 Peck, 122–23.

10 Peck, 126; Myrdal, *An American Dilemma: The Negro Problem and Modern Democracy*, 1003.

11 Peck, *We Who Would Not Kill*, 127–29.

12 Peck, 129.

13 Keve, *Prisons and the American Conscience*, 206.

14 Benedict, *Born Again Radical*, 39–40.

15 Benedict, 39 ff; Benedict, Donald - Interview and Memoir, 67.

16 Benedict, *Born Again Radical*, 41–42.

17 Benedict, 47.

18 The media's handling of the dawning genocide is covered ably in Lipstadt, *Beyond Belief*.

19 Benedict, 46.

Work of National Importance

1 Bennett, *Radical Pacifism*, 98 ff.

2 Sawyer's account is drawn from Sareyan, *The Turning Point*; Sawyer, Warren Sawyer interview, Rutgers Oral History Archives; and Halpern, *Dangerous Medicine*.

3 Warren Sawyer interview, Rutgers Oral History Archives.

4 Sareyan, *The Turning Point*, 52.

5 Frazer and O'Sullivan, *We Have Just Begun to Not Fight*, 190.

6 Sibley and Jacob, *Conscription of Conscience*, 137.

7 Sareyan, *The Turning Point*, 62.

8 Bedlam 1946: MOST U.S. MENTAL HOSPITALS ARE A SHAME AND A DISGRACE" in *LIFE* May 6, 1946, 102-118.

9 Halpern, *Dangerous Medicine* Preface, Introduction, Epilogue.

10 Ehrlich and Tejada-Flores, *The Good War and Those Who Refused to Fight It*.

11 Bateman-House, "Compelled to Volunteer: American Conscientious Objectors to World War II as Subjects of Medical Research," 258.

12 Kampelman, *Entering New Worlds*, 47.

13 Kampelman, *Entering New Worlds*, 48; Tucker, *The Great Starvation Experiment*, 38; Bateman-House, "Compelled to Volunteer: American Conscientious Objectors to World War II as Subjects of Medical Research," 186.

14 Bateman-House, "Compelled to Volunteer: American Conscientious Objectors to World War II as Subjects of Medical Research," 3.

15 "Medicine: The Conscientious Guinea Pigs," *Time* Magazine Dec. 10, 1945.

16 Details on the range of experiments etc. are largely drawn from Bateman-House, "Compelled to Volunteer: American Conscientious Objectors to World War II as Subjects of Medical Research" as well as contemporaneous press accounts in *Time* and elsewhere.

17 Tucker, *The Great Starvation Experiment*; Brody, "Dr. Ancel Keys, 100, Promoter of Mediterranean Diet, Dies."

18 Tucker, *The Great Starvation Experiment*, 31 ff.

19 Tucker, *The Great Starvation Experiment*, 68.

20 Kalm and Semba, "They Starved So That Others Be Better Fed."

21 Kalm and Semba, "They Starved So That Others Be Better Fed."

22 Tucker, *The Great Starvation Experiment*, 103; Ball, "The Minnesota Starvation Experiment."

23 Kalm and Semba, "They Starved So That Others Be Better Fed."

24 Kampelman, *Entering New Worlds*, 52.

25 Tucker, *The Great Starvation Experiment*, 182.

26 Tucker, *The Great Starvation Experiment*.

27 Tucker, *The Great Starvation Experiment*, 177ff. The dialogue between Keys and Brozek is all drawn from Tucker.

Déjà Vu for Rustin

1 D'Emilio, *Lost Prophet*, 88.

2 Levine, *Bayard Rustin and the Civil Rights Movement*, 40; Anderson, *Bayard Rustin*, 101.

3 D'Emilio, *Lost Prophet*, 80–87.

4 D'Emilio, 81.

5 Houser, *Erasing the Color Line (Booklet)*, 48.

6 Anderson, *Bayard Rustin*, 103–4.

7 Anderson, *Bayard Rustin*, 104; Levine, *Bayard Rustin and the Civil Rights Movement*, 42.

8 Clark, "Prison Memoir," 15.

9 Anderson, *Bayard Rustin*, 109.

10 D'Emilio, *Lost Prophet*, 86–87.

11 Anderson, *Bayard Rustin*, 107.

12 D'Emilio, *Lost Prophet*, 86–87; Berg, "Before the Marches."

13 Account of Huddleston episode draws on Houser, *Erasing the Color Line*; Levine, *Bayard Rustin and the Civil Rights Movement*; Anderson, *Bayard Rustin*; D'Emilio, *Lost Prophet*; Clark, "Prison Memoir"; "Huddleston Is Given Five Years."

14 Based on the accounts of Bronson Clark, Levine, Anderson, D'Emilio.

15 Clark, "Prison Memoir," 15.

16 Anderson, *Bayard Rustin*, 101–2.

17 Wetzel, *Pacifist*, 173.

18 D'Emilio, *Lost Prophet*, 94–95.

19 Bennett, *Radical Pacifism*, 130.

20 D'Emilio, *Lost Prophet*, 89; Anderson, *Bayard Rustin*, 102.

21 D'Emilio, *Lost Prophet*, 90.

22 D'Emilio, *Lost Prophet*, 90–91.

23 D'Emilio, *Lost Prophet*, 91–92.

24 Rogne, "The Greatest Generation Revisited," 14–18.

25 D'Emilio, *Lost Prophet*, 96 ff.

26 D'Emilio, *Lost Prophet*, 102.

27 Levine, *Bayard Rustin and the Civil Rights Movement*, 45.

28 D'Emilio, *Lost Prophet*, 104.

29 D'Emilio, *Lost Prophet*, 100–13; Levine, *Bayard Rustin and the Civil Rights Movement*, 44–45.

30 D'Emilio, *Lost Prophet*, 118.

31 Levine, *Bayard Rustin and the Civil Rights Movement*, 47; Rustin, *I Must Resist*, 83.

Doldrums

1 Maidanek, or Majdanek, near Lublin, Poland, was the first major concentration camp to be liberated. It was the site of an estimated 360,000 deaths.

2   Dellinger, David, "Declaration of War," from his book "Revolutionary Nonviolence," Bobbs-Merrill Co., 1970, p. 19.

3   Boyer, *By the Bomb's Early Light*, 215.

4   *Harry S. Truman: Containing the Public Messages, Speeches, and Statements of the President, April 12 to December 31, 1945.* Published by US Govt Printing Offc 1961 in the series Public Papers of the Presidents of the United States.

5   D'Emilio, *Lost Prophet*, 125.

6   Boyer, *By the Bomb's Early Light*, 219.

7   D'Emilio, *Lost Prophet*, 127.

8   Wittner, *Rebels Against War*, 163.

9   D'Emilio, *Lost Prophet*, 141 ff.

10 Harrington, *Fragments of the Century*, 68.

11 D'Emilio, *Lost Prophet*, 184ff.

12 D'Emilio, *Lost Prophet*, 190–93.

13 Levine, *Bayard Rustin and the Civil Rights Movement*, 73 ff; D'Emilio, *Lost Prophet*, 202 ff.

14 D'Emilio, *Lost Prophet*, 206 ff.

15 Loughery and Randolph, *Dorothy Day*, 284; Troester, *Voices From the Catholic Worker*, 75.

Movement

1   Meier and Rudwick, *CORE, a Study in the Civil Rights Movement, 1942-1968*, 35.

2   Meier and Rudwick, *CORE, a Study in the Civil Rights Movement, 1942-1968*, 33ff.

3   Levine, *Bayard Rustin and the Civil Rights Movement*, 65; Young, *An Easy Burden*, 384.

4   D'Emilio, *Lost Prophet*, 237.

5   Scatamacchia, "Politics, Liberation, and Intellectual Radicalism."

6   Smith, "Liberation"; Hunt, *David Dellinger* Chapter Six.

7   Dellinger, "America's Lost Plantation"; Hunt, *David Dellinger*, 120; Miller, *Dorothy Day*, 469.

8   Hunt, *David Dellinger*, 104–5.

9   Hunt, *David Dellinger*, 169.

10 McReynolds, "Remembering Dave Dellinger."

11 Lopach and Luckowski, *Jeannette Rankin*, 202.

12 Wakefield, *New York in the Fifties*, 77 ff.

13 Garrison, *Bracing for Armageddon* Chapters Two and Three.

14 Garrison, *Bracing for Armageddon* Chapters One and Two.

15 Loughery and Randolph, *Dorothy Day*, 266, 338.

16 Loughery and Randolph, *Dorothy Day*, Chapter Nineteen.

17 MacDonald, "Homage to Twelve Judges."

18 Tucker, *The Great Starvation Experiment*, 219.

19 D'Emilio, *Lost Prophet*, 444.

20 Tracy, *Direct Action*, 138.

21 Lelyveld, *Great Soul*, 256; Boteach, "Repudiating Gandhian Pacifism in the Face of Mass Murder."

22 Lelyveld, *Omaha Blues: A Memory Loop*, 177–79.

23 Lelyveld, *Omaha Blues: A Memory Loop*, 188.

24 Gittelsohn's story is drawn from Roland Bertram Gittelsohn, *Pacifist to Padre: The World War II Memoir of Chaplain Roland B. Gittelsohn, December 1941-January 1946*, ed. Donald M. Bishop (Quantico, Virginia: Marine Corps University Press, 2020); Lee Mandel, *Unlikely Warrior: A Pacifist Rabbi's Journey from the Pulpit to Iwo Jima* (Pelican Publishing, 2015).

Epilogue

1 Niebuhr, *Christianity and Power Politics*, 31.

2 Hunt, *David Dellinger*, 124.

3 Dewey, *Freedom and Culture*, 49.

INDEX